PARADOXES OF NOSTALGIA

American Encounters/ Global Interactions

A series edited by Gilbert M. Joseph and Penny Von Eschen

The series aims to stimulate critical perspectives and fresh interpretive frameworks for scholarship on the history of the imposing global presence of the United States. Its primary concerns include the deployment and contestation of power, the construction and deconstruction of cultural and political borders, the fluid meaning of intercultural encounters, and the complex interplay between the global and the local. American Encounters seeks to strengthen dialogue and collaboration between historians of US international relations and area studies specialists.

The series encourages scholarship based on multi-archive historical research. At the same time, it supports a recognition of the representational character of all stories about the past and promotes critical inquiry into issues of subjectivity and narrative. In the process, American Encounters strives to understand the context in which meanings related to nations, cultures, and political economy are continually produced, challenged, and reshaped.

penny m. von eschen

paradoxes of nostalgia

cold war triumphalism and global disorder since 1989

Duke University Press
Durham and London 2022

Printed in the United States of America on acid-free paper ∞
Designed by A. Mattson Gallagher
Typeset in Adobe Text Pro and ITC American Typewriter by Westchester Publishing Services

Library of Congress Cataloging-in-Publication Data
Names: Von Eschen, Penny M. (Penny Marie), author.
Title: Paradoxes of nostalgia : Cold War triumphalism and global disorder since 1989 / Penny Von Eschen.
Other titles: Cold War triumphalism and global disorder since 1989 | American encounters/global interactions.
Description: Durham : Duke University Press, 2022. | Series: American encounters/global interactions | Includes bibliographical references and index.
Identifiers: LCCN 2021043830 (print) | LCCN 2021043831 (ebook)
ISBN 9781478015604 (hardcover)
ISBN 9781478018230 (paperback)
ISBN 9781478022848 (ebook)
ISBN 9781478092629 (ebook other)
Subjects: LCSH: World politics—1989– | History, Modern—1989– | Cold War. | Cold War—Influence. | Cold War in popular culture. | United States—Foreign relations—1989– | United States—Politics and government—1989– | BISAC: HISTORY / World | POLITICAL SCIENCE / International Relations / General Classification: LCC D860 .V664 2022 (print) | LCC D860 (ebook) | DDC 909.82/9—dc23/eng/20211215
LC record available at https://lccn.loc.gov/2021043830
LC ebook record available at https://lccn.loc.gov/2021043831

Cover art: Photograph by A. Mattson Gallagher.

For Kevin and Maceo

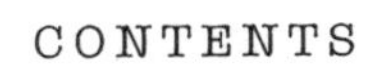

CONTENTS

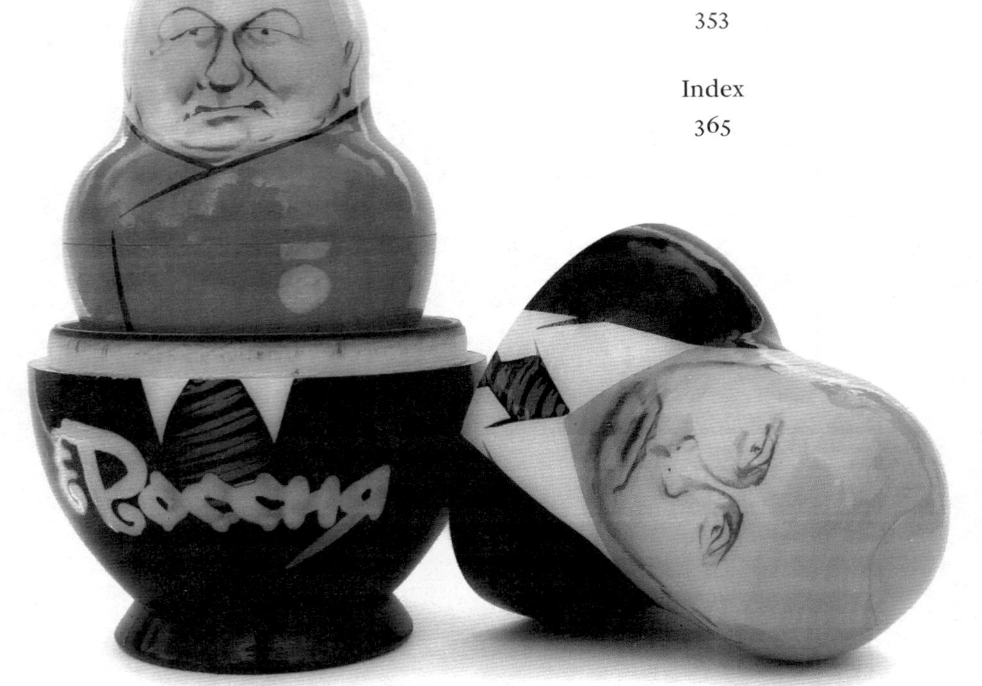

В.В.Путин

ACKNOWLEDGMENTS

This book has been built on the intellectual and material generosity and solidarity of colleagues, friends, and strangers; scholars whose insights and support have sustained a long inquiry into distortions of history across many years and many turns in global politics. The idea for the book emerged as the United States went to war in Afghanistan and Iraq in the early 2000s. As I listened daily to distorted assumptions about past US cold war policies in the mainstream media of record from NPR to the *New York Times*, a 2004 invitation to Berlin for the Black Atlantic conference series organized by Paul Gilroy landed me in the middle of another site of Western triumphalist claims, crystallizing questions about the intersecting afterlives of colonialism and the cold war.

A collaboration with Pamela Ballinger and our international partners in a global cold war course at the University of Michigan, along with Pamela's profound generosity, friendship, and critical advice on the manuscript, has been one of the great pleasures of writing the book. I thank Dong-Choon Kim, of Sung Kong Hoe University in Seoul and director of South Korea's Truth and Reconciliation Commission; Vjekoslav Perica, University of Rijeka, Croatia; and Marta Verginella, University of Ljubljana, along with their students. Dong-Choon Kim's extraordinary generosity on a visit to South Korea allowed me to see the country and the still unresolved Korean War in ways that have deeply shaped the book. None of that would have been possible without the visionary brilliance and intellectual leadership of Monica Kim.

I am deeply indebted to Monica for her intellectual guidance and friendship, along with invaluable comments on drafts at critical stages from start to finish. Thanks also to Deokhyo Choi, Henry Em, Young-ju Ryu, Jae-jung Suh, and Hiro Matsusaka.

Colleagues at Michigan involved in our global history project provided a uniquely generative launch point for the book. Special thanks to Kathleen Canning for her brilliant and erudite engagement with the project from its inception. I also thank Anne Berg, Howard Brick, Juan Cole, Geoff Eley, Dario Gaggio, Will Glover, Gabriela Hecht, Val Kivelson, Matthew Lassiter, Rudolph Mzárek, Farina Mir, Doug Northrop, Damon Salesa, Mrinalini Sinha, Scott Spector, and Ronald Suny. Thanks also to an extraordinary group of graduate students, including Stefan Aune, Ananda Burra, Christina DeLisle, Paul Farber, Brendan Goff, Lauren Hirshberg, Joseph Ho, Jenny Kwak, Cynthia Marasigan, William J. Moon, Marie Nitta, Kiri Sailiata, Hillina Seife, LaKisha Simmons, and Colleen Woods. I am grateful to have shared countless conversations and important research trips with Paul Farber across some of the parallel paths of our work, from Berlin to Los Angeles and Washington, DC.

I am extraordinarily lucky to have had the eyes and erudition of the brilliant global historian of culture and music Connie Atkinson as the book developed. From conference meetings in Salzburg and New Orleans to our research treks through Russia, Lithuania, and Cuba, this book is immeasurably richer because of her.

Feedback at conferences and workshops has shaped my questions and honed my thinking, including those of the Australian and New Zealand American Studies Association and the British American Studies Association. Thanks to Tim Gruenewald and Scott Laderman for hosting me at the University of Hong Kong; to colleagues at Tokyo University, Ehime University, and the Institute for International Studies in Kyoto; and to the Working Group on Memory, Tokyo. Special thanks to Akiko Ochiai, Carl Becker, Hayumi Haguchi, and Yuka Tsuchiya. Thanks to Susan Pennybacker and the participants in the "Global Brexit and Lost Futures" conference at the University of North Carolina. Thanks also to participants in the Columbia University Global History Workshop; London School of Economics, Cold War Studies; University of Chicago Human Rights Workshop; Alexis de Tocqueville Scholar series on internationalizing US history, University of Richmond; and the Harvard University Department of History, Global History Works in Progress Seminar.

Thanks to colleagues and friends for valuable conversations while traveling and at conferences, including: Laura Belmonte, Dawn Berry, Megan Black, Mark Bradley, Tim Borstelmann, Keith Breckenridge, Laura Briggs, Sabine Broeck, Catherine Burns, Frank Castigliola, Bruce Cumings, David Engerman, Clive Glaser, Petra Goedde, Alyosha Goldstein, Pippa Green, Alan Hirsch, Michael J. Hogan, Dani Holt, Richard Immerman, Daniel Immerwahr, Ryan Irwin, Matthew Jacobson, Robin D. G. Kelley, Liam Kennedy, Martin Klimke, Barbara Keys, Paul Kramer, Scott Laderman, Adriane Lentz-Smith, Fredrik Logevall, Sarah Miller-Davenport, David Milne, Christen Mucher, Christopher Nichols, Donald Pease, Barry Shank, Naoko Shibusawa, Cotten Seiler, Brad Simpson, Manisha Sinha, James Sparrow, and Jon Wiener.

American University of Central Asia and Bishkek friends were extraordinary hosts and have given me endless inspiration in their brilliant practice of American studies from the outside in. Special thanks to AUC's Susan Wiedemann and to the US Fulbright Program and US embassy in Bishkek. Thanks also to ASAKG president Chynara Ryskulova at the American University of Central Asia. My deepest gratitude to Valeriy Hardin, Elmira Musuralieva, and Kate Sampsell. I am saddened that technological shifts and xenophobic US policies have not allowed me to stay connected and properly thank others. Masha, Lana, I miss you, and your brilliant engagement, kindness, and generosity have indelibly shaped this project. I am grateful to Georgy Mamedov for introducing me to the remarkable "former west" project. The late Clyde Forsberg, musician, composer, and teacher, enriched my Bishkek experience in his inspired organization of a concert in memory of Dave Brubeck and in honor of the classical and jazz musician Alexandr Yurtaev. Thanks and gratitude to Alexandr Yurtaev, Viktoria Yurtaeva, Nourgghiz Chekilova, and Aziz Gapar.

I am indebted to colleagues and friends who read drafts of chapters. I thank Eric Foner and Nikhil Pal Singh, along with colleagues at Cornell University, including Ernesto Bassi, Judith Byfield, Derek Chang, Raymond Craib, Maria Cristina Garcia, Larry Glickman, Durba Gosh, Isabelle Hull, Julilly Kohler-Hausmann, Oneka LaBennett, Tamara Loos, Shawn McDaniel, Tejasvi Nagaraja, Mary Beth Norton, Russell Rickford, Noliwe Rooks, Aaron Sachs, Eric Tagliacozzo, Robert Travers, Claudia Verhoeven, and Rachel Weil, for commenting on chapters and providing wonderful years of intellectual support and extraordinary community. Special thanks to Aziz Rana for sustained conversations. Thanks also to Abby Cohn and Gretchen Ritter.

Deepest thanks to Andrew Friedman and Melani McAlister for their brilliant and demanding readings of the developing manuscript, the inspiration of their scholarship, and their friendship. Both have shaped the book in critical ways.

The University of Virginia provided invaluable support for research and writing in the final stages of this book. Thanks to Ian Baucom, Sylvia Chong, Claudrena Harold, William Hitchcock, Andrew Kahrl, Kyrill Kunakhovich, Melvyn Leffler, Jim Loeffler, Sarah Milov, Karen Parshall, and Sandhya Shukla. I am especially grateful to Tom Klubock for key suggestions on a penultimate version of the entire manuscript. I thank Garnett Cadogan for his spirited support, friendship, and incisive readings. Anna Brickhouse's brilliant insights, generosity, and infectious energy have been critical to the book's completion.

I am profoundly grateful to Megan Black and Aziz Rana for their brilliant and generous suggestions as readers for Duke University Press. At the press, Gisela Fosado has been a dream editor and Gilbert Joseph has been an inspiring and generous colleague. I thank the excellent editorial and production teams, including Ale Mejia, Annie Lubinsky, Chad Royal, Chris Robinson, Brian Ostrander, and Ashley Moore; and a grateful shoutout to Mattson Gallagher for the strikingly apt cover design.

From the beginning of the project and through its final challenges, Colleen Woods has generously lent her dazzling intellect, humor, and indefatigable passion for setting the historical record right. I am deeply grateful for her timely critical interventions and extraordinary support, and I am honored to include her photograph from our shared time in Hong Kong in the book.

Finally, warmest thanks to my lovely Von Eschen and Gaines extended families. I thank Kevin and Maceo Gaines for traveling with me, taking care of each other while I traveled, and making homes and communities with me where this book began and developed. Maceo's insights, gentleness, and wicked wit have kept me grounded. Not a day has gone by in about 6,574 that Kevin has not brought his spirit, erudition, and love to this book. His boundless creativity, kindness, and wordsmithery humble and inspire every day. Always.

Introduction

On February 11, 1990, Nelson Mandela walked out of Victor Verster Prison near Cape Town, South Africa, where he had spent the last two of his twenty-seven years of imprisonment. Mandela's release capped what many perceived as a breathtaking moment in which the cause of human freedom seemed to be prevailing over tyrannical regimes in rapid succession. Just three months earlier, a groundswell of political change throughout Eastern Europe culminated in the dismantling of the Berlin Wall—part of a sequence of events set in motion by Soviet premier Mikhail Gorbachev's bold calls for glasnost (openness) and perestroika (political reform), challenging an ossified Communist Party. Just days before jubilant crowds of Berliners took sledgehammers to the wall, Czech officials released the dissident author Václav Havel. Sprung from prison in October 1989, Havel was elected president by December. His rapid ascent took him to the United States, where he addressed a joint session of Congress two weeks after Mandela's release. A week after citizens of Berlin laid waste to the wall, it was Polish labor leader Lech Walesa's turn to receive a hero's welcome in the United States. Walesa, leader of Poland's Solidarity movement and soon to be president of his home country, like Havel, addressed cheering members of Congress, as would Mandela some months later.

These exhilarating times saw dissidents elevated to high office. Popular repudiations of tyranny predated the dizzying reversals of 1989. The year before, Chileans voted in a referendum to oust that nation's military dictator, Augusto Pinochet, notorious for his violent and repressive rule. Pinochet stepped down as head of state in 1990. Indeed, as 1989 ended, popular demands for peace, transparency, and accountability had bypassed the political status quo favored by American and Soviet elites, resulting in the unraveling of the cold war.

Mandela's release highlighted the confluence of 1980s global liberation, peace, and human rights campaigns. Little wonder that his release coincided with democratic movements in Eastern Europe, given the global ferment and synergies of the international antiapartheid movement, antinuclear and antimilitarist peace movements, and reform movements. Aspirations for freedom reverberated worldwide through popular music. In 1983, the Irish band U2's hit single "New Year's Day" honored the Solidarity movement, condemning the Polish government's hostility to the trade union–based struggle led by Walesa. U2's anthem of solidarity with striking Polish workers resonated with labor and left constituencies in Margaret Thatcher's Britain and among Americans opposed to Ronald Reagan's aggressive antilabor policies. In 1987, Poland's Solidarity sponsored a world music festival in Gdansk, in support of the South African antiapartheid cause. Performers included the Jamaican-born, British dub poet Linton Kwesi Johnson and reggae bands from the Caribbean diaspora. The August 1989 Music Peace Festival in Moscow at the one-hundred-thousand-seat Lenin Stadium featured several Western heavy metal acts, including the Scorpions, Ozzy Osbourne, Mötley Crüe, Cinderella, and Skid Row, sharing the bill with local bands, including Gorky Park and Brigada S.

By decade's end, such popular soundings of democratic uprisings in Europe reached a crescendo. When George H. W. Bush and Gorbachev jointly declared the end of the cold war on December 3, 1989, hopes of transcending the stultifying restrictions of cold war blocs and the dream of a demilitarized world free of nuclear weapons seemed within reach to many.

The buoyant hopes for democracy and disarmament that accompanied the revolutions of 1989 soon yielded to grave concerns about new conflicts in a rapidly remilitarizing world marked by spiking inequality. Only three years later, the Czechoslovakian poet-turned-president Havel warned that "if the West does not find the key to us … or to those somewhere far away who have extricated themselves from communist domination, it will ultimately lose the key to itself. If, for instance, it looks on passively at 'Eastern' or Balkan nationalism, it will give the green light to its own potentially destructive nationalisms, which it was able to deal with so magnanimously in the era of the communist threat."[1] Havel's prediction that nationalism posed as great a threat to the West as the former Soviet bloc captures his sense that the hopes for freedom and social justice throughout Eastern Europe that were unleashed by the collapse of the Soviet Union were being subordinated to the strictures of Western free market and US military imperatives.

Amid the current global ascendance of authoritarianism and neofascism besetting Western industrial democracies, it remains commonplace in some quarters to look back with nostalgia at the events of 1989 that culminated in the end of the cold war. Many still celebrate that moment of capitalism's purported victory as "the end of history" and as the era of the variously named globalization, neoliberalism, or Washington consensus that followed. Among those more skeptical about the impact of increasingly unregulated capitalism, there is a tendency to regard US global leadership during this period as exemplary. From this perspective, the rise of authoritarianism stems from the abdication of US global leadership. But this view can only be sustained through a geographically and temporally narrow reading of diplomatic history.

While scholarship on the cold war has, in the past two decades, expanded to include numerous accounts of the "third world," historians of the end of the cold war have tended to focus exclusively on US-Soviet or US–Eastern European relations.[2] Treating the end of the cold war and the conflicts in Eastern Europe and Africa that immediately followed as discrete and unrelated events, scholars focusing on the United States, Europe, and the Soviet Union have emphasized the negotiated end to the cold war. Historian Jeffrey A. Engel, for example, concludes his indispensable 2017 book *When the World Was New* with the declaration, "And we all survived the Cold War's surprisingly peaceful ending."[3]

As to the question of who gets to tell the story of the cold war, there is no singular version and no universally agreed on ending. Long before the dissolution of the Soviet Union, new and hotly contested political and cultural narratives about the end of the cold war appeared, claims that cast doubt not only on how we understand the end of the cold war but also about the obfuscating abstraction of the term itself. In addition to the stark inadequacy of using the term *cold war* to describe a period in which millions of combat soldiers and civilians perished in hot wars in Asia, Latin America, and Africa, from the perspective of the Koreas, China, and Cuba, it is misleading to say that the cold war ended when US-Soviet hostilities ceased. Moreover, even in places where former capitalist or communist divides were erased, local manifestations of the cold war unleashed violence in such places as South Africa in the waning years of apartheid, as well as violent aftershocks in Bosnia and Rwanda. Hence, sustained attention to places where the narrative of the end of the cold war does not fit is critical to understanding its contested meaning as well as the erasures of unresolved histories of conflict and violence implicit in the term.

Havel's fear that the West was losing its way stemmed most immediately from his bewilderment over the failure of the United States to intervene in the growing atrocities in Bosnia. Viewed from the global South and much of the former Eastern bloc, the end of the cold war was a markedly violent and unstable process, a story of escalating violence in South Africa; US interventions in Iraq, Panama, and Haiti; and wars of genocide in Bosnia and Rwanda. All of these conflicts were directly and causally related to superpower actions in the last decades of US-Soviet conflict, and to US policy decisions in the waning days of the Soviet Union and its immediate aftermath. These and other policies also produced exponential growth in inequality and the destabilization of entire regions of the globe, which, in turn, produced fertile ground for fascist and authoritarian movements.

Concerns that the United States was becoming directionless also hinted at a general malaise in American political culture and a pervasive disorientation and nostalgia even as the United States was supposedly celebrating its victory. In 1990, the former United Nations official Conor Cruise O'Brien noted, "The death of communism in Europe leaves anti-communism in America bereaved and confused."[4] Indeed, in the wake of the Eastern Europe revolutions but well before the collapse of the Soviet Union, Americans were already awash in nostalgia. Triumphalist boasts that the West had won the cold war coexisted uneasily with speculation about what the United States would do without a clear enemy. Maureen Diodati, a forty-one-year-old English teacher, asked, "Who's our enemy now? Who's going to be the bad guy?" One novelist wondered, "How are we going to talk politics anymore? If Castro goes, I don't know what I am going to do." The writer Henry Allen presciently queried, "Why do we have to look rich, tolerant, and progressive in front of the world if there's no other big country out there competing for hearts and minds?"[5]

Taking to heart Havel's warning that the West was losing its way, and viewing the end of the cold war as a global crisis, this book considers the paradoxical relationship of US nostalgia and triumphalism in the face of the widespread violence that accompanied the end of the cold war. In examining myriad expressions of nostalgia, including US presidents' and Hollywood blockbuster films' assertion, "I miss the Cold War," it is striking that one could "miss" a conflict in which millions died across Asia, Africa, and Latin America. Such assertions betray the limiting bipolar assumptions and Western worldview that distort the lived experience of the era.

Despite triumphalist US assertions that "we won the cold war" through military might, many Americans shared with their counterparts in the former Soviet Union and Eastern bloc complex expressions of loss and nostalgia. The end of the cold war meant the ascendancy of a form of neoliberalism that rejected the existence and possibility of mass society, the idea that individual happiness could align with the collective good. Expressing it as nostalgia for "Soviet times," "Yugostalgia," *ostalgie*, or cold war nostalgia, people throughout the globe articulated a powerful sense of loss and longing for stability, status, and the predictability of everyday life, upheld by the security of social safety nets and the consensus that societies had the responsibility to meet the basic human needs of their citizens. Thus, I am also concerned with interrogating the staying power of this form of nostalgia across former cold war divides.[6]

The processes and events that we associate with the end of the cold war prompted seismic shifts in people's everyday lives—the lived experiences of citizenship, nation, work, and family—and the meanings attached to daily life from the lofty to the mundane. The philosopher Susan Buck-Morss has argued that the dream of mass utopia defines the twentieth century: both capitalist and socialist forms of industrial modernity were characterized by a "collective dream [that] dared to imagine a social world in alliance with personal happiness."[7] As evidenced in the 1959 "kitchen debates" between Vice President Richard Nixon and Soviet premier Nikita Khrushchev, during the cold war era both capitalist and socialist blocs shared a dream of the good life for the masses and competed vigorously over which system could best deliver it.

Beginning in 1917, when Woodrow Wilson responded to Vladimir Lenin's call for a worldwide revolution with his Fourteen Points proposal, the United States and Soviet Union defined themselves in relation to each other with competing universalist promises, each claiming to offer the best and only route to the good life. The bipolar conflict went beyond ideology. Indeed, claims of ideological superiority were based on the ability of a system to deliver a better material standard of living for its citizens. Throughout the era of US-Soviet competition, both sides of the cold war divide set out to prove to their own citizens, those in developing countries, and critics at home and abroad that they possessed the superior route to delivering economic and social prosperity.

Whether dissidents or patriots, people the world over measured their lives and aspirations in terms of the promises of basic needs and human dignity held out by competing cold war blocs. Hence the end of the cold war entailed crises of meaning-making—often expressed as affective popular nostalgia—as well as a global reconfiguration of power. For many on both sides of the former cold war divide, the post-1991 era, unevenly yet consistently, was marked by a loss of hope for collective well-being. Just as critically, a loss of belief in social progress—for many, the loss of political hope itself—seeped into Western and former Eastern bloc sensibilities.

Employing a global and relational frame, this book examines multifarious expressions of nostalgia across former East-West divides. Broadly speaking, some forms of nostalgia posit a mythic past of ethno-nationalism. Other expressions of nostalgia take critical aim at neoliberalism and its discontents, yearning for a time when nonmarket values served as a bulwark against unrestrained materialism, and when many citizens on both sides of the cold war divide believed in the possibility of a collective good.

Cold war binaries proved to be adaptable and mutable, bent to the will of a host of actors, foremost among them George H. W. Bush, whose administration coincided with the dissolution of the Soviet Union. Bush and subsequent officials and pundits transferred the US and Soviet Union superpower conflict to a multiplicity of new enemies, naming new threats abroad and new enemies within.[8] The West's victory in the cold war was pyrrhic at best, with the afterlives of the cold war casting lingering shadows over US and global politics that continue to shape global challenges to liberal democracy.

Paradoxes of Nostalgia tracks three closely related processes: the contested history and memory of the cold war, the thorny political processes through which US cold war triumphalism prevailed over alternative visions of multilateral cooperation and disarmament, and a post-1989 rebooting of "us versus them" binaries, from the 1990s "clash of civilization" foreign policy ideas and the "culture wars" of domestic politics, as they played out in US interventions abroad and in the post-9/11 interplay of domestic and foreign politics. Tracing the rise of the frantic construction of new domestic and international enemies illuminates the historical roots of the global rise of right-wing nationalisms. These historically interwoven processes suggest that the triumphalist and paradoxically nostalgic claims made about the cold war and its demise in the West were necessary conditions for the hegemony of neoliberal economics and unilateral military interventions, epitomized by the US wars in Iraq.

I view this period less as an "age of fracture" dominated by market ideology than as one concretely shaped by an activist state and the weaponizing of global financial instruments to counter and undermine ongoing projects of collective resistance to neoliberal governance.[9] At the same time, much of the recent work on neoliberalism, while illuminating the 1970s and 1980s roots of radical deregulation and the weaponizing of global financial instruments, has obscured the contingencies surrounding the collapse of the Eastern bloc, unwittingly suggesting an economic determinism that diverts attention from the fundamental differences in competing visions of a new global order. Glossing over the political processes by which neoliberal actors marginalized the projects of Gorbachev, Havel, Mandela, and others naturalizes shock therapy and deregulation as the only possible options at "the end of history."

Repurposing the Past

This book explores the uses of history—how historical narratives around the world have been employed in the realms of politics, journalism, and popular culture, from 1989 to the present, to make claims about the cold war. Repurposing the past was critical to George H. W. Bush's conception of American leadership in a "new world order"—a phrase he borrowed from Gorbachev. Enacting their vision of a unipolar world undergirded by US-led militarism, American policy makers consistently favored nationalist over multinational formations. Relying on "clash of civilization" arguments for military spending and intervention, US officials and their policies fueled, at times unwittingly, the short- and long-term development of xenophobic right-wing ethnic nationalisms in the United States and abroad.

The "end of the cold war" needs to be understood not as an event but rather through the global processes by which US unilateralism muscled aside more popular visions of multilateral cooperation and disarmament. Historians of the era's political change have usually emphasized US relations with the Soviet Union or Eastern Europe. But Bush and Congress, and the broader public, witnessing these milestones on twenty-four-hour cable news and print media, experienced Soviet reforms of the mid-1980s and the 1989 revolutions through a complicated unfolding of events in the global South and the nonaligned bloc that had shaped geopolitics during the age of three worlds. This book joins a rich, scholarly literature on US empire and extensive studies on the global cold war, including the magisterial work of Odd Arne Westad. Like this scholarship, which emphasizes the cold war's interconnections with colonialism and imperialism in Africa, South Asia, Southeast Asia, and Latin America, this book examines the fading influence of third-world discourse within a conjuncture shaped by the afterlives of imperialism, nonaligned and national liberation movements, and relations between superpowers.[10]

In addition to investigating the impact of cold war nostalgia on US politics and culture, this book follows the transit of ideas of Western triumphalism across the globe, seeking to assess the reciprocal, local expressions of nostalgia and their impact on US global relations.[11] In other words, I am interested in how foreign audiences answer, or respond to, circulating notions of US triumphalism. Relatedly, I explore emergent expressions of mythic ethno-nationalisms in Russia and the East, constructions of the past that seep into the political void created by the demise of Soviet control. My research examines the interplay between local expressions of nostalgia and assertions of US triumphalism across political geographies shaped by the cold war and the abrupt end of superpower conflict. Whether in the Czech Republic, Germany, Hungary, Lithuania, Poland, Russia, Cuba, South Africa, Kyrgyzstan, or South Korea, each of these sites of cold war history and memory narrates contested views of the past, marking the tension of local histories altered by US or Soviet hegemonic projects.

This book is deeply informed by scholarship on the former Eastern bloc, *ostalgie*, and other forms of postcommunist nostalgia. Indeed, Western and Eastern forms of nostalgia must be understood in relation to one another. Western forms of nostalgia and triumphalism have also appeared in unexpected places. In addition to engaging cold war stories in the much-studied sites of Germany and Russia, this work examines the varieties of Western triumphalism in the international media and sites of public memory, among them Grutas Park in Lithuania (a theme park with a sprawling collection of discarded Soviet-era statues dubbed "Stalin World" by locals); public parks, museums, and cafés in Budapest and Prague; war and security tourist sites in South Korea; and Kyrgyzstan, a former Soviet Central Asian republic and home to the farthest outlying American "lily-pad" airbase, from which US troops deployed to Afghanistan. All of these sites enact a dialogue with US triumphalism; all grapple with alternative histories of the cold war that have been provoked by triumphalist claims, histories in which neither superpower can claim righteousness or victory.

Western and Eastern bloc universalist ideas of the good life and mass society were defined in relation to one another. The unraveling of mass society and of a commitment—however violated—to the common and public good must also be understood relationally. Likewise, new notions of national identity and belonging, deeply bound up with new conceptions of the enemy, must also be viewed in relation to one another.

Examining claims about the cold war is also critical to understanding how the United States conceived of and fought the so-called war on terror, and how Islamophobia became a new wedge issue in US electoral politics. So, too, is it fundamental to grasping the seeming paradoxes of US-Russian relations and the election of Donald Trump. Nationalist and imperial inflections of US and Russian nostalgia put the two countries on a collision course by 2005. At the same time, a growing affinity between the United States and Russia took shape as both nations redefined nationalism in ethnic, racial, and religious terms. In the United States, conservative policy makers promoted faith-based solutions as an alternative to a functioning regulatory and welfare state.

The post–cold war moment sowed the seeds for recent political and cultural affinities between US and Russian conservatives, reaping the whirlwind of the crisis of American democracy under threat as far right extremism found a comfortable home in the Republican Party. Within two years of the collapse of the Soviet Union, a new electoral coalition of "family values" Republicans and gun-rights advocates came together in the Republican Party to win a majority in the 1994 congressional elections—the very combination of gun advocacy and conservative religious and patriarchal values that brought US and Russian conservatives together in the years before Trump's candidacy.

With the Soviet enemy gone, US conservatives promoted family-values rhetoric as part of their political assault on the welfare state and sexuality-based human rights, scapegoating African Americans and LGBT people for electoral gain. Escalating New Right antigovernment rhetoric led many to view the US government itself as the enemy. Antigovernment American conservatives found new, if unpredictable, Russian bedfellows in their attacks on the US government. Christian evangelicals had long been a potent force in the New Right, as well as the GOP electorate. Staunch anticommunists as Reagan lambasted the Soviet "evil empire," members of the Republican Party's Christian right faction, in a striking turnabout, forged business and cultural ties with Russia dating back to the late 1980s. As Trump secured the GOP nomination, he welcomed into his coalition US white Christian nationalists and "alt-right" and white supremacists who were unabashed in their racism, anti-Semitism, and Islamophobia. Pro-Russian positions taken by Trump's campaign prompted intense speculation on his ties to

Russia. Seeking to squelch investigations of possible collusion with Russia, President Trump fired FBI director James Comey, prompting a formal Special Counsel investigation of his campaign's ties with Russia, Trump's alleged acts of obstruction of justice, and possible interference in the 2016 election by Russian intelligence. With the Special Counsel investigation finding well over a hundred contacts between the Trump campaign and Russian oligarchs and intelligence operatives during the campaign, and attendees at pro-Trump rallies clad in T-shirts proclaiming, "I'd rather be Russian than Democrat," the political and cultural affinities between the US far right and Russia were striking and undeniable. A US Senate Intelligence Committee investigation concluded as much, providing a detailed account of extensive contacts between the Trump campaign and Russian officials before and after the 2016 election.

History Battles: Glasnost versus Victors' History

The path leading from the end of the cold war to the shadowy dealings of Trump and his officials with Russian officials and operatives was circuitous, contingent, and improbable, even shocking. Yet much more was at stake in the contested interregnum following the 1989 revolutions and the collapse of the Soviet Union. In the ensuing decades, myriad stagings of the cold war past sprang up in museums and tourist sites throughout the former Soviet bloc as well as in the United States. Analyzing the politicized memory of the cold war entails investigating how narratives about the period have been mobilized and manipulated by politicians and pundits as well as in popular culture.[12] Western triumphalism displaced a much broader range of stories about the cold war and what political possibilities its ending might entail. The revolutions that brought down Eastern bloc regimes began as collective efforts to reform and humanize socialism, not as pro-capitalist movements, and the set of possible futures imagined in the mid-1980s was far more expansive than one can glimpse in triumphalist victors' histories.

One of the greatest impediments to understanding shifts in geopolitics as the Eastern bloc dissolved is the tendency among pundits as well as some scholars to conflate all of Soviet history, as if early Bolshevism, Stalinism, and the era of glasnost and perestroika were all the same thing; and then to merge this with post-Soviet Russian history, as if Russian president Vladimir Putin is synonymous with the USSR simply because of his career's Soviet origins in the notorious KGB. *Paradoxes of Nostalgia* draws on such scholars of the Soviet period as Stephen F. Cohen, who emphasizes the importance of the Soviet reform period.[13] I contend that understanding the intersections of Soviet reform and the radical reform movements of the Eastern bloc and global South—and how and why they were displaced—is vital for comprehending the past decades and writing the history of the end of the cold war.

Ironically, Gorbachev had revived the term *new world order*—invoked by Woodrow Wilson after World War I—to characterize his vision of a demilitarized post–cold war world. Gorbachev elaborated this proposed future in a joint statement with Indian prime minister Rajiv Gandhi in the 1986 Delhi Declaration, which emphasized a strong United Nations and multinational cooperation to secure a nuclear-free and nonviolent world. Also highlighting emergency environmental reforms, the declaration contained sustainable approaches to redress the military and environmental consequences of the cold war race for weapons and mass consumption.[14] The declaration garnered praise in the West for its bracing departure from rigid Soviet ideology and its eclectic adaptation of ideas from the nonaligned world and global South.

Time magazine named Gorbachev its Man of the Year in 1987, praising him for jolting the lethargic Soviet economy, opening the government to scrutiny, and projecting "a new flexibility in Soviet behavior abroad." With millions abroad "growing accustomed to his face" and welcoming the agreement with the United States banning intermediate-range nuclear missiles, *Time* sharply contrasted Gorbachev's dynamic leadership with a United States bogged down by the Iran-Contra affair, recession, and the HIV-AIDS epidemic, where "a White House scandal unfolds, a *contrary* war continues, a boom goes bust, and a plague rages on. It was a year that Ronald Reagan would just as soon forget."[15]

Speaking before the United Nations on December 7, 1988, Gorbachev announced military cuts and a comprehensive plan for disarmament, and elaborated his hopes for international cooperation to alleviate "economic, environmental and humanistic problems in their broadest sense. I would like to believe that our hopes will be matched by our joint effort to put an end to an era of wars, confrontation and regional conflicts, to aggressions against nature, to the terror of hunger and poverty as well as to political terrorism. This is our common goal and we can only reach it together."[16]

Time magazine's Walter Isaacson praised Gorbachev's United Nations speech as "compelling and audacious" and "suffused with the romantic dream of a swords-into-plowshares 'transition from the economy of armaments to an economy of disarmament.'" Gorbachev's vision, Isaacson wrote, had "the potential to produce the most dramatic historic shift since

George Marshall and Harry Truman." Impressed that Gorbachev's proposals "fit together in a world forum to transcend the ideological dogmas that had driven Soviet foreign policy for 70 years," the danger to the United States, for Isaacson, was that it may be unable to "seize the initiative or find an imaginative response." Gorbachev, Isaacson argued, "remains the most commanding presence on the world stage. He is the one performer who can steal a scene from Ronald Reagan, and he did; as they viewed the Statue of Liberty, the visiting Communist played the self-confident superstar while Reagan ambled about like an amiable sidekick and Bush lapsed into the prenomination gawkiness that used to plague him whenever he stumbled across Reagan's shadow. Afterward, Mikhail and Raisa's foray into Manhattan provoked more excitement than any other visit since Pope John Paul II in 1979."[17]

Stressing that Gorbachev had impressively addressed every point of past contention between the United States and the Soviet Union, Isaacson noted that skepticism was prudent, but the greater danger was the possibility that a "wary and grudging attitude could cause the U.S. to miss out on a historic turning point in world affairs."[18]

President George H. W. Bush, however, was not ultimately willing to share the world stage with Gorbachev. He remained fiercely committed to the idea that only the United States could lead the global order. Indeed, in his diplomatic pursuit of international support for the US-led intervention in Iraq, Bush pushed aside Gorbachev's claims to international leadership, along with his vision of multilateral cooperation and the need to address environmental crises. Though Bush developed a rapport with Gorbachev in the months before his resignation and the collapse of the Soviet Union, their testy conflicts over Iraq's invasion of Kuwait highlighted their sharply opposed conceptions of a post–cold war new world order.

Yet it was not simply Gorbachev who lost the argument over the Gulf War, compelled to accept US leadership in a military action anathema to his demilitarization agendas in glasnost and perestroika. It was the defeat of a broader vision, shared by Gorbachev, Havel, and Mandela, of a new world order based on multilateral cooperation and demilitarization.

Gorbachev and Havel's vision of a post–cold war order was based on multipolarity in the context of political glasnost—an official public appraisal of the mistakes of the past. The promising political moment saw the Russian word *glasnost* passed into the English lexicon, defined by the *Oxford English Dictionary* as "literally 'the fact of being public'"; openness to public scrutiny or discussion.[19] Too preoccupied with claiming victory and assuming the role of global hegemon, the United States and its leadership refused the opportunity for its own glasnost—let alone for a peace dividend—in the years following the political openings in the Soviet Union and Eastern Europe.

Bush's proclamation that the United States was now the sole preeminent power—and a trusted power at that—required disengaging from the consequences of military, political, and economic policies of the cold war era. Little wonder that Bush, as former vice president and director of Central Intelligence, was unwilling to revisit recent policies, let alone the troubling covert and illegal actions unearthed by the Church Senate committee during the 1970s. It was a different story in the former Soviet Union and Germany, countries that opened the archives documenting repression and the abuses of the cold war, prompting soul-searching about its chilling effects on society and the human soul. It was dramatically different in postapartheid South Africa, which established the Truth and Reconciliation Commission and multiple official attempts to confront the barbarism of apartheid's past in order to move toward a democratic future.

Victors' History

Havel's unease over what he saw as the West's inability to "get" the East speaks to the dispute between Eastern bloc reformers' vision of a multilateral and disarmed post–cold war order and US cold war triumphalism—the insistence that the United States had won the cold war and was now the lone superpower bestriding a unipolar world. Gorbachev's appeal for political openness entailed a call for a national and international examination of the assumptions and missteps of the cold war past.

By the time of the Eastern European revolutions and fall of the Berlin Wall in 1989, however, Reagan, Bush, and a spate of academics and pundits were already declaring victory. When Francis Fukuyama proclaimed "the end of history" in 1989, he echoed the Bush administration's confidence that capitalist democracy had vanquished all possible alternatives for organizing modern society.[20] Accepting the nomination at the 1988 Republican National Convention, Bush told the crowd that US perseverance and military might, *not* Soviet reforms, diplomacy, and negotiation, made all the difference: "It's a watershed. It's no accident. It happened when we acted on the ancient knowledge that strength and clarity lead to peace—weakness and ambivalence lead to war.... I will not allow this country to be made weak again, never."[21] Just as significant as Bush's intent to carry a big stick was his self-serving account of global politics.

As a former CIA director well aware that the Soviet Union was not the sole cold war actor in southern Africa and Afghanistan, Bush kept silent on US support of white minority governments in southern Africa, CIA actions in Afghanistan before Soviet intervention, and US officials' support of the anti-Soviet mujahideen fighters in Afghanistan.

Like Bush's version of the cold war, the idea that the era was more stable than what followed it ignores the deaths of millions in Asia, Africa, the Middle East, and Latin America. It further overlooks historical connections between cold war policies and post-9/11 conflicts, including the Soviet and US arming of dictatorships in wars of genocide in the developing world.

Reagan's antipathy toward left-leaning anti-imperialism and movements for self-determination and human dignity—along with harsh austerity and structural adjustment programs aimed at the global South and Eastern bloc—amounted to a weaponizing of the Bretton Woods institutions created to bring stability to the international financial markets and prevent war. In effect, the West tried to solve its own stagnation crisis by squeezing the global South and Eastern bloc countries, first calling in debt from loans dating from World War II, then imposing stringent austerity and structural adjustment programs as a condition for restructuring debt.

Economic and political violence intertwined in these intrusive programs promoted by Reagan and British prime minister Thatcher, often imposed on governments and local populations following coups or the use of military force against leftist opposition movements. From the use of covert operations and coups in Chile and Bolivia, to the shock therapy and structural adjustment policies enforced throughout the global South and former Soviet sphere, neoliberal privatization policies effected a reengineering of the state that included a decisive shift in state capacity to the punitive.[22]

Narratives that refuse to critically examine the cold war close their eyes to the proxy wars of the later stages of the conflict that led to US officials' support of the anti-Soviet mujahideen fighters in Afghanistan and enlisted Saddam Hussein's Iraq as allies against Iran after the shah's overthrow.

Through the erasure of such destructive engagements, the cold war's major actors are absolved from responsibility for the vexing problems of the present. In this view, post-1991 wars are attributed to a clash of civilizations, and terrorism is depicted as a product of Islamic history and culture. Such partial and distorted views of the past have misinformed post-1989 foreign policy.

Havel's warning that the United States would give "the green light to its own potentially destructive nationalisms" not only was sadly prescient about the future state of US political institutions but was also a keen observation about American political culture in the moment. It was in the interest of Americans, Havel suggested, to deal "magnanimously" with internal ethnic and racial divides that had festered "in the era of the communist threat." But on the eve of the 1992 presidential elections and beyond, Americans were turning on each other, finding new enemies within.

In 1993, as Havel cautioned the West, liberal capitalist institutions appeared exemplary to most observers within that sphere of influence. The International Monetary Fund, backed by opinion leaders, imposed free market values on the global South and viewed similarly strong medicine as the precondition for aid to the former Soviet bloc. But as neoliberal market fundamentalism conflated democracy and capitalism, it changed the rules of politics, ultimately undermining democracy. State capacities shifted to deregulation, privatization, and increased incarceration. In tandem with accelerating economic inequality, these shifts led to the neglect of investment in public infrastructure, underfunded public education, and helped make daily newspapers and independent media a vanishing resource. In the United States, politicians and journalists saw voter suppression as compatible with the idea of free elections. Behind Havel's enigmatic suggestion that the West would lose itself if it failed to heed the aspirations of the emancipated East, the institutions and credibility of Western liberal democratic regimes were eroding, setting the stage for antidemocratic resentment in the United States.

Celebrations by free market advocates of the rapidity with which a newly unfettered market would lift all economic boats were viewed as an affront to the elderly and vulnerable—those unable to benefit from these new relations—that their lives lived under socialist regimes had been a waste, a mistake, and their lives and livelihoods were now consigned to the dustbin of history. Even the most ardent critics of the old regimes faced a disorienting sense of loss. As Jens Reich, a leading East German dissident, put it in November 1993, "I can't get rid of this feeling of being an outsider, a sense that all of my life experiences are now irrelevant. It's a strange feeling. It's as if you yourself have disappeared, as if you're a relic of a lost era."[23] Films and texts of East German *Ostalgie* further document attachment to the habits, pleasures, and compensations of daily life under communism and the disorientation and longing that developed when this fabric was ripped apart.

As the late theorist and scholar of Soviet nostalgia Svetlana Boym has argued, nostalgia worked, and continues to work, in multiple registers.

Euro-American scholarly discourse occasioned by the end of the cold war highlighted nostalgia as a major subset of memory studies. Although *nostalgia* is a seventeenth-century medical term, the post-1989 scholarly focus on it responded to broad popular expressions of longing in the wake of the collapse of Eastern bloc regimes.

In what we might think of as a restorative, mythic mode, nostalgia played a pivotal and paradoxical role in cold war triumphalism, or what Gorbachev has called America's "winner complex"—the notion that the West "won" the cold war and that alternatives to liberal capitalist democracy were forever vanquished.[24]

Nostalgia also appears in reflective and critical modes that, in interrogating the past in all its sordid and wondrous complexity, can offer trenchant critiques of current power relations. Critical nostalgias in the East have expressed grief over the loss of a commitment to the public good and a longing for a time when money did not seem to rule everything. For some, critical nostalgia entails missing the audacious dream that individual happiness could align with a more equitable and just social world.

Methodology: Sites of Meaning-Making

The story of the end of the age of three worlds is also a story in the crisis of meaning-making and the construction of new narratives and cultural practices across emergent political geographies and cultures. In a globally framed history that examines nostalgia and tracks US triumphalism into former Soviet and Eastern bloc spaces, my research has engaged sites in the United States, Europe, Asia, and Latin America.

To suggest that a history is globally framed is not to claim that it covers the entire globe, or even representative parts of it. The rationale linking these places is the indelible reach and impact of US cold war triumphalism, of US policies as a "unipolar" superpower. The exercise of that power throughout the world is best understood in relation to the places affected by it and the projects and histories that it altered or distorted. The locations I visited and discuss in these pages were chosen to illuminate shifts in geopolitics from the late 1980s onward. If choices were at times dictated by happenstance, through the gift of an invitation or an unexpected opportunity to travel, each offers a critical window into dynamics that are indispensable for comprehending post-1989 shifts in geopolitics. In cases where my analysis draws on museum and site visits, though trained in history and not ethnography, I recognize that it is misleading to write about these engagements as if my presence did not matter, and I use the first person within my descriptions of sites and encounters when relevant.

Furthermore, as a critique of US triumphalism, the book's treatment of US policy does not imply that the United States had absolute power or total responsibility in shaping post-1989 events. Nor do I claim that non-US actors were not politically and morally culpable for their own actions in provoking and shaping wars and shoring up exploitative political, economic, and social structures. Yet as the single most powerful nation in its self-proclaimed unipolar order, more than any other nation or nonstate actor, the United States transformed the terrain and set the conditions on which others acted.

Historians have debated, at times fiercely, the causes, legacy, scope, and significance of the cold war before and after 1989.[25] But an investigation of the politicized memory of the cold war must move beyond the realm of formal politics and ask how and why conservative accounts of the period gained traction with a broader public. Methodologically, this book incorporates diplomatic, political, and cultural history, investigating cold war narratives and assumptions through readings of multiple media representations within intersecting sites of politics, journalism, and popular culture.[26]

In considering post-1989 reshufflings of cold war binaries and, later, a new cold war with Russia, the rise of the internet informs my use of the term *reboot* as both a metaphor and descriptor for a material practice of the post-Soviet era. Representations of the cold war and the war on terror have been largely constructed in a digital world. The first web browser was launched in January 1993, thirteen months after the collapse of the Soviet Union. As personal computers grew ever more popular, the archive of the cold war changed along with technology. Thus, an analysis of the post-9/11 production of cold war history and memory and its mobilization in the war on terror entails an analysis of content on the internet, on television, in film and video games, and in museums, as well as foreign policy discussions and political speech and policy.[27]

Popular culture representations of the cold war were integral in producing cultural understandings of the period. Forms of mass entertainment from Hollywood films and television shows to video games and popular museums were critical in defining a popular discourse on new threats and enemies in the global landscape for consumers and audiences. Narratives of post–cold war anxiety and nostalgia provided fodder for cultural productions that echoed and recycled reductive cold war Manichean binaries and tropes. For example, presumed links between notions of deviant sexuality and political subversion that informed the purge of gay and lesbian people from federal government employment, and structured such 1960s cold war classics as *The Manchurian Candidate* and *From Russia with Love*, were recapitulated in *Skyfall*, the 2012 installment of the James Bond franchise, in which a queer villain with a mommy complex attempts to seduce Bond and wreak destruction on the British government.[28]

My analysis attends to the constitution of power as politicians and cultural producers alike called into being new constituencies that recognized their claims or interests as aligning with their own.[29] I reject any notion of passive reception in this process, recognizing individual participation or recalcitrance in cultural and social practices that seek to recast political reality. Whether thinking about the social dynamics of a Sarah Palin rally or displays of vulgar triumphalism in popular cultural stagings of the cold war, people actively see, hear, smell, and engage the sites. Encounters with representations of the past or participation in reenactments in museums or video games may subtly, perhaps dramatically, reinforce, challenge, or alter prior assumptions and beliefs. As museum visitors, consumers of post-Soviet kitsch, and gamers participate and react, popular culture becomes a fertile arena for the production of knowledge, subjectivity, and alternate realties in ways that may or may not have been intended by the cultural producers and entrepreneurs. Hence a gaming public, like the voting public, is unstable, and neither films nor video games can be said to represent hegemonic American values or interests. Yet at stake in these contested visions of the cold war is the power to reshape political and social knowledge and points of reference, the power to open or foreclose possibilities to imagine the future.

Chapter Outline

Chapters are organized thematically within an overall chronological structure, looking backward to histories that shaped the post-1989 context and forward to the implications of policies and interventions enacted in the wake of the unraveling of the Eastern bloc. The first four chapters consider new geopolitical contests as a new historical bloc replaced the cold war–era structure of competition between universalizing ideologies.

Chapter 1 focuses on roads not taken, juxtaposing the visions and projects of revolutionaries and reformers to the unipolar hegemonic ambitions of the Bush administration and the political and philosophical arguments employed in influential interpretations of the world scene by Fukuyama and

Samuel Huntington. Bush and Congress, like the media and broader public, experienced Soviet reforms of the mid-1980s and 1989 revolutions not in a cordoned-off US-Soviet world but through the more complicated lens of unfolding developments in the global South and the nonaligned bloc that had shaped geopolitics for decades. The later part of the chapter examines how assertions of unipolarity and the end of history played out in Bush's contests with Mandela and the antiapartheid movement.

Chapter 2 traces post-1987 shifts in conceptions of the new world order, from its employment by the Soviets and Eastern European reformers who imagined a multipolar world, to Bush's triumphalist vision of a world policed by a victorious one-world hegemon. Unlike Germany, the Soviet Union, and South Africa, the United States refused a moment of glasnost, a political opening that might have allowed a reckoning with its cold war past. From Bush's manipulation of the cold war past and invocation of "clash of civilizations" rhetoric in the first US Gulf War to US responses to humanitarian crises in Somalia, Bosnia, and Rwanda, both the Bush and Clinton administrations drew on middlebrow ideas that claimed ancient and primordial hatreds as the source of conflicts, leaving the West off the hook for its part in creating the conditions of crisis.

Chapter 3 argues that the collapse of the Eastern bloc prompted a crisis in meaning-making in US society as US politics and culture repositioned American identity in response to the loss of its longtime adversary. As Americans suspiciously tracked early post-Soviet nostalgia in Russia, the end of a bipartisan consensus for New Deal liberalism in the United States and a decline of support for the notion of mass society prompted a rapid construction of internal enemies, an escalation in partisanship, and the erosion of political norms. Chapter 4 turns to expressions of cold war nostalgia in politics and popular culture amid depictions of new threats and enemies by policy makers and cultural producers. As the central cold war commodities oil and uranium escaped their cold war containers, constructions of new enemies defined as rogue states went hand in hand with a rejection of the very idea of diplomacy. New cold war framings produced in popular film, as well as in the political arena, were critical to the consolidation of a popular cold war nostalgia by the end of the 1990s, coalescing in the presidential campaign of George W. Bush.

The final three chapters chart political deployments of the cold war past from the advent of the US war on terror and across the global turn to the right over the next two decades. Chapter 5 examines a thriving global consumer nostalgia along with claims about the cold war found in museums and popular culture in the former Soviet sphere as well as in the former West. Focusing on the instability of nostalgia in the midst of a global turn to the right, I track a shift from expressions of critical nostalgias toward assertions of mythic nostalgia dependent on historical erasures at the behest of right-wing nationalisms. Chapter 6 moves from examining stagings of the cold war past in the post-9/11 war on terror in popular culture and in official rhetoric on war and the "Axis of Evil," to examining implicit and explicit claims about the cold war in places where the war on terror was actually fought. Following the war on terror entails examining the contested presence of Western triumphalism in a former Soviet space, Bishkek, Kyrgyzstan, home of the US base from which most NATO soldiers deployed to Afghanistan. Chapter 7 alternates between geopolitical and cultural registers to probe the seeming paradoxes of the new cold war with Russia. During the 2000s, the two nations' right-wing alliances solidified at the very moment of a new US-Russian cold war over NATO expansion. As the rebooting of a cold war in popular culture resonated with political depictions of Russia during crises in Georgia and Ukraine, the outsize influence of Russia evident in Trump's campaign and presidency represented a twist in a contemporary drama involving new techniques of intelligence, information warfare, and kleptocracy in an era of weakened states and fragmented publics.

The epilogue considers global demands for a genuine reckoning with the past, arguing that an honest accounting of the cold war past is critical to any democratic and just future. Juxtaposing resurgent right-wing nationalist nostalgia to contemporary expressions of critical nostalgia, it emphasizes not longings for flawed past regimes and political projects but nostalgia for hope itself and the possibility of a just global society.

1

The Ends of History

Communism was not defeated by military force, but by life, by the human spirit, by conscience, by the resistance of Being and man to manipulation. It was defeated by a revolt of color, authenticity, history in all its variety and human individuality against imprisonment within a uniform ideology.—Václav Havel, February 4, 1992

It's a watershed. It's no accident. It happened when we acted on the ancient knowledge that strength and clarity lead to peace—weakness and ambivalence lead to war. . . . I will not allow this country to be made weak again, never.—George H. W. Bush, August 18, 1988

As people around the globe celebrated Nelson Mandela's release from prison on February 11, 1990, US president George H. W. Bush called the South African antiapartheid leader to congratulate him and to express "delight" about the news.[1] Yet Mandela's release presented thorny issues for Bush. Only two years prior, the Reagan administration had placed Mandela's African National Congress (ANC) on the US list of terrorist organizations, where it remained until 2008. Just one year earlier, in 1989, a Defense Department publication with a foreword by then-president-elect Bush termed the ANC one of the "world's most notorious terrorist groups," citing Mandela as the organization's leader."[2] Mandela's release was accompanied by reports (later confirmed) that a CIA tip had led to his 1962 arrest; the triumphalist claim that the United States won the cold war because it had always been on the right side of history appeared debatable at best.

A former CIA director and key architect of the cold war order, Bush did not relish the collapse of the Eastern bloc or the upsurge of global demands for democracy. For Bush, the cold war framework had been enabling as well as limiting for US interests, justifying CIA overthrows of democratically elected governments and providing intelligence to white-minority-ruled South Africa for the repression of antiapartheid activists. As head of Central Intelligence in the late 1970s, a period of official scrutiny of the agency's role in foreign assassinations and coups, Bush had contended with the aftermath of those exposés. During the Reagan administration, the mounting evidence against the CIA included reports of then–vice president Bush's covert alliance with Panama's Manuel Noriega and a long line of cocaine dealers—reports that later plagued him during his 1988 presidential campaign.[3]

Such disclosures not only spoiled the triumphalist party, they also fueled questioning of the CIA and the national security state complex in which it was ensconced. During Bush's presidency, the CIA's very existence was questioned by those who saw it as a cold war relic that undermined democratic institutions.

With the cold war over, some suggested, there was no justification for a military-industrial complex. The country could celebrate its dismantling and put the money saved—a peace dividend—to the critical task of rebuilding the physical and social infrastructure neglected as a result of military overspending.[4]

This chapter examines the range of arguments about, as well as the stakes of, the terms of a post–cold war geopolitical order by highlighting visits to the United States of three prominent dissidents in the weeks and months following the collapse of the Berlin Wall: Poland's Lech Walesa in November 1989; Václav Havel, the new Czech president, in February 1990; and Mandela, who toured the country in June 1990. Historians of the end of the cold war have largely focused on US-Soviet or US–Eastern European relations. But no less than the cold war era itself, the end of what Michael Denning has called the age of three worlds was shaped by a conjuncture defined by the intersections of imperialism, national liberation movements, and relations between superpowers.[5] Shifts in US-Soviet relations intersected with unfolding developments in South Africa, Namibia, and the broader nonaligned bloc that had shaped geopolitics for decades. Exploring Bush's conversations with African leaders, including Mandela and his rival, Inkatha party leader Mangosuthu G. Buthelezi; Namibian president Sam Nujoma; and the longtime US ally and dictator of Zaire, Mobutu Sese Seko, I argue that despite Bush's personal admiration for Mandela, his policy toward the ANC and southern Africa was fundamentally shaped by his deep antipathy toward the nonaligned and national liberation projects of Africa. This approach was honed during his days as US ambassador to the United Nations and as director of the CIA in the critical year following the defeat of mercenaries sponsored by apartheid South Africa in Angola at the hands of Cuban and African troops.[6]

Multiple actors in politics, academia, and the world of foreign policy punditry vied to define the interregnum created by the dissolution of the Soviet bloc in the early 1990s. Highlighting the tensions between Bush and his neoliberal allies and the alternative, multipolar visions of Mandela and the Eastern European reformers, this chapter examines the contested ideological process of making the new historic bloc, a world in which Bush believed that the United States should be the sole global hegemon.

Cold war triumphalism—the assertion that Reagan and military might had prevailed—was a shape-shifting narrative, morphing in the hands of Bush administration officials. The chapter then turns to another critical pillar of triumphalism, the claim that free market capitalism had won a decisive and permanent victory over socialist alternatives. Examining the intellectual and political resurgence of neoliberalism, I consider triumphalist and nostalgic "end of history" narratives from the late 1980s as articulated by Francis Fukuyama and other pundits. Amid a welter of heady assertions and mistranslations, neoliberalism constituted the dominant ideas and practices confronting Eastern European dissidents as well as Mandela and the ANC as they sought to bring their own visions and hopes to fruition.

Claims about the cold war—its definitions, who won, how it was fought, how it ended—were fundamental to visions of the future and served to justify political and economic policy decisions and actions in the moment. The end of history of this chapter's title refers not only to the argument that the free market is the only viable path for modern states but also to the "ends" of history—the purposes to which history is put. Articulated at the dawn of the internet age, triumphalist pronouncements of the end of history reverberated through a rapidly diversifying global media.[7]

A focus on the very different visions of freedom that emerged as Bush and Congress responded to the visits of Walesa, Havel, and Mandela illuminates the stakes of the moment as well as roads not taken. Bush's vision of a new world order maintained by US power rested on the claim that all alternatives to free market capitalism had been discredited. But it is wrong to assume that alternate ideas about the optimal organization of society were simply swept away in a celebratory tide of neoliberal ascendency. Reformers such as Mikhail Gorbachev and Havel joined with French president François Mitterrand and others to promote strong multilateral institutions in a demilitarized Europe while shifting resources to human needs.

Much of the recent work on neoliberalism, while illuminating the 1970s and 1980s roots of radical reregulation and the weaponizing of global financial instruments, has tended to obscure the political and ideological contingencies of the collapse of the Eastern bloc, unwittingly suggesting an economic determinism that diverts attention from the fundamental differences in visions of a new global order between reformers such as Havel and Mandela, on the one hand, and US policy makers, on the other. Glossing over the political processes by which neoliberal reformers marginalized the projects of Gorbachev, Havel, and Mandela diminishes the stakes of the debates and the momentous consequences of policies promoted by the United States and the global financial community, naturalizing shock therapy and deregulation as the only possible options at "the end of history."

How, in the midst of vigorous Eastern bloc reforms and the impending victory of an antiapartheid movement defined by the struggle for economic and racial justice, did policy-making elites get to declare that unregulated free market capitalism was the only game in town, so to speak? How were they able to implement such ideas and practices? Deliberate political decisions ultimately enacted radical privatization, deregulation, and the gutting of state capacity, undermining reformist visions.[8]

The development of triumphalist claims about the cold war in political and economic discourse as well as media and popular culture were important factors in the ascendance of neoliberal economic policies and political reforms.[9] Rhetorical constructs of the end of history justified neoliberal economic policies and foreign policy. As these policies took hold, privatization displaced reform hopes in the Eastern bloc, squandered the potential social benefits of the "peace dividend," and forced a fledgling postapartheid South African democracy down the path of privatization. This chapter begins, then, with an examination of triumphalist claims before turning, first, to the visits of the dissidents and then to a more sustained analysis of the tensions between Mandela and George H. W. Bush in the context of US cold war clientelism in southern Africa.

Victors' History and the End of History

Political revolutionaries and reformers of the 1980s imagined a reformed socialist society where economic justice went hand in hand with political freedom. Gorbachev, with his policies of openness and economic reform; Walesa, who led the 1981 strike at the Gdansk shipyards that formed the movement Solidarity; and Mandela, who believed that economic redistribution was critical to the making of a democratic South Africa—all of them confronted a geopolitical terrain where elites forcefully advocated free market solutions and demanded diminished state capacities.

The political scientist Francis Fukuyama became an influential purveyor of triumphalism after writing his 1989 essay titled "The End of History?" Addressing Eastern European reform challenges to calcified pro-Soviet regimes, Fukuyama interpreted movements that sought to democratize socialism as proof that free market capitalism provided the only viable path to modern society. He forecast the end of history as a time of peace and the end of ideological conflict but lamented the prospect of future "centuries of boredom." Predicting that "the end of history will be a very sad time," Fukuyama waxed nostalgic for the high-stakes drama of superpower conflict: "Willingness to risk one's life for a purely abstract goal, the worldwide ideological struggle that called forth daring, courage, imagination and idealism, will be replaced by economic calculation, the endless solving of technical problems, environmental concerns, and the satisfaction of sophisticated consumer demands.... I can feel in myself and others around me, a powerful nostalgia for the time when history existed."[10]

If Fukuyama's nostalgia appeared to some as tongue in cheek, others saw a genuine faith in the market combined with nostalgia for the moral scaffolding of the era as consistent with Fukuyama's training under the political philosopher Leo Strauss. Either way, his confidence that liberal capitalist democracy had decisively vanquished all possible alternatives for organizing modern society offered a vision of the future that reverberated throughout academia, the media, and popular culture, if in ways unintended by the author.[11] Academic and media critics, some amused or indignant, responded to Fukuyama's essay with a healthy dose of skepticism.[12] Nonetheless, the scholar's message was omnipresent in the media and beyond, becoming a key pillar of the emerging Western story about the end of the cold war.

Fifteen years down the road, Fukuyama vigorously objected to those who had linked his "thesis about the end of history to the foreign policy of President George Bush and American strategic hegemony." Rather, he explained, "I argued that, if a society wanted to be modern, there was no alternative to a market economy and a democratic political system. . . . I never linked the global emergence of democracy to American agency, and particularly not to the exercise of American military power."[13] Indeed, Fukuyama broke with his neoconservative allies over the US invasion of Iraq in 2003. His work has also advocated a mix of market and state mechanisms in pursuit of a healthy economy. More recently, in 2016, he denounced the radical privatization of neoliberalism as a perversion of free market ideas and charged neoliberal policies with providing the incubator for the right-wing politics of Brexit and Donald Trump.[14] Yet none of these later developments should obscure Fukuyama's unbridled enthusiasm for liberal capitalism in his 1992 book *The End of History and the Last Man*. There, he didn't recognize the vulnerability of states under what he stipulates as liberal democracy, nor did he manifest concern that neoliberal deregulations required the diminishing of state capacity. In the book, Fukuyama argues that the liberal idea is "emerging victorious." He defines a liberal state as one in which its citizens are protected by the rule of law and have guarantees of free speech, free assembly, and freedom of religion. In its economic manifestation, argues Fukuyama, "liberalism is the recognition of the right of free economic activity and economic exchange based on private property and markets." A liberal state is a state that "protects such economic rights."[15]

In an afterword to the 2006 edition, accounting for a lack of global prosperity despite the dominance of capitalism, Fukuyama maintains that economic development "is not driven simply by good economic policies, you have to have a state to live in that guarantees law and order, property rights, rule of law and political stability before you have investment, growth, commerce, international trade and the like." But for Fukuyama, this was "something that cannot be taken for granted in the developing world."[16] Although he acknowledged a crisis of the welfare state in Europe, he failed to anticipate how quickly neoliberal policies would disrupt state capacities and shred social safety nets in the developed world.

Fukuyama's latter-day regrets and his desire to distance himself from policies of neoliberalism notwithstanding, his influence in the late 1980s and 1990s cannot be denied. Then, one was hard-pressed to find caution about the free market within a range of liberal and conservative social scientists. Nor should it diminish our sense of how fundamentally at odds these ideas were with the ideas and hopes that had sparked change in the Eastern bloc.

Those reforms had begun as movements to improve socialism that preserved egalitarian values—socialism with a human face—not as pro-capitalist free market movements.

Moreover, intentions aside, it is hardly surprising that in the early 1990s, Fukuyama's argument that the free market was the only game in town became neatly yoked to cold war triumphalism and the military policies of both Bush administrations. Despite Fukuyama's desire to separate neoliberalism from US military expansionism on philosophical grounds, in fact, neoliberal economic policies traveled in tandem with, and were often developed in direct political collaboration with, US military intervention.

Most importantly, Fukuyama and his contemporaries assumed that liberal capitalist democracy would survive the collapse of communism. In the early 1990s, liberal capitalist institutions may have appeared robust and spreading globally. But neoliberal market fundamentalism also entailed an ideological and political commitment to draconian cuts in social spending, which, along with accelerating economic inequality, ultimately undermined the capitalist liberal order that Fukuyama and his contemporaries assumed to be triumphant and permanent—allowing the rise of antidemocratic, authoritarian movements to sweep into power over the next decades.

The US invasion of Iraq in 1991 squelched hopes within the United States that reduced military spending would allow investment in domestic social priorities. In addition to securing Western access to Middle East oil reserves, the invasion allowed the Defense Department to craft and enact US strategies for solidifying its status as a one-world hegemon.

The marriage of militarism and free market ideology was given a major boost in what came to be known as the Wolfowitz Doctrine, a Defense Department strategy paper leaked to the *New York Times* in 1992. Authored by the Pentagon's then–undersecretary of policy and longtime Fukuyama associate Paul Wolfowitz, the doctrine outlined a forceful and unprecedented rejection of the collective internationalism central to the vision of such reformers as Havel as well as Gorbachev. The paper asserted that "America's political and military mission in the post-cold-war-era will be to ensure that no rival superpower is allowed to emerge in Western Europe, Asia, or the former Soviet Union."[17] The Wolfowitz Doctrine was considered so extreme that then-president Bush felt obliged to disavow it.[18] Arguably, though, Wolfowitz's aggressive unipolar vision provided the clearest statement of American hegemonic intentions and an accurate description of its actions in the late 1980s and 1990s. In effect, Wolfowitz laid down the principles guiding policy in the years to come.[19] The document's stated intent to assume responsibility for the defense of former Warsaw Pact countries and expand NATO underscored that the document outlined a mentality and policies that, over the course of the next decade, rebooted the cold war, not as a repetition but as a darker do-over. Wolfowitz sanctioned twin pillars of US control: military might and economic hegemony based on radical privatization.

The very idea that Western military power won the cold war, a key tenet in the triumphalist claims of Reagan and Bush, elicited challenges from domestic and global audiences who viewed militarism as dangerous and obsolete. Signs of this challenge to the legitimacy of cold war militarism are evident in a seemingly innocuous event: a White House gala celebrating an intelligence community on the defensive.

Ronald Reagan, Tom Clancy, and *The Hunt for Red October*

On February 18, 1990, a week after Mandela's release from prison and with the Soviet Communist Party about to relinquish control of government, President George H. W. Bush hosted a White House screening of the Hollywood submarine thriller *The Hunt for Red October*.[20] Based on Tom Clancy's 1984 novel of the same name—written at the height of Reagan's cold war—the novel (published by the US Naval Institute after rejection by major publishers) and its author had languished in obscurity until Reagan pronounced the book "unputdown-able" at a press conference. The presidential endorsement made Clancy a household name and a best-selling author. Over the next two decades, Clancy's role as a popularizer of US cold war triumphalism was solidified with nine novels reaching the number one slot on the *New York Times* fiction best-seller list between 1986 and 2003 (often for months at a time). Clancy's military-political thrillers left an indelible mark on American culture.[21]

For Bush, the film's release on the brink of the fall of Soviet communism provided not merely a festive occasion but also proof that the United States had prevailed thanks to its projection of military strength. Popular culture and the media, as much as political speeches and punditry, were fundamental in establishing Reagan and Bush's narrative as cold war victors.

The presidential screening of *The Hunt for Red October* offers a window into how the narrative developed by Reagan carried over into Bush's defense of the new world order. If the screening indicates, at first glance, a simple celebration of triumphalism, a closer look reveals a concerted effort on the part of the administration to control the story of the end of the cold war and to cast the intelligence community in a more heroic light.

Given the ongoing criticism of the role and legacy of the CIA, triumphalism required substantial cultural as well as political work. The agency later worked closely with producers and actor Ben Affleck in the 2002 film adaptation of Clancy's *Sum of All Fears*. The navy advised the producers of *The Hunt for Red October*, and there is ample evidence that the intelligence community recognized in the film an opportunity for badly needed good publicity.

Those present at Bush's "star-studded screening" included Robert M. Gates, then deputy assistant for national security affairs and future secretary of defense for both George W. Bush and Barack Obama. Investigating the relationship between politicians and the entertainment industry, journalist Matt Novak filed a Freedom of Information request with the George H. W. Bush Presidential Library on the screening. His request yielded a trove of redacted photos and a redacted final guest list. Novak writes that the filmmakers insisted on the verisimilitude of *The Hunt for Red October*, "even insisting, in the pre-credit message, that the events of the movie had actually happened." With Gates and CIA officials attending the screening, perhaps the intelligence community regarded the film as a way to improve the reputation of the CIA and to convince the public of the continued relevance of intelligence agencies. In any case, the CIA and navy rarely looked as good as they did in *The Hunt for Red October*.[22]

If Clancy created the most sympathetic CIA agents in the fictional world of intelligence, he was hardly alone among writers depicting cold war and military themes. Around the time of the White House screening, Clancy's *Clear and Present Danger* competed with darker versions of Western actions in the cold war—John le Carré's *Russia House* (1989) and Robert Ludlum's *Bourne Ultimatum* (1990)—all three novels becoming *New York Times* bestsellers in the space of about eight months. As popular as cold war novels and movies were, Clancy maintained a unique relationship with Republican Party leaders and the military establishment, cementing his status as a conservative icon and popularizer of post–cold war triumphalism.

Before *The Hunt for Red October*'s release, producers fretted over whether the cold war theme would resonate with audiences. They added a teaser emphasizing that the film was set in 1984, before Gorbachev came to power. Some critics found the timing of the film odd. Vincent Canby of the *New York Times* called it "an elegy for those dear, dark, terrible days of the cold war, when it was either them or us, and before the world had become so thoroughly fractured that it is no longer possible to know exactly who the thems are."[23]

Canby judged the film "most peculiar" in terms of "logic and politics," but American audiences loved it. *The Hunt for Red October* was one of the highest-grossing films of 1990, earning $122 million in North America and $200 million worldwide. The romance of the Soviet dissident, as fundamental to the US cold war imaginary as any idea of an enemy, could now be consummated in the film as fulfilled desire.[24] When Soviet captain Marko Ramius (Sean Connery) murders his superior officer, to all appearances he is a maniacal enemy commanding a nuclear-armed submarine with unprecedented stealth technology, heading off course toward New York City. As Ramius is pursued by the Soviets (who fear his defection and the loss of their prize technology) and Americans (who fear an attack), the audience learns that the captain is distraught over the death of his wife, for which he blames the Soviets. Moreover, Ramius is Lithuanian, suggesting his motive to defect. As both sides seek to destroy the vessel, the ultimate success of Ramius's sabotage and defection is achieved through a mind meld with CIA analyst Jack Ryan (Alec Baldwin), who defies the order to destroy the runaway vessel when he grasps Ramius's intentions. The bromance imagined in the movie played out an archetypal relationship in cold war culture. The cultural logic of the cold war had never simply posited an absolute enemy; it was also about desire and the possibility of friendship. The affinity between the Soviet dissident and the US hero, who defies rank and protocol to uphold national security, not only remained popular in 1990 as the Soviet Union began to crumble but also represented a new trope of triumphalism. What Canby read as an elegy to the past, others read as an affirmation: in the long (male-centered) flirtation with Soviet dissidents, the Americans had finally gotten the guy.

Declassified British documents provide further insight into the strange career of popular culture and diplomacy in the production of US triumphalism. In 2015, Britain's National Archives published a file marked "particularly sensitive" by Margaret Thatcher's private secretary Charles Powell. The file recorded a conversation between Reagan and Thatcher the day after the 1986 Reykjavik Summit between Reagan and Gorbachev had ended without a deal. At Reykjavik, Gorbachev proposed banning all ballistic missiles, but talks collapsed when Reagan insisted on continued research into the US Strategic Defense Initiative, dubbed "Star Wars" by critics and Reagan alike for its militarization of outer space. In retrospect, the talks were credited with progress leading to the 1987 Intermediate-Range Nuclear Forces Treaty. But not only had Reagan refused to drop his pet project, in his postmortem conversation with Thatcher, Reagan expressed "deep distrust of Soviet motives," arguing that "the Russians don't want war, they want victory by using the threat of nuclear war."[25] "The president," reported Powell, "strongly recommended to the prime minister a new book by the author of 'Red October' called ... 'Red Storm Rising.'" According to Reagan, "it gave an excellent picture of the Soviets' intention and strategy."[26]

Reagan and Thatcher's coordination before the summit had already raised concerns about Reagan's lack of attention to detail, and a British Foreign Office memo to Reagan had been trimmed and "relaxed" in tone to cater to the president's limitations. For a correspondent writing in the *Independent*, Reagan's recommendation to his "political soul mate" confirms that the novel "seems to have influenced his thinking at a critical juncture in the Cold War."[27] The correspondent added, "The Downing Street memo offers a tantalising suggestion that the former film star may have begun to conflate fact with fiction when it came to interpreting Mr. Gorbachev's actions," and that Downing Street had come to suspect as much.[28]

What did Reagan take away from *Red Storm Rising*? In the novel, Soviets seize oil fields in the Persian Gulf after Islamic terrorists destroy an oil production facility in Russia. As NATO fights the Warsaw Pact aggressors, the conflict spirals into World War III. Tracking all too neatly onto Reagan's reading of Gorbachev, the novel "features a slick and duplicitous Politburo chairman who makes Washington a generous offer on arms reduction while all the time secretly planning for war."[29] In the book, the entire Soviet strategy is based on duplicity. The conflict begins when Soviets frame West Germany for attacks actually carried out by the Soviets; as the conflict escalates, Soviet strategy depends on deception about their resources. Only US persistence, a keen eye for Russian vulnerability, and the ability to see beyond Soviet deception prevent the escalation to nuclear war.

How did Reagan interpret Gorbachev as seeking victory through the threat of nuclear war, as he told Thatcher, when Gorbachev had proposed banning ballistic missiles? Perhaps conflating Gorbachev with the character in Clancy's book who proposed peace as a cover for aggression, Reagan, who had actually accelerated the arms buildup, projected the aggression onto Gorbachev. And critically, in the novel the war ends because the West sees through the Warsaw Pact's duplicitous schemes and is subsequently relentless in its military response. As policy makers consumed fictionalized accounts of the Warsaw Pact, they were about to meet that world's real-life dissenters.

A Tale of Two Dissidents: Walesa and Havel in DC

On November 15, 1989, Walesa addressed Congress and an American public that had witnessed the rapid dismantling of the Berlin Wall less than a week before. Opening his address with the words "we the people," the labor leader, immortalized for many Americans in Andrzej Wajda's 1981 film *Man of Iron*, expressed gratitude for American aid and urged a "Marshall Plan to aid Poland and Eastern Europe," as the Soviets had forbidden them from participating in the postwar Marshall Plan. Describing the new noncommunist government's reform efforts, Walesa told Congress that "our task is viewed with understanding by our Eastern neighbors and their leader Mr. Gorbachev."[30] Indeed, Gorbachev had endorsed Solidarity in April 1989, stating that he saw no reason why the Soviet Union could not work with the trade union as well as the government. After all, Gorbachev explained, social democrats and communists are cut from the same cloth; as an example, he cited his cooperation with French president François Mitterrand, and their shared vision of a twelve-member European Union. As scholar Mary Sarotte has argued, this vision, widely shared among European reformers, would have entailed a smaller role for the United States. Although there was no inherent conflict between Walesa's vision of European integration and his eagerness to solicit aid from the United States, ironies abound in his interactions with George H. W. Bush.[31]

Bush was not only determined that US power in Europe not be diminished; he was also antilabor, a fundamental difference papered over by shared anticommunism, and the anticommunist bloc within the American Federation of Labor and Congress of Industrial Organizations (AFL-CIO). Solidarity had emerged in a 1980 strike at the Lenin Shipyards in Gdansk; only a year later, Reagan, with Bush as his vice president, had broken the air traffic controllers' union strike, sending an ominous signal to American labor unions. As *Washington Post* columnist Harold Meyerson reflected, "Employers ... feel little or no obligation to their workers, and employers got that message [from Reagan's action] loud and clear." Meyerson added that employers now had the green light to illegally fire workers who sought to unionize, to replace permanent employees who could collect benefits with temps who could not, and to ship factories and jobs overseas.[32]

On June 13, 1989, Bush vetoed a law passed by Congress that would have raised the minimum wage to $4.55. The following month, he traveled to Poland and met with Solidarity leaders in Gdansk, addressing a crowd of twenty-five thousand at the Lenin Shipyards. Bush was accompanied by Lane Kirkland, the executive director of the AFL-CIO, who held strong anticommunist views. With Bush's Poland trip hailed as a diplomatic success, Walesa's visit to the United States came at the invitation of the AFL-CIO. Perhaps willing to engage in a symbolic gesture, with Walesa still traveling the United States seeking aid and investment for Poland, Bush signed an act on November 17, 1989, raising the minimum wage to $4.25 an hour, lower than the amount he had vetoed earlier in the year.[33]

If seeking Western aid and market reform was at the center of Walesa's agenda, building a new international community was at the heart of Havel's vision. After multiple arrests, including a stint in prison from 1979 to 1983, the dissident had last been arrested by Czech police on October 27, 1989.[34] Two months later, on December 29, the Czech Parliament unanimously elected Havel president. Within weeks, he was in the United States to enlist support for the new government's reforms. Havel immediately set off alarm bells by voicing his hope that NATO and the Warsaw Pact would soon be abolished (ironic, in retrospect, since he later became an advocate of NATO's expansion). "The word spread," reported the *Guardian*, that "the idealistic Mr. Havel wanted to scrap NATO and the Warsaw Pact and let the Europeans organise their own security system and live happily ever after."[35] Havel sought to assure the skittish Americans, explaining that "for another hundred years, American soldiers shouldn't have to be separated from their mothers just because Europe is incapable of being a guarantor of world peace." Europe, perhaps under a "new pan-European structure," would be able to "decide for itself how many of whose soldiers it needs so that its own security ... may radiate peace into the whole world."[36]

Addressing a joint session of Congress, the poet-philosopher befuddled some members with his insistence that "consciousness precedes being."[37] According to the *Guardian*, one hungry member of Congress heard the phrase as "nacho-cheese burrito."[38] Other perhaps less famished and more geopolitically minded lawmakers thought they heard Havel declare, "Confucius precedes Beijing."[39] Another observer reported that some legislators who had actually heard "consciousness precedes being" thought that the statement was an endorsement of their antiabortion position.[40]

The White House pushed Havel to clarify or retract his speech's alarming implications that in a post–cold war world, NATO was irrelevant. Havel sought to reassure Congress and the Bush administration, while insisting on his vision of a new Europe freed of the constraints imposed by a bipolar world. Responding to reported differences with the Bush administration over US troops stationed in Europe, Havel said, "It is not true that the Czech writer Václav Havel wishes to dissolve the Warsaw Pact tomorrow and NATO the day after that."[41]

Asserting his country's independence from the Soviet Union, Havel told Congress, "Czechoslovakia is returning to Europe," and, he added, it is no longer "someone's meaningless satellite." Havel desired "the quickest possible departure of Soviet troops from Czechoslovakia" and sought to make substantial cuts in the Czech army. Again asserting an autonomy for Europe that implied a diminished role for the United States, Havel insisted that "our freedom, independence and our new-born democracy have been purchased at great cost, and we will not surrender them." The audience rose to its feet.[42]

Yet Havel made clear that to assert autonomy from the Soviet Union did not mean replacing one relationship of dependency with another. Havel told Congress, "These revolutionary changes will enable us to escape from the rather antiquated straitjacket of this bipolar view of the world, and to enter at last into an era of multipolarity; that is, into an era in which all of us, large and small, former slaves and former masters, will be able to create what your great President Lincoln called the family of man."[43]

If Congress had been perplexed by "consciousness precedes being," it may have been politically convenient for members to ignore, or mishear, Havel's appeal to move beyond a bipolar world and, in particular, to support Gorbachev's reforms. As to the question of how to create this multipolar world, Havel tested his audience further, explaining, "My reply is as paradoxical as the whole of my life has been. You can help us most of all if you help the Soviet Union on its irreversible but immensely complicated road to democracy."[44] A staunch opponent of communism who supported market reforms, Havel wanted the United States to back Gorbachev's reforms, not turn the economy over to the International Monetary Fund, and certainly not to expand NATO through the former Soviet sphere. The Bush administration tacitly rejected Havel's and Walesa's appeal to the United States to support Gorbachev, whose reforms had facilitated the success of their own agendas. In backing Gorbachev's opponent, Boris Yeltsin, Bush rejected Havel's belief that Soviet stability was critical to the success of Europe. Bush, and later Clinton, conflated Yeltsin's pro-market policies with "democracy"; Yeltsin's autocratic government presided over the rise of a corrupt oligarchy in a frenzy of radical privatization.

Havel later became an ardent supporter of NATO expansion because of his strong belief in the importance of multinational cooperation and his ties to US politicians, chief among them Bill Clinton. The turning point, as we shall see in the next chapter, may have been NATO's belated intervention

1.1 Nelson Mandela's cell, Robben Island, South Africa

in the Bosnian genocide after UN inaction. The 1993 breakup of Czechoslovakia ensued from the conflict between the free market position of Václav Klaus, leader of the monetarist party, and the Slovakian preference for more interventionist economic policies. Havel's position was closer to the Slovakians'. He later regretted that he could not stop the secession, which he regarded as the democratic right of Slovakia. He also rued listening too much to the "experts" in accepting market reforms, not trusting his instincts to urge caution against radical reforms.[45]

The Challenge of Nelson Mandela and the ANC

When Nelson Mandela died in 2013, George H. W. Bush described his June 1990 visit to the White House as the "genuine highlight" of his presidency.[46] Bush's rosy recollection of the event obscures that the South African leader's sudden release by the white-minority apartheid regime, a strong US ally throughout the cold war, presented vexing issues for the US president. As images of Mandela leaving the prison on foot past cheering crowds sparked global celebrations, the turn of events disrupted Bush's determination to control the narrative of the end of the cold war. Mandela's subsequent visit to Washington presented an inconvenient counternarrative for Bush, the intelligence community, and the architects of a new world order based on free market policies.

On the one hand, the end of US-Soviet hostilities promised to make the matter of real and imagined links between the ANC and Soviet communism a moot point. While the Soviets had provided aid to the ANC, the United States had exaggerated Moscow's influence on ANC policy and actions, brandishing anticommunism to resist the international antiapartheid movement.[47] The dissolution of the Soviet Union thus allowed for the possibility of a negotiated end to apartheid. But the cold war wasn't over—not in southern Africa, where pro-apartheid forces unleashed cold war–sanctioned political violence as the now-unbanned ANC tried to move ahead with peaceful negotiations.

As the global antiapartheid movement gained momentum, the regime's defenders held fast to the notion that anticommunism lent a veneer of legitimacy to South Africa's white-minority-ruled police state. But white resistance only intensified with the collapse of the Soviet Union. Those desperate to hold on to power waged and fomented violence aimed at undermining the negotiation process. More than fourteen thousand Black South Africans perished in the orchestrated terror between Mandela's release and the first democratic election in 1994, when Mandela was elected president.

From the moment of Mandela's release, establishment commentators revived the hoary trick of red-baiting, emphasizing ideological differences between Mandela and the United States. When Mandela praised the South African Communist Party as an ally in the struggle, the *Washington Post* disdainfully wondered, "How can a party that now stands revealed almost everywhere else in the world as repressive, corrupt, and bankrupt win top billing at one of the century's great celebrations of freedom?" The short answer, for the *Post*, was that "Mandela is caught in something of a time warp," as the party had been aiding revolutionary guerrilla action at the time of his arrest. The *Post* also took issue with the agenda of economic justice in the ANC's 1955 Freedom Charter, calling it a "lumpily Marxist formulation" and fretting that it remains "the organization's ideological beacon."[48]

Amid debates pitting free market fundamentalism against economic democracy, other troubling legacies of the cold war emerged. On June 10, with Mandela en route to the United States, the *Chicago Tribune* reported, based on a CIA source, that hours after Mandela's August 5, 1962, arrest, Paul Eckel, an agency operative, walked into his office and said, "We have turned Mandela over to the South African security branch. We gave them every detail, what he would be wearing, the time of day, just where he would be. They have picked him up. It is one of our greatest coups."[49] On the eve of Mandela's visit, embarrassed government officials refused to comment on the exposé.[50] From the time of Mandela's release, officials insisted that the United States had always supported Mandela's fight against apartheid and had opposed his arrest. Pressed for clarification following reports of CIA involvement, Bush's White House press secretary, Marlin Fitzwater, commented, "We find no value in reviewing a thirty-year-old history in this case."[51] Here, instead of reckoning with the consequences of a cold war alliance with a tyrannical white-minority regime, the presumed end of history discouraged acknowledgment of past transgressions. Case closed.

In the longer term, the declassification of public memory continued unabated. Donald Rickard, a former US vice consul in Durban and a CIA operative, reported his involvement in Mandela's arrest to British filmmaker John Irvin, director of the 2016 documentary *Mandela's Gun*. The film explores the ANC's shift to armed struggle following the apartheid state's violent repression of nonviolent protesters. Rickard told Irvin that Americans believed that Mandela was "completely under the control of the Soviet Union."[52] Rickard voiced no regrets, stating that the United States believed that Mandela could pull it into a war with the Soviets and "had to be stopped."[53]

As international and US press coverage reported on the CIA's role in Mandela's arrest and imprisonment, Bush went on the offensive, outlining his policy differences with Mandela and demanding that Mandela shift his objectives. Bush called on Mandela to renounce his defense of armed struggle in the fight against apartheid. Furthermore, he demanded a full embrace of "democracy," defined as unencumbered free markets and privatization.

Bush as Shaper of 1970s and 1980s Policy

Bush's demands had roots in long-standing US opposition to Mandela and the ANC and its broader opposition to African and third-world liberation movements. Bush had a direct hand in such policies, first as US ambassador to the United Nations, then as CIA director in 1976, and finally as vice president in the Reagan administration; all shaped Bush's animus toward the ANC and his 1990 confrontation with Mandela.

As ambassador to the UN, Bush had recognized the politicized nature of attempts to distinguish between "terrorism" and "resistance." As the

United States lobbied the Arab world to take action against terrorism, Bush "expected the debate to quickly move to charges of US terrorism in Vietnam."[54] He was also deeply aware that the question of South Africa—the apartheid government's insistence on defining the ANC as a terrorist entity—had a fundamental impact on the ultimate UN resolution. As the historian Paul Chamberlin has shown, Bush believed that the Arab states had outflanked the United States by convincing African nations that the string of antiterrorist resolutions favored by the United States "might be used to target African liberation movements."[55]

Bush's brief tenure as CIA director coincided with an escalation of armed conflict in southern Africa. After the US fiasco in Vietnam, Henry Kissinger had been determined to demonstrate that the United States would not succumb to leftist governments and chose his showdown in Africa, where the United States supported the National Union for the Total Independence of Angola (UNITA) in Angola.[56] Bush was sworn in as CIA director in January 1976, in the wake of what the United States considered a humiliating defeat in Angola at the hands of Cuban troops. As the scholar Piero Gleijeses has written, in July 1975, "Pretoria and Washington had begun parallel covert operations in Angola. . . . Both wanted to crush the leftist MPLA [People's Movement for the Liberation of Angola]." With the MPLA winning the civil war in September, Washington urged Pretoria to intervene. South African intervention turned the civil war into an international conflict. The MPLA began to crumble, until Cuba responded to its appeals for troops on November 4. Though American officials called Cubans "Moscow's mercenaries," the evidence is clear that Cuba had no guarantee of support from Moscow and acted out of support for the struggle against apartheid.[57]

As CIA director, Bush contended with the "tidal wave unleashed by the Cuban victory" and the "great psychological impact and hope it aroused" among opponents of white supremacy, presiding over the agency as President Gerald Ford froze détente with the Soviet Union over Angola.[58] With South African troops forced to retreat from Angola to Namibia on March 27, 1976, the contours of the battle lines over southern Africa were drawn.

UNITA's anticommunist and ruthless guerrilla leader Jonas Savimbi was among a handful of US clients with whom Bush would work closely over the next decades. Doug Smith, the CIA station chief in Kinshasa from 1983 to 1986, recalled believing, like many CIA and Defense Intelligence Agency officers, that Savimbi could overthrow the Angolan government and "push the Cubans out." But, he added, "in retrospect it wasn't a good idea—because of the extent of Savimbi's crimes. He was terribly brutal." Marrack Goulding, the British ambassador in Luanda, characterized Savimbi as "a monster whose lust for power had brought appalling misery to his people."[59]

Yet in the 1980s Republicans openly espoused their support for Savimbi. Writing in support of a bill introduced by Jack Kemp, a Republican congressman from New York, and Democrat Claude Pepper, House minority leader Robert H. Michel wrote to Secretary of State George P. Schulz arguing that US support for UNITA "is not only a geo-strategic but a moral necessity."[60]

US support of Savimbi against the leftist government of Angola was intimately linked to US acquiescence in South Africa's occupation of Namibia. The International Court of Justice had ruled in 1971 that the South African occupation of the former German colony was illegal. The South West Africa People's Organization (SWAPO), the guerrilla group fighting to oust South African rule, operated from Angola, where the MPLA gave them a base.[61] While the Ford administration supported a 1976 UN Council Resolution demanding independence for Namibia, when South Africa refused to comply, the United States withdrew support of the mandatory arms embargo. Namibia would not achieve independence until 1990.[62]

The Cold War Roots of Terror

Asked by Walter Cronkite in a 1981 interview about his support of the apartheid government, Reagan defended the regime as a "country that has stood beside us in every war we've ever fought, a country that strategically is essential to the free world in its production of minerals we all must have."[63] Under Reagan, as Mahmood Mamdani has shown, CIA chief William J. Casey "took the lead in orchestrating support for terrorist and pro-terrorist groups around the world—from RENAMO in Mozambique to UNITA in Angola, and from contras in Nicaragua to the mujahideen in Afghanistan—through third and fourth parties." For Mamdani, these actions constituted the cold war roots of terror, as the "shift from targeting the armed forces of governments to its political representatives and then its civilians blurred the distinction between military and civilian targets. This blurring led to political terror—the targeting of civilians for political purposes—as a sustained strategy in peacetime combat."[64]

The Reagan administration redefined national liberation movements as terrorist threats based on a purported link to worldwide Soviet conspiracy. In 1981, Reagan's secretary of state, Alexander M. Haig, charged Moscow with "the training, funding and equipping of global terrorism," an accusation that struck many as ill-informed. In fact, CIA and FBI reports found "no hard evidence of Soviet involvement in international terrorism." Attempts to revise CIA reports in accord with Haig's statements met with further skepticism.[65]

In 1981, Harry Rositzke, ten years after his retirement from the CIA as a Soviet specialist, excoriated Reagan and Haig for reviving the idea that the Soviet Union was managing a worldwide terrorist conspiracy, and for conflating national liberation movements with terrorism. Writing in the *New York Times*, Rositzke held that Reagan's "conspiracy thesis" misunderstood the Soviet aversion to terrorism. Moscow, he argued, viewed "any violence not directed at transforming society 'anarchic' and they deplore it as pointlessly destructive."[66]

Rositzke found even more deplorable "the equating of terrorism with national wars of liberation." Though no friend of such movements, Rositzke ridiculed the administration's view that liberation movements were directed by Moscow. "With all due respect to the K.G.B.," he argued, "no service can totally control and manipulate a dozen regimes and security services, including [those of] Col. Muammar el-Qaddafi and Fidel Castro."[67] Moreover, this "damaging error" was parroted by the *Wall Street Journal*, which "demands that no one should be allowed to say without challenge that Soviet support for national liberation movements is by definition different than Soviet support for terrorism."[68]

By 1985, Reagan pivoted from the Soviets as he escalated his accusations against a purported international terrorist network.[69] In July 1985, Reagan accused Iran, Libya, North Korea, Cuba, and Nicaragua of forming an international terrorist network that he compared to Murder Inc. Reagan vowed, "We are not going to tolerate these attacks from outlaw states run by the strangest collection of misfits, looney tunes, and squalid criminals since the advent of the Third Reich."[70] At the time, members of his administration as well as the CIA were already in clandestine discussions with Israel that would lead to the Iran-Contra scandal, about the possibility of opening strategic discussions with Iran and selling arms to the country. Viewed as outrageous at the time, the notions of outlaw nations in Reagan's Murder Inc. speech became commonplace in the rhetoric of rogue nations in the George H. W. Bush and Clinton administrations and, later, George W. Bush's 2002 "Axis of Evil" speech.

Throughout the 1980s, Reagan's penchant for labeling his adversaries as terrorists justified the administration's support for apartheid South Africa. In 1986, Reagan vetoed legislation to impose economic sanctions on South Africa, calling it "immoral" and "repugnant."[71] The veto was overridden by Congress. Reagan was joined in his support of apartheid by Dick Cheney, Wyoming representative, soon-to-be secretary of defense in the George H. W. Bush administration, and future vice president in the George W. Bush administration. Cheney opposed a congressional resolution calling for Mandela's release from detention. At the time, Mandela was in his twenty-third year of a twenty-seven-year prison term.[72]

In 1988, the State Department placed Mandela and the ANC on the list of international terrorist organizations. The following year, the ANC was featured in a Defense Department publication, *Terrorist Group Profiles*, with a foreword by then–vice president Bush.[73] This reflexive conflation of terrorism and national liberation groups became a major bone of contention between Mandela and Bush during Mandela's 1990 visit to the United States. Less evident at the time was Bush's behind-the-scenes courtship of southern African cold war dictators, building on decades-long relationships, that informed his approach to Mandela.[74]

Cold War Clientelism

Bush's meetings with Mobutu Sese Seko, president of Zaire (Congo), provide a snapshot of the sordid clientelism in the foreign policy of anticommunism, relationships that Andrew Friedman has characterized as "imperial intimates."[75] At a 1989 meeting in Tokyo, Bush told Mobutu that he was encouraged by developments in Angola and continued to support their ally Jonas Savimbi, adding that "Zaire can take part of the credit for the Cubans leaving."[76] In June, Bush welcomed Mobutu to the White House. Acknowledging their many meetings over the years "and that it was always a pleasure to see him again," Bush congratulated Mobutu on his "visionary leadership" and his "diplomatic triumph in bringing together Angola's President Dos Santos and UNITA's Jonas Savimbi" in a meeting in Zaire.[77]

Having praised Mobutu for his role in negotiating a cease-fire in the Angolan civil war, Bush confronted him on human rights, noting that Mobutu "has some critics in this country, and we can't ignore them." A defensive Mobutu claimed that the UN Human Rights Commission had exonerated Zaire, removing it from the "watch list." Mobutu boasted that Congress had passed a resolution praising him. Indeed, Congress had praised him as "an effective partner with the United States in Africa" who "deserves the heartfelt congratulations and the gratitude of the support of the United States and the American people."[78] Congress proved fickle, however, a year later cutting off all military and economic aid to Mobutu, citing human rights abuses and corruption, over the objections of the Bush administration and the State Department.[79]

Congress's revocation of aid began the process of cutting ties with Mobutu. But in 1989, his importance within a global anticommunist alliance was revealed in his aggressive wrangling with Bush over aid. Noting his role in negotiations in Africa, Mobutu argued, "All of this activity costs money," observing that support for Zaire paled in relation to its contributions "to our joint efforts." Mobutu used Pakistan as an illustration of unfair treatment: "Here is a country [that facilitates US] assistance to an anti-communist freedom group (the mujahiddin), and which also has a human rights problem." Yet, Mobutu complained, "the US gives $400–500 million each year to Pakistan, compared to $4–5 million to Zaire." Despite the tense exchange, the meeting concluded on a cordial note. When Mobutu suggested that Bush meet with Rwanda's president Juvénal Habyarimana, Bush stated that "he recalled with pleasure the time both Presidents Mobutu and Habyarimana had visited the Bushes at their summer home in Kennebunkport (in the summer of 1987)."[80]

As we will see in the next chapter, US relations to these cold war clients soured as the United States increasingly supported Uganda's president Yoweri Museveni, who had come to power in 1986, judging him a bulwark against fundamentalist terrorism in northern and eastern Africa.[81] In events preceding the 1994 Rwanda genocide, the United States covertly funded the Tutsi-led Rwanda Patriotic Front insurgency against Habyarimana's government, while Mobutu supported his friend Habyarimana. But while Bush gently prodded Mobutu on human rights, in 1989 their shared goals still bound them together. Into the early 1990s, the Bush administration continued to defend Mobutu when Congress slashed aid to Zaire.[82] For Bush, the cold war, as an ordering principle of foreign policy and diplomacy, held a familiarity—indeed, an intimacy—akin to that shaping his personal ties with the likes of Mobutu. And the politics of cold war clientelism had a long life. Paul Manafort, the DC lobbyist for Mobutu and Jonas Savimbi, as well as Filipino dictator Ferdinand Marcos, would resurface in 2016 as the campaign manager for Donald Trump.[83]

Imperial Disavowals

Bush's 1990 outreach to ANC allies whom the United States had only recently vigorously opposed provides a glimpse into the president's concerted attempts to control the narrative of fast-unfolding events. Bush solicited advice from ANC regional allies on how to proceed regarding South Africa. On March 21, he presented himself as a neutral party to President Joaquim Chissano of Mozambique, whose government had hosted ANC forces in exile. Regarding South Africa, Bush told Chissano, "I hope we can help. We don't have a colonial background so perhaps we can help where others couldn't."[84]

Three months later, following Namibia's transition to independence, which had been delayed by US support of apartheid South Africa and UNITA in Angola, Bush conveyed a similar message to Namibian president Sam Nujoma. Nujoma, leader of SWAPO during the Namibian War for Independence (1966–89), was elected president after twenty-nine years in exile. At a White House meeting, Bush told Nujoma, "We see a possible role for ourselves with South Africa if Mandela and de Klerk think it useful. We don't have a colonial history and have a slate clean of colonialism. If we can be helpful in Angola, pushing toward reconciliation, we will do that as well."[85]

Nujoma and Chissano must have been amazed by Bush's disavowals of colonialism, his seeming unwillingness to acknowledge that they had been adversaries, and his assertion of innocence. As head of SWAPO, Nujoma had fought the US-backed South African troops from exile in Angola after Cuban forces drove South Africans out of Angola in 1976.[86] Bush was not simply saying, harking back to the 1898 US intervention and occupation of the Philippines, that the United States was not an empire like European colonizers.[87] He audaciously claimed a colonial innocence that flew in the face of Nujoma's experience of the harmful effects of US policies that had supported South African rule in Namibia, prolonging white supremacy for decades and undermining democratic liberation movements.

Chissano may have been equally nonplussed by Bush's professions of colonial innocence. As a founding member of Frelimo, the Mozambique Liberation Front that fought for independence from Portugal, Chissano had negotiated the country's independence and served as minister of foreign affairs before becoming president when Samora Machel died in a plane crash in 1986. In 1990, Mozambique was fighting a civil war against the Resistencia Nacional Moncambicana (RENAMO), a political party "created in 1976 by Rhodesian intelligence officers, who developed it into a military force." RENAMO received covert CIA and Reagan administration support, along with aid from the apartheid South African government. State Department African affairs specialist Chester Crocker broke with Reagan hardliners by challenging their support for RENAMO. He ultimately reversed US policies, supporting Mozambique's socialist government while pushing them toward market reforms.[88] But the US withdrawal of support for RENAMO could not bring back the one hundred thousand civilians killed by the group. Nor did it halt the atrocities waged by RENAMO in Mozambique and South Africa, including the targeting of ANC leaders and civilians in Natal in 1992.[89] Tragically, the cold war roots of terror unleashed by Western alliances with anticommunist dictators spilled into South Africa and cast a pall over negotiations to end apartheid until the eve of the country's first free elections in April 1994.

Not a Victory Tour: Mandela in the United States

For many Americans, June 1990 was etched in memory as the summer of Nelson Mandela's triumphant tour of major US cities. Mandela was warmly received by supporters, and his presence galvanized members of the civil rights, labor, and antiapartheid coalition that constituted the progressive wing of the Democratic Party. During his stop in the Detroit metropolitan area, Mandela donned a union cap and jacket that he received from the president of the United Auto Workers while visiting a Ford Motor plant in Dearborn, and he expressed gratitude and solidarity with factory employees. A capacity crowd of forty thousand jammed an evening rally at Tiger Stadium, where they heard Mandela quote Marvin Gaye's lyrics to condemn political violence in South Africa: "Brother, brother, there's far too many of you dying, / Mother, mother, there's far too many of you crying." The Detroit event raised more than $1 million for the ANC. The message of Gaye's anthem was clear, as it was in Mandela's New York addresses to the UN General Assembly and a huge rally at Yankee Stadium: "Join us in the international actions we are taking. The only way we can walk together on this difficult road is for you to assure that sanctions are applied."[90] At rally after rally, the cheers rung out, "Keep the Pressure On."[91]

Tens of thousands of euphoric American supporters greeted Mandela at rallies in several major US cities over several weeks in June 1990. South Africans traveling with Mandela later recalled that Mandela was received "like a heroic military figure or one of the first astronauts, just back from space."[92] Events in New York City, Boston, Miami, Atlanta, the Bay Area, Detroit, Los Angeles, and Washington, D.C., were all attended by visibly moved crowds, many of them African American, or, according to one account, a "roistering gaggle of thousands of broadcast and print journalists eager to capture every moment." If the trip, in the eyes of South Africans, was something of an "organizational disaster," it was simultaneously an

1.2 "UAW Welcomes Mandela: U.S. Freedom Tour." 1990 Poster. Walter P. Reuther Library, Archives of Labor and Urban Affairs, Wayne State University.

1.3 Nelson Mandela with Owen Bieber. UAW *Solidarity* cover, summer 1990. Walter P. Reuther Library, Archives of Labor and Urban Affairs, Wayne State University.

"overwhelming public affairs triumph," turning Mandela into "a secular saint and political rock star, all rolled into one."[93]

For Mandela, this was emphatically not a victory tour. The purpose of the American trip and the European stops that followed was to lobby for the continuation of US sanctions on South Africa.[94] This was Mandela's message during his historic address to a joint session of Congress on June 26. For members of the Congressional Black Caucus, the moment capped the legislative victory they had achieved when Congress overrode President Ronald Reagan's veto of the Comprehensive Anti-apartheid Act of 1986, which imposed economic sanctions on the apartheid regime. In remarks frequently interrupted by applause, Mandela expressed gratitude for that support and candidly acknowledged the moment's promise and peril: "We have yet to arrive at the point when we can say that South Africa is set on an irreversible course leading to its transformation into a united, democratic, and nonracial country."[95]

Mandela's tour foregrounded alternative histories at odds with Western triumphalism. He proved to be an eloquent and authoritative dissenter from official US narratives. At a White House meeting on June 26, when Bush called on Mandela to renounce the ANC's armed struggle, the antiapartheid leader refused, attributing Bush's remarks to the fact that Mandela had not yet had the opportunity to explain his position to him. No reasonable person, Mandela argued, could fail to understand the need for armed resistance given the thorough denial of political and civil rights by a violent and repressive police state. In a truly democratic, inclusive government, violence would be unnecessary and unjustified.[96]

Years later, following Mandela's 2013 death, and with recourse to the chastening experience of the 9/11 attacks, US diplomat Princeton Lyman, who had served as ambassador to South Africa as Mandela steered the transition to democracy, owned up to the wrongheadedness of branding Mandela a terrorist. For Lyman, "labeling Mandela a terrorist is a misnomer because he didn't see violence as means of seizing power. Nor did he pursue it wantonly like al Qaida or other terrorist groups, but he used it as a way of forcing the white minority rulers to the negotiating table." Lyman pointed out that "the ANC tried very hard not to have civilian casualties" and that most of the bombings that the group staged took place at night against infrastructure.[97]

Ironically, as the Bush administration disavowed its alliance with Iraq's Saddam Hussein and met freely with Mobutu and Savimbi, both notorious for their ruthlessness, media pundits in lockstep with the administration challenged Mandela about the support the ANC had received from those deemed "outlaw nations" by the United States. During a New York town hall interview that was nationally televised on ABC's *Nightline*, Ted Koppel aggressively questioned Mandela's willingness to associate with Fidel Castro, Yasser Arafat, and Muammar Gaddafi. Mandela's answer left Koppel speechless: "They support our struggle to the hilt. Any man who changes his principles according to with whom he is dealing; that is not a man who can lead a nation."[98] Mandela's refusal to bow to cold war protocol generated a remarkable cultural moment, a slap in the face to Reagan-era anticommunism. Before a mainstream television audience, Mandela situated himself and the antiapartheid struggle firmly within a broadly shared politics and culture of third-world national liberation movements.[99] Lyman remembered Mandela's support for Castro and other pariahs in the eyes of the United States as "driven by the gratitude that he felt for their unstinting support of the anti-apartheid movement, and he avoided passing judgment on their own authoritarian rule. He would say, 'these were people who were helping me when you weren't helping me.' "[100]

After his visit to the states, Mandela and Bush continued to clash over Mandela's rival vision of an egalitarian geopolitical world order. Speaking with Bush in a March 1991 telephone conversation, Mandela voiced his opposition to the US war in the Gulf, explaining why the ANC had backed the UN General Assembly resolution of December 6, 1990, asking the Security Council to pursue a negotiated settlement of Iraq's withdrawal from Kuwait. Mandela's position reflected the UN's comprehensive approach to conflict in the Middle East. He told Bush that the ANC's stance was "similar to [that of] the UN" in supporting Iraq's withdrawal from Kuwait, while also calling for the convening of an international conference for a negotiated settlement of the problems of the Middle East, "including the restoration of rights of the Palestinians and the withdrawal of Israel from the occupied territories." Bush responded, "We opposed Palestinian linkage from the beginning. It plays into the hands of the brutal dictator Saddam Hussein.... Maybe we have an honest difference of opinion. But linkage plays into their hands."[101]

Mandela's defense of third-world allies remained an affront to Bush, who engaged in verbal battles with him over the power to name Cuba, Libya, and others as outlaw nations as opposed to sovereign states. Mandela embraced allies that were key targets of Bush's regional defense strategy. Mandela's friendship with Castro (whom he visited in Cuba in 1991) was particularly irksome to Bush. Mandela's defense of Cuba elicited protests by Cuban Americans when Mandela visited Miami. In addition to Cuba's role in defeating US interests in southern Africa, longtime Bush family investments in Cuba ensured that Castro held a special place of enmity for George H. W. Bush. Bush's father and maternal uncle had run several Havana companies during the 1920s and 1930s involved with sugar and rum distilling industries, along with a major railroad that served these enterprises.[102] Historians and journalists debate the origins of George H. W. Bush's relationship with the CIA, some pointing to ties forged during his undergraduate membership in Yale's Skull and Bones society. But whatever the precise origins of Bush's relationship with the CIA, it is clear that his oil company, its operations based near Cuba, served as an intelligence base for the failed 1961 US Bay of Pigs invasion.

Mandela's vision of economic freedom challenged free market dogma. On the eve of his release from prison, Mandela affirmed the ANC's commitment to redistributive justice, arguing that "in our situation state control of certain sectors of the economy is unavoidable."[103] In his June 26 address before Congress, Mandela argued that political change must "also entail the transformation of its economy." A mixed economy was imperative, given the lack of a "self-regulating mechanism in the South African economy which will on its own ensure growth with equity."[104] While Mandela viewed the private sector as a crucial partner, it was "inevitable that the democratic government will intervene in this economy." Condemning the apartheid system, Mandela told Congress, "The extent of the deprivation of millions of people has to be seen to be believed. The injury is made that much more intolerable by the opulence of our white compatriots and the deliberate distortion of the economy to feed that opulence."[105]

Mandela later spoke of the "furious" reaction from the South African business community to his remarks on nationalization, remembering that American business had "put a lot of pressure ... on us ... to reconsider the question of nationalization." There was also pushback from the conservative economics of the Reagan-Bush-Thatcher administrations. Robin Renwick, ambassador to South Africa for the government of British prime minister Margaret Thatcher, recorded what he considered his tutelage of Mandela in neoliberal economics, urging him not to use the word *nationalization* in front of Thatcher. Renwick told Mandela that such ideas of nationalization, promoted during the 1950s, were now outmoded.[106] Keynesianism, let alone redistributive justice, had gone out of style in the years that Mandela had been imprisoned.

In April 1991, amid escalating violence in South Africa, the twelve-member European Union lifted its remaining economic sanctions on South Africa, ignoring appeals from the ANC to keep them in place.[107] In July, against opposition in Congress, Bush followed suit, lifting US sanctions on apartheid South Africa. In response to Mandela's insistence that the "process of dismantling apartheid hasn't proceeded as far as it should have," Bush declared, "I firmly believe that this progress is irreversible."[108] In a telephone conversation, Mandela chastised Bush, telling him, "Your actions are premature," adding that the United States was doing "damage" with its apparent favoritism toward the apartheid regime. For Mandela, even on the terms set by the United States, the conditions had not been met: "There are still political prisoners in prison. It is not correct for the US to have its own definition." Worst of all, Mandela pointed out, "the violence is raging in the country. That is impeding the free political activity."[109]

ANC leaders were gravely disappointed with the international community for removing sanctions. And they were outraged by the political violence in South Africa. Mandela had appealed to Bush for assistance in halting the escalating conflict. The ANC suspended armed resistance in August 1990 in favor of negotiations but soon voiced concern about the existence of a "third force" fomenting unrest with an intent to undermine negotiations. As the scholar Stephen Ellis has argued, "After a brief honeymoon, in which a preliminary accord had been signed between the government and the ANC, Mandela had been incensed by a spate of murderous random attacks on black people, first in the Vaal area, later in the East Rand and on trains running between Soweto and Johannesburg. These attacks, he believed, bore the mark of organized, covert government death squads."[110]

In fact, subsequent inquiries by scholars and the South African Truth and Reconciliation Commission demonstrated that while all parties engaged in violence, the main culprits for the attacks between 1990 and the 1994 elections were security and ex-security force operations, often acting in collaboration with right-wing elements and members of the Inkatha Freedom Party. The "third force" massacres continued until the elections, nearly plunging the country into civil war.[111]

Mandela accused Prime Minister F. W. de Klerk of engaging in political duplicity by pretending to negotiate while allowing government forces to undermine the process. Mandela appealed to Bush to restore sanctions on South Africa, emphasizing the apartheid government's role in the violence. In May 1991, Mandela told Bush that he had "spoken to de Klerk to warn him on the effects of the violence. I have given him concrete examples of the complicity of the police." Mandela continued, explaining that de Klerk never moved on this issue and stating, "We sent him our demands that on May 9th we would halt talks if the government doesn't respond."[112] Bush expressed concern about the violence, emphasizing, "I would appeal to you not to break off the negotiations," and assured Mandela that he would contact de Klerk and would meet with Mandela's opponent, Mangosuthu G. Buthelezi, chief minister of KwaZulu and head of the Inkatha Freedom Party, in June. Buthelezi's Inkatha Party was involved in massacres leading up to South Africa's first free elections in 1994.

Bush met with Buthelezi as promised but did not confront him on his role in the violence. In a June 1991 National Security Council meeting, the president stated that Mandela is "a decent, honest man." But, he continued, "we both have reservations about the ANC. I was concerned by the position they took during the [Iraq] war. I was disappointed by it." Assuring Buthelezi, "You have a lot of respect for you here on this side of the table," Bush asked for his sense of future ANC leadership. In Buthelezi's estimation, Mandela was the plausible leader, as he was committed to negotiation, but Buthelezi warned Bush about the influence of the left, claiming that ANC and South Africa Communist Party activist Joe Slovo was a "colonel in the KGB" and that "half of the Executive Committee of the ANC were card-carrying members of the SACP."[113]

If Buthelezi played to what he understood was Bush's anticommunism, his account on the escalating violence was disingenuous. Despite ample evidence available to Bush on the role of Buthelezi's Inkatha Freedom Party in the violence, Bush broached the issue with an explicit criticism of Mandela and the ANC: "Tell us about the violence problem. Our hearts ache when we see this. The ANC blames it all on de Klerk. That's just not fair. What must be done about it?" Calling the violence in South Africa "endemic," Buthelezi claimed that "a culture of violence is being created by the ANC focus on the armed struggle. Some of them think they can shoot their way into power." Exaggerating his own strength in telling Bush that Inkatha had two million members to the ANC's five hundred thousand, Buthelezi opined that Mandela "sees de Klerk as white" and "wants to go on the basis of race."[114] Whether or not Bush gave any credence to Buthelezi's self-serving account and mischaracterization of the ANC policy of nonracialism, his ease and familiarity of tone with Buthelezi are striking. Both spoke the language of anticommunism, and perhaps Bush, like de Klerk, was willing to look the other way in hope that the elimination of communists would marginalize any remnant of the left in a new government.

With the removal of sanctions and de Klerk's continuing silence as violence soared, in June 1992, Mandela announced that the ANC was suspending negotiations after the June 17 Boipatong massacre, which "left over 40 people dead, after Inkatha members assisted by the security members attacked township dwellers." The international furor that ensued led to some measures to curb government forces, but security and ex-security forces continued to be implicated in the murders that marred negotiations.[115]

Apartheid forces targeted ANC leadership. In October 1992, a Natal ANC leader was shot and killed after disclosing to the *Natal Witness*, a Pietermaritzburg newspaper, evidence that implicated RENAMO in violence in Natal. In April 1993, a Polish right-wing, anticommunist immigrant, Janusz Walús, assassinated Chris Hani, an antiapartheid activist and head of the South African Communist Party. Hani had played a major role in suspending the armed struggle in favor of negotiations. Addressing the nation as the president of the ANC, Mandela appealed for an end to the violence, emphasizing that Hani's assassin was turned in by a white Afrikaner woman. Mandela's speech brought calm and aided in forcing the apartheid government to set a date for elections to appease public anger at the escalating violence.

Less than two months before the April 27, 1994, elections, a white supremacist Afrikaner paramilitary group descended on Mmabatho, the capital of Bophuthatswana. There, Eugene Terreblanche, leader of Afrikaner Weerstandsbeweging, a vigilante group, had threatened a "holy war against 'the godless communists' of the African National Congress." Commandos from Terreblanche's group moved into Mmabatho to join "4,000 white warrior volk."[116] Events at Mmabatho appeared to turn the tide. The police forces that had oppressed Black people in the townships turned on Afrikaner Weerstandsbeweging, killing the organizers as cameras recorded the incident during a live television broadcast. The defiant spasm of white terror and the bloody demise of its adherents at Mmabatho may have bolstered support for Mandela's appeals for calm on the eve of the elections.

Preelection violence kept tensions at a fever pitch. On March 28, clashes occurred outside Shell House, the ANC headquarters, between Inkatha Freedom Party members protesting the upcoming elections and ANC security guards. On March 31, a state of emergency was declared in Natal. Just two days before the election, a car bomb exploded in downtown Johannesburg, near ANC headquarters, killing nine and injuring ninety-two.[117]

Fatal Compromises

The ANC's controversial concessions to banking and financial interests—leading to accusations of selling out—must be seen in the context of the state-sanctioned violence and the premature lifting of economic sanctions during the waning days of apartheid. As political violence threatened to scuttle negotiations, external business and financial interests pressured ANC leaders to avoid actions that would discourage international investment. Mandela recalled "the decisive moment" when, at the January 1992 World Economic Forum in Davos, Switzerland, the finance ministers of the industrialized nations informed him that "we had to remove the fear of business that ... their assets will be nationalized."[118] Mandela continued, "I came home to tell them. Chaps, we have to choose. We either keep nationalization and get no investment, or we modify our own attitude and get investment."[119] Others have pointed to Mandela's meetings at Davos with Vietnamese and Chinese economists whose socialist economies had embraced privatizing government-owned industries as the wave of the future, and who wondered aloud at the ANC's openness to nationalization. Mandela's shift met with considerable skepticism within South Africa.

As Václav Havel had rued taking the advice of pro–free market "experts," in retrospect, South African economists regret having yielded to fears about how the new nation was perceived by others and accepting the "Washington consensus." Some of those involved in economic planning recall the early 1990s as a series of conservative decisions made under duress and preoccupied with ensuring a climate friendly to foreign investors. Others stress that Mandela and ANC leaders hoped for a revival of nonaligned global South alliances and sought investments from prospering Asian tiger economies such as Malaysia. In the end, credibility with foreign investors came at great cost during the 1990s, as the government implemented stringent fiscal policies geared to macroeconomic measures of growth.[120] South African political scientist Adam Habib underlines this point: "The ANC saw the threat of an exodus of investors as more credible and immediate than the challenge of the poor and excluded."[121]

Fateful economic decisions were made in the drafting of the new constitution. As the economist Alan Hirsh has argued, "Not only was the independence of the South African Reserve Bank enshrined within the Constitution, but its mandate was described in the most conservative possible way. There was not a mandate to drive economic development or lean toward full employment." Instead, the mandate was "to protect the value of the currency in the interest of balanced and sustainable economic growth."[122]

Then came the question of debt. Apartheid South Africa was an oligarchy in which four to five companies controlled 80 percent of the wealth. The apartheid central and homeland governments, designed to subjugate the Black majority instead of securing economic growth or efficiency, were heavily indebted, and state budgets were in disarray. But for the incoming ANC government, there was no question that the debts must be paid. To do otherwise would risk the loss of credibility in the eyes of the international community. Much of the debt was to pension funds, affecting the destinies of working people. Mandela and the ANC agreed to pay the debt.

The economic credibility of the postapartheid-ruling ANC was won at great cost. Thabo Mbeki, who succeeded Mandela as the nation's second president, and Finance Minister Trevor Manuel have been accused of pursuing policies one critic describes as "a self-imposed structural adjustment programme ... fairly ruthlessly applied."[123] A key policy program called the Growth, Employment and Redistribution Initiative, "in the contexts of a rising deficit, growing debt, ballooning expenditure by the government and rising inflation," has been similarly characterized as a self-inflicted austerity program, with too little growth.[124] Such growth as was achieved was not in production- or trade-related sectors. Playing by the rules of the international market not only failed to produce significant job growth. As Naomi Klein has put it, the stripping of the new democratic state's assets through privatization resulted in "a twisted case of reparations in reverse."[125]

Once in government, the ANC made vigorous efforts to reform and democratize the International Monetary Fund and global institutions.[126] At the same time, ANC hopes of reshaping investment and trade through global South cooperation continued to inform policy and debate within South Africa. In 1998, Mbeki organized the African Renaissance Conference in Johannesburg, which grappled with issues of a mixed economy similar to those Mandela had raised in 1990. Mbeki warned against treating "the market" as "the modern God ... to whose dictates everything human must bow in a spirit of powerlessness." Mbeki also said, "We cannot win the struggle for South Africa's development outside of the world economy. Thus, we have to attract into the African economy significant amounts of capital."[127] But all of this has played out on a very uneven field. As anthropologist James Ferguson has argued, "However democratic an African government may be in formal terms, its scope for making policy is radically constrained by the nondemocratic international financial institutions themselves."[128]

From Mandela's reluctant embrace of the market economy to the provisions of the constitution, the new government's initial decisions, all with far-reaching consequences, came in the context of enormous pressure from the international financial institutions and a spate of political violence orchestrated by those determined to undermine a negotiated peaceful end to apartheid.

Bush might have recalled with pride his relationship with Mandela, and given the company he had been keeping, Mandela's unimpeachable integrity could not have been lost on him. In 2013, Bush wrote of Mandela as "one of the great moral leaders during that transformative and hopeful time of global change" and characterized his twenty-seven years in custody as "wrongful imprisonment."[129] But Bush's magnanimous memories of Mandela were selective, ignoring Mandela's grave disappointments with US and European politicians and Western business elites as the ANC struggled to build a democracy on fragile foundations of white supremacist oligarchy and terror. A willed amnesia with regard to state violence perpetrated by an apartheid South Africa in its death throes in order to undermine ANC strategy and tactics had been critical to US cold war policy, and it remained critical to a cold warrior's victors' history.

The world rejoiced at the election and inauguration of Mandela in 1994. To global audiences, he won the moral battle over the story of the ANC and apartheid. But Bush and his free market allies succeeded in two crucial ways. First, by publicly deflecting his differences with Mandela, Bush was able to claim Mandela as part of the story of a forward march of universal freedom based on the values of the West, thus severing the history of Mandela and the ANC from a broader story of the struggle for economic as well as political justice. Second, in his one-term presidency, Bush and his allies ensured that future struggles for democracy, including South Africa's transition to democracy, would unfold on a neoliberal, free market terrain. From his rhetoric to his policies, Bush demonstrated a keen sense of the ends of history, the need to control the story of the past to achieve the results he wanted in the present.

Just as the aspirations of many in the third world had been hijacked by cold war dynamics over which most had no say, the global imposition of neoliberalism distorted the aftermath of white supremacist regimes in southern Africa, erasing the history of apartheid South Africa and white-minority-rule governments in southern Africa as part of the Western cold war alliance. Radical privatization was enabled by claims about the cold war that discredited even the most successful mixed economies. The equation of freedom with the free market undergirded devastating policies of neoliberalism, ensuring that from the end of apartheid in South Africa to Russia and the Eastern bloc, reforms that had been grounded in aspirations for economic justice—as well as fundamental political change—played out on a geopolitical terrain of radical privatization and a rapid escalation of inequality. And no region on the globe escaped unscathed.

Out of Order

DISCORDANT TRIUMPHALISM AND THE "CLASH OF CIVILIZATIONS"

There are no longer two superpowers in the world. There's only one.
—George H. W. Bush, 1990

Something has gone out of order, out of new world order.
—Caetano Veloso, "Fora da Ordem," 1992

We are facing a mood and a movement far transcending the level of issues and policies and the governments that pursue them. This is no less than a clash of civilizations.
—Bernard Lewis, "The Roots of Muslim Rage," *Atlantic*, 1990

George H. W. Bush announced his strategic doctrine before Congress on September 11, 1990, in a speech originally scheduled for August 2, the day Iraq invaded Kuwait. In the interval between the invasion and Bush's address, the United States had launched Operation Desert Shield in response to the invasion and Saudi Arabia's request to protect its oil fields. On August 7, US troops and F-15 fighters deployed from Langley Air Force Base in Virginia landed in Saudi Arabia. Ostensibly seeking to liberate Kuwait, the mission also sought to deter Iraq from invading Saudi Arabia to seize control of the Hama oil field near the countries' shared border.[1]

The Persian Gulf Crisis, Bush told Congress, provided "a rare opportunity to advance toward a historic period of cooperation." Out of these "confused times" could emerge a "new world order, a time, freer of threat and terror." Bush yoked his unipolar vision to emergent "clash of civilization" ideas. "Today," Bush asserted, "this new world is fighting to be born ... a world where the rule of law is taking the place of the rule of the jungle."[2] As he disparaged Iraq, a recent ally the United States had supplied with weapons, aid, and strategic advice during its long and costly war with Iran from 1980 to 1988, Bush's reference to the law of the jungle—suggesting a primitive Hobbesian force that must be subdued—was telling.[3] At pains to justify a costly deployment in the Persian Gulf at a moment when many Americans expected the waning cold war would yield a "peace dividend," Bush echoed Ronald Reagan's old saw that the "jungle ... threatens to reclaim this clearing we call civilization."[4] Employing a phrase from the heyday of European imperialism, Bush's reference to the "jungle" portrayed cultural conflict as a threat to global stability, and a call to arms.

Bush's rhetoric of cultural conflict was hardly unique. He may well have been inspired by Bernard Lewis's article "The Roots of Muslim Rage," published just a week earlier in the *Atlantic* magazine. Here, Lewis wrote of a "clash of civilizations," a concept soon to be associated with political scientist Samuel Huntington, first in a 1993 *Foreign Affairs* article, then in his 1996 book. Lewis's *Atlantic* essay alerted readers to a "surge of hatred" in the Islamic world, "a rejection of Western civilization as such," that portended inevitable conflict with the West.[5]

Lewis's essay provoked outrage and incisive critique, much of it due to its influence on policy makers and public opinion. The journalist Steve Coll pinpointed the flaws in Lewis's argument in a 2012 essay: "The notion that a generalized Muslim anger about Western ideas could explain violence or politics from Indonesia to Bangladesh, from Iran to Senegal ... was like arguing that authoritarian strains in Christianity could explain apartheid, Argentine juntas, and the rise of Vladimir Putin. Nevertheless, the meme sold, and it still sells."[6]

As the president conjured an orientalist jungle to make his case for war in the Gulf, his argument papered over past alliances with Iraq. He attempted to squelch any official discussion of continuing US aid to Iraq following its eight-year war with Iran, which ended in 1988. Selling the idea that an

American-led unipolar world would promote peace and stability required jettisoning such unsavory cold war allies as Saddam Hussein and erasing the memory of such alliances. Seizing on a clash-of-civilizations narrative to justify intervention in the Gulf, Bush rebooted cold war binary thinking, telling himself in his diary that Saddam was evil personified and telling his staff "it's black and white, good vs evil."[7]

Declarations of the end of history and a "new world order" by politicians, academics, and journalists during the early 1990s were belied by the political violence of the Balkan wars of independence—notably, the so-called ethnic cleansing of Bosnian Muslims—armed clashes between warlords amid mass starvation in Somalia, and the Rwanda genocide. Here, I focus on narratives invoked by the Bush and Clinton administrations amid lackluster Western responses to these genocides and humanitarian crises. I argue that US interventions and noninterventions—the studied indifference and unwillingness to work with international organizations to stop the slaughter of hundreds of thousands in Bosnia and Rwanda—depended on rewriting the history of the final decades of the cold war, rendering invisible Western culpability in the making of the conditions for these crises.

It should go without saying that US policy makers did not want Yugoslavia or Rwanda to descend into chaos any more than they wanted their anticommunist allies in Afghanistan to turn on the United States. Yet the Bosnian and Rwandan genocides cannot be understood without attention to Western actions during the late cold war. Albeit in very different ways, US economic and political efforts to roll back communism helped to create the conditions for these genocides. For example, Reagan administration policies weaponizing international financial institutions precipitated the collapse of the once-prosperous Yugoslavia.

As political scientist Mahmood Mamdani has argued, "the most intractable internal conflicts in contemporary Africa," as well as those in other places such as Afghanistan and Iraq, "are driven by regional tensions, which are in turn a by-product of the Cold War that led to a regionalization of proxy wars and internal conflicts."[8] Cold war terror spilled over into the 1990–94 Rwandan crisis as the Ugandan dictator Yoweri Museveni funneled US support to provide backing for the 1990 invasion of Rwanda by the Rwandan Patriotic Front (RPF). Through CIA covert aid to the Uganda-based rebel group of Tutsi exiles, the United States had a hand in the instability that led to the genocide lasting from April through August 1994, when hundreds of thousands of Rwandans were slaughtered.[9]

Eliding a complex colonial and cold war history, and unwilling to attend to political and historical causes, the Bush and Clinton administrations fell back on notions of "primordial" hatreds articulated by Lewis, Huntington, and the travel writer turned policy influencer Robert Kaplan. Such atavisms, the logic went, were timeless and intractable, providing the pretext for non-intervention. The clash-of-civilizations trope racializes disorder created by cold war policies while ascribing that disorder to the victims of such policies.[10]

Attention to reinvented civilizationist discourse reveals links between the US intervention in the Gulf and the Bush and Clinton administration responses to political and humanitarian crises in Somalia, Bosnia, and Rwanda.[11] This chapter first considers intervention in Iraq. Then, arguing that Somalia is the exception that proves the rule, I compare US intervention in Somalia—where in Operation Restore Hope, US Marines deployed to Mogadishu in December 1992 to protect UN-sanctioned famine relief efforts—with US hesitance to respond to the slaughter of hundreds of thousands in Bosnia and Rwanda.

As past cold war entanglements were elided in narratives of post-1989 politics, the cold war remained very much present in triumphalist accounts claiming that the collapse of the Eastern bloc proved the superiority of capitalism and vindicated the application of US military force.

Toward a Unipolar World

When Iraq invaded Kuwait, Bush turned the moment into an assertion of unipolar US leadership. His national security adviser, Brent Scowcroft, had been a senior officer in the US Air Force, had served as Henry Kissinger's assistant in the Nixon administration, and had overseen "Vietnamization" and the air force bombing of Vietnam.[12] Appalled that Bush's National Security Council initially reacted to the Kuwait invasion with resignation, Scowcroft steered the discussion away from oil and inter-Arab politics to a focus on the "naked aggression of Iraq" and the broader meaning of the US response, "thinking about the signal that America's response would send to the wider world."[13] As Scowcroft and Bush saw the need for US leadership, Secretary of Defense Dick Cheney chimed in that the "key" was "US military power, the only thing that Saddam fears."[14]

As the historian Jeffrey A. Engel has shown, the first US Iraq War was the moment when Bush defined his notion of a new world order, a unipolar world defined first and foremost, as Scowcroft put it, by "an ongoing process of improvement, as more and more of the world's peoples choose to follow America's lead."[15] Certainly, Bush believed deeply in American exceptionalism; that American values were universal and superior and would eventually be accepted around the world; and that only the United States could safely shepherd the world to a more peaceful and prosperous future. But here, Bush, Cheney, and Scowcroft cloaked their military playbook from the Vietnam War—executing a bombing campaign that targeted Iraqi civilian infrastructure as well as military targets—in the lofty language of a new world order.

When Bush and Mikhail Gorbachev jointly condemned the Iraqi invasion of Kuwait, some observers noted that the cold war was now officially over. But as Engel astutely notes, for Bush, Iraq was also the last act of the cold war, where he made clear to Gorbachev and the world, as he privately told congressional leaders, "There are no longer two superpowers in the world. There's only one."[16]

Cold war triumphalism—the insistence on a conclusive victory—distorted Bush's conception of a new world order, altering it beyond recognition from alternative, aspirational visions of a multipolar demilitarized world. From new justifications for interventions in Central America—now in the name of promoting democracy rather than fighting a communist scourge—to the invocation of clash-of-civilizations rhetoric in Iraq, US justifications for its actions, and inaction, depended on controlling the narrative of the past.

Bush's conception of a new world order built on American leadership was closely tied to his arguments for strengthening the military. Convinced that US military strength had overwhelmed the Soviet Union, he viewed military might as the surest means to tame outlaw nations. At a moment when peace and antimilitarist groups questioned the need for continued expenditures in defense and intelligence agencies, the latter defended their interests by claiming that military and intelligence capacities were needed more than ever to protect the nation from new enemies. Bush's view of anarchic threats to global stability extended the Reagan administration's concept of outlaw states, which, in turn, morphed into the idea of rogue states that underlay policy-making during the Clinton administration.

First Interventions: From Panama to Iraq

Bush's readiness for unilateral military action was evident as early as the 1989 invasion of Panama, two years before the dissolution of the Soviet Union. For Bush, a former CIA director and key architect of the cold war order, the bipolar framework had been enabling as well as limiting. The military and economic rollback of communism during the Reagan era—including support of the state terrorism of such right-wing dictatorial regimes as General Augusto Pinochet's in Chile—had been justified by Reagan national security adviser and US ambassador to the UN Jeane Kirkpatrick. Arguing that supporting right-wing authoritarian governments was acceptable as long as they were anticommunist, Kirkpatrick believed such dictatorships could be reformed from within, whereas left "totalitarian" governments could not.[17]

Kirkpatrick's assumptions were belied by the internal reforms of the Soviet and Eastern bloc regimes. And cold war–weary critics were eager for US interventions to end. In 1990, the former United Nations official Conor Cruise O'Brien viewed the post–cold war transition as an opportunity for the United States to end its reflexive support of anticommunist dictators. For O'Brien, as evidenced by the recent electoral defeat of the Sandinistas in Nicaragua, the doctrine of containment had lost all credibility. O'Brien hoped that "the disarray of American anticommunism" would also imperil right-wing dictatorships "once it can no longer be plausibly maintained that their demise would lead to an extension of Soviet power in the Western hemisphere."[18]

Suddenly and unexpectedly bereft of their main communist adversary, Bush and his advisers struggled to justify their interventionist instincts. Determined to put the stamp of American power on a rapidly changing geopolitical landscape, and drawing on the triumphalist idea that the United States had prevailed in the cold war through the assertion of might, less than six weeks after the Berlin Wall fell, Bush ordered the invasion of Panama in late December 1989, ousting the dictator and former CIA asset Manuel Noriega.

As historian Greg Grandin has asserted, the unilateral invasion of Panama, done without the sanction of the United Nations or the Organization of American States, provided a model for future interventions. Before that, the 1983 US invasion of tiny Grenada, under Reagan, had tested the waters for intervention, facilitating a surge of patriotism that in some circles had banished post-Vietnam malaise. But as Grandin notes, while the United States had frequently violated national sovereignty during the cold war, Panama marked a departure. Noriega was toppled not in the name of anticommunism; instead, democracy was given as the pretext. "It was overtly argued," explains Grandin, "that national sovereignty was subordinated to democracy, or the United States' right to adjudicate the quality of democracy."[19]

Panama thus provided a model for intervention carried out in the name of democracy, setting the stage for the Iraqi invasion that followed. But just as important was the assertion of control over former cold war assets who no longer served the purposes for which they had been cultivated. Bush, who had been directly involved with Noriega in Panama and with Saddam Hussein in Iraq, employed the time-worn CIA standard of "deny everything" to craft a new story.

During Bush's 1988 presidential campaign, *New York Times* and *Rolling Stone* investigations tracked the use of the vice president's office as a cover for Operation Black Eagle. Noriega made available Panamanian airfields and front companies in exchange for the use of the operation's "fleet of cargo planes to smuggle cocaine and marijuana into the US on behalf of the notorious Medellín cartel of Colombia."[20] From the time the Iran-Contra scandal broke in late 1986, provoking scrutiny of possibly related covert operations such as Operation Black Eagle, Bush and members of his office vehemently denied their involvement. "There is this insidious suggestion that I was conducting an operation," Bush said. "It's untrue, unfair and totally wrong." *Rolling Stone* described Bush "[sticking] to his basic story, insisting that he and his staff were exonerated by the Iran-*contra* committee." However, *Rolling Stone* charged, the Iran-Contra hearings focused only on Oliver North's operation and its Iranian connections, not on Black Eagle. Bush, however, considered the whole issue to be "old news." He said, "You get sick and tired of saying, 'I've told the truth.'"[21]

After his election, with critics observing the president targeting out-of-control cold war clients (as in Panama and Iraq) while using covert means and economic pressure to punish the remnants of communism or nonaligned movements (as in Cuba, Haiti, and Libya), many accused Bush of acting like the world's police officer.

But as Bush sought intervention in Iraq, Gorbachev's vision of multilateral cooperation through a revived UN stood in the way. Overcoming the initially widespread support for a negotiated settlement in Iraq depended as much on Bush's control of the narrative of history as it did on his energetic global diplomacy in search of support for intervention.

Turning Allies into Enemies: The US Gulf War and the Genesis of Popular Islamophobia

As Bush ordered US troops to Saudi Arabia and launched a military operation against another former US ally, Saddam, his arguments for intervention concealed US cold war alliances with Iraq, as well as ties to Saudi Arabia. As historian David Vine has argued, the US buildup of military bases in the Gulf region began in earnest with the 1980 Carter Doctrine. Facing grim reelection prospects and chastened by failed efforts to curb American energy consumption, Jimmy Carter intended to secure Middle Eastern oil and gas "by any means necessary." Vine writes that, presented as preemptive moves to keep the Soviets out of the Gulf, "[the] Pentagon build-up under Presidents Carter and Ronald Reagan included the creation of installations in Egypt, Oman, Saudi Arabia, and on the Indian Ocean Island of Diego Garcia."[22]

The Bush Doctrine constituted an active forgetting, airbrushing from public memory cold war–era alliances with Saddam and Iraq. The US had intervened in Iraq as early as 1963, with CIA involvement in a coup that brought the Baathist government and later Saddam to power.[23] With the 1979 Iranian revolution and the fall of the shah, the United States lost its most dependable ally in the region, and Iraq became a critical US ally. As a sign of the normalization of US-Iraq ties, Mayor Coleman A. Young of Detroit awarded Saddam the key to the city in 1980 after Saddam donated over $200,000 to the Chaldean Sacred Heart Church.[24] Donald Rumsfeld's 1983 and 1984 meetings with Saddam in Baghdad while serving as Reagan's special envoy to the Middle East cemented the alliance. The United States supported Iraq in its long war with Iran following Iraq's September 1980 invasion of its rival and continuing until August 1988. The United States played both sides, covertly and illegally selling arms to Iran to raise funds for the Contras in Nicaragua while aiding Iraq with extensive military and strategic assistance. As Seymour M. Hersh reported in the *New York Times* in 1992, "The Reagan Administration secretly decided to provide highly classified intelligence to Iraq in the spring of 1982—more than two years earlier than previously disclosed—while also permitting the sale of American-made arms to Baghdad in a successful effort to help President Saddam Hussein avert imminent defeat in the war with Iran, former intelligence and State Department officials say."[25] Later, declassified CIA documents revealed that then-CIA chief William J. Casey and other top officials were repeatedly informed about Iraq's attacks with chemical weapons and its plans for launching more such attacks against Iranian troops and towns near the border.[26]

The US-Iraq relationship appeared strong until Iraq's invasion of Kuwait. On July 25, the United States informed Saddam that it had no stake in Kuwait, an act that many saw as encouraging Iraq's aggression.[27] Iraq's invasion of a sovereign state produced new fissures in Middle Eastern politics, with Jordan and Yemen refusing to back the US position while Egypt and Saudi Arabia backed US intervention. The Iraqi invasion also played into the hands of Bush and Cheney's determination to secure control of the region by preemptive action if necessary. From Operation Desert Shield in August 1990 to Operation Desert Storm in January and February 1991, hundreds of thousands of US troops were deployed to Saudi Arabia and surrounding countries.[28]

At a moment of global reckoning when places as disparate as the Soviet Union and South Africa were reexamining their pasts, the Bush administration balked at interrogation of its cold war past. Critics, in fact, including some in Congress, pointed to the ironies and hypocrisy of the administration's abruptly turning on a recent ally. During the congressional debate on the Gulf in January 1991, Senator Daniel Patrick Moynihan challenged what he viewed as an about-face on Kuwait. As a former US ambassador to the United Nations, he remembered Kuwait as "a particularly poisonous enemy of the United States." Moynihan insisted that "one can be an antagonist of the United States at the United Nations in a way that leaves room for discussion afterwards. But the Kuwaitis were particularly nasty."[29] Such challenges were brushed aside by the Bush administration.

National and international calls for diplomacy over the use of military force resounded in the fall of 1990. The UN General Assembly resolution of December 6, 1990, asked the Security Council to pursue a negotiated settlement seeking Iraq's withdrawal from Kuwait. It also called for convening an international conference for a comprehensive settlement of Middle Eastern problems, including the restoration of the rights of Palestinians and the withdrawal of Israel from the occupied territories.[30]

Rejecting such a course, Bush invoked a clash-of-civilizations frame to drum up support for intervention. His reference to "laws of the jungle," positing a clash with a lawless, Hobbesian threat, animated the narrative leading up to the war. Before the US invasion, Bush advanced a lurid fabrication of Iraqi atrocities to justify the onslaught against Iraq.[31] Nayirah, later identified as the fifteen-year-old daughter of Saud Nasir al-Sabah, the Kuwaiti ambassador in Washington and a member of the royal family, posed as a nurse and testified before Congress on October 10, 1990, that Iraqi troops were entering hospitals, removing babies from incubators, and throwing them on the floor to die. These falsehoods, repeated in the media and frequently invoked by Bush in his discussions of Iraq, provided a crucial pretext for launching Operation Desert Storm on January 18, 1991.[32]

Nayirah's unfounded tales of Iraqi atrocities exploited the political potency of orientalism and Islamophobia. Critics have dissected Lewis's sweeping assumption that "all of Islam is, by nature, based on a religious obligation to slay the infidel," an assumption that made him unable to "distinguish Wahhabi extremism from other forms of Islam."[33] Though appallingly wrongheaded, Lewis's ideas lent authority to Bush's appeal for domestic and international support for military intervention in the Gulf. To be sure, Bush did not traffic in Islamophobia. But his naming of inscrutable threats in the service of his regional defense strategy resonated with Lewis's ominous portrayal of an irrational and threatening Muslim world. Bush's policy also seemed a fulfillment of Huntington's 1989 dire forecast of increased instability and violence in international affairs.[34] As the administration confronted what National Security Advisor Brent Scowcroft described as "a very messy world," Bush's rhetoric reverberated with that of Lewis and Huntington through media and popular culture.[35]

The terror attacks of 9/11 dramatically escalated the Islamophobic rhetoric of 1990 by pundits and policy makers. In 2010, Newt Gingrich elevated Islam itself as an existential threat, arguing that Islamic sharia law was "a mortal threat to the survival of freedom in the United States."[36] But well before 9/11, from the time of the Gulf War, the Bush administration's vague but unrelenting suggestions of new shadowy threats helped set the terms for a weaponized Islamophobia that would take root in 1990s popular culture.

The Rage of Lewis

Lewis's "Roots of Muslim Rage" reinvigorated discussions from the previous decade that, as Melani McAlister has shown, had asserted that Islam had a "special relationship" with terrorism. International conferences on terrorism—the first in Jerusalem in 1979, and the second in Washington, DC, in 1984—"highlighted the supposedly special relationship between Islam and terrorism." And despite wide-ranging talk of terrorist activities in Europe, Latin America, and Asia, "no other cultural or religion group was singled out this way."[37] The purported special relationship followed from Lewis's characterization of Islam as a "political religion." Lewis and other participants posited a "particular fusion of state and religion" as inherent in the "'nature' of Islam," a relationship that was not attributed to Judaism or Christianity.[38] Later, a May 1993 conference sponsored by the Social Science Research Council in Istanbul posed the question, "Is Islam the new enemy?"[39]

Lewis's 1991 essay, rooted in stereotypes rather than history, assumed rather than demonstrated "Muslim rage." Putting a homogenized and dehistoricized Islam on trial by jurors from an equally ill-defined "West," Lewis dismisses any possible political causes for what he terms "rage," waving away criticisms of Western policy and historically specific grievances responding to those policies. Particular policies, he acknowledged, have provoked hostility, but "when these policies are abandoned and the problems resolved, there is only a local and temporary alleviation." For example, he argued, "The French have left Algeria, the British have left Egypt, the Western oil companies have left their oil wells, the westernizing Shah has left Iran—yet the generalized resentment of the fundamentalists and other extremists against the West and its friends remains and grows and is not appeased." Rejecting claims that American policies toward Israel fuel anti-American sentiment, Lewis maintained that the United States was slow to embrace Israel while the Soviet Union granted Israel immediate de jure recognition and support. For Lewis, since Soviet policy in the region caused no ill will, he concluded that resentment toward the United States cannot be explained by US policies. Lewis also hastily dispensed with racism, sexism, slavery, and imperialism as possible causes for criticisms of the United States. Defining imperialism narrowly as ruling over Muslim subjects, Lewis argued that if imperialism were the issue, then again, it would be the Soviet Union, the last surviving empire with Muslim subjects, that would be the object of attack, not the United States. Clearly, Lewis reasoned, "something deeper is involved than these specific grievances, numerous and important as they may be—something deeper that turns every disagreement into a problem and makes every problem insoluble." Invoking the phrase "clash of civilizations," Lewis continued, "It should by now be clear that we are facing a mood and a movement far transcending the level of issues and policies and the governments that pursue them. This is no less than a clash of civilizations—the perhaps irrational but surely historic reaction of an ancient rival against our Judeo-Christian heritage, our secular present, and the worldwide expansion of both."[40]

In one short article, Lewis, while claiming to be an expert on Islam, absolved the West from any serious inquiry into history. His cultural and historical distortions of the Islamic world deflected attention from the ways that US cold war policies, in their fight against "godless communism," had reshaped Islam in multiple regions by funneling money and support to fundamentalist groups. As Emran Qureshi and Michael A. Sells state in their introduction to *The New Crusades: Constructing the Muslim Enemy*, "For many Muslims it is a bitter irony that the dominant stereotype of Islam is based upon the Saudi model of police-state repression, religious intolerance, oppression of women, moral hypocrisy among the male elite, and an aggressive and highly funded export of militant anti-western ideology—and that the Saudi monarchy is kept in power by the very Western nations that display fear and loathing at that stereotype."[41]

Western powers were more than complicit in maintaining the most repressive forms of Islam in power. They had a hand in producing such fundamentalisms. Thanks to the work of historians and journalists, the contours of the US role in fomenting militant fundamentalism are well known. The policy had roots even before the funding of jihadists beginning in the Carter administration and accelerating under Reagan.[42] In 1951, as conservative Christian groups lobbied to print "In God we trust" on all US currency and to insert the phrase "One nation under God" in the Pledge of Allegiance, the CIA targeted its Radio Liberty programs in Central Asia, attempting to incite Islamist groups against the Soviet Union. In 1952, the Saudi American oil company Aramco paid for the printing of religious propaganda in Riyadh.[43] In the 1950s and early 1960s, the United States funded Islamist groups in Egypt, Syria, and Iraq, mostly branches of the Muslim Brotherhood, hoping to weaken Gamal Abdel Nasser's secular, nonaligned government and undermine Arab nationalism.[44] The CIA funded the Muslim Brotherhood and helped the organization's Egyptian leaders migrate to Saudi Arabia when they were banned by the Nasser government.[45] And after the United States began funding the mujahideen in Afghanistan during the 1980s and well into the 1990s, the US government "spent millions of dollars to promote resistance to Soviet occupation among Afghan schoolchildren."[46] As part of these efforts, the CIA produced violent jihadist textbooks for Afghan schoolchildren through the University of Nebraska in the 1980s.[47]

Whether he subconsciously feared the return of the violence that the United States had inflicted on others—psychological projection on the part of a paranoid empire—or whether he was simply engaging in outright denial, civilizationist assumptions continued to animate Bush's rhetoric as he moved toward invading Iraq.

A Thousand Points of Light and a "Big Idea"

By January 15, 1991, the date of the UN deadline for Iraqi withdrawal from Kuwait, more than nine hundred thousand troops in a US-led coalition were positioned in the region, most along the Saudi-Iraq border. Bush announced the start of Operation Desert Storm on January 16. The following day, coalition forces began what became a five-week air and sea bombardment of Iraqi targets.

The 88,500 tons of bombs dropped on Iraq by coalition forces targeted civilian and military infrastructure, attacking electric, water, and sewage treatment facilities. After the bombing campaign, Bush imposed what a journalist termed "the most sweeping economic sanctions in history, leading to skyrocketing cancer rates while hospitals could not import basic medicines, analgesics, and cancer treatment."[48] By the end of 1992, one US government official estimated that two hundred thousand Iraqis had died as a result of the war and the destruction of the civilian infrastructure. A 1995 UN report found that "as many as 576,000 Iraqi children may have died since the end of the Persian Gulf war because of economic sanctions imposed by the Security Council."[49]

On January 29, 1991, twelve days after the operation's launch, Bush invoked the concept of a "thousand points of light" in his State of the Union address. More was at stake in this war than "one small country," Bush told the nation. "It's a big idea: a new world order where diverse nations are drawn together in common cause to achieve the universal aspirations of mankind—peace and security, freedom, and the rule of law." Striking a high-minded tone meant to quell the war's many critics, Bush pledged to guide the world to the realization of its "universal aspirations." He further declared that "the end of the cold war has been a victory for all of humanity."[50]

Bush's lofty, luminous rhetoric and talk of a new world order did not conceal the fact that this was a belligerent war speech. His uplifting message coincided with the height of aerial and naval bombardment of Iraqi troops in Kuwait, followed by the movement of ground troops into Kuwait and then Iraq. Bush's speech and other utterances erased the longtime military alliance with Iraq. It concealed the determination to control oil reserves in a facade of feigned righteousness. Bush marshaled forgetting into the creative power of making and creating a new world.

"We stand at a defining hour," Bush told the nation. "Halfway around the world, we are engaged in a great struggle in the skies and on the seas and sands. We know why we're there: We are Americans, part of something larger than ourselves. For two centuries, we've done the hard work of freedom. And tonight, we lead the world in facing down a threat to decency and humanity." Declaring that "the cost of closing our eyes to aggression is beyond mankind's power to imagine" and that "our cause is just; our cause is moral; our cause is right," Bush elaborated his vision: "The winds of change are with us now. The forces of freedom are together, united. We move toward the next century more confident than ever that we have the will at home and abroad to do what must be done—the hard work of freedom."[51]

Two phrases stand out in this speech. First, "the winds of change" signaled Bush's attempt to yoke the moral authority of Eastern European reform and the antiapartheid movement to his war. Likewise, the repeated phrase "hard work of freedom" summoned the aura of the antiapartheid and civil rights movements. But by "the hard work of freedom," Bush meant militarism.

Squandering the Peace Dividend

The 1991 Gulf War ended on February 28 with the withdrawal of defeated Iraqi forces from Kuwait. The United States stopped short of toppling Saddam, but the region was transformed by the expanded US footprint. Thousands of US troops and an expanded base infrastructure remained in Kuwait and Saudi Arabia, and the US Navy's Fifth Fleet was stationed in Bahrain. The Pentagon launched air installations in Qatar and regular operations in the United Arab Emirates and Oman.[52] As Hal Brands has argued, "The long-term stationing of American troops in Saudi Arabia would become increasingly destabilizing for the Saudi regime over time, while also motivating lethal jihadist attacks against a perceived occupation of the Muslim holy land." As the US presence became a recruiting device for "an al-Qaeda organization that was now setting its sights on American targets in the region and beyond," foreign policy analysts eventually regarded installing bases in the Gulf as a strategic mistake.[53]

Bush's regional defense strategy worked in tandem with broader economic and political national security objectives, policies that came to be known as the Wolfowitz Doctrine after its leak to the press in February 1992. The doctrine held that no counterhegemonic challenge to US political and economic dominance could be allowed to emerge in the former Soviet sphere. Some claim that the administration walked back from the policy after the leak, as critics judged it too extreme. But the strategy is evident in the administration's policies, and its influence is borne out by subsequent developments.

Preventing counterhegemonic challenges required a robust military, blocking the much-anticipated "peace dividend." With the collapse of the Soviet Union, many in the United States and Europe had hoped that military spending could be redirected toward social programs—everything from health and education to shoring up decrepit infrastructures. A 1991 UN human development report described a great surge of hope "brutally dashed" when Iraq invaded Kuwait. It nevertheless waxed hopeful at the opportunity to "recapture the peace dividend that was tragically lost in the shifting sands of the Gulf region."[54] The report estimated that global defense spending cuts of 2–4 percent a year could free up $200–$300 billion a year, a projected savings of $2 trillion over the 1990s. "Even taking into account increased social spending," reported the *Independent*, "Western countries would be able to increase their foreign aid . . . cautiously welcoming a new era."[55]

Instead, as the country pivoted toward new targets, combatting regional threats required military spending. In a nationally televised speech on September 27, 1991, seven months after Operation Desert Storm, Bush again declared victory in the cold war but warned of "regional instabilities, the spread of weapons of mass destruction, and . . . territorial ambitions of power-hungry tyrants." Such dangers, Bush argued, required "a strong military to protect our national interests and to honor commitments to our allies."[56] By 1993, critics lamented that opportunities for a peace dividend had been squandered.[57]

Along with Bush's mopping up of cold war allies who had outlived their usefulness, the scope and speed of the administration's targeting of left-leaning reformers was dizzying. Two days after the president sounded the alarm about "regional instabilities" and new threats, Haitian president Jean-Bertrand Aristide—the former Roman Catholic priest elected by 70 percent of the population in the country's first free election—was overthrown in a military coup d'état. If the matter of direct US involvement in the coup is still debated, there is no doubt that the CIA poured millions into organizations run by the thugs who ousted Aristide.[58] Despite international outrage over the coup, it would be three years before the United States, under the Clinton administration, provided political and military support for Aristide's return to power.

Under Bush, the lack of support for Aristide appears sadly overdetermined. The United States had a long history of intervention in Haiti, including US occupation from 1915 to 1934 and decades of supporting Haitian dictator François Duvalier and his successor and son, Jean-Claude, both staunch cold war allies.[59] In 1986, the CIA created a Haitian intelligence unit intended to combat cocaine trafficking. The unit (Service d'Intelligence National) became a corrupt instrument of political terror, its officers engaging in trafficking drugs, targeting supporters of Aristide, and directly supporting the military junta that overthrew him. The United States stopped funding the service only after Aristide was overthrown.[60]

There is no evidence that the CIA directly supported the coup, and in some cases US officials acted to protect Aristide and some of his supporters. What is clear emerges from the reporting of Stephen Engelberg, Howard W.

French, and Tim Weiner of the *New York Times*: "The agency paid key members of the junta now in power for political and military information up until the ouster of Father Aristide in 1991. A review of the C.I.A.'s activities in Haiti under the Reagan and Bush Administrations, based on documents and interviews with current and former officials, confirms that senior C.I.A. officers have long been deeply skeptical about the stability and politics of President Aristide, a leftist priest."[61]

Indeed, in aiding Aristide's foes and refusing to protect a democratically elected government, the Bush administration settled scores with a version of the Catholic liberation theology that had indicted cold war massacres in El Salvador and Guatemala and continued to advocate redistributive social justice. With Fidel Castro still in power in Cuba, the administration's animosity toward left-leaning governments, and its ongoing conflation of social justice movements with an international communist conspiracy, fundamentally shaped its responses to democratic movements such as Aristide's. Thus, as Bush warned of regional instability, a government guided by the principles of liberation theology and social justice appeared a greater threat to the administration than violent and corrupt elements in the Haitian military.

1992: A New Chapter in Victors' History

Bush's celebratory vindication of the Gulf War epitomized his evolving cold war triumphalism. In 1991, he universalized that triumphalism, declaring that "the end of the cold war has been a victory for all of humanity."[62] Yet by 1992, in his last State of the Union speech, he seemed less magnanimous, more inclined to spike the football. "Communism died this year," he bragged, "but the biggest thing that has happened in the world, in my life, is this: by the grace of God, America won the cold war.... For the cold war didn't end: it was won." Some of those who "won it ... in places like Korea and Vietnam," he told his audience, "didn't come back." For Bush, the collapse of the Soviet Union had altered the meaning of the deaths of Americans in Korea and Vietnam, burnishing the memory of those military quagmires. "Back then," he explained, "they were heroes, but this year they are victors." A "world once divided into two armed camps now recognized one sole and preeminent power, the United States of America.... The world trusts us with power.... They trust us to do what is right."[63]

In many respects, Bush's election-year victory lap struck a discordant note, out of touch with recession-weary Americans who, yearning for the peace and prosperity promised by Clinton, booted the Kennebunkport patrician from office. Bush's bravado also tried the patience of overseas allies. His rejection of the promise of a multipolar world was not lost on Václav Havel, who was dismayed by the actions of those he had trusted as democratic allies and defenders of human rights. In his one-term presidency, Bush had remade the global order in the image of a remilitarized and unipolar world. His triumphalism fell flat among the electorate but endured in the neoconservative worldview of the Republican majority that took over Congress in 1994 and found renewed expression in George W. Bush's presidential campaign in 1999–2000.

As Clinton assumed office, one critical trope of George H. W. Bush's repackaged enemies—the idea of a clash of civilizations—carried forward into the next administration, informing responses to political and humanitarian crises in Somali, Bosnia, and Rwanda.

From Bush to Clinton

After establishing new bases in the Middle East, continuing the US military presence in Asia, and ordering soldiers to Somalia in December 1992, Bush bequeathed to Clinton an expanded global military presence. Surveying the international scene on the eve of Clinton's inauguration, Andrew Marshall, a correspondent for the *Independent*, observed that "the real tragedy is not just that there was no peace dividend in 1992, but also that there was no peace." Given the "different possible conflicts and the range of tasks—peacekeeping, humanitarian operations, enforcing sanctions or simply guarding borders," "defense planning has become even more of a black art than normal."[64]

Bush and Clinton differed profoundly in their approach toward the exercise of US power. Bush ran for reelection on the conviction that the United States should use military power as a force for good in the world. Clinton, employing a belief in "soft power," as his assistant secretary of defense Joseph Nye would later name the strategy, hesitated to employ military force.[65] As Corey Robin has observed, Clinton, "a southern governor with no foreign policy experience—and a draft dodger to boot . . . concluded that his victory over Bush meant that questions of war and peace no longer resonated with American voters the way they might have in an earlier age." Clinton, Robin writes, believed that "globalization of the free market [had] undermined the efficacy of military power. . . . Power now hinged on the dynamism of and success of a nation's economy and the attractiveness of its culture."[66]

If Bush was the dedicated author of the triumphalist political narrative, Clinton, unschooled in a cold war world of CIA political orchestration, extolled a free market capitalist triumphalism and was a cheerleader for "free trade" policies. His seeming dovishness effaced the violent economic dislocations that often accompanied what he regarded as soft power. He was often inattentive to the negative consequences of past and ongoing US policies abroad. Clinton ruffled feathers in Guyana when he appointed as US ambassador the CIA operative involved in the 1963 ouster of Prime Minister Cheddi Jagan. Whether unaware of policies in Yugoslavia and Somalia—ignoring conditions that led to war and genocide—or consistently embracing economic structural adjustment policies that thwarted genuine intentions to support democracy as in Haiti, Clinton's policies betrayed a culture of cold war innocence and reflected his sense that the past was irrelevant.[67]

Clinton, ironically, was more akin to Reagan in his belief in the need to liberate the market. Indeed, continuities with Reagan-era global economic policies are critical to understanding how 1990s crises developed and played out. In *The Shock Doctrine*, Naomi Klein explains that in the 1970s and 1980s, the Reagan and Thatcher administrations harnessed the International Monetary Fund (IMF) and World Bank "for their own ends, rapidly increasing their power and turning them into primary vehicles for the advancement of the corporatist crusade." National Security documents of the Reagan administration, National Security Decision Directive 133 and National Security Decision Directive 54, laid plans to "employ commercial, financial, exchange, informational, and diplomatic instruments," including credit policy, IMF membership, and debt restructuring, toward achieving the goal of weakening Soviet control in Eastern Europe and integrating Eastern European economies into what was termed an effective, market-oriented structure.[68] After enforcing liberal lending policies, the IMF and World Bank decided to call in the debt.

Driven by the ideology of the so-called free market while ironically imposing a massive top-down program of social and economic engineering—one might think of it as centralized planning on steroids—the IMF and World Bank attached conditions to desperately needed debt relief that required developing nations to implement structural adjustment programs (SAPs). In what Klein calls "the dictatorship of debt," SAPs forced governments to impose a package of austerity, privatization, and massive deregulation. In Mexico, for example, as Walden Bello has shown, "The contraction of government spending translated into the dismantling of state credit, government-subsidized agricultural inputs, price supports, state marketing boards and extension services. Unilateral liberalization of agricultural trade pushed by the IMF and World Bank also contributed to the destabilization of peasant producers." Consequently, "interest payments rose from 19 percent of total government expenditures in 1982 to 57 percent in 1988, while capital expenditures dropped from an already low 19.3 percent to 4.4 percent."[69]

This blow to peasant agriculture was followed by an even larger disruption when the North American Free Trade Agreement went into effect in 1994. Although NAFTA had a fifteen-year phaseout of tariff protection for agricultural products, including corn, highly subsidized US corn quickly flooded in, reducing prices by half and cementing "Mexico's status as a net food importer."[70]

In 2008, the World Bank acknowledged that structural adjustment from the 1980s was a failure that "dismantled the elaborate system of public agencies that provided farmers with access to land, credit, insurance inputs, and cooperative organization." The bank's stated intention was to "free up the market" so that the supposedly more efficient private sector could take over, but "that didn't happen." The bank confessed that the beneficiaries of privatization were commercial farmers, which threatened the survival of smallholders.[71]

African countries were saddled with an additional burden. As Bello argued, structural adjustment in Africa, as in Mexico and the Philippines, "was not simply underinvestment but state divestment." But there was one major difference. In Africa, the World Bank and IMF micromanaged, making decisions on how fast subsidies should be phased out, how many civil servants had to be fired, and even, as in the case of Malawi, how much of the country's grain reserve should be sold and to whom. According to Oxfam, the number of sub-Saharan Africans living on less than a dollar a day almost doubled, to 313 million, between 1981 and 2001—46 percent of the whole continent. The role of structural adjustment in creating poverty was difficult to deny. As the World Bank's chief economist for Africa admitted, "We did not think that the human costs of these programs could be so great, and the economic gains would be so slow in coming."[72]

In the context of the subsequent massive economic and political destabilization of much of the global South, the Bush and Clinton positions mirrored each other in their reluctance to intervene in humanitarian crises and wars of genocide. Critical decisions about how the United States would or would not act in the Somali, Bosnian, and Rwandan crises occurred across both the Bush and Clinton administrations. Contrasted with Bush's statement on Bosnia that "we don't want to put a dog in that fight," Clinton campaigned on the moral necessity for intervention in Bosnia but then vacillated, leading French president Jacques Chirac to describe Clinton's position as "vacant."[73] With the wars and genocides overlapping in real time, Clinton's painful experience with Somalia influenced his hesitant approach to Rwanda. But attention to the particulars of each crisis is critical to illuminating how cold war policies continued to shape events in a supposedly post–cold war world.

Somalia: Humanitarian Intervention or Mini–Operation Desert Storm?

In contrast to US reluctance to intervene in Bosnia and Rwanda, the deployment of troops to Somalia in 1992 was hailed as a humanitarian intervention. The notion that military force achieved benevolent ends was central to Bush's conception of a new world order. In his December 4 address, he described the mission's objective to save thousands of lives and fleshed out his vision of the United States as a global police force: "One image tells the story. Imagine 7,000 tons of food aid literally bursting out of a warehouse on a dock in Mogadishu, while Somalis starve less than a kilometer away because relief workers cannot run the gauntlet of armed gangs roving the city." Telling his audience that it is "now clear that military support is necessary to ensure the safe delivery of the food Somalis need to survive," Bush explained that "our mission is humanitarian, but we will not tolerate armed gangs ripping off their own people, condemning them to death by starvation."[74]

Armed supporters of Mohammed Farrah Aidid, who had overthrown Somalia's US-backed president Siad Barre in January 1991, were exacerbating a crisis of mass starvation by blocking food relief efforts. Bush's portrait of the humanitarian crisis suggested that it had been caused by an anarchic warlord and "armed gangs roving the city," and that their removal would restore order and resolve the crisis. Indeed, when the UN began relief efforts in Somalia in 1992, the starvation of three hundred thousand people was portrayed as the result of a warlord's cruelty.

But food insecurity had been a critical *cause* of Aidid's overthrow of Barre, not simply the *result* of the overthrow. The crisis in Somalia cannot be understood without the context of cold war politics and the structural adjustment policies imposed by the IMF and World Bank. After the 1974 socialist revolution in Ethiopia, the United States began supporting Somalia under Barre's leadership, bringing the previously Soviet-client regime into the West's column.[75] According to the *Los Angeles Times*, the United States provided $600 million in aid between 1978 and 1985 to Barre. In 1980, the United States made a $100 million commitment along with a ten-year access agreement for Somalia's Berbera port, intending to develop the port's airstrip for access in the case of instability in the Middle East. Diplomats reported that the United States had soured on the port project after military exercises with the Somali army in 1983 had gone badly.[76] But the United States continued to supply $50 million in arms to Barre yearly. When repression and social unrest led to the outbreak of civil war in 1988, rival factions fought with US-supplied arms.[77]

Barre's overthrow created a power vacuum, with rival factions vying for control.[78] By this time, reported the *Los Angeles Times*, "nearly two-thirds of Somalia was allocated to the American oil giants Conoco, Amoco, Chevron and Phillips." Industry sources reported that the companies holding concessions were hoping that "the Bush Administration's decision to send U.S. troops to safeguard aid shipments to Somalia [would] also help protect their multimillion-dollar investments there."[79] After US intervention, the Houston-based Conoco Oil company, involved in extensive oil exploration in north-central Somalia since 1981, aided in the US relief efforts and profited as the government subsidized the company's facilities.

As critics charged that Bush, a former Texas oilman, sent in the troops to secure oil reserves, John Geybauer, spokesman for Conoco Oil, claimed the company was acting as "a good corporate citizen and neighbor."[80] The *Los Angeles Times* reported that "the close relationship between Conoco and the US intervention force has left many Somalis and foreign development experts deeply troubled by the blurry line between the U.S. government and the large oil company." Some compared the Somalia operation to "a miniature version of Operation Desert Storm, . . . to drive Iraq from Kuwait and, more broadly, safeguard the world's largest oil reserves."[81]

The chaos in Somalia, Rania Khalek has argued, grew from the combination of "the neoliberal dismantling of Somalia's agro-pastoralist economy" and sectarian violence fed by US arms sales, leaving Somalia "extremely vulnerable to famine when faced with a drought in 1992, causing the mass starvation of 300,000 people."[82] Despite frequent droughts, Somalia's economy, led by small-scale farmers and pastoralists, or "nomadic herdsmen," was self-sufficient in food production well into the 1970s. The pastoralists proved quite successful as livestock produced 80 percent of Somalia's export earnings through 1983. The IMF played a significant role in undermining Somalia's subsistence agriculture, and World Bank–imposed policies further disrupted the pastoral and agricultural economy of the country.[83] These SAPs privatized veterinarian services for livestock, depriving herders in rural grazing areas of access to health care for their animals, which devastated pastoralists who made up half of the population. They also mandated imports of rice and wheat that displaced small farmers, and resources were diverted to grow export commodities. Worst of all, the privatization of water sources by local merchants and large farmers restricted access to water points and boreholes.[84]

The Somali crisis was created by a congeries of global, regional, and local disruptions. The first UN humanitarian intervention augmented by US military forces in December 1992 restored food distribution networks, saving an estimated three hundred thousand people from starvation. However, the next phase of the UN intervention was radically different, aimed at the restoration of the Barre government. Madeleine Albright, as UN ambassador, described this undertaking as "an unprecedented enterprise aimed at nothing less than the restoration of an entire country."[85] A UN resolution, adopted unanimously by the fifteen-member Security Council, ordered UN commanders "to complete the disarmament of Somalia's heavily armed factions begun by the Americans throughout the entire country." Under Chapter 7 of the UN Charter, the resolution "empowered the peacekeeping troops to use whatever force is needed both to disarm Somali warlords who refuse to surrender their weapons and to ensure that relief supplies reach needy people." In addition, it directed UN troops to enforce the Security Council's existing embargo on new arms deliveries.[86]

In August 1993, four US soldiers were killed in Somalia, following the killing of others involved in the UN force, including twenty-four Pakistani peacekeepers, four journalists, two Italian peacekeepers, and six Somalis. In response to the killings, Albright called for "the capture, detention and trial of Mr. Aidid." Failure to take action, she argued, "would have signaled to other clan leaders that the UN is not serious."[87]

On October 3, 1993, US special forces launched Operation Gothic Serpent, intended to capture two of Aidid's top lieutenants in Mogadishu. Although the two were captured, the anticipated one-hour operation dragged into the next day, and eighteen US soldiers perished as two Black Hawk helicopters were shot down and the bodies of several US soldiers were dismembered and paraded through the streets.

As Americans watched in horror, on October 7, Clinton, saddled with a debacle initiated by his predecessor, made the case for sending more troops but promised a complete US withdrawal by March 31, 1994. He declared that if the United States pulled out now, “within months, Somalis again would be dying in the streets.... All around the world, aggressors, thugs and terrorists will conclude that the best way to get us to change our policies is to kill our people. It would be open season on Americans.”[88] On March 25, 1994, the last US troops left Somalia.

Less than two weeks later, on April 6, Rwandan president Juvénal Habyarimana and the president of Burundi, Cyprien Ntaryamira, were killed when their plane was shot down, setting in motion the government-organized genocide. US responses to the Rwandan crisis were conditioned by Bosnia as well as Somalia. Before turning to Rwanda, I consider the historical and immediate context of US responses to the breakup of Yugoslavia and the crisis in Bosnia. Clinton's reluctance to intervene in Rwanda was conditioned by his view of the Bosnian genocide as rooted in primordial ethnic hatreds.

From Yugoslavia to the Bosnian Genocide

Václav Havel, in his 1993 admonition that the West “would ultimately lose the key to itself” if it underestimated the threat of Balkan nationalism, warned that in doing so, the West would “give the green light to its own potentially destructive nationalisms.”[89] Havel registered his dismay with the Western response to the breakup of Yugoslavia. As the country imploded, Bush's lofty rhetoric of humanitarian action in Iraq and Somalia contrasted with his indifference to the political violence engulfing Yugoslavia, expressed in the statement, “We don't want to put a dog in this fight.”[90] By some accounts, Clinton fell under the spell of Robert Kaplan's 1993 book *Balkan Ghosts*, which depicted the region as a tinderbox of seething ancient ethnic hatreds, “spooking” Clinton from putting troops in Bosnia.[91] In any case, the administration did not act decisively until, in the words of historian Susan Woodward, the Europeans “tricked them” into intervention through NATO obligations to defend the security of Europe.[92]

But as Woodward has compellingly shown, Western European policy had contributed to the breakup of Yugoslavia. “Having ignored the crisis during 1989 and 1990 ... the international community took actions in 1991 that redefined the crisis as ethnic conflict and nationalist revolution. The result was self-fulfilling.”[93] Ignoring the “many citizens' groups working to foster countrywide cooperation,” and with the United States bowing to pressure from ethnic lobbying groups, the West prejudged the actions of the Yugoslav People's Army to restore order in the republics as “illegitimate intervention."[94] Hence, as Havel implied, Europe, recognizing only nationalist claims based on ethnicity, gave the "green light" to nationalist politics, destroying extant structures of multinational shared sovereignty.

As an Eastern European dissident, Havel would have appreciated the unique position of Yugoslavia in the geopolitics of the cold war, and the role of the West in plunging a recently prosperous country into chaos. Through the 1970s, Yugoslavia experienced a 6.1 percent growth rate, and its achievements included free health care for all citizens of its six republics and a 91 percent literacy rate. And as Balkan expert Misha Glenny has written, despite the many times that the Balkans have served as a proxy for broader European conflict, the various ethnic and religious groups—Serbs, Croatians, Muslims—traditionally got along with one another. Coexistence, not hatred, was the historical norm.[95] For many Yugoslavs, economic collapse followed by war and genocide was a deeply shocking and traumatic loss of the good life, once characterized by security, stability, interethnic harmony, and international prestige.

How, as Woodward asks, "did the good life devolve into genocidal hell?" The answer began with the radical shift in IMF economic policies from 1980 onward. The anti-Soviet socialist government of Yugoslavia had played a critical role for the West during the cold war, serving as a buffer to Soviet expansion and influence among third-world nations, many of whom shared Yugoslavia's nonaligned politics.[96]

In Yugoslavia, World War II was largely fought as a civil war between communist Partisans led by Josip Broz Tito against occupying Axis forces, while Serbian royalist Chetniks, Croatian fascists, and Slovenian Home Guard troops collaborated with the Axis. With support from the Western Allies and ground support from the Soviets, the Partisans eventually gained control of the country. The Partisans' role in defeating the Axis powers won international recognition at the Allied summit in Tehran. After the war, Tito had wide popular support. He ruthlessly eliminated his opponents, and after he was expelled from the Cominform in 1948, he purged nearly 20 percent of party members who supported Stalin.

Tito had been ruthless, but he commanded wide legitimacy by glorifying brotherhood and promoting an expansive memory of World War II as a unifying struggle to heal wartime divisions.[97] His leadership was also defined by his success in delivering the good life, as measured by access to consumer goods, travel, and cultural amenities, including world cinema.[98] Tito's cult of personality borrowed from Hollywood with, for example, *Battle of Sutjeska*, a 1973 film restaging Partisan battles against Axis forces.

Tito chose Richard Burton to play the Partisans' leader (and unsuccessfully sought to cast Sophia Loren and Elizabeth Taylor). In Yugoslavia, the good life was glamorous and steeped in international prestige born of leadership in the nonaligned movement.

Tito's death in 1980 coincided with an economic downturn. Yugoslavia's socialist, mixed economy, characterized by its worker-owned enterprises, free health care, and high degree of prosperity, was deliberately targeted by the international finance community, which aimed to pull the country into the free market capitalist world. The Reagan administration's National Security documents National Security Decision Directive 54 (1982) and National Security Decision Directive 133 (1984) stipulated use of global financial instruments—banks, the IMF, and the World Bank—to push Yugoslav and Eastern European economies toward capitalist market economies and to weaken their links to the Soviet Union. International creditors called in Yugoslavia's debt, imposing austerity measures that included the gutting of its welfare state and privatizing publicly owned banks and businesses. By the late 1980s, as Western powers ignored the growing economic crisis, the Yugoslav standard of living had plummeted.

The IMF instituted shock therapy in 1990, effectively controlling the Yugoslav central bank with tight money policies undermining federal Yugoslavia's ability to finance its economic and social programs. The federal Yugoslavian government was forced to send money to European banks instead of the republics, straining its relationship with the latter. Worsening political and economic conditions in the republics provided the tinder for secession movements and the breakup of the country.[99] Furthermore, the IMF's shock therapy froze wages, which fell by 41 percent in the first six months of 1990.[100]

Yugoslavia's severe economic crisis and its weakening of the federal government set the stage for such ethno-nationalist politicians as Slobodan Milosevic to seize power, exploiting real grievances. Emerging hatreds were not ancient but had historical roots, first in the broader context of wartime resistance to European fascism, and more recently in politicians' manipulation of historical memory in service of their quest for power.[101] As Milosevic aimed to cannibalize the Yugoslav state to create a greater Serbia, the West conflated Serbian nationalism with Yugoslavia, failing to recognize the efforts of citizens' groups to preserve federated Yugoslav structures. Hence, concludes Woodward, in 1990 and 1991, the West abandoned the Yugoslav government that "depended on international support for economic and political reforms."[102]

From a foreign policy or national security standpoint, it made no sense for the United States to encourage the breakup of Yugoslavia. Yet Reagan's determination to destroy communism did not make fine distinctions between state-planned economies and mixed economies such as Yugoslavia's that had worker self-management, worker-owned enterprises, and strong social welfare benefits. Departing from previous cold war policy that distinguished between the Soviet Union and anti-Stalinist European socialism, the Reagan administration took aim at all forms of worker and trade union organizing, redistributive social programs, and the welfare state. Reagan's domestic agenda to undermine trade unions and social welfare programs, in effect, was pursued around the world. And having once been a bulwark of containment, Yugoslavia became expendable in Bush's triumphalist new world order.

In July 1990, six months into the shock therapy experiment, the republics of Slovenia and Croatia declared their right to sovereignty and secession. One year later, on June 25, 1991, Slovenia and Croatia announced their independence from Yugoslavia. When Yugoslavia attempted to defend its territorial integrity, hostilities broke out between Slovenia and the Yugoslav People's Army, and then between the Croatian government and the Yugoslav People's Army.

In May 1992, two days after the United States and the European Community recognized Bosnia's independence, Bosnian Serb forces backed by Milosevic, who gained power as president of Serbia in 1989 by promoting a Serbian nationalism then anathema to most Yugoslavians, launched a military offensive against Sarajevo, the Bosnian capital. In a policy dubbed "ethnic cleansing," the armies terrorized and removed Muslim Bosnian citizens—murdering, raping, and torturing them.

Many in the international community pleaded with the Bush administration for intervention to stop the Bosnian genocide. On December 5, 1992, the day after Bush's speech outlining the commitment of troops in Somalia, Turgut Ozal, the president of Turkey, implored Bush to stop the slaughter in Bosnia, stating that the "rapes and massacres have reached terrifying levels," and "the world is looking to your leadership." Bush had justified intervention in the Gulf and Somalia on humanitarian grounds. Why Iraq and Somalia, but not Bosnia? Earlier, Bush told Ozal and Havel that his hands were tied in Bosnia because he was under pressure at home, and that Americans were looking inward and wanted a peace dividend. Bush now told Ozal, "I am trying not to saddle Clinton with major new commitments. Somalia was so appalling."[103]

Ignoring the ways in which the US and international finance community had already intervened in Yugoslavia, Bush posed as the pragmatist, always careful, as the historian Hal Brands has argued, "to reiterate that the United States had neither the intention nor the capability to intervene in every conflict or address every problem."[104]

There is no evidence that the Bush or Clinton administration ever acknowledged the role of US policy in breaking up Yugoslavia, appearing instead to view the United States as a passive observer. Yet the ideologically driven destruction of a once-successful and internationally prestigious socialist alternative to capitalism is fully consistent with the policies advocated in the Wolfowitz Doctrine. Rather than dictating any particular action, the doctrine described the worldview, sensibility, and broad approach of the administration's defense policy. Seeking as a cornerstone of US foreign policy the prevention of any counterhegemonic bloc capable of challenging US military, economic, or political leadership, the document laid out imperatives in "non-defense areas": "We must account sufficiently for the interests of the advanced industrial nations to discourage them from challenging our leadership or seeking to overturn the established political and economic order. We must maintain the mechanism for deterring potential competitors from even aspiring to a larger regional or global role."[105]

Splintering ethno-nations were hardly "aspiring to a larger regional or global role." But the former Yugoslavia had aspired to and achieved all of these things. A federated Yugoslavia with a mixed market and social welfare economy could have remained a powerful model and economic partner for Eastern European economies freed from the stultifying planned economies of the Soviet era. Most importantly, freed to trade with a reforming Soviet Union and a Europe partnering across former East and West divides, such a bloc would have challenged the status of the United States as a one-world hegemon.

Bush's unwillingness to act in Bosnia underscores the unipolar slant of his new world order, his resistance to US action in accord with the interests of a multipolar world. While Havel and Gorbachev had hoped for a strengthened UN and stronger European and multilateral cooperation, at the moment of the Bosnian crisis, the UN was weakened because the United States had not paid its bills. From 1985 on, with the Reagan administration and Republicans resentful over the perceived strength of a nonaligned bloc, the Senate blocked funds to the organization. Bush and Clinton squandered the chance to redress the neglect before Republicans took control of the

House in 1994 and made hostility to UN peacekeeping actions a central tenet of its foreign policy.

From the point when Clinton took office in 1993 through 1995 when the United States intervened through NATO, the crisis in Bosnia had further deteriorated. The Siege of Sarajevo continued, with scorched-earth raids by the army of the Bosnian Serb secessionists terrorizing small Muslim towns. Thousands of refugees flooded the town of Srebrenica, guarded by UN peacekeeping volunteers from Europe and elsewhere.[106] Although it was declared a safe area in 1993, in July 1995, the UN forces failed to prevent the town's capture by the Bosnian Serb Army and the subsequent massacre of eight thousand Bosnian Muslims, mainly men and boys.

Although Clinton saw the Bosnian conflict as warranting diplomatic attention, he believed that it did not justify putting American lives on the line.[107] Hence, following the Srebrenica massacre, when the United States intervened in Bosnia in Operation Deliberate Force from August 30 to September 20, 1995, it was under the auspices of NATO, a cold war military alliance, with assistance from the United Nations Protection Force.

Elizabeth Drew and Richard Reeves have argued that Clinton read Kaplan's *Balkan Ghosts* and concluded that "these people have been killing each other for 10 centuries," leading Clinton to shift away from campaign promises to intervene on humanitarian grounds.[108] Indeed, by Clinton's own account, Kaplan's books shaped his view of global conflict.[109] Clinton enthusiastically recommended the work of Kaplan, as well as Samuel Huntington's *Clash of Civilizations and the Remaking of World Order*, to members of his administration.

Kaplan informed Clinton's thinking on Rwanda as well as Bosnia. Before turning to Rwanda, it is worth examining the assumptions of Kaplan's *Balkan Ghosts*. In a saturnine portrait based on travels in the region when living in Greece, Kaplan depicted the Balkans as riven by ungovernable ancient and timeless hatreds. He has said that *Balkan Ghosts* has been misunderstood. But the book teems with examples of how his purported inquiries, and his conclusions, fall back on his initial assumption that the people of the Balkans live in a world predetermined by ancient conflict and outside history, unchanged across millennia. While he claims intimate knowledge of the region's countries and communities, in Kaplan's world, every person encountered, every story told, is simply another homogenized foil to an assumed Western modernity. In one passage, part of an extended attempt to expose the "myth" that Greece is part of Western civilization and to place it firmly in a timeless Eastern past, Kaplan describes crossing the border between Greece and Albania and encountering a community of ethnic Greek Albanians, writing, "Every man-made object—the rough cakes of soap, the water taps, the door handles—manifested a primitive, just-invented quality. Lignite and lead fumes clouded the landscape, giving it the grainy and yellowy aura of an old photograph. Under sodium lamps, I examined the faces of these ethnic Greek Albanians. The expression in their eyes seemed far away." After Kaplan visited a family, as the elder son accompanied him back to his hotel, the son confessed, in this avowedly atheist country, to having been secretly baptized. "I am a Greek. What else can I be? I believe in God." Four days after this conversation, Kaplan recounts, two Greeks were shot as they attempted to cross the border into Greece, their bodies then hung upside down in the public square. For Kaplan, "this was a time-capsule world; a dim stage upon which people raged, spilled blood, experienced visions and ecstasies. Yet their expressions remained fixed and distant, like dusty sanctuary." Recalling that a former Bulgarian foreign minister had told him, "Here, we are completely submerged under our own histories," Kaplan explains his investigative methods: "Thus, I developed an obsession with medieval churches and monasteries, with old books and old photographs. On the road, when I met people, I asked them about the past. Only in this way could the present become comprehensible."[110]

Seeking the key to the present in medieval churches and old photographs, as Kaplan turns his attention to Greece, it is unthinkable to him to read the post-1945 history of Greece in terms of the 1946–49 civil war, the first proxy war of the cold war, when the United States and Britain supported the right-wing, anticommunist Greek government army against the military wing of the Greek Communist Party. And it is equally unthinkable for Kaplan to read the economic crisis in 1980s Greece in terms of the global political economy and the austerity plans imposed by the IMF on the socialist government of Andreas Papandreou. Indeed, it is unthinkable for Kaplan to pose questions that would place the history of Greece inside a dynamic geopolitical and global economy. Instead, argues Kaplan, "in the autumn of 1990, Greece was as much a part of the Balkans as it had been during the days of direct Ottoman rule in the early nineteenth century.... Papandreou was the most original of the Balkan ghosts, a man of our own times who moved in the depths of the darkest past."[111]

Kaplan closes his *Balkan Ghosts* with a loaded question: "Had the poison of eastern despotism and decline, seeping from Byzantium, to the Sultan's Palace, to the Kremlin, finally expended itself?" Kaplan answers his own question with a bizarre paradox of hope emerging only through apocalyptic violence: "I felt it had. Here at the world's end, at a place whose very collapse gave the twentieth century its horrifying direction. . . . As I observed the violent disintegration of Yugoslavia and the turmoil that was bound to continue in other Balkan states, I was reminded of a line from Shakespeare's *Life and Death of King John*: 'So foul a sky clears not without a storm.'" For Kaplan, writing at the moment that ethnic cleansing had been instituted in Bosnia, it was only with the cleansing storm of violence that "the Enlightenment was, at last, breaching the gates of these downtrodden nations. A better age would have to follow."[112]

Kaplan's denouement imbues the violence of ethnic cleansing with positive necessity, the storm required for "a better age." Although Kaplan's assumptions about timeless, unbridgeable difference and innate violence have long precedents in Western orientalism, it is important to stress how such tropes were remade and reinvigorated in a profound moment of geopolitical shift. The ideas of Kaplan, Lewis, and Huntington reverberated throughout politics and the media. As Tom Bissell asserted in "Euphorias of Perrier: The Case against Robert D. Kaplan," "Not many authors can expect blurbs from senators, former Department of Defense secretaries, the Director of Central Intelligence, or Tom Brokaw, but Kaplan can."[113] For those policy makers influenced by Kaplan, his views discouraged examination of the role of Western powers in breaking up Yugoslavia and rendered any consideration of actual historical dynamics irrelevant.

The Rwandan Genocide as Cold War Afterlife

In 1998, Clinton regretted his failure to halt genocide in Rwanda when hundreds of thousands of Rwandans were murdered between April and July 1994. Clinton recalled not "fully appreciat[ing] the depth and the speed with which Rwandans were being engulfed by this unimaginable terror."[114] In a 2008 interview, Clinton ruefully acknowledged that three hundred thousand lives could have been saved.[115] US officials in Rwanda had been warned a year earlier that Hutu extremists were contemplating the extermination of ethnic Tutsis, and had briefed the administration months before it was carried out.[116]

Clinton's sense that he might have done more to save lives suggests a cold war political culture of innocence, unable to recognize, name, or act to redress the consequences of its past policies and actions. The cold war and its afterlives mattered in the genocide. At the time, some argued that a lack of interest in Rwanda was related to the end of the cold war, citing Secretary of State James Baker's defunding the African Bureau to establish more than a dozen new embassies in the former Soviet Union. But the elimination of civilian and political personnel in Africa went hand in hand with increasing military commitments to new African clients such as Uganda's president Yoweri Museveni as fundamentalist terrorism was replacing communism as a primary security concern. Shifting resources from civilian and diplomatic to military operations, the end of the cold war entailed yet another remilitarization.

The political scientist Mahmood Mamdani has argued that in much US writing on the genocide, the casting of the Hutus as perpetrators and the Tutsis as victims is devoid of any historical context, positing "an eternal clash between evil and innocence." Citing Philip Gourevitch's best-selling *We Wish to Inform You That Tomorrow We Will Be Killed with Our Families*, Mamdani states that "this kind of journalism gives a simple moral world, where a group of perpetrators faces a group of victims, but where neither history nor motivation is thinkable because the confrontation occurs outside of history and context."[117]

Mamdani argues that the Rwandan genocide had political causes, "born of a civil war," rooted in the broader regional and global dynamics of the cold war and its afterlives.[118] The immediate cause of mass killings had been the assassination of Rwandan president Juvénal Habyarimana. But the West was implicated through overt and covert intervention in Rwanda's civil war, as well as the longer history of colonialism and the cold war that shaped the region's politics.

For Rwanda and its larger neighbors to the north and west, Uganda and Zaire, the cold war prolonged the effects of colonialism and imperialism in Africa through US support of dictators as well as IMF and World Bank SAPs. From 1990 to 1994, similar to the challenges faced by the African National Congress and the political transition in South Africa, cold war terror carried into Rwanda.

Colonial policies constructed hardened ethnicities from what had been shifting and fluid identifications. Rwanda was created as a trust territory of the League of Nations following World War I, when control over the colonial possessions of the defeated imperial forces (the Ottoman empire, Germany, and Italy) was ceded to the victorious powers.[119] Before colonialism, "Tutsi" and "Hutu" designated not ethnicity but social status, with the king's inner circle considered Tutsi, and everyone else Hutu. In Rwanda, Mamdani explains, Belgium, with the blessing of the League of Nations, forced people to carry ID cards classifying them by ethnicity and instituted policies favoring Tutsis, reifying Hutu and Tutsi into "racialized identities" and institutionalizing discrimination between them. Belgian colonialism cultivated a small, educated, and economically empowered Tutsi elite along with forced Hutu labor, laying the foundation for the genocide that occurred fifty years later. The system of indirect rule not only denied sovereignty to Rwanda; "it also remade their administrative and political life, creating a regime based on group identity and rights."[120]

Festering Hutu resentment led to violent upheavals in 1959 in which twenty thousand Tutsis were killed, with many others fleeing to Burundi, Tanzania, and Uganda. After independence in 1962, Hutus took over the government. Systematic discrimination and the scapegoating of Tutsis by the majority-Hutu government fueled a mass exodus, with an estimated nine hundred thousand Tutsis fleeing by 1990.

With neighboring Zaire as the closest US cold war client, the Habyarimana regime retained close ties with France, which benefited from selling arms to Rwanda. As Helen Epstein has documented, as US attention turned from the cold war to the war on terror in the late 1980s, new proxy armies were needed to fight America's new battles. Before fundamentalist militants vied for power in Somalia after Barre's overthrow, the United States had increasingly supported Uganda's president Museveni after he came to power in 1986. "Wedged between Congo/Zaire, with its enormous mineral wealth, and eastern Africa's Muslim fringe, predominantly Christian Uganda occupied a crucial geostrategic position."[121] The United States embraced Museveni as a bulwark against Islamist militants who seized power in Sudan in 1989, assisting Ugandans in training and arming antigovernment rebels, the Sudanese People's Liberation Army.

Trained by US-backed Ugandan forces, the Rwandan Patriotic Front formed in Uganda, consisting mostly of Tutsi exiles. The RPF invaded Rwanda in October 1990 with a force of over four thousand troops. At the time of the invasion, Paul Kagame, the future leader of RPF forces, was training at Fort Leavenworth, Kansas. During the nearly four years of civil war preceding the genocide, Ugandan operatives violated several peace agreements and UN and Organization of African Unity restrictions by supplying the RPF with weapons.[122]

Mamdani rejected the premise that the US failure in Rwanda was epitomized by inaction: "What the humanitarian intervention lobby fails to see is that there were two Western interventions in Rwanda, both self-serving." France's intervention, Operation Turquoise, created a sanctuary both for ordinary Tutsis fleeing the killings and for the political leaders responsible for the genocide. US intervention came by proxy through the invading RPF, led by US-trained Kagame and augmented by Ugandan Army forces.[123]

During this period, US embassy officials in Kampala, Uganda, monitored the traffic in weapons crossing the border between Uganda and Rwanda. However, Washington not only ignored Uganda's assistance to the Rwandan rebels, it also increased military and development aid to Museveni, then praised him as a peacemaker once the genocide was underway.[124] US foreign aid to Uganda nearly doubled, as that nation purchased ten times more US weapons than in the preceding forty years combined.[125]

The Rwandan Civil War intensified when a 1992 cease-fire and a 1993 settlement to contain the conflict broke down.[126] Well before the plane crash that precipitated the genocide, the CIA knew that the rebels' growing military strength was escalating ethnic tensions within Rwanda, placing hundreds of thousands of Rwandans at risk from widespread ethnic violence. The CIA, reports Epstein, "accurately predicted that panicked Hutus could unleash extreme violence, resulting in up to a half a million deaths."[127]

On April 6, 1994, the airplane carrying Rwandan president Juvénal Habyarimana and Burundian president Cyprien Ntaryamira was shot down as it prepared to land in Kigali, Rwanda. Over the next four months, hundreds of thousands of Rwandans were murdered. In the words of Epstein, "The killers used simple tools—machetes, clubs and other blunt objects, or herded people into buildings and set them aflame with kerosene. Most of the victims were of minority Tutsi ethnicity; most of the killers belonged to the majority Hutus."[128]

Deploring the barbarism unleashed by the Hutu *génocidaires*, Epstein argues that the violence was not spontaneous. It was the product of a century or more of injustice and brutality on both sides, and although the killers targeted innocent civilians, they had been traumatized by "heavily armed rebels supplied by Uganda, while the US looked on."[129] The slaughter was initiated by the majority-Hutu government-sponsored militias "intent on carrying out large scale massacres" and relying on imported automatic rifles and hand grenades. After the 1990 invasion, with the civil war underway, Rwanda had become the third-largest importer of weapons in Africa, buying weapons from Egypt with French financing, from France itself, and from apartheid South Africa.[130]

The politics of the IMF also contributed to the crisis. First, Tutsis had been scapegoated by Rwanda for an economic crisis when a global collapse in the price of coffee—Rwanda's largest export—led the IMF to impose a painful currency devaluation just as the RPF invasion ignited the civil war. Displaced farmers and public employees plunged into the ranks of the unemployed were among those recruited for the killing militias.[131] The government was directly involved in the killing of the Tutsi minority, as Andy Storey has argued, inciting the massacres with radio propaganda blaming Tutsis for the economic crisis. Throughout the civil war, aid to Rwanda through IMF SAPS claimed to support the peace process. Yet during the civil war the main beneficiaries of IMF aid were elites and the military.[132] The United Nations Security Council did not impose an arms embargo on Rwanda until May 17, over five weeks into the genocide.

The problem, as Mamdani notes, was not that Western and US powers had failed to act. Western powers *had* been actively participating in the creation, not of "a problem from hell," as Samantha Power would have it, but a hell born of decades of colonial policies, proxy war politics, and neoliberal economic involvement.[133] Most critically, ignoring the political causes of genocide, Mamdani and former president of South Africa Thabo Mbeki contend, has led to an international response based on Nuremberg-style criminal courts. Unlike the Holocaust, during which the victimized Jewish population was largely killed or uprooted from Europe (exiling Europe's colonial problem to Palestine), in Rwanda and other African countries where perpetrators and victims must live together, the model of criminal courts establishes a self-perpetuating cycle of reproducing perpetrators and victims. Problems with political causes require political solutions.[134]

In February 1994, as US officials received warnings of impending violence and government-led plans to carry out genocide, Clinton read Kaplan's "The Coming Anarchy," published in the *Atlantic*. Arguing that the twenty-first century would be characterized by "environmental scarcity, cultural and racial clash, geographic destiny, and the transformation of war," Kaplan painted a bleak portrait of "tyranny" and "lawlessness" ravaging African cities, where "criminal anarchy emerges as the real strategic danger." He raised the bar on his earlier sensationalized portrait of the Balkans. Kaplan compared the Balkans with Africa, maintaining that in the former "the threat was the collapse of empires and the rise of nations based solely on tribe." In Africa, "the threat is more elemental: nature unchecked." Kaplan foresaw an unremittingly bleak African future: "The coming upheaval, in which foreign embassies are shut down, states collapse, and contact with the outside world takes place through dangerous, disease ridden, coastal trading posts, will loom large in the century we are entering."[135]

Clinton pronounced the essay "stunning," foisting it on White House aides. Vice President Al Gore led a task force on "countries at risk." The *Atlantic* issue became one of the highest selling in the magazine's history.[136] Had Clinton been under the spell of Kaplan as reports warning of a coming genocide went unheeded? The UN's Canadian force commander, Lieutenant General Roméo Dallaire, author of a cable warning of the massacre, holds Clinton accountable, claiming that the president's so-called policy was "that he didn't want to know."[137] Clinton maintained that his administration acted decisively as soon as the genocide became known, and that the United States did the right thing. "We have worked on this for months," Clinton told a reporter. "We are doing the best we can. We are going to do more."[138]

Lacking expertise in foreign affairs and knowledge of covert US intervention in the regional conflict as the United States actively pivoted to northeast Africa and Uganda as a proxy in a clash-of-civilizations war on terror, Clinton crafted a culture of innocence.

Out of Order

To some observers, there was something profoundly amiss in the new world order. This sense of distress over the disparity between official optimism about the possibilities of the new world order and the lived reality of spiking inequality, poverty, drug trafficking, and violence registered in popular culture as well as politics. Brazilian singer-songwriter and poet Caetano Veloso identified these alarming trends, concluding that "something has gone out of order, out of new world order." Prompted by the violence unleashed by states on people protesting neoliberal austerity and genocidal war, the British-based, Afro-Jamaican reggae poet Linton Kwesi Johnson's "New World Hawdah" exploded cold war triumphalism. Johnson surveyed the dislocations of political violence from Bosnia to Rwanda, as well as in Shatila, the Palestinian refugee camp in Lebanon, the scene of an infamous 1982 massacre by the Israeli Defense Force:

> di killahs a Kigale [Central Rwanda]
> mus be sanitary workaz
> di butchaz a Butare [South Rwanda]
> mus be sanitary workaz
> di savijes a Shatila [Palestine]
> mus be sanitary workaz
> di beasts a Boznia

mus be sanitary workaz
inna di new world hawdah[139]

For Johnson, the so-called new world order amounted to state-sponsored mass murder and a new language that naturalized mass atrocities.

is a brand new langwidge a barbarity
mass murdah
narmalize
pogram
rationalize
genocide
sanitize
an di hainshent clan sin
now name etnic clenzin[140]

The obscenity of these modern technologies of genocide and mass murder, in Johnson's view, was heightened by their being carried out against the backdrop of celebratory claims of the "end of history" and George H. W. Bush's acting "as if the US was the world's policeman."[141]

Clinton, like other American policy makers, unwitting of the Rwandan genocide's complex roots in the cold war, voiced a sense of regret born of willed amnesia. The killing of the US soldiers in Mogadishu in 1993 prompted Clinton to acknowledge "failing to enlist the nation more fully in 'the great national debate' over America's role in the post–cold war world."[142] Drawing attention to a widely shared nostalgia among policy makers for the anti-Soviet framework in which the West operated for decades, Clinton warned that finding a new workable framework could take decades. "I even made a crack the other day . . . Gosh I miss the cold war."[143] "It was a joke," Clinton continued, "I mean, I really don't miss it, but you get the joke."[144] Clinton's remarks provoked harsh criticism by Republicans, who blasted the president's "alibi" for an incoherent foreign policy.[145] But judging from public anxiety as well as popular culture's fascination with new threats and enemies—the subject of the next chapters—many in fact did get the "joke."

3

Losing the Good Life

POST–COLD WAR MALAISE AND THE ENEMY WITHIN

There is a religious war going on in our country for the soul of America. It is a cultural war, as critical to the kind of nation we will be one day as was the cold war itself.—Patrick Buchanan, 1992

Never again will people trust planners and paper shufflers more than they trust themselves.—1992 Republican Party platform

Once the Berlin Wall fell and the Russians fell apart on us, we've sort of looked within for enemies. The natural faceless enemy we picked was the government.—Brian Helgeland, 1997

Communism is no longer the quintessential enemy against which the nation imagines its identity. . . . Of course, the enemy within is far more dangerous than the enemy without and a black enemy is the most dangerous of all.—Angela Davis, 1997

In 1993, the neoconservative critic Irving Kristol, formerly a managing editor at *Commentary* and professor of social thought at New York University, argued, "Now that the other 'Cold War' is over, the real cold war has begun. We are far less prepared for this cold war, far more vulnerable to our enemy, than was the case with our victorious war over a global communist threat." Who did Kristol imagine as the enemy in this new, evidently more urgent cold war? "There is no after the Cold War for me," Kristol continued. "So far from having ended, my Cold War has increased in intensity as sector after sector of American life has been ruthlessly corrupted by the liberal ethos." The idea that the defeat of global communism abroad necessitated the escalation of an even more dangerous war at home resonated in grassroots Republican politics. Kristol's conviction that the liberal ethos "aims simultaneously at political and social collectivism on the one hand, and moral anarchy on the other," echoed consistent attacks on "bureaucratic collectivism" in the 1992 Republican Party platform as well as Patrick Buchanan's culture war parlays at the convention.[1] As cultural historian Andrew Hartman has written, "Cold War convictions bled into culture war convictions, especially as the Cold War wound down."[2]

Kristol explained his conversion to neoconservatism as an "experience of moral, intellectual and spiritual liberation." He "no longer had to pretend to believe ... that liberals were wrong because they subscribe to this or that erroneous opinion.... No—liberals were wrong—liberals are wrong—because they are liberals."[3] But if Kristol's attack appeared tautological, his righteousness captured a sense of American malaise as the Soviet Union disappeared from the globe, formally dissolving on December 26, 1991.

Judging from commentary surrounding the 1992 US elections, one might have thought that it was the United States that was collapsing. Looking back, the 1990s economy appears supercharged, marked by spiking inequality but also with a dynamism born of colossal sums of money appearing unpredictably in new places. At the decade's dawn, however, many economists predicted that the United States was headed into a prolonged recession, and few anticipated the robust growth and rapid expansion of wealth for the few.[4] Not only did the US economy seem stagnant, but Americans, devoid of the Soviet nemesis, turned inward on themselves—on perceived enemies within—with surprising speed and acrimony.

Surveying the post–cold war landscape, the *Times* of London noted a "chastened" United States after the Ronald Reagan years. Damning with faint praise, it credited Reagan with ending the cold war on a gamble because his dangerous intransigence convinced the Soviets "that the new arms race would bankrupt their country." Moreover, President George H. W. Bush was culpable for invading Iraq while allowing domestic "racial and social troubles to fester," culminating in the Los Angeles riots. The fiscal irresponsibility of Reaganomics did not deliver the promised trickle-down of wealth. Job growth and broad prosperity failed to materialize under Bush. A visit to any part of the country, from the once-booming Sun Belt to the shuttered factories of the industrial Midwest, reveals "gleaming 1980s towers" dominating "cityscapes surrounded by squalor and anarchy and then by outer rings of increasingly fortified suburbs. Roads and bridges are crumbling from neglect, as are the schools. About 30 million people live in fear of medical bills for which they have no insurance. Hard times are hitting the middle classes more severely than any time since the 1930s."[5]

As domestic and foreign observers chronicled the United States' economic insecurity and post–cold war malaise, the anemic economy fueled Bill Clinton's electoral victory over President Bush in November 1992. The *Times*' grim assessment points to a nation adrift in the wake of a supposed cold war victory. Americans won the cold war but had little to show for it, and a country once remarkably united, if only by the idea that the American political system was superior to that of Soviet and Eastern European alternatives, was riven by deep divides of class and culture.

American political culture underwent a sea change following the collapse of the Soviet Union and the loss of the United States' main external adversary. The United States and USSR had defined themselves in relation to each other since 1917, when President Woodrow Wilson responded to Bolshevism and Vladimir Lenin's call for a worldwide revolution with his Fourteen Points, a rival vision of global order defined by capitalist trade, peace, and diplomacy.[6] For the duration of the US-Soviet rivalry, each antagonist set out to prove to its own citizens, to the colonized world, and to all domestic and foreign critics that it and only it could lead the rest of the world to economic and social prosperity: the good life. Whether in Louisville, Leningrad, or Leopoldville, those living under the cultural logic of the cold war measured their lives and hopes by universalizing promises held out by the competing cold war blocs.

For people in the West, as well as those in the Soviet bloc, cold war geopolitical competition structured not just the culture and political economy of citizenship and work but that of everyday life, providing a sense of meaning and, for many, self-identity. As seen in the 1959 Kitchen Debate between Soviet leader Nikita Khrushchev and Vice President Richard Nixon at the US exhibition in Moscow, the race to consumer supremacy was as critical to the cold war as the space race—both linked to a military-industrial economy.[7] Just as US and Soviet versions of the good life for the masses developed in relation to one another, conservative political attacks on the consensus of New Deal liberalism as "collectivism" and their scorn for a commitment to the social good filled the vacuum created by the loss of a rival Soviet vision of the good life.

The end of the cold war brought a far-reaching epistemological crisis—a crisis in what people believe we can know and how we can know it. Doubling down on support for cold war–era fossil fuel industries, politicians and CEOs impugned the integrity of environmental scientists. Widespread skepticism about scientific knowledge and paranoia about the status of truth itself entered the American mainstream.[8] Conspiracy theories had long existed at the fringes of American culture. Now, newly proliferating antigovernment theories were reflected in such popular culture arenas as *The X-Files* television series (1993–2002). A growing segment of the American public rejected the very notion of truth, turning to individual spirituality and religious faith as more reliable sources of knowledge.

The crisis over disputed notions of truth and scientific knowledge was in part a by-product of cold war obfuscation. With "plausible deniability" at the heart of national security practices, the 1947 creation of a covert arm of government (the CIA) erected barriers between government activity and public knowledge—and trust. But the tenuous status of truth in 1990s American culture, whether in *The X-Files* or among climate deniers, was not predetermined. Its cold war roots notwithstanding, the crisis surrounding "facts" was reshaped by political choices made at a dramatic moment of geopolitical upheaval, as these choices played out within a new media and technological landscape.

There is no inherent reason why the dissolution of the Eastern bloc could not have prompted a broader examination of the environmental and political consequences of the cold war and a reimagining of the good life. Indeed, there was considerable will to reimagine the good life in environmentally sustainable terms. But rejecting such inquiry in favor of corporate profit and undermining the authority of scientists, politicians and corporations discredited science, feeding conspiracy theories and paranoia.

This chapter explores a crisis in meaning-making—how people understood their place in a post–cold war world—locating shifts in US politics and culture in the early post-Soviet world in a global and relational frame. On the one hand, American and Russian experiences of the early 1990s diverged dramatically. The collapse of the Soviet Union was catastrophic for Russian society and many in the Soviet republics, while sharply rising inequality in the United States was, for many, tempered by increased access to credit. Russians got shock therapy while Americans got credit cards. Yet whether shock therapy for the former Eastern bloc, structural adjustment for the former third world, or deregulation for the former West, the privatization of the 1990s destroyed the political impediments to sharp increases in inequality. Moreover, the imposition of these policies undercut the social and moral scaffolding on which people had based their worldviews and framed their hopes for the future. With jobs and real wages in decline while unprecedented wealth appeared in new places, millions of people found themselves in an existential wilderness where familiar signposts, rules, and currency didn't work or had simply disappeared.

With many in the Eastern bloc facing the sudden loss of jobs, Americans confronted an uncertain economy of vanishing living-wage manufacturing jobs. Social welfare policies fell into disfavor, and student financial aid, pensions, and health care eroded or disappeared. Fueled by declining wages and standards of living, nostalgic narratives expressing a pervasive sense of unease, uncertainty, and loss gained traction and quickly became bound up with the elaboration of enemies both abroad and at home.

In both the United States and the Soviet Union, early expressions of nostalgia gave voice to radical ruptures in daily life. Neither Russian nor US nostalgia was inherently conservative or reactionary. In the spirit of glasnost (openness), Russian expressions of loss often sought to reanimate socialist values as a bulwark against savage capitalism and authoritarian rule as well as voicing a longing for the former prestige of a global superpower. And while much US cold war nostalgia expressed a longing for military might, it also looked back to the relative stability of a social compact where people trusted government to provide such agreed-on necessities as quality public education and affordable health care. Against the dehumanization and destruction of social bonds engineered by neoliberal policies, people on all sides of former geopolitical divides sought to defend a collective good life.

With the disappearance of the Soviet bogeyman, prominent politicians set about the construction of new enemies at home and abroad. In the anxious context of recession, declining standards of living for the middle class, and accelerating globalization in the geopolitical economy, many Americans began turning on each other.

During his 1992 presidential campaign, Bush sought to discredit the Democratic Party nominee Bill Clinton as a socialist and a central planner, posing a threat to liberty as great as that of the vanquished communist "command economies." Bush's attempts to tar his Democratic opponent with the brush of socialism and centralized planning fell flat with the electorate. In retrospect, his failed strategy might appear comical in light of

Clinton's centrist politics. Yet such rhetoric proved durable, as repurposed histrionic binaries developed in the campaign continued to reshape politics. The 1992 Republican Party platform provided the logic and foundation for the radical dismantling of government regulation and social safety nets, along with new forms of social control and policing. At the same time, it discredited expertise and the idea that government solutions were critical for securing the common good in such areas as health care, education, and environmental regulation.[9]

At the 1992 Republican National Convention, Patrick Buchanan's speech declared a cultural war and Republicans targeted new internal enemies in LGBTQ and poor people, setting the stage for a renewed assault on the social safety net by the 1994 Republican Contract with America and an acquiescent Clinton administration.

I emphasize the uneven but global effects of neoliberal policies, outlining parallel tracks: a diminishment of government-backed social safety services, and a related dependence on conservative institutions such as family and faith-based institutions.[10] The roots of a later convergence between American and Russian conservatives can be seen in the early 1990s. With the Soviet enemy gone, in addition to promoting "family values" and scapegoating Black Americans and LGBTQ people, many came to see the US government itself as the enemy. Rebooting another cold war dynamic, the notion that the enemy of one's enemy is one's friend, antigovernment Americans found new, if unpredictable, cultural bedfellows from Russia in their attack on the US government.

As the end of US hostilities with the Soviet Union enabled the construction of internal enemies, an escalation in partisanship rapidly outweighed the rules of compromise in Congress, as seen in the takeover of the far right of the GOP and the subsequent federal government shutdowns of 1995 and 1996.[11] While these dynamics have earlier roots that have received sustained attention from historians, the end of the cold war mattered. It was only after the collapse of the Soviet Union and Eastern bloc that the long-standing consensus between Republican officials and social welfare state defenders was broken. With the idea that social problems can only be solved through market solutions enshrined in Bush's 1992 campaign and in the Republican platform, a spate of legislation shifting the social safety net from communal to individual and family obligation followed.[12]

Finally, US responses to the collapse of the Soviet Union unfolded in a context of economic crisis, disorientation, and a struggle to find meaning in a post–cold war world. For Americans who had constructed their political sense of belonging and patriotism in relation to a Soviet other, however, the sudden disappearance of that state meant grappling with a new Russia and former Soviet sphere. The emergence of a new disdain for a weakened Russia diverted attention from Americans' own maladies. If cancer rates and birth defects were elevated near Three Mile Island, Pennsylvania, and the nuclear testing grounds of New Mexico, the meltdown of the reactor at Chernobyl was truly catastrophic.

Contempt for a vanquished Russia reflected American fear and anxiety about what many Russians called wild capitalism. On the one hand, the nationalist and imperial inflections of US and Russian nostalgia put the two countries on a collision course by 2005 in the "new cold war." At the same time, however, new efforts to define nationalism in ethnic and racial terms—along with a growing dependence on conservative nonstate institutions in lieu of a regulatory and welfare state—set the grounds for a cultural convergence of the US white nationalist self-proclaimed alt-right and Russian conservatives, a dynamic that became particularly visible in the period before and after the election of Donald Trump as US president in 2016. Within two years of the collapse of the Soviet Union, a new US electoral coalition of family-values Republicans and gun-rights advocates came together in the Republican Party to win a majority in the 1994 congressional elections, the very combination of gun advocacy and conservative religious and patriarchal values that brought US and Russian conservatives together in the years before Trump's candidacy.

In the United States no less than the Soviet Union, the relationships among citizenship, race, gender, sexuality, and family were upended by the end of the cold war. I thus provide a sketch of a world in turmoil—a world of post–cold war malaise—before turning to the ways in which the making of new enemies spilled into American culture and politics and rewrote the social contract, and finally turning to new US-Russian relations.

Snatching Defeat from the Jaws of Victory: How the Grinch Stole Christmas

For many Americans, triumphalist rhetoric rang hollow. If we won the cold war, what did we win? People throughout the West and Eastern bloc had hoped that reduced military spending would lead to domestic economic reform along with social spending and investment in public infrastructure. But retrenchment in the defense industry did not yield social and environmental benefits. Reporting in the *Independent* in 1993 that in "Britain alone, tens of thousands of jobs have been lost in the past two years," Andrew Marshall argued that "the transitional costs of the end of the Cold War, combined with an utter lack of coordination between state and industry or among governments" in Western Europe, have meant "that we are worse, not better, off."[13]

Journalist David Beers, who grew up in Silicon Valley, where his father worked in the aerospace industry, described his father's disorientation as he contemplated retirement in 1990. The end of the cold war confronted him with a sobering realization: "Your adult working life has been spent in a futile pursuit. You are not needed anymore." Even before its end, Beers's father lamented the cold war's "dissipated energies" and "wasted technical talent," wondering, "What the hell is this doing for the species?" As his father faulted himself for lacking the "moral compass" to find an alternative to a career that now seemed dubious at best, Beers thought it tantamount to a national secret that a technician, "averse to mush, could feel such doubt and yearning."[14]

Many lost jobs as US bases closed and defense contracts expired or were canceled; others found hope in the much-talked-about peace dividend. With billions of dollars potentially to be freed up from military spending, Americans looked to benefit from the rebuilding of crumbling infrastructure and schools. Yet such social benefits never arrived.

As hopes for a peace dividend, widely reported in the press, were dashed by the US intervention in Iraq and a global reshuffling rather than reduction in military bases, advocates for a dividend proved no match for Bush's new world order. Commenting on Bush's 1991 arguments for a leaner military, columnist Sandy Grady likened the president to the character Lucy in the *Peanuts* comic, referencing her habit of holding a football for Charlie Brown to kick, only to withdraw it. Bush withdrew the peace-dividend football when he told the nation in a televised address, "Some will say that these initiatives call for a budget windfall for domestic programs. But the peace dividend I seek is not measured in dollars but in greater security. In the near term, some of these steps may even cost money."[15]

The sleight of hand was dryly noted by Grady: "Wait a minute, did I miss something? ... You mean we're going to destroy all our tactical, short-range missiles, eliminate all nuclear-tipped cruise missiles from Navy ships, take B-52 bombers off alert, end two expensive mobile-missile programs—and we end up with no money? That's as depressing as paying off a house mortgage over 40 years and hearing your banker say, 'Sorry, pal, you owe us.' Talk about the Grinch that stole Christmas."[16]

The day after Bush's address, reporters asked Defense Secretary Dick Cheney how he magically made the peace dividend vaporize into thin air. "There are added costs in terminating contracts, moving systems around, destroying missiles, et cetera," Cheney replied. As he insisted that programs critical to security were not cut, he provided fodder for critics with his sales pitch for the B-2 bomber. Cheney explained, "We need a bomber that carries a payroll worldwide. Uh, I meant payload. A slip of the tongue."[17]

As suggested by Cheney's gaffe, strategies for a "leaner, meaner defense" entailed not shrinking the defense industry but instead diversifying and privatizing the industry as the Pentagon shifted priorities and established new bases.[18] Demands to maintain defense jobs and what Beers described as contractors' "colossal financial leverage in [electoral] campaigns underscored how difficult it was to reform an economy thoroughly imbricated with military interests." For Beers, "the evidence clearly shows a lack of political will to diminish rather than re-fashion and privatize the military."[19]

Cheney's slip of the tongue revealed that stewardship of a global military-industrial political economy remained the Bush administration's priority. As talk of a peace dividend faded, ordinary Americans and observers alike noted a growing malaise in a country still smarting from the Reagan recessions.

Losing the Good Life

In the United States during the age of three worlds, politicians and corporate leaders tied the superiority of the US political system and consumer capitalism to the idea of the good life for the masses: mass production, consumption, and government-guaranteed public education along with security and dignity in old age. But the political, economic, and cultural shockwaves accompanying the collapse of the Eastern bloc revealed that in the United States, the former promises of the social contract were now tenuous at best.

During the 1980s, rising inequality along with the Reagan New Right agenda of deregulation and the attack on government programs—the erosion of the idea that government was an active steward of the good life—built on a revolution in financing and credit underway from the early 1980s. In 1979, when Paul Volcker, the Federal Reserve chair appointed by Jimmy Carter (and serving under Reagan until 1987), sought to rein in inflation, Democrats as well as Republicans panicked as inflation and unemployment temporarily spiked before bottoming out and decreasing over the next two

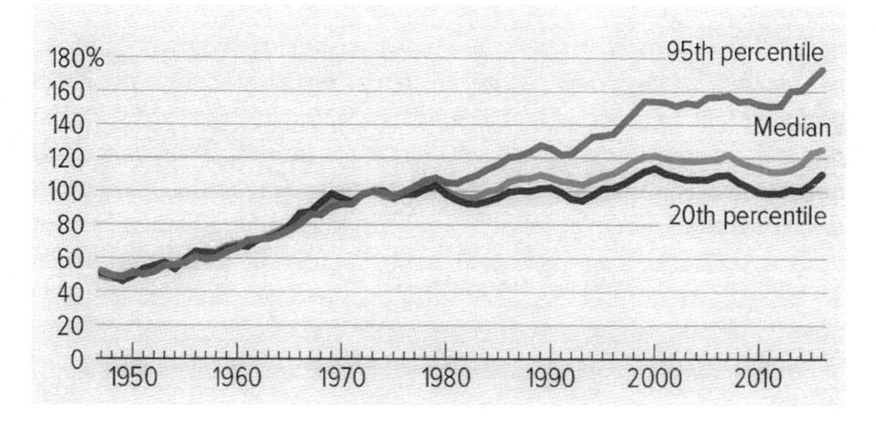

3.1 Spiking inequality accelerating after 1990. "Income Gains Widely Shared in Early Postwar Decades—But Not Since Then; Real family income between 1947 and 2014, as a percentage of 1973 level," Center for Budget and Policy Priorities, based on US Census Bureau data

years. Many policy makers realized that the rising prosperity many Americans had come to see as their birthright under a Fordist economy—based on mass production and mass consumption—could only be sustained by "democratizing credit and stimulating asset inflation."[20] If the middle class could no longer afford the good life, they could borrow it, taking the heat off politicians to deliver on traditional living standards.

But the biggest spike in inequality in the United States, and globally, came when American policy makers no longer had to answer Eastern bloc rivals' criticisms of capitalist inequality. As Boris Yeltsin embraced Western-imposed shock therapy and rapid privatization of the Russian economy, the US defunding of public institutions and the commons—and increases in inequality that had begun during the Reagan and Thatcher years in the West—accelerated dramatically. Income inequality "first started to rise in the late '70s and early '80s in America and Britain (and also in Israel)." The ratio between the average incomes of the top 5 percent and the bottom 5 percent in the world increased from 78 to 1 in 1988 to 114 to 1 in 1993. During the Thatcher and Reagan era, income tax rates were lowered for higher earners, trade unions were broken, and the financial sector was deregulated, all with devastating consequences. Already a trend, inequality spiked in the late 1980s, wrecking, in the words of one observer, "the social fabric of countries throughout the world, including more egalitarian nations, like Sweden, Finland, Germany and Denmark." From 1988 to 2008, people in the world's top 1 percent saw their incomes increase by a staggering 60 percent, while those in the bottom 5 percent had no change in their earnings.[21] Income inequality widened most dramatically in the first decade after the collapse of the Soviet Union—from 1991 to 2000—continuing to grow after that but not at the 1990s rates following the radical privatization of shock therapy and deregulation.[22] Soaring stocks, with an 18.6 percent annualized return for the decade overall, punctuated by years such as 1996 with a 27 percent growth, created unprecedented wealth for some Americans, while others eked out a semblance of the good life using credit, and others still tumbled out of reach of a middle-class life entirely.[23]

American disorientation as communist regimes collapsed took many forms, sometimes to the mild amusement of foreign observers. A correspondent in the *Independent* noted, "In the past two years, the American perception of the threat has been turned upside down—from three-quarters believing that the Soviet Union is the biggest threat to US security, to three-quarters believing that it is not." Attesting to "a great debate" unfolding in America, journalist Peter Pringle wondered what issue "could possibly take the place of Soviet communism as a focus for the nation's energies; what could be the unifying force of America for the 1990s as it undergoes its own perestroika?" Pringle emphasized US economic anxieties and scattershot polling data. "Will the U.S. plunge into a depression or benefit from a peace dividend?" With "one poll finding that 70% of Americans believe that the Japanese now pose the greatest threat to future well-being," will America seize on another external enemy, or "be brought together by domestic issues such as drugs, health and education—or even garbage?"[24]

From Environmental Redress to Climate Change Denial

A puckish Pringle explained that American suburbanites "are talking about how to dispose of trash with the same kind of intensity they once devoted to the 'commie menace.'" After Reagan presided over a decade of deregulation, a throwaway society was running out of landfills. As environmentalists and city managers moved to confront the waste through recycling, for others, garbage was a telling metaphor for the cold war, an era marked by "large-scale waste everywhere." Pringle thought it was no accident that the new "preoccupation with waste has come at the same time as Mikhail Gorbachev has been dismantling the main American obsession of the century, the threat of communism."[25]

The environmental damage wrought by the detritus of cold war militarism, industrial chemicals such as plastics and pesticides, and accumulated nuclear waste—and the inability of states to ensure public safety—was brought most sharply into public view by the nuclear accidents at Three Mile Island (1979) and Chernobyl (1986), and the deadly toxic gas leak in Bhopal, India (1984). As some contemplated new possibilities for a post–cold war world, they confronted a profoundly toxic and fragile environment, fueling demands for redress and environmental restoration and protection.

As the Eastern bloc unraveled, many on both sides of the former divide confronted the environmental contamination caused by towering landfills, incinerated garbage, discarded consumer goods, and nuclear waste. The sense that the race for superiority in weapons and appliances was unsustainable led some to propose a radical rethinking of the good life. This sense of the harmful effects of cold war consumerism founded on cheap, readily available fossil fuel energy was the backdrop for the growing scientific consensus on climate change. Reagan fought environmental protections; in one of his first acts as president, he removed thirty-two solar panels Jimmy Carter had installed on the White House roof, calling them a "joke." By 1988, discussions of the greenhouse effect and the banning of ozone-depleting aerosol sprays had shifted public opinion. On the campaign trail in 1988, during the hottest summer ever recorded, George H. W. Bush declared himself an environmentalist, embarking on a five-state tour that began on Lake Erie and ended in Boston. He challenged complacency in the face of climate change, arguing, "Those who think we are powerless to do anything about the greenhouse effect are forgetting about the White House effect."[26] Once in office, Bush and a bipartisan group in Congress moved to immediately cut emissions in the United States.

On November 6, 1989, three days before the unexpected breaching of the Berlin Wall, an international gathering of scientists and diplomats met in Noordwijk in the western Netherlands to forge a comprehensive treaty to address climate change through strict emissions restrictions. On the advice of Bush political adviser John Sununu, the United States withdrew from the treaty, despite Bush's support of emissions controls. The United States, "at the urging of Sununu, and with the acquiescence of Britain, Japan and the Soviet Union, had forced the conference to abandon the commitment to freeze emissions."[27]

The Noordwijk convention marked a major reversal in the perestroika-era resolve of major superpowers to clean up their cold war mess. While the Soviet Union and Eastern European countries were slow to acknowledge the environmental damage wrought by their arms and development race, by 1989 a "public awakening about environmental problems" was taking hold in the Soviet Union and Eastern Europe "comparable to that triggered by Earth Day in the United States in 1970."[28] In addition, Sununu's rejection of the international scientific consensus as "technical poppycock" signaled a new attack on science that would take more extreme form in climate change denial.[29] Although Sununu's position reflected oil and gas executives' determination to shield their enormous profits, the fateful decision to side with extractive energy industries over the scientific community had far-reaching consequences in attacks on science.

As the presidential elections approached, despite warning signs of an unregulated market imperiling the environment and exacerbating US economic and social problems, Republicans plowed ahead, seeking to advance their free market agenda in what they called, in their platform, "liberation through deregulation."[30]

From Cold War to Culture War

Bush's sensibility clashed with the antigovernment sentiment taking over the Republican Party. More inclined to a Wilsonian approach, Bush favored government intervention (sometimes covert) to shape the domestic and global order. During his first presidential campaign, his vision of a "kinder, gentler nation" offended conservative Republicans who believed that the phrase, in the context of federal programs for childcare, education, and the environment, ceded ground to the domestic agenda of liberal Democrats. As they pondered the implications of his words, establishment Republicans appeared as alarmed as the right wing of the party.[31]

On the eve of the first national election conducted after the "twin epoxies"—Reagan and the Soviet Union—that held the party together were no more, the press observed internal warfare breaking out among Republicans. Under siege from the right, Bush tacked in that direction and soon settled on a unified plan of attack against Democrats.[32]

The cold war triumphalism and nostalgia saturating the 1992 Republican presidential campaign did not go unchallenged, with the challenges sometimes coming from surprisingly authoritative sources. The experienced Soviet observer George F. Kennan wrote in the *New York Times* that campaign rhetoric boasting that "the United States under Republican leadership had 'won the cold war' is intrinsically silly." To the architect of containment policy, "nobody—no country, no party, no person—'won the cold war.' It was a long and costly political rivalry, fueled on both sides by unreal and exaggerated estimates of the intentions and strength of the other party. It greatly overstrained the economic resources of both countries, leaving both, by the end of the 1980s, confronted with heavy financial, social, and in the case of the Russians, political problems that neither had anticipated and for which neither was fully prepared."[33] Bush, preoccupied with reelection, could ill afford to consider the ways in which cold war policies created the present malaise. Rather than engage critical perspectives such as Kennan's, Bush's stump speech chalked up the challenges facing the United States to a yet-unresolved political battle against centralized planning and state bureaucracy at home.

Bush played to his strength, compensating for his awkwardness as a campaigner. Triumphalist crowing came naturally. "Imperial communism became a four-letter word: D-E-A-D, dead," Bush proclaimed at his re-election campaign announcement on February 12.[34] The Republican Party platform conjured an internal threat, warning that "centralized government bureaucracies" threatened the family, the individual, and the economy. In an attack on the welfare state and social programs, Republicans equated government spending for the public good with failed Soviet centralized planning.

"We Republicans saw clearly the dangers of collectivism: not only the military threat, but the deeper threat to the souls of people bound in dependence. Here at home, we warned against Big Government, because we knew concentrated decision making, no matter how well-intentioned, was a danger to liberty and prosperity." "Free markets," the Republicans contended, offer "true liberation," freeing "poor people not only from want but also from government control."[35]

On the stump, Bush embraced this line of attack with relish, linking his Democratic opponent, Clinton, to socialism so tenaciously that journalists took note. A *New York Times* analysis parsed the logic: "Now that Moscow has abandoned all claim to the mantle of socialism, President Bush tried hard today to drape it over his Democratic rivals."[36] A *Los Angeles Times* correspondent portrayed Bush's Oklahoma campaign speech as a "calculated . . . assault" of "rhetorically charged descriptions of Clinton and his economic advisors as unrepentant heirs to failed European-style policies of social engineering."[37] Indeed, opening his stump speech by reminding audiences that America had won the cold war, Bush quickly pivoted to charges that American institutions were on "the wrong track." In Tampa, he told the audience, "The cold war is over, and America won, and the Soviet Union collapsed." But if "imperial communism, the communism with outreach ... is dead all around the world," its central features still imperiled the United States. Americans, Bush admonished, must use the "same spirit" and "same leadership" that won the cold war "to change America."[38] In San Diego, indicting government as the source of America's ills, he charged that "the welfare system ... perpetuates dependency instead of personal responsibility." Labeling a proposed Universal Health Care Act as "nationalized socialized medicine," Bush declared, "I will not allow those people to give America a prescription for failure."[39] The choice, Bush argued at an Oklahoma event, was between himself, "the entrepreneur, the risktaker," and Clinton, "the government planner," who advocated the same "command-and-control economies [that] have been dismissed as failures."[40]

The campaign's attack on "planning" was related to a more general attack on expertise. Charging that "from kremlins and ivory towers ... planners proclaimed the bureaucratic millennium," the 1992 Republican platform declared that "centralized government bureaucracies created in this century are not the wave of the future. Never again will people trust planners and paper shufflers more than they trust themselves."[41] In equating expertise with "a failed scoundrel ideology" and equating the ivory tower with the Kremlin, they made anti-intellectualism and contempt for expertise central to Republican Party identity.

Blaming Poor People

Historians have noted the irony of Reagan, an antigovernment politician, creating the largest government to date through increased military spending. Another ironic aspect of the era is that those who condemned "social engineering" as communist employed such policies on a massive scale in reshaping the global economy through failed structural adjustment programs abroad and through welfare reform and carceral policies that targeted poor people, disproportionately African Americans.

The radical Black feminist activist Angela Davis observed that, during the 1990s, "an ideological space for a racialized fear of crime was opened by the transformations in international politics created by the fall of the European socialist countries." In regulating the bodies of women and Black, brown, and poor people, racism was the glue that held together the purported antistatism. For Davis, "Communism is no longer the quintessential enemy against which the nation imagines its identity. This space is now inhabited by ideological constructions of crime, drugs, immigration, and welfare. Of course, the enemy within is far more dangerous than the enemy without and a black enemy is the most dangerous of all." Davis's analysis of a post–cold war shift to an internal enemy helps explain the seeming paradox of how antigovernment politicians and constituencies enacted a massive expansion of the carceral state. Widespread fear of crime, Davis argued, attained a status akin to the fear of communism. Under such a siege mentality, "anything is acceptable—torture, brutality, vast expenditures of public funds," so long as it is done in the name of public safety.[42]

Just as the cold war order gave leverage to nonaligned nations such as Yugoslavia, the competition between capitalism and communism had at times allowed strategic leverage for racially marginalized Americans.[43] But the end of the cold war brought a swift end to even the limited support for civil rights rooted in national security considerations. With no Soviet Union to publicize racial injustices before world opinion, the Los Angeles rebellion in 1992 provided Republican leaders ideological ammunition against the civil rights and social justice agenda of Great Society liberalism.[44]

The uprising began on April 29, 1992, following the acquittal of four police officers whose savage beating of Rodney King, an unarmed African American motorist, had been caught on videotape one year earlier on March 3, 1991. For months as the case garnered national and world publicity, cable news networks had repeatedly broadcast the videotaped evidence of police brutality. But when hopes for justice for King were thwarted by the acquittals, furious Angelenos took to the streets, hurling rocks at police and setting fires. With sixty-three lives lost, over twelve thousand arrests, and estimated property damage of over $1 billion, the multicultural rebellion sparked mini rebellions in other cities, including Iowa City.

Bush's response to the rebellion was predictable. Wishing to be perceived as compassionate, he made vacuous claims about problems of "hatred, poverty, and despair." He had nothing to say about the frustration born of decades of systemic police abuse of power and discrimination in housing and employment that had fueled the unrest. Instead, he declared government the source of the problem. On May 8, in South Central Los Angeles, Bush declared, "Things aren't right in too many cities across the country, and we must not return to the status quo." Bemoaning what he deemed a lack of personal responsibility, he argued that "we must start with a set of principles and policies that foster personal responsibility."[45] He portrayed poverty and discrimination, once seen as problems requiring state action, as the *results* of public policy and state activity.[46]

Bush's assessment of the rebellion as the result of cultural pathology rather than systemic poverty and injustice signaled a changed relationship between foreign policy and civil rights. Cold war–era claims that the United States was the legitimate leader of the democratic "free world" had provided strategic leverage for civil rights, antiracist, and anti-imperialist activists, who across decades called the United States to account for failing to live up to its professed ideals of equality. With no Eastern bloc adversary to denounce racism, poverty, and violence as failures of capitalism, emboldened conservatives placed the onus for systemic racism on oppressed people of color, and the onus for poverty on poor people.

Following the release of Nelson Mandela and the unbanning of the African National Congress in 1990, conservatives redoubled arguments they had been making since the 1980s that the struggle against structural forms of racial domination was over—it had been won. Declaring victory in the international struggle against racism disavowed the long-standing synergy between antiapartheid, anti-imperialist, and US antiracist struggles. For Bush and his fellow conservatives, by 1992, apartheid and racism were vanquished, and any remaining problems were due not to systemic injustice but to personal failings.

Bush's emphasis on personal responsibility paved the way for those armed for the culture wars with punitive intent. Vice President Dan Quayle's "family values" speech in San Francisco asserted that poor African Americans' lack of virtue had become a national crisis. Asserting that poverty was an individual and cultural choice, Quayle yoked his law-and-order rhetoric with a call for policies that would "reinforce values such as family, hard work, integrity, and personal responsibility."[47] Blaming the Los Angeles rebellion on "a culture of poverty," and perhaps seeking to confound critics of the anti-Blackness inherent in his argument, Quayle charged the fictional television character Murphy Brown, an unmarried white professional woman, with mocking the importance of fathers by bearing a child alone and calling it just another lifestyle choice. Asserting that intergenerational poverty "is predominantly a poverty of values," Quayle argued, "Marriage is probably the best anti-poverty program there is."[48]

The White House initially refrained from comment on Quayle's salvos against a program with thirty-eight million viewers. But Bush endorsed Quayle's racially coded campaign for family values. A *New York Times* analysis claimed that by attacking "Hollywood, the news media, academics, abortion rights activists, East Coast liberals, gay couples, New York City and Mario M. Cuomo," Quayle not only got "what he so badly craves—press attention as something more than Mr. Malaprop"—but he "polarized the 1992 election into an 'us versus them' battle. The strategy is clear: by dividing the country, he and his Republican advisers hope to conquer it."[49]

The Passion Is Gone: The Enemy Within

The 1992 campaign prosecuted the culture wars with a marriage of triumphalism and nostalgia that sought to redefine the enemy within. In August 1992, as the Republicans gathered in Houston for their nominating convention, the party platform declared, "The greatest danger to America's security is here at home, among those who would leave the Nation unprepared for the new realities of the post-Cold War world."[50]

Patrick Buchanan led the chorus lamenting the loss of the old enemy and a consequent lack of clarity in American politics. Failing to wrest the party's nomination from Bush, Buchanan gave the keynote speech after the president extended an olive branch to the right wing of the party. Buchanan rallied Republican forces against new enemies in his infamous culture war speech. "There is a religious war going on in our country for the soul of America," the political commentator told his audience. "It is a cultural war, as critical to the kind of nation we will be one day as was the Cold War itself."[51] Charging that a Clinton administration would impose "abortion on demand," "homosexual rights," and "discrimination against religious schools," Buchanan cloaked his racial and religious bigotry within his vision of imperiled families, who were at the center of his defense of a white Christian America. Journalist Jeff Sharlet, an expert on Christian fundamentalism and conservative politics, helps place Buchanan's remarks in perspective. Sharlet observes that anticommunism had once been the organizing principle of American fundamentalism. After the cold war, he argues, Christian fundamentalists no longer defined godless communism as the enemy; instead, "sex provided a new battleground."[52]

Attendees of the Houston convention basked in the glow of triumphalism and nostalgia. Buchanan, who had worked in the Nixon and Reagan administrations, linked his moral crusade with cold war triumphalism. It was under Reagan, he told the crowd, that "the Red Army was run out of Afghanistan." It was "under our party that the Berlin Wall came down" and "the Soviet Empire collapsed."[53] Sellers at a flea market outside the Astrodome hawked post–cold war souvenirs and tchotchkes ranging from "genuine" chunks of the Berlin Wall to political memorabilia from the Soviet Union. Ruble notes were on sale for five dollars each. "There's almost a nostalgia for the old enemy in Houston," observed the *Irish Times*. "With the Cold War over, Republicans must now grapple with less simple, unifying issues, and an enemy within which includes the media, liberal Democrats, pro-choice and gay-rights groups and their most dangerous foe, Mr. Bill Clinton."[54] Former Reagan staffers lamented a loss of moral certainty. "Back then," one staffer explained, "there was passion ... we were the Good Guys and they were the Evil Empire."[55]

To Buchanan, Reagan was not getting his due for winning the cold war, a sentiment that resonated inside and outside the Astrodome. Lou Cordia, executive director of the Reagan-Bush administrations and Campaign Alumni Association, groused that "you have Gorbachev getting named Man of the Decade, and Reagan getting no credit for planting the seed" of the Soviet Union's dissolution.[56] An Irish journalist contextualized the Republican defensiveness. Having left the economy in shambles, four years out of office, the Great Communicator registered unfavorable ratings by 63 percent of Americans. Reagan's appearance late in the convention, in what many anticipated to be his last public appearance, allowed Republicans to wallow in nostalgia.[57]

Resenting Reagan's faded favorability among the broader public, Republicans seized on triumphalism in a campaign to mythologize his image. And after Clinton defeated Bush, Republicans redirected their nostalgia for bashing communists to a new round of accusations that the Clinton administration harbored socialists.

A New Script for a New Enemy: Socialism in the Doctor's Office

In the 1930s, an advertisement for Scott tissues famously asked, "Is your washroom breeding Bolsheviks?" Reproduced in the following decades as an absurdist spoof of McCarthyite paranoia, the ad in its original context illustrated the promise of the good life, and consumerism as a key terrain of US-Soviet competition. Warning that "employees lose respect for a company that fails to provide decent facilities for their comfort," the ad promises that using Scott towels and tissues will prevent employees from turning into radical communists. Before describing the "amazing cellulose product" with "thirsty fiber," the ad explains the social and political costs of bad tissue.[58]

"Try wiping your hands six days a week on harsh, cheap paper towels or awkward, unsanitary roller towels—and maybe you, too, would grumble.

Towel service is just one of those small, but important courtesies—such as proper air and lighting—that help build up the goodwill of your employees. That's why you'll find clothlike Scott-Tissue Towels in the washrooms of large, well-run organizations such as R.C.A. Victor Co., Inc., National Lead Co. and Campbell Soup Co."

If Scott's 1930s ad touted comfort as a gift of corporate largesse and a bulwark against communism, perhaps nothing better illustrated how far Republican ideology had traveled from cold war–era promises of the good life than its 1993 campaign against Clinton's health care reform proposals. Superficially reminiscent of the Scott tissues ad, the anti–health care reform campaign hysterically posed the question, is there a socialist in your doctor's office? But far from advocating excellent care in the interest of satisfied employee-citizens, attacks on the health care plan as a "blueprint for tyranny" and "cradle-to-grave slavery" demanded a disciplining of the consumer-citizen, whose needs were restricted to what they could afford to pay in a competitive market.[59]

Given the Clinton administration's part in dismantling the welfare state, the expansion of the prison-industrial complex, the embrace of free trade policies, and the ruinous deregulation of the financial sector, it may appear ironic in retrospect that it faced accusations of socialism as it put forth comprehensive health care reform. The Clintons themselves, with the feminist implications of their ostensible marriage of equals (the reality was more complex), elicited the visceral hatred of Republican culture warriors. It followed naturally that conservatives would seize on cold war Manichean logic in attacking Bill Clinton's health care reform plan. As Theda Skocpol has argued, the 1993 Clinton health care proposal provided an ideal foil for concerted antigovernment countermobilization.[60] During the 1992 campaign, the *New York Times* reported, Bush tried to paint Clinton's plans as "socialistic" and the Republicans "pummeled Clinton "as an advocate of ... socialized medicine."[61]

Conservative pundits repeated their claims that the collapse of the Soviet Union proved that markets work and government policies had failed. William Kristol charged that the Clinton health plan "would guarantee an unprecedented federal intrusion into the American economy," signaling the "rebirth of centralized welfare policy at the very moment that this policy is being perceived as a failure in other areas."[62]

The rise of right-wing radio and television provided venues for Rush Limbaugh and other conservative broadcasters to emerge as popularizers of a rebooted cold war. For months on radio and television, Limbaugh derided the health care reform plan as "socialist."[63] Echoing Kristol's accusation, he charged, "This health care plan is all about the destruction of the creation of wealth in America and the socialization of this country, and it won't work—never has anywhere else—and we're going to see to it here that they don't succeed."[64]

In the run-up to the 1994 midterm elections, an army of pundits mobilized by right-wing think tanks railed against the proposed reforms. One critic accused the Clinton plan of "coercion" and "controlling the conduct of state governments, employers, drug manufacturers, doctors, hospitals, and you and me."[65] Resuscitating the 1950s language of NSC-68 and its framing of the Soviet Union as a slave state, Jarret Wollstein of the Future of Freedom Foundation called Clinton's health care plan "a blueprint for tyranny" and "cradle-to-grave slavery." Portraying a dystopian communist nightmare, Wollstein warned that Clinton's plan would give the government "life and death power over you" and "change the way you and your children live." "You could find it impossible to get medication necessary for your health and life or to get an operation if you're injured or in an accident."[66]

The complex reasons for the ultimate failure of HCR, from its cumbersome provisions to the ways in which it provoked interest groups that it attempted to appease, have been thoroughly explored by Skocpol and other scholars.[67] The mortal blows dealt by antisocialist hysteria found further elaboration in Newt Gingrich's 1994 Contract with America, signaling a sharp departure from political norms of compromise and bipartisan respect for the legitimacy of the opposition party that had held through the end of the cold war.[68]

Launched during the 1994 congressional campaigns, the Contract with America aimed to finish the job Reagan started in dismantling domestic welfare programs. Signed by more than three hundred Republican congressional candidates, it mobilized a coalition of advocates of family values and gun rights, a coalition held together by profound suspicion of government and contempt for the idea of the public good. Building on Reagan's antigovernment ideology, the Contract with America radically reimagined the relationship between the family and the nation. A key trope in cold war discourse since the 1950s, the family had been idealized as a microcosm of the nation-state.[69] At once a model for international relations in which sovereign democratic nations should freely choose to follow the leadership of the United States just as a wife freely chooses to follow her husband's guiding authority, and purportedly a microcosm of democracy with its patriarchal hierarchy harmonized by a separation of powers (gendered division of labor), the nuclear family was a powerful symbol of belonging and citizenship in the cold war national imaginary.[70]

In the 1970s, as Natasha Zaretsky has shown, images of the patriarchal family in peril became analogous to fears of national decline, a shift that enabled the Reagan revolution.[71] To be sure, the idea that the government threatened the sanctity of the white nuclear family had been a defining element of white southern resistance to court-ordered desegregation during the 1950s. This once-regional strain of conservatism rose to national prominence under Reaganism and the Christian right. By the 1990s, with the Soviet threat removed, the sense that family, patriotism, and nation were under moral assault by government became conservative dogma, even seeping into mainstream discourse in unexpected ways.

The Truth Is Out There: *The X-Files*, Conspiracy, and the Imperiled Family

Accusations of government conspiracies threatening family and nation were a prominent theme of 1990s popular culture. Brian Helgeland, the screenwriter for Richard Donner's 1997 film *Conspiracy Theory*, starring Mel Gibson and Julia Roberts, asserted that the proliferation of conspiracy thinking "stems from the Cold War being over. Once the Berlin Wall fell and the Russians fell apart on us, we've sort of looked within for enemies. The natural faceless enemy we picked was the government."[72] Director Paul Verhoeven explained in 1996, "The US is desperately in search of an enemy. The communists were the enemy, and the Nazis before them, but now that wonderful enemy that everyone can fight has been lost. Alien sci-fi films give us a terrifying enemy that's politically correct. They're bad. They're evil. And they're not even human."[73]

Conspiracy theories did not begin in the 1990s; they have long occupied the fringes of American culture. The phenomenon became a staple in the decade's mass entertainment. The popular science-fiction television series *The X-Files* (1993–2002) portrays an out-of-control government as a threat to families within a sprawling and politically ambiguous storyline. The series signaled a coming explosion in alien science-fiction television and film productions.[74] Though tongue-in-cheek, Verhoeven's comment that science-fiction alien enemies were sublimated versions of actual pariah groups rang true. In *The X-Files*, the aliens' coconspirators are not only human, they are deeply embedded within the US government.

The X-Files engages cold war legacies in multiple and obfuscating ways. The show's creator, Chris Carter, explained in a 1994 interview, "Now that Russia is no longer our very recognizable enemy, we suddenly need to find other enemies and other sources of discontent. That's when we start looking to the skies."[75]

Considered by television critics and media scholars alike as mining the era's cultural zeitgeist, *The X-Files*' twin mottos, "Trust no one" and "The truth is out there," recast the gritty shadows of the cold war where truth was a casualty in the quest for national security. The series plumbs the depths of public mistrust, linking shadowy accounts of the paranormal with government duplicity. As captured by *New York Times* critic Joyce Millman, *The X-Files* set the tone for the 1990s: "Perpetually underlighted and rain-slicked, rich with cynicism, almost Hitchcockian in its command of tension and release, it was the defining series of the 90's. It hauntingly captured the cultural moment when paranoid distrust of government spilled over from the political fringes to the mainstream, aided by the conspiracy-theory-disseminating capability of the Internet."[76]

The X-Files taps into ideas of a global clash of civilizations as well as domestic anxieties about race and immigration—all by positing a government conspiracy involving extraterrestrial aliens. On the one hand, the show's individual monster stories often portray African Americans sympathetically as victims of heinous plots, overtly raising actual histories of enslavement and victimization by the government in the Tuskegee experiments in which African American men with syphilis were intentionally not treated in order to study the effects of the disease over time.

Yet repeatedly in the series, main characters, as well as those featured in subplots, are found infected with alien DNA, promulgating narratives obsessed with contagion and racial purity. Thus, despite multiple episodes portraying African American and minority victims of alien and government conspiracy, *The X-Files* frequently raises the question of who belongs and who does not; and the answers are consistently ambiguous, stoking anxieties that cannot be resolved through reason.

In the main characters' search for truth, nothing is more important than defining the enemy. When George W. Bush raised the specter of an unseen enemy in his 2000 presidential campaign, his rhetorical gambit drew as much from *The X-Files*' sensibility as from the neoconservative project to promote another US intervention in Iraq. "When I was coming up," Bush told college students in Iowa, "it was us versus them and you knew who them was. Today we're not so sure who the they are, but we know they're there."[77]

Seemingly endorsing critical inquiry into government claims as well as unexplained phenomena, *The X-Files* seduces the potential dissenter with routine references to actual historical events in the cold war past while conflating actual cover-ups with fictional acts of government suppression of alien activities. "With its high-level cover-ups, Deep Throats and adherence to the watchwords 'Trust no one,'" argues Millman, "'The X-Files' tapped into still-fresh memories of Iran-contra and Watergate, not to mention Ruby Ridge and Waco."[78] In the context of official US effacement of the history of the cold war and politicians' feigned innocence about past actions, FBI agent Fox Mulder seems a welcome and credible historical investigator. As the United States refused a reckoning with its cold war past, the fictional Mulder operates as the US simulacrum to the political opening of glasnost as he attempts to run his own truth and reconciliation commission.

In the first season's finale, which aired in May 1994, the Watergate-era figure Deep Throat appears, reporting that in 1987, American children had been injected with a "clone DNA." When Deep Throat asserts that there are things so horrible and vast they must be kept from the American people, Mulder insists on the people's right to know, further asserting that the reaction will be "outrage."[79] With Mulder cast as the defender of democracy and government transparency, the historical thoroughness of his inquiry, along with his demand for transparency, provides comfort. A dedicated investigative reporter, Mulder promises credible knowledge, just like the *Washington Post*'s Bob Woodward and Carl Bernstein. Yet in Mulder's account of outrages—mixing the verifiable cover-ups of Watergate and Iran-Contra with the fictional injection of alien DNA into US children—the "truth" is so "out there" that it cannot be known. In the impossible quest for truth, the well-meaning citizen-investigator is left not only exhausted but thoroughly disempowered.

In the episode "Jose Chung's from Outer Space," written by Darin Morgan, an air force pilot abducted by aliens confesses to Mulder in a fit of frustration, "I can't be sure of anything anymore!"[80] Citing the conspiracy scholar Peter Knight, cultural critic Jonathan Kirby argues that modern conspiracism is ruled by a "vertigo of interpretation" where "nothing is certain; everything can be reinterpreted. . . . The final revelation is constantly deferred, with a complete view of the overarching conspiratorial design always just slightly out of reach. The truth is, literally, out there."[81]

As the series developed, weaving ever-greater conspiracies within conspiracies, it engaged spiritual and religious themes, further putting any hope of a resolution through verifiable facts out of reach. The descent into investigative rabbit holes required the scientific medical doctor FBI agent Dana Scully to abandon her skepticism and to rely on paranormal and spiritual phenomena. Emphasizing her Catholic faith, the series suggests that truth and meaning are located in spirituality and religion. In the series, which asserts that everything is up for questioning instead of encouraging critical thinking, the truth, paradoxically, can only be found through absolute faith.

With the series based on the premise that a government-alien conspiracy is carrying out abductions, and Mulder personally driven by the quest to find his abducted sister, *The X-Files* pits a lying government against the sovereignty of the American family. Further sustained by romantic and sexual tension between temperamental opposites Scully and Mulder, *The X-Files* is also a story of repeatedly frustrated heteronormative desire, a narrative with an uncanny resemblance to American fringe and increasingly mainstream politics.

The X-Files premiere in September 1993 came in the wake of a fifty-one-day standoff between the FBI and a polygamous Christian cult, the Branch Davidians, and its leader, David Koresh, in Waco, Texas. The series and the standoff not only constituted the most popular conspiracy narratives of the 1990s; they also shared narratives of patriarchal families under siege, with modes of religious and spiritual belief posited as the only solution to the crisis of the family.

Beginning with an attempted FBI raid to recover illegal firearms, the Waco standoff ended when a botched police action prompted an apparent mass suicide, leaving seventy-six dead when the cult's compound burned to the ground.[82] Events at Waco spawned hundreds of conspiracy theories with a common theme, as described by journalist Jonathan Tilove: that an out-of-control government agency had decided to put on a big military-style show targeting innocent people to serve its sinister ambition.[83] Some viewed Koresh and the Davidians as martyrs, an innocent "community of God-fearing if unconventional Christians whose freedoms should have been guaranteed by the US Constitution, but who were instead killed by an ever more controlling government."[84] Waco galvanized the right-wing militia movement and became a rallying cry that helped Republicans gain control of Congress in 1994.

Koresh and the Davidians were odd heroes for Americans. Those who championed Koresh extolled a leader who had children with women as young as twelve and had fathered at least fifteen of the children in the compound. Waco nevertheless became a focal point for gun rights activists, many of whom maintained that the federal government was bent on confiscating firearms. The defense of the authoritarian Koresh as a worthy Christian prefigured the marriage of gun rights and patriarchal religion that marked the 1994 Republican congressional campaign and its central policies in the years to come.

Two years to the day after the Waco tragedy, on April 19, 1995, domestic terrorist Timothy McVeigh claimed to avenge the Davidians when he killed 168 people in his attack on the Alfred P. Murrah Federal Building in Oklahoma City.[85] In the tightly intertextual and paranoid 1990s, some critics accused Chris Carter, the *X-Files* creator, of promoting antigovernment sentiment, compounded by the series' direct references to McVeigh's act of terrorism.[86]

From *The X-Files* to Congress

With the 1994 Republican takeover of Congress, *The X-Files*' dramatization of sinister government threats was mimicked in the form of congressional antigovernment hostility. In a departure from norms of compromise, Republican House Speaker Newt Gingrich shut down the government in 1995 and 1996 because President Clinton refused to yield to Republican demands to privatize Medicare.[87] Such battles left Clinton vulnerable, setting the tone for his compromises with far right ideologues in his welfare reform legislation.

In his 1992 campaign, Clinton had promised anticrime policies and "an end to welfare as we know it." Despite his antiwelfare campaign rhetoric, as president he proposed legislation that expanded social services in health care, childcare, and jobs. His proposals were doomed when the Republicans took control of Congress. Clinton vetoed the first two of three bills seeking to end the welfare system established during the New Deal, which would have abolished Aid to Families with Dependent Children, food stamps, and Medicaid. But on the eve of his reelection, though acknowledging that it was "bad legislation," he nevertheless signed the third. Although it restored Medicaid and food stamps, the abolition of federal aid to families with dependent children shifted responsibility to the states and put a five-year limit on cash assistance.

Despite Clinton's reluctance, as the sociologist Melinda Cooper has argued, the bill constituted the "most comprehensive attempt to substitute the private responsibility of the family for the public responsibility of the state," further removing barriers between church and state by placing much of what remained in government services in the faith-based "Charitable-Choice organizations" that were later greatly expanded in the George W. Bush administration.[88]

In the United States, the shifting of responsibility for the health, education, and well-being of citizens from the state to the family may not have appeared as abrupt as the collapse of the Soviet Union. But for those who found themselves in need, it could be shockingly unsettling. Clinton's welfare program, Cooper argues, "radically overhauled the existing child support system, transforming it into the comprehensive federal enforcement regime that Reagan had dreamt of."[89] The legislation that replaced Aid to Families with Dependent Children, Temporary Assistance for Needy Families (TANF), was dubbed by some applicants as "Torture and Abuse of Needy Families." The TANF requirements stipulated a forty-hour-per-week job search for those with no car or gas money and no resources to care for their children in their absence.[90] In what became known in the media as the deadbeat dad law, rather than aiding women directly, TANF stipulated that funds for aid would be collected from men delinquent on child support. Under TANF, Cooper explains, "the administrative costs dedicated to the identification of father and collection of child support are enormous.... The average amounts collected on behalf of each applicant are minimal—not surprisingly given that 'absent' fathers are often poor or unemployed themselves."[91]

In refusing to disburse welfare funds directly to impoverished women, the new laws "appear to be motivated as much by a will to punish and deter as any concern with fiscal burdens; by detouring the payment of welfare benefits via legally designated fathers, the state reminds women that they cannot hope to find economic security without entering a relationship of personal dependence on a man."[92]

Dependence on patriarchy and conservative institutions was exacerbated by the state-sanctioned rise of faith-based welfare. Section 104 of the Clinton 1996 welfare reform act, explains Cooper, "exhort[ed] federal and state government to contract with religious nonprofits—without infringing on their rights to religious expression."[93] The faith-based initiatives of the George W. Bush administration further consolidated an elaborate infrastructure that entrenched faith-based options in all social services.[94] With Bush's faith-based initiative, Copper asserts, "the moral and economic obligations of work and family have been refashioned in the religious idiom of faith, conversion, and redemption."[95]

Ironically, these avowed antigovernment ideologues harnessed the levers of state power, using institutions for their own purposes while eviscerating the social contract. And as Clinton's anticrime legislation in effect targeted Black and brown Americans, who were disproportionately imprisoned, the racialized carceral and coercive state grew apace with the reduction in spending on education, welfare, and environmental protections.[96]

With race, faith, and family structurally woven into meager residues of a US social safety net, the post-Soviet world's sudden loss of jobs, housing, and health care also transformed the family into a locus of crisis and dependence. With the parallel loss of social safety nets and new dependencies on patriarchal family structures, the stage was set for the US far right to build ties to its Russian counterparts, over time developing robust ostensibly pro-family, antigay, pro-gun, white nationalist alliances.[97] Conditions allowing the flourishing of far right politics in both countries developed in tandem with close US observation of, and sometimes hands-on involvement in, post-Soviet society.

Recasting Russia: Shock Therapy and New US Views of Russia

Gorbachev's perestroika reforms sought to streamline centralized planning by introducing market competition while preserving social programs that protected basic human needs such as health care, housing, and education. Proponents of shock therapy rejected the very notion that reform of state-planned economies, transitioning to mixed-market economies, was possible. Reform, in their view, could only be achieved by the sudden ending of price controls and government subsidies and by the privatization of public-owned enterprises. Shock therapy also demanded tighter fiscal policies, including higher tax rates and decreased government spending, with the goal of reducing inflation and budget deficits.[98]

In the waning days of the Soviet Union, neither Gorbachev nor Bush was in control of events. Gorbachev was squeezed by both an international finance community impatient for rapid market reforms and, from the left, by Soviet communist hardliners. When hardline communists mounted a coup against Gorbachev in August 1991, his opponent, Boris Yeltsin, had intervened to prevent Gorbachev's ouster. Yeltsin had been elected president of the Russian Soviet Federative Socialist Republic on June 12, 1991, after he led a Russian nationalist breakaway from the USSR. Welcomed by the radical proponents of shock therapy, Yeltsin lacked Gorbachev's commitment to perestroika's mixed-market reforms and yielded to Western implementation of shock therapy policies.

The USSR formally dissolved on December 26, 1991, the day after Gorbachev resigned as president, turning over his office and functions to Yeltsin.

Although Bush, mindful of the destabilizing potential of post-Soviet nationalisms, did not appear to relish the collapse of the Soviet Union, he welcomed Yeltsin's embrace of radical market reforms. Yeltsin was lionized by neoliberal triumphalists, who gleefully anticipated the dismantling of the Soviet state. He embarked on shock therapy upon assuming office. As a rising elite of organized crime bosses and oligarchs capitalized on the unregulated chaos of early shock therapy, the West refused any aid that would have preserved social safety protections. By 1994, even Yeltsin described the country as "the biggest mafia state in the world" and the "superpower of crime," where corruption had "penetrated the political, economic, judicial, and social systems so thoroughly" that it "ceased to be a deviation from the norm and became the norm itself."[99]

Harvard economist Jeffrey Sachs, the chief architect of shock therapy, advised the governments of both Gorbachev and Yeltsin in their transition from centrally planned economies to market economies. As Francis Fukuyama has done, Sachs has since vigorously repudiated neoliberalism. Sachs's 2012 recollection provides a chilling account of what went wrong. He distinguished between his shock therapy recommendations and what he termed the "extremely different" neoliberal version, which he rejects. According to Sachs, the shock therapy policies that he advocated in Bolivia, Poland, and Russia "[refer] to the rapid end of price controls in order to re-establish supply-demand equilibrium in a context of pervasive rationing and blocked trade." The neoliberal version, rejected by Sachs, "refers to the dismantling of all government interventions in the economy in order to establish a 'free-market' economy." In 2012, Sachs maintained, "I have never been an advocate of shock therapy in its second, neo-liberal context. I regard a pure 'free-market' economy as a textbook fiction, not a practical or desirable reality." Defending himself against critics who blamed him for Russia's corrupt privatization, Sachs blamed the disastrous US and International Monetary Fund (IMF) refusal to provide sustained and timely foreign assistance to Russia in 1991, as had happened in Poland. Instead, the G-7 insisted "that the Soviet Union should continue to service its external debts at any cost." The only source of funds for debt servicing was through reduced state capacity. For Sachs, successful economic reform depended on aid from the West to ensure a "a strong social safety net.... This was not accomplished. The health care system for example, fell into shocking collapse." Emphasizing that the IMF spurned his advice, Sachs added that Russians "ignored his directives for a strong monetary and fiscal policy to fight against hyperinflation" (as Sachs's policies had done in Bolivia).[100]

Sachs insisted—both in the 1990s and in retrospect—that a social safety net was vital to successful reform, and he despaired when aid for Russia's health care system was not forthcoming. But like the IMF, Sachs never supported the gradual economic reforms of perestroika. For him, revolution was the preferred mode of economic change. "If you look at how reform occurs," he said in 1993, "it has been through the rapid adaptation of foreign models, not a slow evolution of modern institutions." And if he later decried the lack of transparency and corruption that had accompanied privatization and had bred the rise of Russian oligarchs, he had been far more sanguine during the Yeltsin reforms. Featured in a 1993 *New York Times* account of Moscow, Sachs was confident that controlling inflation and jump-starting an economy through radical reductions in government spending could benefit economies "with no collective memory of free markets or history of even handed rules of contract law and property rights."[101]

Shock therapy was not without critics, as World Bank and IMF policies wreaked havoc on fledgling Eastern bloc economic reforms. Warning that classic market economics had no more to offer than orthodox Marxism, British economist Will Hutton described the market onslaught faced by the Eastern bloc. Hutton asserted, "It is the citizens of Eastern Europe and the Soviet Union that have first claim on our sympathies. Into their capitals have flooded a bunch of intellectual carpet-baggers, free-market advisers, and officials from the World Bank and IMF, who have set about imposing a series of crash economic reforms, careless of society, the existing stock of capital and trade relations, or even what a nodding acquaintance of economic history and theory might suggest could be successful." As price deregulation and trade liberalization went to new extremes in draconian adjustments to living standards and working practices demanded by the reforms, Hutton reported that "anyone preaching caution or gradualism—like Czechoslovakia's Václav Havel, has been scorned for lack of daring."[102]

Reading the Crisis

Hutton's critique of the imposition of reforms "careless of society" exhibited a sensitivity rare in the Western press. At its best, Western reporting on the collapsing Eastern bloc contributed to a broader ethnography of deregulation and privatization. The *Washington Post*'s Margaret Shapiro, writing from Zagoriye, Russia, in July 1992, documented tenuous support for Yeltsin as he plunged ahead with shock therapy. Interviewing Ludmila Ulyanova, thirty-six, an engineer at a state-run electronics plant, Shapiro described a shifting and unpredictable environment: "The hours she spent last fall and winter waiting in sullen lines for a piece of fatty ham or a loaf of bread are a distant nightmare ... but in many other ways, she says, life has gotten much worse."[103]

Ulyanova had been "dazed and disoriented by changes she and her family have had to cope with since the Soviet Union shuddered to a collapse last December. She is dismayed at the wars that threaten relatives on the edges of the Soviet orbit [and] skeptical of every politician." Shapiro noted Ulyanova's ambivalence, her sense of loss. "Despite a relatively liberal temperament," she felt "nostalgic" for the security, predictability and what she remembers as the relative prosperity of her youth under Soviet socialism. "I can hardly believe in anything any longer," Ulyanova told Shapiro. "We are just dragging on." Anxious as another harsh winter approached, her family purchased rabbits and pigs to provision themselves. Echoing a widespread dismay that suddenly everything was about money, Ulyanova explained, "This is how we live now. We think every day of how to sell ourselves and our labor at the best price."[104]

In the popular, mass-mediated Western imagination, the end of the cold war was about walls coming down and borders opening. But for those who were suddenly "no longer a citizen of the mighty Soviet Union," it was also about painful new borders and boundaries. Those like Ulyanova were left by the overnight transition "with a loss of identity and documents issued by a country that no longer exists."[105] Ulyanova could no longer travel to her family's vacation spot in Crimea, where she had gone on holiday throughout her life. Such ruptures met with disbelief. "It's just impossible to declare that this or that is a foreign land in one day," she commented. "It simply cannot be like that."[106] The anthropologist Serguei A. Oushakine has recounted the story of a mother from Altai village in Siberia whose son had been drafted into the Soviet army in July 1991. From boot camp in the Urals, he was sent to Germany and, in August 1992, to Estonia. On July 16, 1993, she received notice that her son had been killed, but with communication between Russia and Estonia cut off, she went through months of bureaucratic dead ends as she sought to recover his remains, receiving no information about his death. For such people, says Oushakine, "the dramatic confrontation with the internal vacuity of Soviet ideology could hardly justify their personal ordeals associated with releasing a son's body from a country that had just become independent.... The institutional collapse of the country, in other words, was also experienced as a fundamental rupture in people's *daily* lives."[107]

In the early 1990s, triumphalism drowned out dissenting voices and genuine debate about the wisdom of capitalist shock therapy. For the most part, the stories of Ulyanova and others like her went largely unremarked in the West. And despite growing attention by scholars and journalists to the working poor in the United States as safety nets crumbled, the ways in which Ulyanova's story mirrored those of people around the globe experiencing, however differently, the impact of capitalism run amok went unexplored.[108]

Western journalists tracked the collapse of Eastern bloc states with nervous fascination, a touch of schadenfreude, and contempt for expressions of loss and nostalgia. Despite celebrating the supposed triumph of free markets, a profound anxiety about the viability of markets emerged, mixed at times with a voyeuristic fascination with black markets and organized crime. With capital increasingly unmoored from the nation-state, in a world of speculative bubbles and untranslatable derivatives, the chaos of the former Eastern bloc functioned as a doppelganger to the West, *not* as a mirror image, as in one prevalent contemporary usage, but in the sense of a ghostly counterpart of a living person, a disavowed self that one is afraid to confront, that one fears being consumed by.

The End of History or a Return to History?

The so-called end of history touted in the US media did not simply hail the supposed end of ideological conflict; it discredited the very notion that people in the former Soviet sphere had existed as historical subjects. After four years as Moscow correspondent for the *Christian Science Monitor*, Daniel Sneider declared that "decades of communism, of forging a 'Soviet' identity, had produced nothing fundamentally different than centuries of czarism."[109]

The idea that the Soviet Union was an unnatural form of society had existed from the time of the 1917 revolution, elaborated in the 1947 Truman Doctrine and the 1950s depictions of the USSR as a "slave society." Reagan resurrected the idea of the Soviets as fundamentally aberrant, declaring in 1981 that "the West won't contain communism ... it will dismiss it as some bizarre chapter in human history whose last pages are even now being written."[110] In this view, true history was manifested in the development of capitalist, liberal institutions; interrupted by the Bolshevik revolution, history resumed only after the collapse of the Soviet Union.

The historian and anthropologist Kate Brown has argued that emphasis on the differences between capitalism and communism has ignored parallels produced by the industrial-capital expansion of the twentieth century.[111] Asking, "can the West afford to clean up the mess left by Mr. Marx?" a Toronto *Globe and Mail* reporter, Peter Cook, documented environmental devastation across the crumbling Eastern bloc. Citing the destruction of trees in East Germany and in the Ore Mountains on the Czechoslovakian–East German border by acid rain, this account described chemical plants in Leipzig that "darken the sky during the day and cause visitors to wake up vomiting after an overnight stay in the city."[112]

Ignoring the environmental emphasis of Gorbachev's reforms as well as a growing consciousness of environmental damage in the West, Cook pitted an undeserving East that had brought destruction on itself against a West meriting praise for placing environmental pollution "on capitalism's agenda." According to him, Marxist theory was responsible for Eastern bloc degradation because it held that "environmental problems cannot occur in socialist countries because man and nature work in harmony." Declaring "aid to countries in such a desperate condition" a task "beyond the capacity of the West to finance," Cook argued that capitalism did not produce environment problems but was inherently problem solving.[113]

Cook's punitive triumphalism, along with his assumption that capitalism was self-regulating, echoed throughout the Western press during the last year of the Soviet Union under such headlines as "Soviets Learn the Hard Lesson of 'Self-Deceit'" and "Communism, Exposed."[114] After communist hard-liners' failed attempt to overthrow Gorbachev in August 1991, ordinary Americans voiced panic about the return of communism. *USA Today* reported that "stunned Americans shivered with a collective chill for the 'New World Order' and the man they fondly nicknamed 'Gorby.'" Others worried about the return of the cold war. Mike Ward, the manager of a suburban St. Louis pub, told *USA Today* that people are "wondering how this is going to affect our lives here." Philadelphia waiter Brendan O'Hara worried that the coup "brings back the possibility of war" if the Soviets do not "stick to recent arms treaties."[115]

Expressions of concern for Gorbachev quickly gave way to dismissals of any vestiges of nostalgia for the old regime. While more sympathetic observers acknowledged the deprivation of Eastern Europeans as long as they blamed communism for their plight, for many Western commentators, any protest against shock therapy was dangerous.[116] The *Boston Globe* reported in 1992 that "20,000 nationalists and pro-Communist demonstrators vented their anger over the disintegration of the Soviet Union and the collapse of their own living standard." Protesters carried "pictures of Lenin and Stalin," along with "religious icons or flags emblazoned with the hammer and sickle," while marching "through the center of Moscow to the accompaniment of a scratchy recording of the heroic Soviet marching songs of their youth." Acknowledging an "unlikely coalition" of communists and "extreme nationalists, many of whom are as anti-communist as they are anti-Semitic," the correspondent conflated economic grievance and racist nationalism, concluding that opponents of Yeltsin suffered from "ideological confusion."[117]

Dismissing the validity of economic grievances, in this account, those protesting shock capitalism were by definition "extremists"; their "drawing power" could only be explained by "racism." Demonstrations, the report concluded, simply allowed "people the chance to display their pro-Russian, anti-Semitic views and meet sympathetic, like-minded people."[118]

Viewing economic cooperation across the post-Soviet world as threatening, *Washington Post* foreign correspondent Jim Hoagland worried in March 1992 that Paris and Bonn "continue to be knee-deep in nostalgia for Mikhail Gorbachev." Declaring the post-Soviet Commonwealth of Independent States a mere "fig-leaf" for continued bureaucratic collectivism, he hoped for its rapid demise, ridiculing the "faint hearts and Cold War nostalgia buffs" who "will again bemoan this fragmentation of state authority."[119]

Even critiques of Bush-style triumphalism frowned on expressions of disorientation and nostalgia. Paul Goble, a former State Department analyst, found the Bush administration's "triumphalism, the notion that we were somehow responsible for what has occurred," unattractive and disingenuous.[120] Yet Goble worried "that two-thirds of all Muscovites now suffer from 'nostalgia' for the USSR." In a lesson that George W. Bush would take to heart in his 1999–2000 presidential campaign, Goble recommended getting tough with Russia, declaring that the West needs to make clear that we would oppose any effort to re-establish the empire.[121]

With some observers positing that an aberrant Soviet regime had overridden supposedly natural and transhistorical Russian national identities, many Western observers celebrated the restoration of czarist and Russian Orthodox symbols. But as Leningrad reassumed its original name, St. Petersburg, in 1991, the acknowledgment that Russia had been a vast empire before the Bolshevik revolution proved vexing. For those who imagined multiple sovereign nations following a US-led, free market global order, a resurgent Russian empire was intolerable. Sneider asked in the *Christian*

Science Monitor whether Russia could define itself "distinct from empire." Warning that "imperialism and authoritarianism are the Siamese twins of Russian history, appearing and expanding always in tandem," for Sneider, it was imperative that Russian expansion be prevented: "If the door is not barred to Russian expansion, can the West really help establish democracy in Russia?"[122]

Triumphalism, bordering on contempt for those who still felt a stake in the former Soviet order, became the common sense of the West in the 1990s. But most people in the Soviet Union and Eastern bloc states were neither evil communists nor dissidents biding their time to defect to the West. American commentators are often adept at grasping contradictions within US society, understanding, for example, how a citizen may be critical of certain features of US society (racism, gun violence, lack of health care) and still avow patriotism and what they understand to be the core values of American democracy. US observers rarely granted the possibility of such complex outlooks to inhabitants of Eastern bloc countries.

Scholarship by historians and anthropologists working on the former Soviet bloc has highlighted the socialist idealism shared by many citizens of the Soviet Union and Eastern bloc countries. Glasnost and perestroika—openness and restructuring—like the 1989 Eastern European revolutions, took hold as movements to reform socialism, to recast "socialism with a human face." These movements were decidedly *not* pro-capitalism. As Alexei Yurchak has put it, "An undeniable constitutive part of today's phenomenon of 'post-Soviet nostalgia' . . . is the longing for the very real humane values, ethics, friendships, and creative possibilities that socialism afforded—often in spite of the state's proclaimed goals—and that were as irreducibly part of the everyday life of socialism as were the feelings of dullness and alienation."[123] Yet such complexities in people's relationship to power and political change were often elided in Western accounts of post-socialist transitions.

A Love-Hate Relationship: The United States and Russian Nationalism

With expansion and collectivism seen as clear threats, Russian nationalism presented a conundrum for some US observers. On the one hand, Western observers worried about Russian "ultra-nationalist" challenges to Yeltsin's pro-Western policies, most clearly manifest in the right-wing populist Vladimir Zhirinovsky's "ill-named" Liberal Democratic Party.[124] Discussing 1994 plans to rebuild the Cathedral of Christ the Savior in Moscow,

London's *Observer* reported that "nostalgia for a past that might have been, had there never been a Soviet Union, is widespread in Russia. It is a longing that has been hijacked by the extreme right—the Black Hundreds, monarchists, anti-Semites, fascists, and free-lance mercenaries fighting with the Bosnian Serbs—who voted for . . . Zhirinovsky in the last election, winning him 24 percent of the vote."[125] Indeed, the Russian ultranationalist soon emerged as a stock villain in American culture even less trustworthy than the former Soviet Union and an alarming harbinger of global insecurity.[126]

Despite worries about right-wing nationalism, just as US policy tacitly supported and sometimes goaded on Serbian, Slovenian, and Croatian nationalism in Yugoslavia, US public opinion tended to support post-Soviet nationalism—Russian, Ukrainian, and so on—over any mode of political and economic coordination within the former Soviet bloc that might challenge the American position as the sole hegemon in a unipolar world. The roots of a later convergence between the US alt-right and Russian conservatives can be seen, in part, in early sympathy with Russian nationalism as a default mode of opposition to any vestiges of Soviet internationalism. Even before the collapse of the Soviet Union, right-wing Americans and right-wing Russians collaborated by 1990 to form new institutions such as the American University in Moscow, the innocuously named Center for Democracy, and the Krieble Institute. These organizations ran initiatives to spread rightist propaganda; they also abandoned alliances with Gorbachev to support Yeltsin.[127]

Grim Choices

Deep dissatisfaction with Yeltsin's austerity programs brought tens of thousands into the streets in Moscow in the fall of 1993 in support of Parliament's attempt to impeach Yeltsin. Russian voters had voiced their objection to shock therapy in a referendum earlier that year when 44 percent of voters rejected Yeltsin's economic program. The conflict came to a head in Parliament when it refused to confirm Yegor Gaidar, the unpopular Russian architect of shock therapy, as prime minister in September 1993. In response, Yeltsin disbanded the Parliament—the Supreme Soviet—and called for new elections, leading to his impeachment. As his opponents locked themselves in Moscow House, Yeltsin declared a state of emergency and ordered a military assault on the Supreme Soviet.[128] With the country on the brink of civil war and hundreds of protesters killed, Gaidar, now a vice minister, posed the question of support of Yeltsin as a choice between democracy and returning to concentration camps. Critics of shock therapy, in the eyes of US policy makers, were "hard-liners."[129]

In December 1993, Yeltsin eked out a victory in a referendum on his draft constitution. Zhirinovsky's right-wing nationalist Liberal Democratic Party shocked observers by winning sixty-four seats, enough to keep pro-government parties or Yeltsin from setting the agenda in the Duma. Jonathan Steele argued in the *Guardian* that the surge of support for the right wing indicated anger at Yeltsin's austerity plan as well as resentment over the loss of the "inner empire" in the last three years of Gorbachev's reform.[130]

"A huge mountain of bitterness," Steele reported, has built up over "the loss of Russia's status as a superpower." While withdrawal from Eastern Europe contributed to the "feeling of a world turned upside down," the "collapse of the Soviet Union and the loss of the Baltics, the Transcaucasus, and Central Asia was a shock." Not only did Russians who "used to have their holidays in the Baltics dare not go there," but the many Russians who had lived there are now "treated as second class citizens." In Central Asia, the "situation is even worse. Hundreds of thousands of Russians have been driven out or are hastily emigrating. They have become refugees in their own countries."[131]

Like Steele, some Western observers acknowledged the trauma caused by the imposition of national boundaries and ethnic identities for people who had previously lived in multiethnic and multilinguistic communities. But on the whole, US politicians and pundits regarded nationalism as the only legitimate mode of political belonging. And over time, US policy makers' disregard for Russia's centuries-old ties with Crimea and Ukraine—which had been absorbed into the Russian empire *before* the 1804 Louisiana Purchase in the United States—animated the view that the United States had a more legitimate right to engage in commerce and extraction in the former Soviet sphere than did Russia.

NATO and Foreign Policy Fissures

As the United States defended Yeltsin's deeply unpopular economic policies, policy makers further undermined his political standing by exposing weakness in Russian foreign policy. James Goldgeier has suggested that Russian confusion over US policies on NATO expansion in particular stemmed from indecision among top American officials about which path to pursue.[132] Goldgeier identified internal dissension within the Clinton administration between such figures as US secretary of state Warren Christopher, wary of

3.2 NATO surrounding Russian bear. *Newsweek*, November 1, 1993. Museum of Political History, St. Petersburg, 2017

antagonizing Yeltsin's Russia, and National Security Advisor Anthony Lake, who pushed for NATO expansion. In November 1993, with Yeltsin clinging to power after his impeachment, Clinton and Christopher assured him that their priority was partnership, not NATO expansion. The international, English-language edition of *Newsweek*, launched earlier that year, detected the pulse of the expansionist hawks with a cover feature: "The New NATO: Should East Europe Be Let In?" As the cover feature of the US edition explored the secret life of dogs, the international edition cover graphic displayed a tiny Russian bear with a hammer-and-sickle hat, encircled by guns, missiles, and bombs pointing at it from all directions.

As the US media promoted advocacy for NATO enlargement, and with Yeltsin fending off opposition from the right as well as the left in Russia, Clinton promised Yeltsin that NATO would pursue the Partnership for Peace for all, rather than expand through a membership track for some. Affirmed at a January 1994 NATO summit, the Partnership for Peace began to unravel when Lake and others pursued expanded membership. Lake urged the president to tell Central Europeans in Prague that "the question is no longer whether NATO will take on new members but when and how." In September 1994, not even a year after Yeltsin had been promised "partnership for all, not NATO for some," Clinton informed Yeltsin of NATO's expansion.[133]

By this time, Republicans had elevated NATO's expansion to a key issue in the 1994 midterm elections, central to the Republican Party's Contract with America. When the Republicans swept both houses of Congress, it sealed the deal for a more aggressive expansion.

Expressing his "displeasure" at the December 1994 meeting of the Organization on Security and Cooperation in Europe, which took place in Budapest, Yeltsin shocked his American and European colleagues. Europe, he charged, "is risking encumbering itself with a cold peace" without managing "to shrug off the legacy of the Cold War." Charging NATO with creating new divisions and undermining European unity, Yeltsin asked, "Why sow the seeds of distrust? After all, we are no longer adversaries, we are partners."[134]

The confrontation coincided with the first Russian-Chechen war, beginning with Russian aerial bombardments and ground attacks on Grozny in December 1994. Yeltsin continued to voice his grave concern, telling Clinton in a May 1995 meeting at the Kremlin, "I see nothing but humiliation for Russia if you proceed" with NATO expansion. "How," he asked, "do you think it looks to us if one bloc continues to exist while the Warsaw Pact has been abolished? It's a new form of encirclement."[135]

Over the next decade, American oil interests, their sights set on Caspian oil reserves, embraced NATO expansion, as well as the corollary that US corporations had a legitimate claim to extraction in the former Soviet sphere. At the same time, other US politicians and businesspeople were reaping the benefits of wild capitalism, Russian-style.[136] And throughout the 1990s, as many Republicans insisted that only government regulation blocked market equilibrium, actual markets, including criminal black markets, defied utopian forecasts rooted in free market fundamentalism. As the Clinton administration backed the radical privatization of Yeltsin's Russia, it also confronted a brave new world where untrammeled markets intersected with shifting political borders, recasting threats and upsetting the containers of the most familiar commodities in a post–cold war nuclear landscape. It is to this world in motion, and how it allowed the production of robust and politically focused nostalgias by decade's end, that I now turn.

4

"God I Miss the Cold War"

BUSTED CONTAINERS AND POPULAR NOSTALGIA, 1993–1999

Many things that were anchored to the balance of power and the balance of terror seem to be undone, unstuck. Things have no limits now. Money has no limits. I don't understand money anymore. Money is undone. Violence is undone, violence is easier now, it's uprooted, out of control, it has no measure anymore, it has no level of values.

—Klara in Don DeLillo's *Underworld*, 1997

Oil is unique in that it is so strategic in nature. We are not talking about soapflakes or leisurewear here.

—Dick Cheney, speech for the Institute for Petroleum, 1999

In the 1997 film *The Peacemaker*, Colonel Thomas Devoe (George Clooney) and US nuclear specialist Dr. Julia Kelly (Nicole Kidman) join forces to prevent the detonation of a nuclear bomb at the United Nations building in New York City. Opening with an unexplained assassination in a church in Sarajevo, the film cuts to a nuclear explosion in Russia, a distraction, it turns out, from the theft of a nuclear bomb from the southern Urals, the weapons-producing region of the former Soviet Union. As Devoe begins his investigation, the US national security adviser declares Russia a "fucking mess," adding, "God, I miss the cold war." Hinging its suspense on the idea of the former Soviet Union's nuclear stockpiles left unguarded, the film contrasted that threat with an era portrayed as one of relative stability when both antagonists had a stake in order, and one knew who and where one's enemies were. The London *Daily Mirror*'s critic declared the plot "firmly grounded in reality. With many Russian soldiers and nuclear scientists living in abject poverty, the likelihood of nuclear weapons being sold to the highest bidder grows each day."[1]

The previous year, the PBS documentary series *Frontline* warned viewers that endemic corruption and chaos in Russia had put "tons of nuclear material at risk." Precisely who was smuggling uranium and plutonium into Germany and Czechoslovakia was murky, but investigative journalist Sherrie Jones believed that Russian scientists and officials were involved.[2] Jones featured a Russian scientist who compared uranium with spaghetti: "You may just put it in your pocket. I don't know anyone who carries spaghetti in a pocket, but one smuggler reportedly put a batch of uranium in his underwear on a train trip from Moscow to Minsk to Warsaw and finally to Prague, where he was caught."[3] Paradoxically, uranium, this dangerous, sequestered commodity, has become horrifyingly mundane and mobile, transformed as a new source of terror. As many heralded the triumph of the market where buyers and sellers met in perfect equilibrium, trafficking in nuclear material had become a chillingly opaque operation.

The Peacemakers was one of several 1990s films that imagined the smuggling of nuclear weapons, complicating rosy market scenarios of the unfettered movement of people and goods on a global scale. It portrayed a world with nuclear arsenals no longer controlled by powerful nation-states but subject to the covert will of the highest bidder. In the film, the stolen bomb is smuggled across the Russian border in an ordinary backpack. *The Peacemaker* dramatizes the chaos of a borderless black market in post-Soviet security. I will return to a discussion of "loose nukes" and such films later in this chapter, and their portrayal of regional crises such as the Bosnian war and the conflict between Russia and Chechnyan nationalists. For now, I note the film's Western nostalgia, expressed by staging the circulation of weapons through new and shadowy markets. How was security understood and maintained in a world of changing, permeable borders? How does one measure value in undercover, shape-shifting markets with hidden commodities and transactions? With planned economies replaced by new speculation and organized crime, where costs might triple or quadruple overnight, how was one to know what anything was worth? Transformed boundaries and borders necessitated new containers for the quintessential cold war commodities—uranium and oil. With vast oil reserves yet unexploited in the former Soviet region of the Caspian, oil, too, had escaped its cold war containers, and the scramble was on to capture it in new geopolitical ampoules.

The collapse of the Eastern bloc coincided with the dawn of the internet. With the World Wide Web's creation in 1989 and people's surging use of it in their daily lives from 1993 onward, the allure of the internet, along with the disruptions of online existence, signaled a loss of control. Shopping, friendships, bill-paying, work, intimacy, sex, community—the most familiar routines of life—were escaping their lived spaces and boundaries and happening somewhere else. Nothing seemed to be where it used to be.

Don DeLillo's sprawling 1997 novel, *Underworld*, brilliantly captures the chaotic lived experience of an unhinged market. The book meditates on a loss of the certainties of political order and moral and material worth. Klara Sax, an artist who creates assemblages from discarded military hardware, feels unmoored by a world no longer tied to the rules and regulations of the cold war geopolitical economy. "Many things that were anchored to the balance of power and the balance of terror seem to be undone, unstuck," she says. "Things have no limits now. Money has no limits. I don't understand money anymore. Money is undone. Violence is undone, violence is easier now, it's uprooted, out of control, it has no measure anymore, it has no level of values."[4]

Jumping into this transformed, unsettled, unsettling world, this chapter moves from political and media framings of new threats—loose nukes, terrorism, and "rogue states"—returning to cultural representations of a robust popular nostalgia evident in the United States as well as the Soviet Union by the mid-1990s. As in US interventions in Iraq and Somalia, definitions of new enemies in the scramble for the postwar containment of nuclear weapons and oil depended on stark distortions of US cold war–era relations and of past interventions in multiple regions. Policy responses to such problems as terrorism and loose nukes were handled—and hampered—through a framework of rogue states, a framework promoted and reinforced in the media and popular culture. The assumption that the United States contended with outlaw states beyond the pale of the international order fine-tuned the notion of the clash of civilizations, justifying policy prescriptions for targeting states construed as recalcitrant actors.

With the 1993 terrorist bombing of the World Trade Center, militant Islamic fundamentalism rose to the forefront as a threat, eventually exposing the cold war–era US backing of fundamentalist and anti-American forms of Islam in the 1970s and 1980s. As the Republican Contract with America's push for the expansion of NATO heightened tensions with Russia, aggressive moves by US government and corporate interests to wrest control of Caspian oil from Russia were highly consequential in the long run for US alliances and enemies in the Middle East. The quest for control over Russian oil led the United States to forge corporate and government alliances with the Taliban in Pakistan and Afghanistan.

As the United States and former Soviet sphere contended with new threats to global security during the late 1990s, each produced robust if divergent forms of nostalgia. Western filmmakers expressed lament via nightmare scenarios of mass destruction against the backdrop of a supposedly more stable cold war era. This was worlds away from the quotidian lament of many in the former Eastern bloc for the loss of human security and a material standard of living central to a bygone egalitarian era in which it seemed that not everything was about money. Longing in the Russian and Eastern bloc contexts shifted from initial expressions of trauma to poignant elaborations of loss. Such feelings of loss reflected on changes in sexuality and intimate life, influencing not only politics but a range of cultural productions and a new political economy of desire.

Mass-mediated Hollywood potboiler narratives of cold war nostalgia could not have been further from the palpable feelings of loss attested by members of the former Soviet-Eastern bloc. Nevertheless, by the end of the 1990s, there was a convergence between US and post-Soviet societies. Both sides evolved a shared, conservative sense of popular nostalgia. Building on grievances based on perceptions of the West's humiliation of Russia, Vladimir Putin cultivated a conservative Russian nostalgia largely based on the traditional values of the Russian Orthodox Church. Soviet global ambitions coalesced around his 1999 appointment as acting president and his subsequent election in 2000. In the United States, a conservative version of nostalgia congealed in the 1999–2000 George W. Bush campaign. Both elections were preoccupied with the nationalist enterprise of identifying new enemies and internal and external threats. Neither the United States nor Russia entered the new century with a reaffirmation of the social good that had shaped cold war competition and that might have checked the disruptive privatization that upended so many lives in the 1990s. That would have required implementing post–cold war visions akin to those of Mikhail Gorbachev, Nelson Mandela, and Václav Havel. Instead, electoral coalitions in the United States and Russia asserted nostalgia for the might of empire and the supposed stability of traditional morality. The US expansion of NATO crystallized Russian resentments, putting the two on a collision course.

Loose Nukes

After a truck bomb detonated below the North Tower of New York City's World Trade Center on February 26, 1993, the what-if character of films imagining nuclear terrorism echoed press accounts of loose nukes. As A. M. Rosenthal put it in the *New York Times* the following month, "Suppose Mideast terrorists make the U.S. a constant target. Suppose the U.S. knows they are sponsored by a state with access to *portable* [my emphasis] nuclear weapons."[5] A 1995 *Christian Science Monitor* editorial warned that "the superpower discipline of the cold war has been replaced by shadowy new types of proliferation possibilities—from smuggling fissile materials to nuclear terrorism and acquisition of dual-use nuclear technology."[6]

What-if scenarios portrayed in Hollywood films reverberated throughout the press, and for good reason. The theft of nuclear weapons and material due to unguarded arsenals and power plants in the former Soviet Union was at once real and surreal. In "Bottling Up Nukes," the *Christian Science Monitor* pondered the catastrophic result if the terrorists behind the World Trade Center attack had used an atomic weapon. "Just 12 pounds of fissile material could have created an explosion the size of Hiroshima."[7]

Underscoring the chaos of a market untethered to the rules and regulations of the cold war geopolitical economy, the *Moscow Times* reported on the 1994 arrest in St. Petersburg of three people, including a butcher and factory worker, accused of trying to sell $600,000 worth of stolen enriched uranium on the black market. Although nuclear physicists determined that the uranium was reactor fuel and could not be repurposed for nuclear weapons, Western governments feared that in post-Soviet Russia, criminals might obtain nuclear technology.[8] According to the Federal Counterintelligence Service, the men took no safety precautions, storing the uranium in glass jars in the refrigerator.[9] The FBI set up a Moscow office, reported the London *Independent*, "prompted by fears that Russia's criminal gangs may be able to steal nuclear weapons which could be sold to terrorists for use against the US and other countries." Director Louis Freeh told the Senate Government Operations Committee, "We have all been lucky that there have apparently been no nuclear [weapon] thefts so far. But any nation on earth could be in jeopardy."[10] Later that year, German police intercepted small amounts of nuclear material on Europe's black market. In February 1995, after Prague police seized highly enriched uranium stolen from the Soviet Union, German intelligence services reported "a quantum leap" in smuggling of nuclear materials from the Soviet Union over the previous year.[11]

US and Soviet nuclear production fostered genuine cooperation in the post-Soviet period, as Kate Brown's work has shown.[12] In what the anthropologist Joseph Masco calls the "intimate power" of a perverse international gift economy, weapons scientists at Los Alamos met with their counterparts in the Russian nuclear weapon lab Arzamas-16. As the forty-year struggle "dissolved into a proliferation of concern by Los Alamos weapon scientists for the fate of their Russian counterparts in a rapidly disintegrating political situation," their research collaboration, financial support for Russian scientists, and sharing of technology led Masco to conclude that "American and Russian [weapons designers] were perhaps more closely linked in technoscientific culture and worldview than any two such communities on earth."[13]

Underlining the psychological intimacy of the US-Soviet cold war relations that had coexisted with fear, by 1995 Los Alamos and Arzamas-16 (now Sarov, its pre-Soviet name) had become official sister cities, and the residents of Los Alamos were investing in medicine, clothing, and food drives for its counterpart.[14]

Nuclear Sludge and Garbage Dumps

In the absence of transparency by government and corporate entities, artists and activists also examined cold war environmental destruction and imagined the conditions in which harms could be acknowledged and relationships reassessed. DeLillo's novel *Underworld*, a postmortem on the cold war, makes a bold plunge into the waste products of the era. The race for superiority in nuclear weapons and consumer lifestyles produced a human and environmental catastrophe of a world littered with nuclear sludge, unexploded bombs, and mountainous garbage dumps. One character in DeLillo's portrayal of a post–cold war hangover obsessively tracks a container ship with contents so foul it is repeatedly rejected at every port, while attempting to identify its sinister origins and content. Frequently changing flags and names in an effort to gain docking and unloading rights, the ship is eventually revealed to be American and its contents, human excrement.

As pundits dilated on the end of history, DeLillo's garbage archeologist Detwiler theorizes that true history is measured in what a civilization throws away. A fringe figure notorious for "snatching the garbage of J. Edgar Hoover from the rear of the director's house in northwest Washington,"

Detwiler teaches at the University of California, Los Angeles, taking his "students into garbage dumps" to make them understand the civilization they live in. "Consume or die."[15]

Confronted with the existential vacuity of the cold war, the novel's protagonist Nick Shay, a waste management executive, seeks meaning and selfhood by rummaging through the objects and relationships of the past, hoping to cobble together a sense of the future. In 1992, he finds Klara, an artist and former lover, working on a project in the desert, "Long Tall Sally," collecting and painting discarded B-52s. Framing her work as "an art project, not a peace project," Klara is preoccupied with the meaning of power after the cold war, in "shatters and tatters" now that the "Soviet borders don't even exist in the same way." Her artistic repurposing of the military aircraft attempts to retrieve a submerged emotional memory, a "sense of awe and a child's sleeping feeling of mystery and danger and beauty." "Power meant something thirty, forty years ago. It was stable, it was focused, it was a tangible thing. It was greatness, terror, all those things. And it held us together, the Soviets and us. Maybe it held the world together. You could measure things. You could measure hope and you could measure destruction. Not that I want to bring it back. It's gone, good riddance. But the fact is."[16] In a post-Soviet interregnum, Klara is unable to complete her thought. "The fact is" an inexpressible existential void. In one sense, Klara makes art in the spirit of Detwiler's embrace of waste as the essential artifact of civilization.

But Klara's project lacks the confident resolve of the garbage guru. For Klara, the weight of the bomb, the threat of nuclear destruction, had measured the world. Insisting that she is not an artist, that her collection of B-52s does not seek to "disarm the world," Klara explains her painting as "putting our puny hands to great weapons systems" to "unrepeat" the homogeneity of factory-produced weapons, "to find an element of felt life . . . a graffiti instinct—to trespass and declare ourselves, show who we are."[17]

If Klara tries to imprint herself like graffiti on the destructive detritus of cold war militarism, Nick follows his work with Waste Incorporated—Whiz Co—into the belly of the unhinged, out-of-control market. In the cold war, "we built pyramids of waste above and below the earth. The more hazardous the waste, the more we tried to sink it." The word *plutonium*, as the garbage guru explains, "comes from Pluto, god of the dead and ruler of the underworld."[18]

Within Nick's corporate mission of waste disposal, he follows the market to the Semipaltinsk bomb-testing site in Kazakhstan, home to the first Soviet hydrogen bomb explosion. An area closed off to outsiders in the

Soviet period, like sites in the US West, its thorough contamination has resulted in widespread cancers and deformities. As Nick teams up with Viktor, his Kazakh business partner, in the logic of profit—the more dangerous and toxic the waste, the more profitable its management—their preferred disposal method for nuclear waste is blowing it up. The former Soviet nuclear testing site and its contaminated, dilapidated grounds, itself abandoned by the disappeared Soviet state that had produced the toxic weapons and waste, is now purely commodified, sold to the highest bidder. Conducting an underground explosion, the waste managers extract profit from environmental and human damage, reenacting the violence of cold war in the service of profit. DeLillo presents the afterlife of cold war competition as a cooperative, stateless, and ruthless pursuit of wealth, with no ideology to justify it, nor any political container to hold it. Like John le Carré's Western and Eastern bloc spies, who come to resemble each other in their shared logic of the end justifying the means, Nick and Viktor confront the vacuity of their earlier allegiances. As the two approach the test site, Nick asks, "Viktor, does anyone remember why we were doing all this?" "Yes," Viktor replies, "for contest. You won. We lost. You have to tell me how it feels. Big winner."[19] Viktor finds the words for what Klara struggles to articulate—the terrible emptiness of the West's "victory" in the cold war. Absent the contest, Americans and Russians answer to the same master: the raw, unadorned free market.

Like many in the antinuclear and environmental justice movements, Nick begins to see past the shiny illusion and allure of consumer goods. Garbage is the currency of his thinking. "Marian and I saw products as garbage even when they sat gleaming on store shelves, yet unbought. We didn't say, What kind of casserole will that make? We said, What kind of garbage will that make?"[20] But DeLillo offers no happy ending in the form of Nick's redemption or the feel-good embrace of suburban recycling.

DeLillo provides a critique of environmental racism, satirizing Lawrence Summers's leaked 1991 trade policy memorandum produced when he was chief economist of the World Bank. Discussing the ship with the foul waste, Nick and a colleague marvel that even the LDCs—Less Developed Countries, or "the little dark countries," in the colleague's words—will not accept the waste for pay. Nick is surprised because he had assumed that "terrible substances were routinely dropped in LDCs."[21] In what Rob Nixon called Summers's "win-win scenario for the global North," the economist argued that global economic efficiency required that toxic waste be dumped in third-world countries.[22]

Referring to "dirty industries," Summers wrote in his leaked memo, "Just between you and me shouldn't the World Bank be encouraging MORE migration of the dirty industries to the LDCs [Least Developed Countries]." Declaring "underpopulated" African countries "vastly UNDER-polluted," Summers argued that the "economic logic behind dumping a load of toxic waste in the lowest wage country is impeccable and we should face up to that." He dismissed moral arguments against dumping more pollution in LDCs, stating that such arguments "could be turned around and used more or less effectively against every bank proposal for liberalization."[23]

Nick and his colleague's discussion of the ship with the toxic cargo turns to rumors of a ghost ship. Asked, "How toxic is the cargo?" the colleague tells Nick, "I hear rumors. This isn't my area of course. Happens in some back room in our New York office. It's a folk tale about a spectral flying ship. The Flying Liberian."[24] Evoking the US slave trade and colonial past, DeLillo also figures the 1989–96 Liberian Civil War as a toxic by-product of the cold war. The civil war, which attracted the West's attention for conscripting child soldiers, was part of a global surge of human trafficking in forms old and new, as new internet technologies enabled new criminal enterprises capitalizing on collapsed borders and new markets.[25] A seismic shift in the global political economy of human trafficking—from sexual slavery, to boys forced into combat, to trade in human organs—had consequences on every continent.

Slow Violence of Environmental Destruction

Nixon has explored the work of the dissident writer, environmental justice activist, and television producer Ken Saro-Wiwa, a founder of the Movement for the Survival of the Ogoni People, whose execution in 1995 by a Nigerian military tribunal with the collusion of the multinational Shell Oil corporation galvanized a global environmental movement. Taking on Shell as well as the broader "consolidation and increasingly unregulated mobility of transnational corporations," Saro-Wiwa, argues Nixon, "understood that environmentalism needs to be reimagined through the experience of the minorities who are barely visible on the global economic periphery, where transnationals in the extraction business—be it oil, mining, or timber—operate with maximum impunity."[26]

Saro-Wiwa described the destruction of the Ogoni land by Shell's oil exploration and drilling: "Oil blow-out, spillages, oil slick and general pollution accompany the search for oil.... Oil companies have flared gas in

Nigeria for the past thirty-three years causing acid rain.... What used to be the breadbasket of the [Niger] Delta has now become totally infertile."[27]

Arguing in 1992 that the Ogoni were victims of an "unconventional war" prosecuted by ecological means, for Saro-Wiwa, the end of the cold war had brought increasing attention to the global environment, "and the insistence of the European community that the minority rights be respected, albeit in the successor states to the Soviet Union and in Yugoslavia." Saro-Wiwa called for the international community to apply the same standards on behalf of the minority Ogoni peoples and their victimization at the hands of the Nigerian dictatorship and Shell.[28]

But post–cold war calls for minority rights and corporate accountability were no match for capitalism on steroids. The new round of deregulation granted oil and extractive industries greater latitude in exploration and extraction, backed by Nigerian military forces when activists sought to stop them. With Shell owning 47 percent of Nigeria's oil and close ties with the Sani Abacha dictatorship that allowed Shell to operate without the environmental regulations protecting first-world nations, a 1994 Nigerian government memo acknowledged that Shell could not operate without "ruthless military operations."[29] Saro-Wiwa's execution elicited global outrage, sparking an international campaign to boycott Shell.

At a moment when US-Russian cooperation was desperately needed for environmental containment and security, lack of international cooperation was exacerbated by the opening of dark commodity chains. Despite scientists and politicians on both sides promoting coordination, many factors hindered cooperation. As a US-proposed Caspian oil pipeline bypassing Russia and the expansion of NATO undermined goodwill, the unending cold war on the Korean peninsula also blocked political and scientific cooperation. As with the US war in the Gulf, US policy toward North Korea reflects the clash between advocates for diplomacy in the United States and abroad, and a doubling down on cold war militarism, elaborated by US policy makers through the idea of the rogue state.

Rogue States and the Unending Cold War

Responses to terrorist threats and loose nukes were interpreted through a policy framework of rogue states, a new formulation constructed by policy makers and circulated in popular culture. The rhetoric of rogue or outlaw states whose conduct placed them beyond the pale of the international community refined the broader notion of the clash of civilizations into policy prescriptions for targeting recalcitrant states.

The idea of the outlaw or rogue nation posited a malevolent and irrational enemy with whom any negotiation or compromise was impossible. Any posture of routine diplomacy with such actors was rejected as appeasement, discrediting the very notion of political and diplomatic solutions, and seeming to foreground the option of armed conflict. Just as important, the idea of a rogue state constituted a new geopolitical framework that distracted from and obfuscated cold war histories and peculiar post–cold war continuities that should have raised eyebrows.

The threat of loose nukes was real. The idea of a rogue state was a political invention. Scholars have astutely commented on the incoherence of the idea. Linking vastly different states that the United States essentially didn't like, the accusation often centered on nuclear capability. Given the strength of US treaties with Gorbachev, those concerned with multilateral cooperation on controlling nuclear proliferation had a strong foundation to build on. In May 1990, the Non-proliferation Treaty, in effect since 1970, was expanded indefinitely, with its 191 signatories agreeing not to acquire weapons in exchange for peacefully applied benefits of nuclear power. Well before the 1991 dissolution of the Soviet Union, the Soviet-led nuclear research bloc that had included North Korea had broken up, and the new treaty sought to preserve the commitment of former Soviet bloc members. Sustained political cooperation between the United States and Russia enjoyed broad support from a host of commentators and citizens who viewed joint action as essential for securing loose nukes and numerous cold war–era weapons throughout the world. But advocates of international cooperation were increasingly disregarded by those who pushed for the military removal of recalcitrant leaders of rogue states.

The concept of the rogue or outlaw state was formally defined in 1994 by the Clinton administration's Anthony Lake. However, as Michael Klare has argued, its central precepts had been adopted by 1990, informing the 1990 George H. W. Bush regional defense doctrine. Later, when George W. Bush named Iraq, Iran, and North Korea as the "Axis of Evil" in January 2002, the precursor of that belligerent position had been the George H. W. Bush administration's attempts to curb outlaw nations.[30]

Lake's "Confronting Backlash States," published in *Foreign Affairs* in 1994, named North Korea, Cuba, Iran, Iraq, and Libya as "backlash states." "Our policy," Lake argued, "must face the reality of recalcitrant and outlaw states that not only choose to remain outside the family but also assault its basic values." Lake described such nations as "aggressive and defiant, the ties between them ... growing as they seek to thwart or quarantine themselves from a global trend to which they seem incapable of adapting."[31] As policy makers reinscribed colonial racial hierarchies that posited some people as living outside the "family" of civilized nations, their map of rogue entities was invoked in the media. Urging tighter controls on enriched uranium, a *New York Times* editorial cautioned that Georgia is "precisely the kind of unstable place where nuclear materials should not be stored. It is close to Iran and Iraq ... and not far from Chechnya." The danger was that "rogue states or terrorist groups intent on making a nuclear weapon would not need sophisticated bomb-making technology."[32]

Critics of the concept charged that characterizations of "rogue states" precluded policy makers' objective assessments of regimes that would provide the basis for sound policy decisions. Robert S. Litwak, then director of the Division of International Studies at the Woodrow Wilson International Center for Scholars, charged that the rogue state framework simplistically demonized and lumped together disparate nations, neglecting rational analysis and distorting policy-making.[33]

As Klare has demonstrated, policy recommendations based on the idea of rogue and outlaw states were a bipartisan affair, but from 1990 and especially after 1994, Republicans emboldened by their majority in Congress denounced diplomatic engagement with so-called rogue states and called for aggressive measures to undermine the regimes. Building on Reagan's and Bush's emphasis on "strength" as the route to peace and complementing the Republican agenda of NATO expansion, repeated warnings about outlaw states could and did undermine support for treaties and international cooperation.[34] Klare outlined the issue in his 1995 op-ed for the *Christian Science Monitor*. Republicans and Democrats alike, Klare charged, "seem to share the same delusion: that America's national security interests are best secured by preparing for an unending series of conflicts with 'rogue states' in the Middle East and Asia." Unable to live in a world without enemies, Klare argued, US policy makers characterized a number of third-world states as "rogue and outlaws, living outside of 'the family of nations.'" "Such states—notably Iran, Iraq, Libya, Syria, and North Korea—are said to support terrorism or radical insurgent forces, to seek weapons of mass destruction, and to violate various international 'norms.'" For Klare, the unwillingness to rethink the antirogue strategy inhibited policy makers from making realistic assessments of security threats and hence developing an appropriate and effective defense strategy.[35]

Designating states as rogue actors absolved policy makers and the public of any responsibility for examining past relations as a basis for diplomatic and policy alternatives. Historical and political knowledge of one's adversary was irrelevant. Even verifiable facts, such as whether weapons of mass destruction actually existed in Korea in 1990 or in Iraq in 2003, were immaterial if such states, a priori, threatened national security. Calling North Korea a "Stalinist Jurassic Park," the moderator of National Public Radio's *America and the World* show argued that "there is something surreal about North Korea as a nuclear menace."[36] Media narratives of mysterious and inscrutable enemies had made Americans susceptible to falsehoods about incubator babies in Kuwait in 1990 and, later, weapons of mass destruction in Iraq in 2003.

Just as critical was the reliance on cold war amnesia in mobilizing political support for military action against so-called rogue states. The inconvenient facts of US alliances with now-discredited states were not to be spoken of, all but banished from public discourse. Just as the moral and political argument for the 1990 US troop buildup in the Gulf and 1991 invasion of Iraq downplayed the US alliance with Saddam Hussein, accounts of Iran shrouded the past. One account waxed nostalgic for the cold war "containment" of Iran. It was misleading, at best, to suggest that the United States had "contained" a regime that in fact was its strongest and most dependable strategic ally in the region from 1953 to 1979. Moreover, such revisionism erases the US overthrow of the democratically elected government of Mohammad Mosaddegh in 1953 and subsequent support of the twenty-five-year dictatorship of the shah.[37] Ironically, given the prominence Iran has occupied in US affairs since 1979, the silence on the US coup in 1953, and US support for dictatorships in Egypt, Bahrain, and Saudi Arabia, left the American public ill-prepared to understand popular resentment in the Middle East of US interference in the region. The only explanation for the deep resentment toward US policy among the Iranian people that was fit for public consumption was an irrational rogue state.[38]

Instead of reexamining cold war assumptions that had guided earlier foreign policy, powerful members of the Bush and Clinton administrations placed those who did not fall in line behind US military and economic hegemony beyond the pale of the international community. Perhaps nothing is more illustrative of the cost of constructing a rogue state at the expense of informed diplomacy than the case of North Korea. But before turning to this particular "outlaw" state, it is necessary to consider the broader regional dynamics of the unending cold war in Asia.

The Unending Cold War

The Chinese government's violent military suppression of the pro-democracy student movement in Tiananmen Square on June 3 and 4, 1989, following weeks of protest sparked by the visit of Gorbachev, shocked Americans. The crackdown reversed years of American goodwill toward China and ushered in a new dark age in US-Chinese relations.[39]

Tiananmen and its aftermath left Western commentators feeling "like a jilted lover," as *New York Times* reporter and witness to the bloody crackdown, Nicholas Kristof, put it in 1991. After Richard Nixon's audacious overture to the long-coveted China market, the gift of the pandas Ling-Ling and Hsing-Hsing to the National Zoo cemented American goodwill and paved the way for harmonious trade relations between the countries. Pandamania and ping-pong diplomacy melted American hearts, helping forge what Bush's national security adviser Brent Scowcroft called the "American love affair with China." It was a durable bond until it wasn't, beginning "with Nixon's trip and ... last[ing] until Tiananmen."[40] Throughout, for many, American admiration for China's veneer of orderliness, seemingly well-behaved children, and adorable pandas had seemed to be a two-sided affair.

Robert L. Suettinger, a national security and intelligence expert on China in both the George H. W. Bush and Clinton administrations, has argued that because Beijing withheld documentation of the events, Tiananmen took on meanings for the United States and China that were out of proportion to what actually happened. Following Tiananmen, outraged by the violent repression of Chinese students, Congressperson Nancy Pelosi led a bloc in Congress imposing sanctions on Beijing. Bush dispatched former president Nixon and former secretary of state Henry Kissinger to Beijing in a failed attempt to reprise their diplomatic successes of 1971 and 1972 détente.[41]

In the aftermath of Tiananmen, as the world appeared to embrace market reform, insisting that markets and political democracy went hand in hand, China was not having it. Dismayed at proclamations of communism's demise, Beijing believed that Gorbachev had introduced political reforms too rapidly without providing economic benefits, leading to massive instability. At the same time, Beijing took issue with US pressure to quicken the pace of reform by tying human rights concessions to economic and trade relations.[42]

Moreover, the older China Lobby had resurfaced in the 1980s, opposing détente and reviving the assertion that Taiwan, not Beijing, should be the sole Chinese government recognized by Washington. In the later years of the Reagan administration, "patience with Beijing was already wearing thin for many American foreign policy elites well before June 4."[43] In addition, a still powerful China Lobby had never reconciled itself to recognition of Beijing over Taiwan as the legitimate Chinese government.

From a cold warrior perspective, China, not unlike Cuba, was the ultimate recalcitrant state, defying the US insistence on the equation of capitalism and democracy at every turn. But with the United States already committed to economic interdependence, China was simply far too powerful to be a rogue state. North Korea, on the other hand, provided a perfect rogue state justification for continued US military presence on the Korean peninsula.

Reenacting Cold War Division in the Koreas: The Almost Hot War

In 1991, hard-won achievements of the South Korean democracy movement, along with glasnost in the Soviet Union, renewed hopes for ending the Korean War and moving toward reunification. After decades of US-backed dictatorship in South Korea, the democracy movements in the 1980s pushed for direct presidential elections in 1987, as political elites sought to polish the image of Korean civic politics for the 1988 Olympics. During the Soviet era, North Korea had been involved in the Soviet consortium of nuclear research. Breaking from that cold war alliance, Gorbachev met with South Korean officials in 1991. Although that angered North Korea, the regime at the time was seeking friendlier ties with the West. In 1990, discussions between the leaders of North and South Korea resulted in cultural exchanges, including the formation of joint sports teams for international matches in table tennis and youth soccer in 1991. The countries joined the UN as separate members on September 17, 1991. As reported by the *New York Times*, on December 13 of that year, leaders of North and South Korea "signed a treaty of reconciliation and nonaggression ... renouncing armed force against each other and saying that would formally bring the Korean War to an end, 38 years after the fighting ceased."[44]

Despite these promising developments, Secretary of Defense Dick Cheney inflamed cold war divisions. Seeming to offer withdrawal of US nuclear weapons in South Korea, along with US troop reductions, Cheney made both contingent on inspection of North Korea's nuclear facilities and Pyongyang's "forswear[ing] development of nuclear weapons and allow[ing] international verification teams to visit facilities." Speaking in Seoul, Cheney opted for confrontation over negotiation, charging North Korea with a "40-year history of terrorism, aggression, and irresponsible weapon sales."[45]

Most accounts place the first North Korean test of a nuclear device in 2006, but listening to Cheney and the echo chamber of media punditry in 1991, one would have believed the existence of such weapons was imminent. Earlier that year, despite no evidence of nuclear arms development, a *New York Times* editorial called for strong action against North Korea, labeling it "renegade, and perhaps [the] most dangerous country in the world today ... the next Iraq," if not stopped by the world community.[46] Hinging US policy on an exaggerated threat of nuclear capability, Cheney rejected diplomacy for measures that would quickly cripple the regime.

North Korea–bashing came easily to the US news media. The historian Bruce Cumings has explained that "the North Korea that Americans see is the one that a CBS news correspondent chose to highlight after his 1989 trip there." North Korea, to that observer, "is a society where individuality is the greatest crime"; "forty years of nationalism, state terror, and brainwashing" has turned the people into "thousands of cogs in an Orwellian wheel." Cumings writes, "There is another way of thinking about this country: as a small, Third World postcolonial nation that has been gravely wounded, first by forty years of Japanese colonialism and then by another sixty years of national division and war, and that is deeply insecure, threatened by the world around it. And so it projects a fearsome image."[47]

Media accounts of North Korea seldom address the partition of the Korean peninsula in August 1945, when two American generals took out a National Geographic atlas and arbitrarily divided the peninsula at the thirty-eighth parallel without consulting the Korean provisional government that had formed during the war.[48] When superpowers chose divided military occupation, the United States moved into the South, and the Soviet Union took control of the North. In mainstream US accounts, the division is naturalized, its origins as an arbitrary cold war creation obscured to American audiences. Viewed internally by Koreans, within the historical frame of Korea's long struggle against Japanese colonialism, the partition appears as a violent imposition of a cold war geography on a colonial and decolonizing landscape.[49]

Emerging from an anticolonial struggle, North Korea had long sought national independence and, like other small states, tried to play stronger powers against each another to its advantage. Against all odds, North Korea eked out a measure of economic self-reliance in the late 1950s, as "an economic miracle" following the end of combat in 1953 lifted the country from the devastation of war and UN bombing. Between 1950 and 1953, UN forces had dropped 635,000 tons of bombs on North Korea, leaving "a scale of urban destruction that exceeded [that of] Germany and Japan" in World War II. The North's infrastructure of an estimated fifteen thousand underground military installations cannot be seen apart from the horrific reality of mass-scale aerial bombardment by the United States in the span of only three years. By US government accounts, at least 50 percent of the "North's twenty-two major cities were obliterated," including 75 percent of Pyongyang.[50]

The scale of destruction should give pause to smug characterizations of North Korean paranoia and irrationality. In 1990, the United States could have followed the lead of South Korean advocacy groups seeking reunification to reassess the cold war assumptions that had led to the arbitrary 1945 partition. Then, too, the United States could have reexamined its support for the dictatorship of Park Chung-hee in South Korea. Certainly, the Park dictatorship fomented the anticommunism that in turn sustained the regime. But in their accounts of the regime, US hawks flattened South Korea into a simplistic anticommunist monolith, ignoring internal democratic opposition and calls for reunification.

On October 19, 1991, the same month George H. W. Bush and Cheney declared that there would be no peace dividend, the *New York Times* reported that US officials were "turn[ing] the screws on Pyongyang," making the withdrawal of US nuclear weapons and a reduction of US troops in South Korea contingent on nuclear inspections.[51] In November Cheney embarked on an Asian tour aimed at justifying the US postponement of troop reductions until "uncertainties about North Korea's nuclear program are addressed."[52]

Some observers noted parallels between the squeeze on North Korea and the US intervention in Iraq earlier that year. Declaring that "the Gulf War had come just in time to spare the world" the "nightmare of Iraq obtaining nuclear capability," the Australian *Sydney Morning Herald* reported US and South Korean claims that "North Korea is 12 months away from producing about 50kg of weapons grade plutonium and about another year or two from having the technology to turn that plutonium into six or seven nuclear warheads." Admitting skepticism on unsourced reporting, the *Herald* nonetheless concluded, "The experience with Iraq shows that it is better to err on the side of caution than generosity in calculations of this nature."[53] But Cheney's contention that North Korea was close to having nuclear weapons proved as deceitful as George H. W. Bush's fabricated story of Iraqi soldiers throwing babies out of incubators.

Seemingly oblivious to reunification hopes and ongoing negotiations between North and South Korea, the *Washington Post* described the border between North and South as "one of the very few hostile boundaries unaffected by the end of the Cold War." For the *Post* opinion writer, "Kim Il Sung's isolated and deeply strange state has repeatedly resorted to assassination and terrorism in its rivalry with South Korea. Nuclear weapons in those hands is a terrible thought."[54]

Cheney and his allies reaffirmed the existence of the border despite the end of the cold war. Cheney had no interest in Korean reunification, let alone any significant reduction of US troops in South Korea. Of course, he could not be expected to take actions undermining a critical US strategic position, as well as the military-industrial political economy that structured US–South Korean relations, after relations with China had soured. Cheney's interests in a "leaner and meaner" war economy, strengthened in key strategic areas, are clear. But in the historical context of the superpower division of a colonized country, "turning the screws" on North Korea disrupted cooperation between North and South Korea, further naturalizing Korea's artificial division by cold war superpowers and reinflicting the wound of division.

Refusing Resolution

North Korea's cooperation with US demands failed to satisfy Bush administration hawks. In 1991, North Korea agreed to a weapons inspection, and approximately one hundred American tactical nuclear weapons were withdrawn at the end of 1991. On January 31, North and South Korea signed the Joint Declaration on the Denuclearization of the Korean Peninsula. Yet US officials in the Bush administration were unhappy with the inspections. Convinced that key information was withheld, they continued to pressure North Korea. By the end of 1993, North Korea was threatening to pull out of the Non-proliferation Treaty and forge ahead with nuclear arms development. The tensions inherited by the Clinton administration played out in contests between hawks and diplomats, as well as across the media.

Media and policy makers' rhetoric on North Korea reveals both a battle over historical narrative and the rebooting of 1950s cold war orientalist tropes. With US attention centered on Kim Jong Il, son of the ailing president Kim Il Sung and commander of the North Korean Army, officials openly debated whether the younger Kim was "crazy" or "canny."[55] Some officials described him as "a dangerous eccentric—a spoiled, shy, immature leader with a reported penchant for wild parties, fast cars, violence, and sexual liaisons—who might eventually provoke a war to stay in power." Another senior US official thought Kim "crazy, but like a fox—a wily statesman whose isolation masks a canny understanding of how to tweak the world into giving his nation the political independence and economic assistance it needs." The *Guardian* described the appearance of the elder Kim as that of "Octogenarian Mutant Ninja Turtle," while the *Irish Times* reported that "Mr. Kim Jong-Il is short and pudgy and tales of him being a spoiled and sadistic playboy have certainly been helped by his permed hair, Elvis blow Wave and platform heel boots."[56] When in doubt, suspect the worst. Paul Wolfowitz, the undersecretary of defense under George W. Bush, said, "What little we know suggests he makes his father look moderate and his father started the Korean War. We are dealing with extremely tough characters."[57]

Wolfowitz's statement that Kim Il Sung "started the Korean War" is also dependent on a historical sleight of hand. To consider the Korean War as beginning only in June 1950 when North Korea invaded the South is to willfully ignore the five years of previous foreign military occupation on the post-1945 artificially divided Korean peninsula. As Heonik Kwon has argued, "For people who date the origins of the war to 1950, the culpability rests unquestionably with the northern Communist regime.... For those who associate the origin of the Korean War with the end of the Pacific War in 1945, however, the main responsibility for the war lies with the United States and the Soviet Union, which partitioned and separately occupied the postcolonial nation after the surrender of Japan."[58] The division of the peninsula at the thirty-eighth parallel and the US and Soviet occupations touched off profound economic and political turmoil. Significant numbers of Koreans were killed during the three years of US occupation in actions including lethal US military violence toward civilians, as in the Yeongcheon massacre of October 1946. Wolfowitz's account naturalizes the division of Korea, rendering the US military presence in South Korea a natural part of the landscape.

Only rarely did speculation about Kim's personality draw on the context of Korea's colonial history. A *Washington Post* reporter explained, "What many experts say is Kim's extraordinary suspicion of the outside world may stem from the difficult circumstances of his early life. He was born on a commune in the Soviet Far East at a time when Japanese occupiers were implementing a harsh policy of forced assimilation for Koreans back home. His father had fled the country after protesting Japanese efforts to virtually wipe out the indigenous Korean language, religion, and culture." An unnamed US government analyst told this reporter, "His father's underground existence produced exaggerated traits [in Kim], including a conspiratorial view of the world, a sense that the world is a frightening place, that there are few people that you can trust."[59]

Yet the historical elisions in this candid and even sympathetic analysis of the impact of Japanese colonialism are striking. On the one hand, the account portrays Kim's father as motivated against Japanese attempts to destroy his entire culture. Yet appreciation of an "underground existence" to escape Japanese colonizers obscures the terror inflicted in the 1950–53 UN/US bombing of North Korea, which forced people to flee underground and resulted in the construction of extensive underground military installations.

The portrayal of Kim's mental state as paranoid and conspiratorial also ignores the fact that US policy makers made no secret of their desire to destroy him and the regime. In December, a headline in the *Washington Times* declared, "U.S. diplomacy [is] not the answer in North Korea, two experts say: Kim called 'evil,' son half-crazy." According to Fred C. Ikle, undersecretary of defense for the Reagan administration, two top Reagan-era Pentagon officials said, "There's one and only one solution to the North Korean nuclear problem, and that's the demise of this evil regime.... To think that you can make a deal with that kind of beast is the wrong road. I would put all of the efforts into undoing the regime." Frank Gaffney, who had worked under Ikle during the Reagan administration, believed that "the Clinton administration's diplomatic approach" was "playing to Kim Il-Sung's worst tendencies."[60]

The Diplomats and the Hawks in the Almost War of 1994

With US policy on North Korea divided between hawks who viewed the collapse of the Soviet Union as an opportunity to overthrow communist regimes in Korea and Cuba, and those who saw the moment as an opportunity for diplomacy, continuing concerns over North Korea's nuclear facilities nearly led to another military outbreak in the still-not-ended Korean War in June 1994.[61] In January of that year, CIA director James Woolsey warned the Senate Select Committee on Intelligence about North Korea's military buildup, estimating (wrongly) that "the DPRK [Democratic People's Republic of Korea] had built one or two nuclear weapons, produced weapons-grade plutonium, and exported missiles with a range of 625 miles or more." Reprising 1950s depictions of the "Oriental Mind," Defense Intelligence Agency director James Clapper said North Korea was one of the intelligence community's biggest challenges because of "mysteries, things that are not predictable, not even knowable."[62]

With the Clinton administration actively reviewing war contingencies and estimating at least one hundred thousand dead should war break out, including ten thousand US troops, conflict was averted when former president and special envoy Jimmy Carter talked with Kim Il Sung. Making an agreement to halt the weapons development program at Yongbyon, the negotiators charted a path to "harmonious relations" and eventual reunification in what became the Agreed Framework, signed by the United States and North Korea in Geneva on October 21, 1994. Though it was not a treaty, the document's goals included ending the armistice, developing a peace agreement, and establishing a framework for continuing talks.

Even in the midst of Carter's negotiations, hawks and members of the press insisted on the impossibility of diplomacy.[63] The *Scotsman* wrote that Kim's ruthless efficiency as a dictator "makes Saddam Hussein seem sober and judicious."[64] A *Philadelphia Inquirer* account, attacking the younger Kim, contrasted the "shrewd and ruthless" yet "articulate, forceful, and clear-headed" elder Kim to the "spoiled brat ... playboy and dilettante ... notorious for his mistresses and numerous illegitimate children."[65] Such caricatures of Kim buttressed the constant assertation that diplomacy is impossible, serving as a dress rehearsal for the insistence in the George W. Bush administration that regime change is the only possible way forward. In other words, regime change is rational, while diplomacy is irrational. One cannot be a rational person if you argue for diplomacy.

One might expect portrayals of a rogue state to fasten onto anti-American rhetoric or actions. In the case of North Korea, however, Kim Jong Il's interest in American culture was used against him. Press accounts, such as the 1994 report in the *Philadelphia Inquirer*, made mockery of Kim's love of American cinema, charging him with a "fanatical interest in ... American movies from the 1930s and 1940s." The critical preoccupation of commentators with Kim's predilections suggests a rare, if not singular, instance in which a foreign leader's affinity with American culture was made a point of derision instead of a basis for engagement or negotiation. Moreover, such media portrayals from the 1990s would be rehashed in the formulation of the axis of evil a decade later.[66]

Following President George Bush's 2002 naming of North Korea as a part of the axis of evil, PBS's *Frontline* gathered the players in the 1994 US North Korean dispute for an assessment that demonstrated the incompatibility between the "rogue nation" worldview and the very possibility of diplomacy. The 1994 agreement had created the Korean Peninsula Energy Development Organization, an international entity, to build light-water reactors. In exchange for North Korea's putting a halt to weapons-grade development, the United States, South Korea, and Japan were to assist in the building of light-water reactors and provide aid for oil to help with energy needs.

Richard Perle, of the Defense Policy Board, believed Americans were "being jerked around by North Korea, and we're appeasing them with feckless diplomacy." But for Perle, any diplomacy with North Korea was feckless: "Sometimes there are regimes that you cannot reliably enter into an agreement with, and the North Korean regime at the time, looked to me to be an example." He believed that there were "alternatives to negotiation," including a "precision strike."[67]

Robert Gallucci, the chief US negotiator with North Korea, recalled being accused of submitting to blackmail. Critics demanded to know whether he and Carter understood this was a rogue regime, asking, had they learned nothing about the failures of appeasement? After the Republican takeover of Congress, a lack of political will all but ensured the demise of the agreement, and Gallucci conceded the validity of North Korean accusations of foot-dragging on the part of the United States.[68] Similarly, William Perry, US secretary of defense from 1994 to 1997 and special envoy to North Korea in 1999, recalled that Senator John McCain called the framework "appeasement and called the Clinton administration treasonous. He called the President a traitor." McCain wasn't alone, as other hawks in Congress, Perry recalled, said, "Let's overthrow the North Korea regime. It's an evil regime."[69]

Donald Gregg, former national security adviser to Vice President George Bush (1982–89) and ambassador to South Korea from 1989 to 1993, believed that the North Koreans upheld their end of the Agreed Framework. Although he faulted such hostile North Korean acts as sending "their submarines down the east coast of the Korean peninsula," angering Republicans and South Koreans, Gregg blamed the United States for "foot dragging on our part." Promised "oil shipments came late and there was a real lack of enthusiasm for ... getting them off the terrorist list. I wouldn't say we reneged. But it was not implemented with any great enthusiasm." Gregg added, "I think the North Koreans can say with a straight face that, 'We think that you have never really been enthusiastic about improving relations with us. We think you have contributed to the delay of the building of the [light]-water reactors. This has contributed to our power shortage. And you are to blame for the sad state of our economy.'"[70]

Despite US foot-dragging and pressure from Republican hawks, diplomacy prevailed during the Clinton administration and was then buoyed by South Korea's 1998–2008 Sunshine policy under Kim Dae-jung, president from 1988 to 2003 and winner of the 2000 Nobel Peace Prize. Kim had been a critic of the Park dictatorship and involved in the democracy movements that accelerated after Park's 1979 assassination. Despite US Republican sabotage of the Agreed Framework, the Sunshine policy, with its goal of normalizing political and economic relations and easing military tensions through bilateral and multilateral diplomacy and negotiations, achieved considerable success.

As Bruce Cumings has asserted, from 1994 to 2002 North Korea produced no plutonium, and in October 2000, the Clinton administration worked out a deal "to buy all of its medium and long range missiles." Writing from the vantage point of a Donald Trump administration–induced crisis in March 2017, Cumings compellingly argued that if George W. Bush had not unraveled years of diplomacy by naming North Korea as part of his axis of evil in January 2002—and then announcing, in September 2002, a preemptive doctrine aimed at North Korea and Iraq—North Korea would have no nuclear weapons in 2017.[71]

From the disruption of North and South Korean negotiations in 1991 to US hawks undermining the Agreed Framework, the United States bears no small measure of responsibility for the unresolved division of the Korean peninsula—namely, there are at least three instances: the definition of North Korea as an outlaw nation at a moment of significant thawing in North-South Korean relations; the Republican undermining of the Agreed Framework; and Bush's condemnation of North Korea as part of the axis of evil in 2002, also at a moment of South and North Korean cooperation. Through repeated abandonment of diplomatic openings, hardliners in the United States reinflicted the wounds of 1945.

The history of US relations with North Korea illustrates how acknowledging the profound costs of the cold war—and the mistakes made on all sides—could foster public awareness and democratic support for a political, diplomatic solution to international problems. Placing rogue states outside history and outside the family of nations obscured the actual successes of past diplomacy, inflamed public fears, and made Americans susceptible to wars rooted in deception. It also distracted attention from genuine threats to security.

Oil versus Oil: Sleeping with the Enemies

On February 26, 1993, Eyad Ismoil, a Jordanian national, and Ramzi Yousef, a Kuwaiti, detonated a 1,300-pound bomb laced with cyanide in the parking garage of the North Tower of the World Trade Center in New York City. The blast blew a thirty-meter hole in the ground, killing six people and injuring another one thousand.[72] Each of the seven people convicted of the bombing had ties to a radical Egyptian cleric, Omar Abdel Rahman. A State Department investigation revealed that he had been issued four US visas by the CIA, the first in 1986.[73] He was in fact traveling as part of an international network of Arab groups supporting jihad—a group that had become even more important to the CIA after the Soviet withdrawal from Afghanistan in 1989. Abdel Rahman had been recruited by the CIA to preach radical Islam in Afghanistan, and in return for the favor had been granted multiple visas to the United States.[74]

As the historian Nick Cullather has shown, from 1946 onward, US policymakers had courted Afghanistan as a critical buffer between the Soviet Union and the vast oil and mineral resources to the south. Initially, the United States faced little competition from the Soviets as they recovered from World War II. But by the early 1950s, the Soviets were pouring technological support into Afghanistan. A modernizing monarchy that tilted to the west co-existed with the technocratic prime minister, Mohammed Daoud, who welcomed Soviet aid. Director of Central Intelligence Allen Dulles advocated Daoud's overthrow, modeling the idea on the CIA's 1953 disposal of Mossadegh in Iran. Opting for diplomacy over a coup, President Dwight Eisenhower visited Afghanistan in 1959, flying into the Soviet-built Bagram airport. And in September 1963, King Mohammad Zafir Shaw visited the Kennedy White House, with Kennedy and the king issuing a joint statement on Afghan nonalignment.[75] In the 1970s, impatient with the slow pace of modernization, left-leaning Afghans overthrew the monarchy, with their own factional differences leading to a Soviet invasion in 1979. Even before the Soviet invasion, the United States had begun to arm anticommunist Islamicist factions.

In the late 1970s, the CIA supported mujahideen, including Osama bin Laden, as a way of drawing the Soviet Union into war in Afghanistan. In July 1980, five months before the Soviet invasion of Afghanistan, Carter formally authorized the CIA to provide aid to the mujahideen. During the 1980s, in Operation Cyclone, the CIA worked with Pakistan's Inter-services Intelligence, furnishing arms to mujahideen fighters in Afghanistan. In January 1980, Secretary of State Zbigniew Brzezinski visited Egypt, attempting to mobilize Arab support for the Afghan war. Within weeks of the visit, Egyptian president Anwar Sadat began mobilizing arms and recruiting fighters from the Muslim Brotherhood, further allowing the United States to station its air force base in Egypt; these actions were steeped in layered and tragic ironies since members of the same groups assassinated Sadat eighteen months later. US Special Forces trained Islamist militants in bomb-making, sabotage, arson, and guerrilla warfare.

Reagan met with mujahideen in the Oval Office in 1983, declaring, "To watch the courageous Afghan freedom fighters battle modern arsenals with simple hand-held weapons is an inspiration to those who love freedom."[76] "Many of the Islamist Arab recruits, including Osama bin Laden, who were trained as fighters by Green Berets and Navy Seals for the Afghan War, would go on to form the backbone of Al-Qaeda."[77]

Before Soviet and Western meddling, Afghanistan had a secular government in which women were granted relatively equal rights. The People's Democratic Party of Afghanistan was formed in 1965, during the 1963–73 period of constitutional reform, and took power in 1978 through a military coup. The United States and Soviet Union stepped into a power struggle between two factions of the party: the Soviet-preferred Parcham (The banner) and the more globally oriented Khalq (The people), whom the Soviets found threatening for their nonaligned tendencies as they sought trade and development ties with states outside the communist bloc. After the Parcham faction was ousted by Khalq, the Soviets invaded and reinstated Parcham. With US support, the Islamist insurgency that had existed before the Soviet invasion became far more concerted. Despite factional differences, Afghani governments had made considerable developmental strides in the postmonarchy reform period, gains that were obliterated as mujahideen and then Taliban forces took over the country.[78]

Brzezinski, President Carter's national security adviser from 1977 to 1981, defended the US support of the mujahideen, arguing that the "secret operation was an excellent idea. It had the effect of drawing the Russians into the Afghan trap. . . . We now have the opportunity of giving to the USSR its Vietnam war.... Moscow had to carry on a war unsupportable by the government, a conflict that brought about the demoralization and finally the breakup of the Soviet empire." Further pressed on whether he regretted aiding and training militants, Brzezinski replied, "What is most important to the world, the Taliban or the collapse of the Soviet empire? Some stirred-up Moslems or the liberation of Central Europe and the end of the cold war?"[79] Brzezinski's defense underscores the perceived need to defeat communism by any means at any costs, and the inability to question that assumption despite evidence to the contrary.

When the last Soviet troops were withdrawn in 1989, the mujahideen did not simply leave; a civil war followed, with various Islamist militant groups fighting for control. US funding of the mujahideen continued for another three years. The Taliban prevailed and established a theocratic regime to replace the former "godless" socialist government.[80] Renewed CIA collaboration with Pakistani intelligence during the 1990s extended the power of the Taliban across the Afghanistan-Pakistan border, efforts that increased after the United States went to war with Afghanistan in 2001.

The year 1993 would have been an opportune moment to reexamine US support for fundamentalist Islamist groups. Instead, the quest to control oil supplies—this time in the Caspian—lured corporate and government officials into covert relationships with the Taliban. In 1995, for example, the US oil company Unocal was among several companies that formed a cartel in Washington, DC, to further their interests in the Caspian.[81] Unocal sought to build oil and gas pipelines from Turkmenistan to Afghanistan and through Pakistani ports.

Officials justified oil alliances with undemocratic regimes through the logic, as Cheney put it to oil executives at an Institute for Petroleum lunch in 1999, that "oil is unlike any other commodity"; it is the "basic, fundamental building block of the world economy," essential, therefore, to national security.[82] A convenient policy for their own pocketbooks, it was certainly not conducive to the development of alternative forms of renewable energy. Beyond this, these powerful shapers of policy refused to budge from assumptions that force is the route to peace and stability and that their fundamentalist anti-American allies could be controlled in the face of massive evidence to the contrary.

After the Taliban seized power in Kabul in 1996, oil executives invited Taliban leaders to Houston, citing the pipeline as the basis for Pakistan's amity toward the Taliban, which also seemed to enjoy US support.[83] Marjorie Cohn, a law professor and scholar at the Institute for Public

Accuracy, reported in 2000 that instability in the Middle East led Cheney and oil executives to focus on the Caspian region. The Washington-based American Petroleum Institute called the Caspian "the area of greatest resource potential outside of the Middle East." Cheney told a gaggle of industry executives in 1998, "I can't think of a time when we've had a region emerge as suddenly to become as strategically significant as the Caspian."[84] Indeed, the thirst for Caspian oil would guide the George W. Bush administration's approach to the war on terror as well as its relation to Russia from beginning to end. Toward the end of his vice presidency in September 2008, Cheney traveled to Azerbaijan and met with its president, Ilham Aliev (who maintained power through rigged elections and the brutal suppression of protest), at his residence on the Caspian Sea, followed by talks with executives of British Petroleum and Chevron.[85]

US corporate and official determination to control Caspian oil by routing a pipeline through Afghanistan and Pakistan, bypassing Russia, informed cooperation with the Taliban in Pakistan and Afghanistan up to two weeks before the 9/11 attacks. The scramble for Caspian crude also reveals US duplicity in its partnership with Russia in the post-9/11 war on terror, as US officials deemed Russia unworthy to compete for oil reserves it might legitimately claim through business ties built on long regional relations. The United States' courting of the Taliban in its Faustian pursuit of Caspian oil provides an important context for the Republican Congress's push to expand NATO and to contain Russia, as outlined in the 1994 Contract with America.

Cold War Nostalgia and the Expansion of NATO

As in the thwarting of détente with North Korea, efforts by policy makers and others to secure nonproliferation treaties met resistance from conservatives and the GOP. The Republicans' Contract with America made the expansion of NATO a central tenet of the party's foreign policy agenda, along with its goal of limiting US involvement in United Nations peacekeeping actions. A 1995 *New York Times* editorial deplored the "Cold War nostalgia" of Republican legislators, who "press[ed] ahead with a mischievous piece of legislation that would undo the Clinton Administration's modest efforts to adjust U.S. national policy to post-cold war realities." The legislation, the *Times* went on, called for increased defense spending and the revival of efforts to develop the Star Wars missile defense system. Judging the proposals impractical and wasteful, the editors warned, "The legislation takes a dangerously simplistic approach to expanding NATO."[86]

In 1999, the Czech Republic, Hungary, and Poland became the first former Soviet bloc states to join NATO. Leaders of these countries had actively sought membership in NATO. After initially doubting the relevance of the alliance and the Warsaw Pact as outdated cold war creations, Havel had come around to NATO expansion as an important form of cooperation, perhaps as a consolation prize for his unfulfilled dream of robust multilateralism. Yet NATO's 1999 expansion set in motion greater expansion in 2002, when seven nations were invited to accession talks, provoking the 2006–7 first new cold war with Russia.[87]

While one group of primarily Republican congressional members followed the money into new relations with the Taliban, another group followed a different pot of money by transnationalizing US pay-to-play lobbying practices, pursuing lucrative relations with the very Russian oligarchs their colleagues sought to contain. During the late 1990s, Tom DeLay, Republican House member from Texas and future House majority leader, visited Moscow several times with the lobbyist Jack Abramoff. According to Salon, the trips "were organized by Russian oil and gas executives who wanted to lobby the US government for more foreign aid. The trips were paid for by a shadowy group in the Bahamas, associated with Abramoff and suspected of being financed by these Russian players. DeLay subsequently voted for the bill the Russians were pushing." The Russians had also given $1 million to the US Family Network, an "advocacy" group that was part of DeLay's "political money carousel" and also received $0.5 million from the Republican National Campaign Committee.[88] During an investigation in 2005, DeLay's spokesperson claimed that the main purpose of DeLay's trip to Russia from August 5 to August 11, 1997, was "to meet with religious leaders there." DeLay claimed that the US Family Network, which raised $2.5 million during its five years of existence but kept its list of donors secret, was a grassroots organization.[89]

A US Family Network associate acknowledged that "the payment was meant to influence DeLay's vote in 1998 on legislation that helped make it possible for the IMF [International Monetary Fund] to bail out the faltering Russian economy and the wealthy investors there." The pay-to-play politics had high stakes for Russians. The Russian stock market fell steeply in April and May. In June, Moscow announced that it needed $10 billion to $15 billion in new international loans. Throughout the spring, House Republican leaders opposed allocating to the IMF the funding needed for new bailouts. The IMF and its Western funders, meanwhile, pressed Moscow, as a condition of any loan, to increase taxes on major domestic oil concerns such as Gazprom, which had earlier failed to pay billions in taxes to the Russian government.

In August 1998, the Russian government devalued the ruble and defaulted on its treasury bills. DeLay, appearing on *Fox News Sunday* that same month, criticized the IMF financing bill for "trying to force Russia to raise taxes at a time when they ought to be cutting taxes in order to get a loan from the IMF. That's just outrageous," DeLay said.[90]

In the moment, DeLay got his way when the Russian legislature refused to raise taxes and the IMF approved the loan anyway. With DeLay now supporting the foreign aid bill, his spokesperson defended the lawmaker's decision and legislative priorities as "based on good policy and what is best for his constituents and the country."[91] As such transnationalizing of pay-to-play politics aligned US lawmakers and businesspeople with conflicting interests abroad, it was clear that the end of cold war containment opened a Pandora's box of shadowy and sketchy uranium and oil deals, and corruption, dynamics that resulted in DeLay's conviction on charges of illegal campaign finance activity and his resignation from Congress in 2006.

As politicians, lobbyists, and oil companies maneuvered their way across the post-Soviet landscape, as I discuss in the next sections, novelists, Hollywood screenwriters, and directors fashioned their own new world of global threats and US-Russian relations out of the unraveling of the old.

Tom Clancy and the New Enemy

Victory in the cold war brought new paranoia. Samuel Huntington's warnings of a clash of civilizations and the anarchic phantasmagoria of Robert Kaplan's influential travel writings found a popular parallel in Tom Clancy's best-selling novels. In a series of 1990s novels positing Middle Eastern and Muslim threats to the United States and rebooting older Asian enemies, Clancy was a major exponent of popular Islamophobia and racialized xenophobia. His *Sum of All Fears*, released in 1991 following the US Gulf War and debuting at number one on the *New York Times* best-seller list, imagines a conspiracy of Palestinian and East German terrorists seeking to carry out a nuclear attack on US soil. (A 2002 film adaptation starring Ben Affleck, which restages the villain as an Austrian neo-Nazi fascist, credits members of the CIA as consultants.) Clancy's 1994 *Debt of Honor* invents a Japanese enemy who, seeking revenge for defeat in World War II, has secretly developed a nuclear weapon. Some critics charged Clancy with racist depictions of Japanese people; others thought he was on to something. One praised him for issuing a clear warning "that recent downsizing in the defense establishment has so depleted our military resources that the country is vulnerable to aggression that could arise anywhere anytime."[92] *Debt of Honor* closes with a Japanese pilot's kamikaze attack on the US Capitol building, killing the US president and nearly all the cabinet. The inexperienced vice president, master CIA agent Jack Ryan, is sworn in as president.

Clancy's sequel, the 1996 *Executive Orders*, picks up the story from the cliffhanger conclusion of *Debt of Honor*. *Executive Orders* sold over 2.3 million copies. Dedicated to "Ronald Wilson Reagan, fortieth president of the United States: the man who won the war," Clancy's novel is an exercise in feverish paranoia.[93] Spinning a dense, far-fetched web of global threats, the plot features a crisis that is touched off by Iran's assassination of the leader of Iraq and its formation, with the assistance of India and China, of a United Islamic Republic that launches a full air, land, and sea attack on the United States. Taking no chances, the enemy onslaught includes a weaponized release of the Ebola virus into the United States and an attempt to kidnap President Ryan's daughter. Declaring martial law, the fictional president thwarts the kidnapping and attempts on his own life, and leads the nation to victory over the foreign attacks.

Reviewing *Executive Orders* in the *New York Times*, the antiestablishment producer, writer, and filmmaker Oliver Stone, whose antiwar feature *Platoon* was based on his combat experience as a Vietnam veteran, accused Clancy of crossing a line, from harmless popular entertainment to the transformation of imagined threats "into a political reality." For Stone, Clancy's fictional enemies suggest "the perpetual war he is fighting in his own mind against all foreign demons, be they Arabs, Chinese, the drugged veins of our own populace, or crazed Hollywood liberals." Stone feared the political influence of Clancy's best sellers: "To thrive in such a climate means precisely to help create such a climate. Create the terror, then rescue the terrorized, and you will be a hero forever. In such a way does the white knight Tom Clancy (a k a Jack Ryan) save his bride (the U.S.A.) from the clutches of the Evil Arab, Oriental, Outsider, and so on."[94] As Clancy depicted an America under siege and foreign attacks subdued and order restored by the superspy American hero, other cultural producers imagined a Russia-bashing joyride through the post-Soviet world.

Post-Soviet Geography: Loose Nukes and Elusive Oil in Hollywood

In the mid-1990s, a host of action movies and spy thrillers remapped the post-Soviet world. Here, I emphasize not the plotlines per se but a remapping of geopolitics and shifts in narrative structures that, taken together, tell a story about the aftermath of the cold war. As perestroika and glasnost gained momentum in the late 1980s, US-Soviet conflict provided a familiar narrative vessel for the James Bond franchise. In the film *The Living Daylights* (1987), Bond is captured in Czechoslovakia and tricked into attempting to aid a phony KGB defection. The hero is taken to a Soviet airbase in Afghanistan. He escapes with a female Soviet agent also betrayed by the villain, the fake defector. The two join forces with a local mujahideen leader. As part of the film's representation of the political and sexual trope of the seduction of potential defectors, Bond works with the Soviets, who rank lower in the hierarchy of enemies than the supreme villain of international crime syndicates. He defeats the Soviet criminal masquerading as a KGB defector. At the same time, he helps the mujahideen defeat the Soviets in an important battle. The film sends the reassuring message that the morally superior West is winning the cold war, and that England, though deprived of its empire, is in control. And once again, the loyal communist woman falls for Bond and the film ends in an embrace (and so on).

With glasnost, perestroika, and Mikhail Gorbachev himself capturing the global imagination by 1988, the 1989 Bond film *License to Kill* dispensed with the Soviet backdrop altogether as cocaine smugglers replaced the Soviet nemesis. But if cocaine smuggling was Soviet neutral, the film's climactic resolution in Cuba signaled a recalcitrant communist enemy while displacing recently exposed CIA drug trade onto Cubans. Indeed, in the next Bond film, *GoldenEye* (1995), the villains again get their comeuppance in Cuba, further criminalizing the "rogue" holdout.

In the six-year Bond hiatus before the release of *GoldenEye*, the Berlin Wall had come down and the Soviet Union and Yugoslavia had collapsed. The unprecedented time lapse between the consistently lucrative films reportedly resulted from legal disputes, though one has to wonder whether radically altered geopolitics muddled visions for next steps, diminishing incentives to quickly resolve contract disputes. With a new Bond, Pierce Brosnan, and a new and female M, Judi Dench, the first post-Soviet James Bond film opens by communicating to audiences its location in a post–cold war world through a visual triumphalist party that simultaneously signals new threats. Opening theme credits feature seminude women in silhouette dancing, their gyrating bodies superimposed on the heads of statues of Stalin and images of the hammer and sickle. As red flags and communist symbols hover and move through the frame, crashing and dissolving, the go-go dancers take sledgehammers to the statues, indicating—just in case audiences have slept through the past six years—that communism has fallen.

The cold war might be over, but the Bond franchise's deployment of campy sexuality returned in full force. The lyrics of the opening theme song, composed by the Irish band U2 and performed by Tina Turner, provide a hint of what is to come: "See reflections in the surface," "found his weakness," "bitter kiss will bring him to his knees," "smoke and mirrors," "honey trap." The theme song—like the film's femme fatale, Xenia Onatopp, a former Soviet fighter pilot who has joined the crime syndicate Janus and murders a Canadian naval officer while having sex with him by crushing his head with her thighs—continues the franchise's portrayals of the sexual deviancy of communism (replete with puns aimed at adolescent boys, "Onatopp" recalling *Goldfinger*'s lesbian gang leader and eventual Bond conquest, Pussy Galore).

The film presents audiences with a new villain in place of the earlier stodgy and overbearing Soviets, a post-Soviet loser bent on revenge and seething with frustrated desire. Rogue MI6 agent Alec Trevelyan had previously worked with Bond in a 1986 infiltration of a Soviet chemical weapons plant. Bond thought he had been killed, but he had disappeared with the long-range goal of exacting revenge on Britain. His parents had been Cossacks, Nazi collaborators who had been sent back to the Soviet Union after their capture by the Allies. Implausibly, as a six-year old orphan, Trevelyan had been sent to Britain and cultivated by MI6. Here, the collapse of the Soviet Union reanimates World War II–era grievances, pursued not by nation-state actors but by shadowy crime syndicates that steal a Soviet-era satellite weapon to use in an attack on London aimed at destroying global financial markets.

In a triumphalist set piece, Bond commandeers a Soviet T-55 tank for a chase scene through the streets of St. Petersburg and topples a Russian military statue, which somehow adheres to his tank, conveniently allowing him to use it to crush his opponents. The film's visual iconography of post-Soviet monuments is reproduced in the acclaimed video game adaptations of the film that followed in 1997 and were rebooted in 2010, in which the first-person shooter fights through a labyrinth of fallen Soviet-era statues in a St. Petersburg statue park.

A box office as well as critical success, *GoldenEye*, featuring Bond's triumphalist mastery over the remnants of the Soviet Union, clashed with the real-world Western pursuit of containment through control of nuclear weapons and oil. After gala openings in London and New York, Brosnan boycotted the French premiere screening in protest of French nuclear testing in the South Pacific. Infuriated French planners canceled the party, regretting that the French Navy had cooperated extensively with the film's production, lending a helicopter and granting permission for the country's Naval and Defense Ministry logos to appear on promotional materials.

Reinforcing the chaos of the post-Soviet geography, the opening theme of the franchise's next installment, *Tomorrow Never Dies* (1997), incorporates images of undulating scantily or unclad women moving through a tableau of miscellany, replete with hovering guns, ammunition, diamonds, and patterns of computer board circuitry that sometimes give visual definition to the contours of objectified nude women. The film opens at a terrorist arms bazaar on the Russian border where the British military had ordered a missile attack. After discovering nuclear warheads on a Czechoslovakian-produced L-39 Albatross jet trainer, Bond steals the plane and flies it away, averting a nuclear disaster caused by the British bombing.

The Bond movies were just a few among many to chart a post-Soviet geography. With the most elaborate map of the post-Soviet world to date, dramatizing the black market in weapons and nuclear materials, *The Peacemaker* (1997) joined *Under Siege* (1992), *Broken Arrow* (1996), and *The Rock* (1996), a cluster of films in which nuclear weapons are no longer controlled by nation-states but increasingly goods coveted by nonstate actors in an illicit trade. In *The Peacemaker*, as in *Broken Arrow*, a stolen nuclear bomb goes onto the black market. News analyses gaming out scenarios of nuclear warheads falling into the hands of rogue actors were already pervasive. Hollywood took notice, green-lighting films that mined the emotional lives of generations raised on nuclear anxieties, fallout shelters, and bomb drills.

The suspense of *The Peacemaker* hinged on the nightmare scenario of the black-market loose nuke falling into the wrong hands, highlighting the chaos of post-Soviet security. To this I would add that the film unsettled triumphalist talk about free markets by dramatizing a crisis in markets. As if to mock notions of a new world order, and the cessation of cold war hostilities, *The Peacemaker* and similar films portray an unpredictable world in which it is still a possibility that violence from unknown foreign threats might materialize on US soil.

The Peacemaker drew on familiar American narratives about the post–cold war world, with villains torn from the headlines, including Serbians, Croatians, and the usual suspects, Russians and former Soviet bloc members, all posing sinister threats to the United States and to a peaceful, civilized international order. The terrorist villain remains mostly offstage but identifies himself as a Yugoslav without a country, not Serbian, Croatian, or Muslim. His backstory endows him with moral ambiguity; he seeks vengeance against the West for tacitly enabling the sectarian violence of nationalist politicians who destroyed his home and family.

As in *The Peacemaker*, other Hollywood movies used the story of Bosnian conflicts as a dramatic backdrop for essentially American and British stories, years before filmmakers from war-torn Bosnia and Serbia had an opportunity to produce their accounts.[95] The acclaimed 1997 *Welcome to Sarajevo*, a British film directed by Michael Winterbottom and based on the book *Natasha's Story* by Michael Nicholson, centers on comradery among Western journalists in 1992 Sarajevo as ITN reporter Michael Henderson risks his life to smuggle an orphan to safety in London.

As the post-Soviet sphere provided the setting for a spate of Hollywood action thrillers and fictional terror threats, some critics felt Hollywood was adrift without its classic cold war villains. Having "stumbled through the complex mine-field of the post-Cold War moral landscape," producers, screenwriters, and directors could not figure out "who to cast as villains now that the once dastardly commies are doing nothing more evil than benignly pushing up the daisies of our collective nostalgia," wrote Christopher Goodwin in the UK's *Sunday Times*. Screenwriters "have desperately scoured the dark recesses of their and our psyches for enemies as compelling as the power-crazed psychopathic red menaces who gave James Bond and his ilk so many hours of innocent fun from the 1950s until the late 1980s. But they have come up almost empty-handed."[96]

The scenario of the blockbuster thriller *Air Force One* (1997), impatiently noted a reviewer for the *Independent*, "is still rooted in the Cold War. The terrorists are communist Russians, long out of power in Moscow, but ruthlessly ruling the former Soviet republic of Kazakhstan under the dictatorship of General Ivan Radek, until being deposed by a joint Moscow-Washington coup."[97] When US president James Marshall (Harrison Ford) leaves a celebration of the joint overthrow of the communist hard-liner in Moscow, traveling home on Air Force One with his family, the plane is hijacked by Radek loyalists who have boarded the plane disguised as journalists. The president, who has seemingly escaped in a pod but has actually hidden away, demonstrates remarkable physical and military prowess as he rescues civilian hostages on board while wresting control from the hijackers. With the damaged plane leaking fuel and unable to land, US parachutists come to the rescue with tether lines. But after getting the president's family and wounded civilians off the plane, in one of the film's many absurd plot twists, the president's trusted bodyguard, Gibbs, the last man on board with the president, turns out to be a Radek plant. In a final scuffle, the betrayed president tells him, "I trusted you with my life." "And so will the next president," replies the guard, before the president overpowers him, seizing the last transfer line before Gibbs and Air Force One crash into the Caspian Sea.

Bill Clinton confessed to seeing the movie twice. One reviewer suggested that it addressed deep American anxiety, allowing "Americans to believe that the president, while endangered, is still omnipotent."[98] Trashed by some critics as patriotic tripe, the movie nevertheless struck a raw nerve with visceral appeals to fear and power in much of its audience, a potent mix that would fuel George W. Bush's consolidation of a hawkish brand of popular cold war nostalgia in the coming years.

The 1999 James Bond film *The World Is Not Enough* gestures toward a le Carré–like exploration of fallout from the moral compromises of the West. Instead, despite its setting spanning Britain and the oil-rich Caspian region and the post-Soviet republics, it obscures the Caspian region's history and ongoing political rivalries over rights to its vast oil reserves. The film delivers the spectacles that audiences have come to expect of Bond films, with a deranged villain motivated by terror and revenge, and with its opening theme depicting women's bodies dissolving and reconstituting in and out of crude oil, the commodity driving the plot. When Electra—an heiress and daughter of British oil tycoon Sir Robert King and an Azerbaijani mother whose family had fled to England after the Soviets came to power—is kidnapped, M (Judi Dench), the head of MI6, refuses to negotiate with the kidnappers. We meet Electra in Azerbaijan, where she is seemingly overseeing the construction of a pipeline under the Caspian Sea, thus continuing her father's work and guaranteeing access to oil for Europe's benefit. In fact, she has fallen in love with her captor and seeks revenge against her father, who, along with Britain, abandoned her. What she's really doing is providing cover for a nuclear attack to blow up the pipeline. In a clash-of-civilizations twist, and a garbled reference to psychoanalytic theory, Electra is not simply exacting revenge on the land of her father; she is choosing to side with her mother's people. Of Azeri descent, Electra has come to believe that her father stole her mother's family's oil.

The Bond franchise has adeptly focused on geopolitical hot spots, only to obfuscate and trivialize their history and politics. *The World Is Not Enough* invites attention to important issues for US and global audiences—new political alliances marshaled in the quest for control of Caspian oil. To be sure, the Bond franchise can be expected to exercise its license to kill geopolitical realities in providing audiences with its escapist fantasies and pleasures. But it is worth noting the contrast between fact and fantasy. Post-Soviet political fissures in the region were not produced by ancient hatreds as the film suggests, but were in no small part created by US lobbyists and politicians, courting politicians in the Caspian region and sleeping with the enemy in Pakistan and Afghanistan to get their coveted Caspian pipeline.

The United States and the 1996 Russian Election

As US oil companies and politicians forged ahead with their designs for the Caspian region, in the months leading up to the 1996 Russian election, most observers thought Boris Yeltsin had no chance of winning. Joint Brookings Institution and Russian polling indicated that Russians overwhelmingly rejected Yeltsin's reforms, by 90 percent, predicting that the Communist Party candidate Gennady Zyuganov, who promised a return to social values such as justice, honesty, and solidarity, would be the likely winner. According to the polls, "61 percent of the Russian voters agreed with the statement that the West had the goal of weakening Russia with its economic advice."[99] Oleg Bestikov, a thirty-eight-year-old judge from Vladivostok, told a *New York Times* reporter, "I know life is no longer fair here.... This is now a country without ideals. If you know how to do it, life can be easy. If you are caught on the farm or the factory, though, you are dead."[100]

With Yeltsin's campaign faltering badly, a $10.2 billion IMF loan to Russia was announced in February, intended to carry forward the country's free market reforms.[101] The loan, reported the *Washington Post*, "is widely viewed as the West's best chance of influencing the outcome of the June election, in which Yeltsin faces a strong challenge from Communists and Nationalists."[102] Yeltsin hired three American political consultants that same month. Two of the consultants, George Gorton and Joseph Shumate, had been aides to California governor Pete Wilson, and the third, Richard Dresner, had worked for Wilson's failed presidential campaign. The consultants, paid $250,000

4.1 "Yanks to the Rescue," *Time*, July 15, 1996. Museum of Political History, St. Petersburg, 2017

each, later took credit for Yeltsin's victory, with Shumate boasting of their success in overcoming "a classic Soviet mind-set."[103] In the first round of voting, Yeltsin got 35 percent of the vote against 32 percent for Zyuganov. Yeltsin narrowly won in a runoff vote, with 53.8 percent.

Postelection commentary suggested that the consultants might have had help. Some speculated that Yeltsin had benefited from dirty tricks. A 2012 *Time* magazine exposé reported, "Powerful oligarchs in Yeltsin's circle have said on the record before that their goal was to get Yeltsin a second term by any means necessary." *Time* reported that Dmitry Medvedev, president of Russia from 2008 to 2012 (and then prime minister), told opposition leaders, "We all know that Boris Nikolaevich Yeltsin did not win in 1996."[104] Indeed, the perception that the West had stolen the election for Yeltsin would become a staple in the Russian story of humiliation by the West.[105]

Pushing Back against Western Triumphalism

With Hollywood awash in triumphalism, and Americans trumpeting their role in Yeltsin's improbable victory in the presidential elections, many Russians had had enough. Initially, they voiced nostalgia in response to disruptions in daily life and the imposition of boundaries and political identities that to many felt arbitrary. By the late 1990s, a culture of nostalgia centered on critiques of Western capitalism and longing for the material comforts of life under socialism. In July 1997, the Moscow correspondent for the UK *Sunday Times* reported that "in a trend unthinkable only two years ago, Russian state and private television channels are flooding the airwaves with communist-era films." Dating back to the 1920s, such films were scoring record ratings on prime-time television. Sergei Fiks, a buyer of foreign films for NVT, the most successful commercial channel, explained that "Russians are sick and tired of American blockbusters" and "fed up with cheap violence and sex. They've seen it a hundred times and the novelty has finally worn off."[106] For audiences, the "old films evoke a gallantry and nobility of spirit lacking in today's cut-throat world of consumerism." Such films as Vladimir Motyl's *Zhenya, Zhenechka, and Katyusha* (1967), in which a communist kills a ruthless aristocrat and rescues the latter's seven wives from a life of slavery, so popular within the Politburo that it became compulsory viewing for cosmonauts, enjoyed a revival.[107] Some resurgent films, such as the 1970s romantic comedy *Irony of Fate*, poked fun at the uniform apartments and drunken spa outings associated with the old system. But in the bleak present, explained film critic Danil Dondurei, the appeal of such characters as Katya, the main protagonist of the 1979 cult film *Moscow Doesn't Believe in Tears*, lies in their heroic overcoming of great odds. "She is hope. And that's what Russians long for above all else in today's uncertainty and misery."[108]

Nostalgia for the stability of jobs and steady incomes included a yearning for hope itself. Soviet-era cultural artifacts became the subject of a bidding war in the privatized world of the 1990s, as "sudden affection for old films led to a very post-communist commercial battle," with networks competing for the rights to over one thousand Soviet films in the archives of Moscow's state film studio. Rival media entrepreneurs in search of advertising revenues scrambled for exclusive rights to classic films, now hot properties, including some commissioned by Vladimir Lenin and epic dramas such as Sergei Eisenstein's *Ivan the Terrible* and Sergei Bondarchuk's *War and Peace*.[109]

The nostalgia for Soviet film extended to the "good values" of children's television shows, such as *Gina the Crocodile* (1969) and *Cheburaska* (1971). The opening ceremonies for the 1997 exhibit "Toys of the Soviet Childhood" at the Antique Dolls Museum featured a twelve-year-old girl "wearing a red Pioneer scarf," who talked about the cultural significance of the toys as the Soviet anthem played in the background. Sergei Romanov, owner of the collection, was committed to introducing the toys to a new generation of children. From stuffed bears and Red Army soldiers to characters from popular children's books, toys became repositories of memory, of Soviet history and values. The Young Chemist set encouraged children to pretend that they were doing pioneering research at their local scientific institute, and models of Soviet-made cars and trucks harked back to shared beliefs in science and technology as the material achievements of mass society. In the board game Pioneer, children played at building the Soviet future through such symbols of infrastructure as homes, bridges, and heavy machinery.[110]

The sense of abandonment to the vicissitudes of the market, and dependency on family resources in lieu of state-subsidized employment and housing, was experienced as a loss of the individual and sexual autonomy that women had experienced under socialism. For Katya, the hero in *Moscow Doesn't Believe in Tears*, who had arrived in Moscow from the provinces searching for a better life, marrying the man of her dreams is the icing on the cake, not the means to survival. She had already raised a child on her own and had been promoted to the top at a Moscow factory.[111]

Anthropologist Kristen R. Ghodsee argued that women of the Eastern bloc benefited from personal and sexual autonomy under socialism. She reported that a "comparative study of East and West Germans conducted after reunification in 1990 claimed that Eastern women had twice as many orgasms as Western women." Ana Durcheva, sixty-five in 2011, had lived for forty-three years under communism and "often complained that the market economy had hindered Bulgarians' ability to develop healthy amorous relationships." She explained, "Some things were bad but my life was full of romance.... After my divorce, I had my job and my salary and I didn't need a man to support me. I could do as I pleased." For Durcheva, her life as a single mother compared favorably to that of her daughter, born in the late 1970s. "All she does is work and work.... When [her husband] comes home at night she is too tired to be with [him]. But it doesn't matter, because he is tired too. They sit together in front of the television like zombies. When I was her age I had much more fun."[112]

Czech-born photographer Hana Jarhlova, in her twenties and living in Prague in 1989, described the shock of an overnight shift to a market economy, and the cost to intimate relations. "Prior to the fall of the Berlin Wall, . . . you were always physically restricted. You couldn't move around. You could go to Yugoslavia once in five years if you were lucky. But what you could control was your body. . . . The freedom of sleeping around was a way to express yourself. In other areas of life you were not free. It wasn't about exploring. Life generally sucked. But people found joy in sex and relationships."[113]

As US politics was upended by sex scandals, and American working women contended with the "second shift" of uncompensated household labor, some new to privatized post-Soviet economies declared that a harried free market life was not good for the libido.[114] "Where has all the sex gone?" queried a *Moscow Times* article. "Despite unprecedented freedom," the correspondent reported, "some Russians say sex was more abundant and exciting under the Communist regime." Vera Pagodina articulated "the cry of her generation of Muscovites," explaining, "Before, sex was the main outlet for all of our inner energy. You could feel the vibes when you walked into a party. But nowadays Russian men are just not interested, all their strength, time, and desires are channeled into their work." An organizer of art exhibits, with a good job, her own flat, and the money to travel, Pagodina "realized what a dire state her sex life was in when she had to go to America to have an affair. 'It is really ironic.'"[115]

Pagodina's sense of a crisis in social and intimate relations mirrored a crisis faced by economically vulnerable post-Soviet women as a sudden loss of jobs, housing, and health care transformed the family into a locus of privation. And while Western women did not experience a sudden rupture, women in the United States reported widespread dissatisfaction as they sought relief from the hardship of the second shift. Professional as well as working-class women found themselves facing greater economic insecurity and often increasing cross-generational care-giving responsibilities with dwindling government support.

Politicized Nostalgia: The Elections of Vladimir Putin and George W. Bush

Longing for a lost world of egalitarian and antimaterialist values could coexist with simplified longings for lost power and empire. In 1999, as IMF loans failed to stabilize the Russian economy and Yeltsin engaged in bouts of public intoxication in the last months of his presidency, Western reporters regarded burgeoning Soviet nostalgia with bemusement and worry. Richard Beeston reported in the *Australian* that "an opinion poll found that 85% of Russians regret the collapse of the Soviet Union." The sentiment was on view in themed restaurants and popular television shows and, surprisingly, a poll showing Leonid Brezhnev as the most popular leader of the twentieth century. In the West, observed Beeston, Brezhnev is known as the Soviet hard-liner who reversed Nikita Khrushchev's brief experiment in reform. "But most Russians recall the era as a time when the State provided the basics of life, such as housing and a job, and when a few luxuries were possible via the thriving black market."[116] A *Christian Science Monitor* reporter noted that "Marxist-Leninism has given way to a hodgepodge of nationalism, welfare state populism, and nostalgia for the good old days of Soviet social order and superpowerdom."[117] Looking ahead to the 1999 Ukraine elections, the *Economist* lamented that candidates "say they want to go back, more or less, to the old days. And at least three out of the seven ... say they want to recreate the Soviet Union in one guise or another—with Ukraine inside it."[118] When Yeltsin's presidency imploded in December 1999, he turned the position over to then–prime minister Vladimir Putin, who was elected president on March 26, 2000. But as Western observers vigilantly tracked post-Soviet nostalgia, they appeared oblivious to the nostalgic narratives spun out in their own midst.

Rebooting the Cold War: George W. Bush

The 1999–2000 presidential campaign of Texas governor George W. Bush codified a simple, conservative story about the cold war that had been developing for over a decade. Backed by a brain trust of cold warriors from the Nixon, Reagan, and George H. W. Bush administrations, Bush invoked cold war triumphalism, telling a crowd at the Ronald Reagan Presidential Library, "We live in the nation President Reagan restored and the world he helped to save. A world of nations reunited and tyrants humbled."[119]

Throughout his campaign, Bush punctuated cold war nostalgia with dire warnings about the unknown enemies of the present: "When I was coming up, it was a dangerous world, and you knew exactly who they were," he told a group of students in Iowa. "It was us versus them and you knew who 'them' was. Today we're not so sure who the they are, but we know they're there."[120] As Bush lamented the loss of the cold war's clarity and sense of mission, such neoconservatives as editor William Kristol, Secretary of State Donald Rumsfeld, Undersecretary of State John Bolton, and Vice President Dick Cheney had contemplated another invasion of Iraq as early as 1998. In an open letter to Clinton, the Project for the New American Century called for removing Saddam Hussein by military means. Signers included Kristol, Wolfowitz, and Francis Fukuyama (although Fukuyama later minimized his signing, stating that the Project for the New American Century "is basically just Bill Kristol and a fax machine"). Arguing that the current strategy of "containment" would not prevent the development of weapons of mass destruction in Iraq, the letter claimed that diplomacy had failed, and called on the president to "enunciate a new strategy that would secure the interests of the U.S. and our allies around the world."[121] Eager to return to government, these hawks scorned Clinton's retreat from Reagan's massive military buildup that had vanquished the Soviet enemy.[122] Bolton and Kristol in particular demanded that Clinton overthrow Saddam Hussein. It wasn't enough for them that Clinton, throughout his presidency, bombed Iraq on average once every three days under the guise of the so-called no-fly zones.[123]

Promising a more active US role in the world, Bush's campaign rhetoric foreshadowed the 2003 invasion of Iraq, as he emphasized "defend[ing] America's interests in the Persian Gulf . . . and check[ing] the contagious spread of weapons of mass destruction." He also foreshadowed a collision course with Russia. Though naming Russia as a potential partner in facing rogue nations, Bush placed "*a condition*" (my emphasis) on cooperation: "Russia must break its dangerous habit of proliferation." With Russia on the verge of war with Chechen separatists, Bush warned that "when the Russian government attacks civilians—killing women and children, leaving orphans and refugees—it can no longer expect aid from international lending institutions." The United States, Bush told the crowd at the Ronald Reagan Presidential Library, wants to "cooperate with Russia on its concern with terrorism, but that is impossible unless Moscow operates with civilized self-restraint." Warning of "a return to Russian imperialism," Bush demanded a larger US role in the former Soviet sphere, calling on the United States to "actively support the nations of the Baltics, the Caucasus and Central Asia, along with Ukraine, by promoting regional peace and economic development, and opening links to the wider world."[124]

Bush's talk of threats did not convince a majority of American voters to cast their ballot for him. Losing the popular vote to Al Gore, Bush gained the presidency when the Supreme Court ruled in his favor, ensuring his victory in the Electoral College. Following the September 11, 2001, terrorist attacks on the World Trade Center and Pentagon, Bush mobilized a potent combination of the clash-of-civilizations theory and a nostalgic revival of cold war binary thinking in the service of policies destabilizing large swaths of the globe. With the elections of Putin and Bush, both the United States and Russia entered the new millennium on a path toward the erosion of civil liberties in both societies and strong reassertions of imperial might. To appreciate the resonance of nostalgia in the United States as well as in the former Soviet sphere after 9/11, it is necessary to examine the robust production of nostalgia in public and commercial spheres.

5

Consuming Nostalgia

LAMPOONING LENIN, MARKETING MAO, AND THE GLOBAL TURN TO THE RIGHT

As Joerg Davids, an East German entrepreneur, put it, "It all started with communist condoms." Out of a job in 1992 like so many of his comrades, Davids wondered whether there was a living in marketing nostalgia for the East German state. Surmising that "East Germans didn't want heavy reminders of the past[,] ... we started with funny products like condoms. I guess you could say we were trendsetters." Along with tomes on perestroika and busts of Lenin, by 2003, Davids was selling sixty thousand T-shirts a day, emblazoned with images of such East German products as Mondo condoms, Ata pot cleanser, and portraits of the "wooly bearded socialist grandfather, Marx."[1] He may have added that his Mondo-brand condoms were all the more authentic in being internationalist as well as socialist.

If Davids brought irreverent humor to his marketing of objects or replicas associated with former communist regimes, those tangible relics were soon at the center of a weighty transnational debate over the meanings of the communist past. The Soviet Sculpture Garden at Grutas Park, in Lithuania, dubbed "Stalin World" by locals, consists of a sprawling expanse of discarded statues of Vladimir Lenin and other Soviet leaders. Two hours away, in the forests outside Vilnius, the entrepreneur Rutha Vanagaite has salvaged an underground Soviet bunker, convinced that the acres of Soviet-era monuments at Grutas Park send the wrong signal about the Soviet past. Six meters underground, with the help of a theater troupe, Vanagaite offers tourists two-to-three-hour enactments of the "real" Soviet experience. In an immersive reenactment of the ordeal of Soviet citizenship, after signing a health waiver warning of "psychological and physical abuse," one's identity is stripped before one is forced down a narrow corridor with threats of flogging. Vanagaite boasts that at least one tourist per tour faints (the record stands at five in a single tour), hastening to add that smelling salts are provided. After their ordeal, tourists are offered a shot of vodka. For those with enough cash, one can experience the corruption of the Soviet regime by playing a party bureaucrat, with a feast that includes caviar and high-end vodka.[2]

If the simulation of terror and corruption leaves one still curious about the Soviet past, a short flight from Vilnius to St. Petersburg affords the opportunity to dine in such Soviet-themed restaurants as Dachniki, or Soviet Café Kvartirka, the latter meaning "little apartment." Both re-create the decor, cuisine, and ambiance of 1960s and 1970s Russia. Soviet life, Kvartirka's owners explain, was much more than being part of a drab "military industrial complex," albeit one with "great ballet and hockey." They tout an ineffable experience of "people behind the system who lived, loved, and died like anywhere else on the planet. These people also cooked food—rich, solid, simple dishes that satisfy every taste possible." Here, nostalgia re-creates the culinary comforts of Soviet-style cosmopolitanism. On the menu are Soviet barbeque (*shaslyk*) from the Caucasus Republic, Ukrainian borsch, and Russian *pelmeny*—a meat dumpling—"all the elements come from a different Soviet Republic and are united on the table of Kvartirka customers."[3] Like the debates over the expansion of the European Union (EU) and NATO, cultural contestation over the memory of the Soviet and Eastern bloc past occurred far from the negotiating table of summit meetings.

In the United States, cultural remnants of the Eastern bloc have been displayed as gimmicky spoils of war. Just steps from the US Capitol, a toppled, decapitated statue of Lenin imported from Tevriz, Russia, was displayed near the entrance of what had been the Newseum (now defunct). Visitors encountered the statue in a corner, near a photograph depicting the removal of another Lenin statue. On the adjacent wall, visitors could view a photograph of yet another statue of a Bolshevik leader from Bucharest,

5.1 Toppled, headless statue of Lenin imported from Tevriz, Russia. Newseum, Washington, DC. By Lvova Anastasiya (Львова Анастасия, Lvova), CC BY 3.0, https://commons.wikimedia.org/w/index.php?curid=20363168

this one with a noose around the neck. At the Mandalay Bay Resort in Las Vegas, between 1999 and 2019, diners strolled past a gargantuan upright statue of a headless Lenin to dine in Russian imperial splendor at the Red Square Restaurant and Vodka Lounge. For $14, a triumphalist tippler could order such cocktails as the "Chernobyl" or "Rude Cosmo-not" martini. Those seeking a more rarified experience entered the "exclusive" Vodka Vault, where patrons "do shots off Vladimir Lenin's head" (the one missing from the statue) with a choice of two hundred varieties of top-shelf vodka, starting at $200 per shot. Operating with a sister restaurant in Atlantic City, New Jersey, the Las Vegas location closed in November 2019, two years after a gunman staying at the Mandalay Bay Hotel killed fifty-eight people.

In the two decades following the 1989 revolutions and the collapse of the Soviet Union, myriad stagings of the cold war past sprang up in museums and at tourist sites and attractions. Some enacted triumphalism with a vengeance, presenting defaced statues as trophies. Others mourned the loss of familiar tokens and touchstones of daily life or invited reflection on the complexities of the past. Whether nostalgic, celebratory, or ambivalent, constructions of the past have circled the globe in the form of objects large and small, from massive toppled statues to toy reproductions of the East

German Trabant automobile. Images, objects, and artifacts caught the wave of thriving global markets increasingly mediated by the internet.

The marketing of cold war–era objects and cultural evocations occasioned a rehashing of the era's bipolar competition over which system delivered the material and cultural benefits of the good life. Amid the era's race for supremacy in space, technology, and nuclear weapons, and its breakneck exploitation of land and labor, competing utopian visions of the good life hinged on consumerism and the material benefits of everyday life. These became tokens of the respective virtues of the competing systems. As American blue jeans and jazz and rock LPs were associated with the West, in what Eli Rubin has called "synthetic socialism," colorful plastic kitchen implements brightened flats in East Berlin.[4]

The marketing of artifacts from the past, along with reproductions of vintage objects and symbolic images, also points to a process of commodity fetishism, as objects representing unresolved social contradictions take on unexpected and often powerful social meanings. These emotionally and politically charged objects continued working their magic on hearts and minds in museum shops as well as flea market tables laden with socialist-era mementos.

With an eye to contested narratives, materialized history, and altered landscapes, this chapter focuses on constructions of the past in museum and tourist sites in Lithuania, Budapest, Prague, and Berlin. It further considers cold war–themed artifacts that circulated more widely, recontextualized and staged for global audiences in the United States and beyond.

Drawing on a rich literature on nostalgia and stagings of the past in the former Eastern bloc, I examine how Western triumphalism entered these spaces, influencing the terms by which new national narratives were constructed. I analyze explicit and implicit claims made about the cold war in a range of museum and tourist sites, including Szoborpark (Memento and Statue Park), in Budapest; and Grutas Park, outside Vilnius, Lithuania, the Stalin World theme park. All are indicative of an explosion of cold war museums, memorials, and consumer kitsch. In each case I consider the nature of its intervention in the history of the cold war. At their best, such sites do not simply offer information but also invite the visitor to engage in critical reflection about the past and its myriad representations.

The meanings of these interventions are necessarily generational and resonate differently for different people at different political and cultural moments. Nevertheless, all of these sites engage with local as well as global and national histories. Grutas Park, for example, is suffused with the anti-Russian and nationalist politics and history of Lithuania, and Szoborpark abides in a memory landscape of local narratives of nostalgia, nationalism, and the changing politics of Hungary.

Yet these sites embody more than local and national narratives. They engage global debates, including those over the expansion of NATO and membership within a broader European or global community. I focus on two pivotal moments in the staging of the cold war past. The first is the mid- to late 2000s, marked by a robust consumer nostalgia and the initial signs of a global turn to the right. At this juncture, engagements with the material culture of the past mourned the loss of the good life and attendant ideals of solidarity, even as narratives of nostalgia for a mythic past were creeping in. By the second moment, 2016–19, right-wing governments had risen to power, notably in the United States, Poland, and Hungary.

In the 2000s, many sites of cold war memory in the former Eastern bloc sought meaning in the recovery of daily lives under socialism. Others, however, disavowed socialist pasts and were framed with an eye to joining the EU and NATO. Most of my site visits took place in the mid-2000s amid controversy over the expansion of NATO and the EU. With NATO expansion underway, representations of the past not only dramatized past relations with the Soviet Union but also curated a vision of the future, with hopes to shape new relations with Europe and the United States.

Much of what media and travel guides—websites and brochures—characterize as nostalgia is more accurately described as triumphalist enactments and representations of the purported victory of the West. Such triumphalist statements posit a natural affinity with the West and emphasize victimization by the Soviets. Yet the most seemingly straightforward of such framings are never stable, and slippages in triumphalist and nostalgic claims point to unresolved pasts. I focus on the ambivalent claims of these sites, noting their uneasy relationship to wartime antifascist struggles, as well as with the Soviet past, revealing the instability of triumphalism and nostalgia caused by submerged and unresolved histories that belie victors' claims. And this instability yielded unexpected outcomes. Museums and even objects could provoke a critical nostalgia, perhaps the questioning of why positive social goods such as health care had disappeared with the less desirable aspects of the old regimes. At the same time, articulations of a triumphalist joining of the West often relied on nationalist narratives of victimization that morphed into a xenophobic chauvinism, which later turned against European and liberal institutions and values.

Narratives of victimization were critical in these turns to the right, from shifting inflections in museums to developments such as the establishment of Victims of Communism legislation by the European Parliament during 2004–9 and the Victims of Communism Foundation and Memorial in the United States. To be sure, there were victims of repressive communist regimes. The problem is that the proponents of these acts, and the subsequent uses of them, homogenize "communism" to equate all regimes and movements, from the worst oppression of Stalinism to left anti-Nazi resistance. In conflating communism and fascism, proponents of the legislation posited their own victimization by communism, which often depended on a complete denial of their nation's complicity in fascism. The Florence-based critic Jamie Mackay has parsed the historical distortions of current conflations of Nazism and communism. First, Mackay argues, "the horrors of Soviet Communism are well known." Yet while communism "has been a form of state-based oppression ... [it] has also played [a] role in a pluralistic conversation about social justice, and as such has deep links to democracy in a way that is simply not true of far-right ideologies." For Mackay, current conflations of communism and Nazism rewrite the history of World War II, glossing over the fact that Nazism was defeated by a coalition of the United States, Britain, and Soviet Union, involving "millions of Russian soldiers who died on the eastern front, not to mention the Italian, French and other partisan movements, most of which were motivated by some vision of communism." As seen in the partisan movements that were critical to Adolf Hitler's defeat, "communism has a quite different meaning in Poland than in France, in Romania than in Italy; and neither are these meanings fixed within such geographical confines. In many parts of Europe, communist ideology has long been mixed up with philosophies of anarchism, socialism, liberalism, and, so, democracy." This, for Mackay, "is the biggest differentiating point with Nazi-Fascism."[5]

The first laws in the European Parliament conflating the victims of fascism and Nazism were punctuated by a 2009 resolution calling for all member states and other European countries to implement the European Day of Remembrance for Victims of Stalinism and Nazism. And the homogenization of communism mattered in this rightward turn. These acts, often accompanied by the banning of communist symbols (Nazi symbols were already banned), undermined the critical explorations of the past that had framed many of the museums that sprang up in the 1990s and early 2000s.

This chapter concludes by considering the restaging of history in sites I visited during pronounced right-wing turns from 2015 to 2017, finally turning to a triumphalist staging of the Berlin Wall at the University of Virginia in Charlottesville, where I have taught since 2018.

The Perils of Global Kitsch: "FYI: Don't Bring Your Mao Bag to Peru"

As China was sprucing up for the 2008 Beijing Olympics and seemed to be opening up politically, Chinese Communist Revolution kitsch and Mao Zedong in particular had a retro revival with poster reproductions and sundry revolutionary insignia available in Chinese markets and online. One such site, Good Orient in Spring, featured a "Mao Series," with a Red Army shoulder bag selling for $28.99. Chairman Mao watches and clocks, ranging from $19.99 for a small alarm clock to $37.99 for a Chairman Mao rectangular clock, vied with Mao statues, a "Marching with Chairman Mao Decorative Ashtray," and, of course, Mao's Red Book.[6] Collectors and observers noted that the circulation of the material culture of revolutionary China consisted mostly of reproductions, as much of this material was destroyed by the Chinese state after Mao's death and the arrest of the Gang of Four. One collector surmised that despite the Mao boom, Mao-themed objects had not reached the popularity of images of Che Guevara, whose ubiquitous presence on T-shirts and posters increased with the 2004 release of the film *Motorcycle Diaries*, which chronicles his 1952 journey from Argentina to Peru, a trip that played a key role in his radicalization.[7]

With the increased demand for "CultRev stuff," it was a matter of time before an American celebrity strayed into controversy. In the spring of 2007, actor Cameron Diaz was in Peru filming a television show celebrating Peruvian culture. While visiting Machu Pichu, Diaz sported a Mao shoulder bag she had purchased as a tourist in China. Like those readily available on the web, the olive-green bag bore a red star and a phrase from Mao's Red Book, "Serve the People." Diaz was oblivious to the history of Peru, where nearly seventy thousand people were killed during the Maoist Shining Path insurgency in the 1980s and early 1990s. Diaz apologized for the slogan's "potentially hurtful nature" and wished Peruvians "continued healing."[8]

At the height of the circulation of "commie kitsch," what many called Diaz's "fashion faux pas" sparked a wide range of reactions. The controversy raged in venues as diverse as Russia's *Pravda*, *USA Today*, Chinese-based blogs, Christian blogs, such celebrity fashion blogs as the *Purse Blog:*

Shallow Obsessing Strongly Encouraged, and the self-avowed Maoist journal *Monkey Smashes Heaven*.[9] The *Purse Blog* noted a "huge fashion don't," asking, "Should she have known better ... or is this no big deal?"[10] To its credit, the *Purse Blog* quoted a prominent human rights lawyer, Pablo Rojas. Rojas spoke to *Pravda*, explaining, "I don't think she should have used the bag where followers of the ideology" claimed so many lives and caused so much damage.[11] Defenders of Maoist ideology were especially enraged at Diaz for her apology.[12]

Cold war nostalgia consumption seemed to peak in roughly 2007–9. Before laws banning such objects, their presentation in multiple museums sparked provocative discussions of the Eastern bloc past. At their best, these museums spurred public discussions of history in the spirit of glasnost, an open-minded quest for historical truth through political debate. As kitsch objects proliferated, even with rumblings—however faint—of the turn to the right, there were still political formations demanding a return to government-subsidized health care and education, the social safety net that had been lost with the onset of shock therapy and privatization. These voices and demands informed the engagement with material culture. In what follows, I first consider the framing of museums in Budapest, Lithuania, and Prague before turning to the kitsch commodities of these sites.

"No Irony: Memento"

Szoborpark, located on the outskirts of Budapest, opened on June 29, 1993, the second anniversary of the withdrawal of Russian troops from Hungary. After a competition run by the Budapest General Assembly, the park, also known as Memento Park, was designed by Hungarian architect Ákos Eleod.[13] The park, said Eleod, represents "a reconstituted and symbolic rendering of the atmosphere of dictatorship." Eleod described the challenge of building a "counter-propaganda park out of these propaganda statues.... This park is about Dictatorship—but in the very same moment when it becomes utterable, describable, and possible, then suddenly, this Park is about Democracy!"[14]

The entry to the park is a brick Greek facade, said to represent the emptiness of communism, an ideology with nothing behind it. Visitors cannot enter through the front gate, symbolizing the corruption of regimes in which one had to bypass official channels to find work or achieve advancement of any sort. The main road of the park is shaped in a figure eight to represent the belief that communism would exist for infinity. The park is organized

5.2 Entrance to Szoborpark, Budapest

so that if one leaves the path, one must return, reenacting the communist taboo on freedom of thought as ideological deviation. A road on the far end of the park departs from the figure eight but is a dead end, forcing the visitor back to the path of infinity.[15]

In addition to statues of Lenin, Karl Marx, and Friedrich Engels, the park displays what its promotional literature describes as an "endless parade of liberation monuments" and "endless parade of personalities in the workers' movement," such as Hungarian communists Béla Kun, Jeno Landler, and Tibor Szamuely, that formerly dotted the Budapest landscape. The city's only statue of Joseph Stalin was destroyed in the 1956 uprising, leaving only the figure's iron boots. The whereabouts of those boots are unknown. An enormous sculpture re-creation of Stalin's boots outside the main entrance to the park commemorates the uprising.[16]

The Hungarian government owns Szoborpark, but like Stalin World in Lithuania, it is entrepreneurial, self-consciously marketing itself to both tourists and Hungarians. Defining the park as a "museum" and not a "memorial," promoters of the park do not shy away from presenting the complexity of "utterly . . . ambivalent political matters" to "the touristic market." They are sensitive, however, to "hurting the feelings of those who haven't been able to forget their grievances engendered by the communist regime."[17] Unlike the over-the-top artifice of Stalin World, whose fine art exhibits and zoo animals are surrounded by barbed wire, guard towers, and Siberia-bound trains, Szoborpark's slogan promises an undiluted history: "No irony, memento."[18] Both parks have responded to criticism over what some have seen as an affront to those who suffered under authoritarian communist regimes. They argue in their defense that the parks represent a mastery over a past that shouldn't be forgotten but needn't any longer be feared. Szoborpark's contention is that visitors "know that these statues belong to the history of Hungary and it would be useless to deny them. At the same time, it is good to know that they do not deface the most beautiful squares of Budapest any longer."[19]

The removal of some of the statues from the city itself to the outlying park proved controversial. One such lightning rod was the removal of the Hungarian Fighters in the Spanish International Brigades Memorial. Many felt the resistance to Francisco Franco and the Spanish fascists had been honorable and had nothing to do with subsequent communist oppression. Others claim that the monument's socialist realism aesthetics gave such offense that it was deemed unfit for remaining in the city, regardless of the context. Similarly, the removal from the city to the park of a bust of Endre Ságvári, a Hungarian communist and ardent antifascist killed in 1944, led some to question the indiscriminate lumping of all those who had communist affiliations.

I will return to Szoborpark's fraught relation to evolving Hungarian politics later by considering the park's gift shop and comparing it with shops at Grutas Park that present objects within the context of rising Lithuanian nationalism in and around Vilnius.

Lithuanian Nationalism in Three Acts

Three different sites, Stalin World, the Soviet Bunker, and Vilnius's Museum of Genocide, document and memorialize Lithuania's Soviet past. Differences aside, all espouse—or default to—Lithuanian nationalism that downplays its multiethnic history and a deeply violent past, with the exception of Soviet repression. The theatricality of the Soviet Bunker is matched at the Soviet Sculpture Garden at Grutas Park, Lithuania, only on the first day of April, when actors dressed as Stalin and Lenin roam the grounds. Yet the park flirts with infotainment with its quirky juxtapositions. Approaching the entrance, visitors are greeted by barbed wire and guard towers. Opposite

5.3 Entrance to Grutas Park ("Stalin World"), Lithuania

the barbed-wire fence is a petting zoo with a zebra and giraffe, making the visit family friendly.

Founded and operated by the Lithuanian entrepreneur Viliumas Malinauskas, who prospered by exporting mushrooms to the West, Stalin World is a private venture, with statues leased from the state for a twenty-year period. From the discarded statues of Lenin and other Soviet Union leaders, laid low after 1991 and scattered throughout Lithuania, Malinauskas sensed a business opportunity in memory making.

The vastness of the park, inviting visitors to amble among the repurposed monumental statues, busts, and relief and group sculptures of Soviet leaders, soldiers, workers, and partisans sprouting from a leafy wooded landscape, gives the effect of walking through the ruins of a bygone civilization. The varied sculptures, marked not only by their location in the communist era but by information about the artist, amount to a primer of early Soviet modernism. The renowned Lithuanian sculptor Konstantinas Bogdanas, known for his sculptures of Lenin and, later, for his rendering of Frank Zappa commissioned by a well-heeled fan of the composer and guitarist in 1995, disputes the view that Grutas Park's display of communist-era sculptures condones the regime.[20] For Bogdanas and other Lithuanian sculptors,

Grutas Park is simply a museum of socialist realist sculpture, "an art era tarnished by political censorship but nonetheless worthy of preservation." For Bogdanas, "you can't reject those past 50 years because intelligent people made art and it's still art, whatever its flaws are." Intentionally or not, the park documents much of the substantial artistic production of the communist era.[21]

Amid the expanse of statues, a café serves an austere menu of communist-era dishes: "Nostagija Borscht," vodka and potatoes, more borscht, more vodka. An indoor museum documents life under communism, with stunning lithographs and wood-block prints representing Soviet modernism, official documents of party life, and representations of everyday life. Posters depicting international solidarity and exhibits of multiethnic dolls recall the elaborate ethno-nation-building projects of the early Soviet era.

Like the architects of Szoborpark, the founder of Grutas Park embraces controversy and differences of opinion, emphasizing such contestation in the park's publications. In the April 2002 edition of the Grutas Park *Tiesa*, Ona Voverienė, chairperson of the Lithuanian Women's League, called Grutas Museum "the height of cynicism, a mockery of the perished, political prisoners, totally innocent civilians who were murdered, tortured and deported to gulagos of Siberia." In the same edition of *Tiesa*, defenders asked, "If we decide to drown these monuments in sewage, wouldn't we resemble those who after the war used to throw away tortured and naked partisans?"[22]

Despite an avowed commitment to the liberal ideal of representing all sides in a debate, other features of the park conjure a primordial Lithuanian nationalism at cross-purposes with critical investigation of the Soviet era. Beyond the barbed-wire fence and train near the entrance, visitors encounter carved wooden statues of Lithuanian folk heroes. Also displayed at the entrance is a picture of the thirteenth-century king Mindaugas, who first brought Christianity to Lithuania. With these works, the park digresses into a heroic narrative of the Lithuanian nation, obscuring the multiethnic history of the region. Also elided is the diverse religious history of its capital city, Vilnius, once called the Jerusalem of the North and considered the heart of learning in the Yiddish-speaking world.

Vilnius's Museum of Genocide, housed in a former KGB prison, documents the 240,000 killed during the Nazi period, including 200,000 Jews and the 74,000 people who were shot or died in prison or during deportation under the Soviets. Emphasizing repression under the Soviets, the museum has no exhibits on the Holocaust. Indeed, none of the three Lithuanian sites touches on the destruction of over one hundred synagogues and Jewish institutions of learning in Vilnius. Nor do they acknowledge the shifting borders that brought Vilnius in and out of Poland with a Polish ethnic majority at the time of the Nazi and Soviet occupations. The Lithuanian Activist Front, formed after the 1940 Soviet annexation, attempted to purge remaining Jews from the country, as well as oust the Polish majority population from Vilnius during the June 1941 uprising that began the day that the Nazis invaded the Soviet Union. Before the Nazi invasion, Lithuanian Activist Front partisans killed 3,800 Jews and thousands of Poles, torching synagogues and Jewish settlements. While the Nazis did not, as the Lithuanian Activist Front had hoped, support Lithuanian independence, it is estimated that tens of thousands of Lithuanians collaborated with Nazis during World War II, when Lithuanians assisted Germans in one of the largest pogroms of the Holocaust. Three times more people were killed during the Nazi occupation than during the Soviet occupation. Yet the emphasis on Soviet domination in all three sites in Vilnius and surrounding areas minimizes the brutal collaboration with Nazis to a footnote at best. Some Lithuanians have claimed that the small Jewish Museum in Vilnius adequately represents the Holocaust and that treatment of such wartime atrocities is not needed in the other museums.[23]

Instead of confronting, let alone acknowledging, Lithuania's tortured modern history, an idealized past of Lithuanian nationalism is pitted against representations of Soviet occupation. When I visited Grutas Park in 2008, an image of King Mindaugas seemingly torn from a magazine was prominently displayed in the ticket booth window. Was it placed there by a worker or donated by a sympathetic visitor? Such acts of political memory-making are ongoing, but along with the carved wood statues of traditional folk heroes, they reinforce the park's evasion of the dark complexities of Lithuanian history.

That evasion is starkly illustrated in the story of a statue of Marija Melnikaitė (1923–43), by J. Mikėnas and architect G. Valiuskus, once displayed on Lenin Street (now D. Bukanto Street) in Zarasai from 1955 to 1992. Melnikaitė was born in Zarasai, and after the 1940 Soviet annexation of Lithuania, she joined the Communist Union of Youth. Evacuated to Russia when the Nazis invaded in 1941, she took a job as a machine tool maker in Tyumen and joined the Sixteenth Lithuanian Division of the Red Army in 1941. Sent back to her native Zarasai, she became a leader of the Komsomol underground, taking the name Ona Kuosaite. Less than two months later, Lithuanian police turned her over to Nazi authorities. Melnikaitė was ex-

5.4 Monument to Soviet Partisans and Underground Workers, J. Kalinauskas and A. Zokaitis, originally on Reformed Square, Vilnius, 1983

5.5 Marija Melnikaitė (1923–43), by J. Mikėnas and architect G. Valiuskus, once displayed on Lenin Street (now D. Bukanto Street) in Zarasai, Lithuania, from 1955 to 1992, Grutas Park, Lithuania ecuted after five days of torture. The text panel by her statue explains, "On May 23, 1943, [she] was sent to Lithuania with the detachment of saboteurs." On July 8 she was taken prisoner and "shot dead for diversion on July 13th, 1943.... After death she was awarded the name of the Hero of the Soviet Union in 1944." Plaques in the park never acknowledge communists as part of the antifascist resistance. Instead, the death of Melnikaitė is portrayed as a tragedy, due to the folly of youth. In a thinly veiled reference to the complicity of Lithuanian authorities in her capture and execution, the plaque contains the words, "We didn't want to kill the students ... we warned them ... we had no alternative."[24]

The framing of a purist Lithuanian nationalism and the consistent evasion of the history of Lithuanian collaboration with Nazis inhibit public recognition of the connection between the execution of Melnikaitė and antifascist resistance. When the Soviets annexed Lithuania in 1940, some Jews and leftists actually welcomed the government as delivering them from the collaborationist regime and willingly joined the anti-Nazi resistance.

To be sure, visitors will derive multiple interpretations from Grutas Park's presentation of the contested past. Nevertheless, the selective account of the nation's divisions, on both sides of the conflict during the global war against fascism, exemplifies the displacement of once-powerful, albeit flawed, narratives of internationalism by equally flawed nationalisms. Unlike Szoborpark in Budapest, the Political Museum in St. Petersburg (discussed later in this chapter) or the US International Spy Museum (discussed in the next chapter), it is difficult to get to Grutas Park without a car (and my return bus to Vilnius arrived two hours late). Though the park was initially popular, its attendance is now lower, but it continues to draw school groups and Lithuanians from abroad, along with assorted international tourists. For all of its complexities, Grutas Park may be read as an expression of the fierce anti-Russian politics of Lithuania, including Lithuania's campaign to keep Russia out of the EU (at a moment when that seemed a possibility). Like the US encouragement of the expansion of NATO, contravening prior agreements with Russia, the turn inward to nationalist narratives and policies has thwarted international cooperation necessary for stabilizing the post-1989 world. Perhaps the sculptors and other artists pursued a forward-looking antidote to insular nationalism in the unlikely choice of Zappa as a universal symbol of rebellion, seeking to break out of the strictures of a contested past. One departs Grutas Park wondering

5.6 "Marx despised agrarian workers and Lenin liked them even less." Museum of Communism, Prague

whether the expansive, internationalist, and antifascist commitments that animated many of these artists are being suppressed once again.

If Lithuania's Grutas Park and Szoborpark invite discussion and controversy, in Prague, the Museum of Communism, located over a McDonald's off Prague's Old Town Square, offers straightforward triumphal tales of the West. It has been criticized for emphasizing repression under communism while ignoring Czech complicity in Nazi rule. Visitors to the spare Museum of Communism, owned and operated by an American, encounter a decrepit plow and are lectured on the evils of communism: "Marx despised agrarian workers and Lenin liked them even less." A half-empty shelf of canned goods seeks to establish the shortages endemic to socialism. The museum's constant depiction of decay and misery is lightened somewhat by the dark humor of postcards in the gift shop. One in socialist modernist style features a man with a work implement thrown over his shoulder and a woman with a loaf of bread, with the caption, "Sometimes there was no toilet paper in the shops. Luckily there was not much food either." In another postcard, designed as a Soviet-era poster, a beaming woman worker

5.7 "Like their sisters in the West, they would've burnt their bras, if there were any in the shops." Gift shop, Museum of Communism, Prague

is foregrounded in a brightly colored T-shirt and overalls, providing the sole burst of color against a drab, gray-scale background that includes a group of smiling women behind her dressed in 1950s-style frocks: "Like their sisters in the west they would've burnt their bras, if there were any in the shops."[25]

Kitsch and the Banned Object

Milan Kundera has famously defined kitsch as the "absence of shit." Perhaps the power of this pithy statement is that the very description "the absence of shit" evokes the violence and deception—all the shit—necessary to present corruption and hypocrisy as ideologically pure. Indeed, objects displayed in the museum as well as those available in gift shops traffic in a murky border between innocence, parody, and fear.

The gift shop at Grutas Park (Stalin World) offers a kitschy assortment of communist paraphernalia: hot water bottles, posters, and T-shirts emblazoned with "CCCP" and the hammer and sickle; cheap busts of cosmonauts; toy models of ballistic missiles; and vintage vodka bottles, most of them reproductions devoid of parody or humor. In 2008, one could see vendors on the streets of Vilnius and at countless outdoor tables in Russian cities selling a host of similar souvenirs, including a miscellany of Soviet medals and pins, many featuring the hammer and sickle or praising achievements in industry, space exploration, or athletics; commemorative stamps; and pamphlets, their declining value as tokens of Soviet might limited to whatever price tourists are willing to pay for them. In St. Petersburg's open-air markets, for example, objects are sold on tables grouped in threes: one table of Russian holiday ornaments, one of dolls, and one of communist memorabilia that includes the pricier originals and cheaper reproductions.

I was at Grutas Park in May 2008. The following month, the Lithuanian government banned the display of the hammer and sickle and all communist symbols, with Poland following suit in 2009. As critics charged that such laws falsely equated Nazism and communism and infringed on free speech, Poland attempted to extend its ban on the symbols throughout Europe, introducing legislation that would prohibit them throughout the EU.[26] In these cases, as the banned objects are newly fetishized by the state, imbued with the potential for independent public interpretation, these commodities are peculiar things, deemed threatening and dangerous by state officials. As seen in the outdoor markets dotting the former Eastern bloc, objects that some wished to contain in the park, relics of an inherently contested past, have spilled over into the streets.

The Redstar Store, Szorborpark's gift shop, sells everything from parodic T-shirts and coffee mugs that revel in irreverence toward once-hallowed communist symbols, to relics of quotidian life under communism, including toy models of the East German Trabant, a car once ubiquitous not only in East Germany but throughout the Eastern bloc. Notions of world historical influence, for better and for worse, adhere to medals of honor from the Red Army that prominently feature such Soviet icons as Lenin and Stalin. In the irreverent mode, playing off the satirical US cartoon, a coffee mug displays *South Park*–inspired caricatures of Marx, Engels, and Stalin under a red sign with black letters: "East Park." T-shirts available in multiple colors similarly feature Marx, Engels, and Lenin under the sign "Marx Park." Such merchandise conveys the sense that the park has safely contained communism within its borders. Other items are more ambiguous. A dilapidated vintage Trabant

5.8 Gift shop, Szoborpark, Budapest

sits close to the shop; a visitor can sit in it to experience the ripped seats and insubstantial, cardboard-like interior. In one sense, the Trabant is another demonstration of communist ineptitude. Yet steps away, the shiny new toy Trabant models are available in four colors, displayed next to Communist Party and Red Army memorabilia and red-star coffee mugs. The mugs replicate the Starbucks logo but replace the green-colored design with red and an image of Lenin. On the opposite side, bold letters declare, "I'm from the old School: I like my coffee BLACK and my communism RED." Do such objects, in keeping with the objectives of the park's organizers, assure the observer and purchaser that the past is past? Or does this complex assortment of souvenirs elicit longings for the familiar and predictable in an often frighteningly unpredictable world? In 2007, when rising health care, food, and housing costs resulted in a rally of thousands in Budapest demanding the return of social welfare programs of the old regime, is it possible that these objects might have signified unresolved social contradictions? Perhaps Marx's significance had not been contained in the park after all, but was instead haunting the place, conspiring with the miniature Trabies and Lenin mugs in their secret social life of things, mischievously upending any comfortable or settled sense of history. Soon after, Viktor Orbán, who was elected prime minister in 2010, tapped into widespread structural economic uncertainty and Hungarians' feelings of having been the losers in the global economy. Orbán rejected citizens' demands for a return of social protections. He increasingly espoused xenophobic nationalism.

Szoborpark exists within a range of engagements with Hungary's communist past. The tone struck by my Hammer and Sickle walking tour offered by a private tourism company was an even-handed recovery of the texture of everyday life, rather than a grim preoccupation with deprivation, unfreedom, and terror. "Socialism was a great idea that did not work very well," our guide told us. Discussions of the history of Hungary were interspersed with conversations about contemporary Hungary. Most guides were university students or postgraduates. They loved their jobs, but they were more concerned with finding employment that had health care. Hungary joined the EU in 2004, and the socialist-led coalition of Prime Minister Ferenc Gyurcsany had been returned to power in 2006. Widespread protests broke out later when Gyurcsany, part of the elite that had benefited handsomely from the privatization of the 1990s, admitted that he had lied about the health of the economy during the election. At that point, neoliberal policies were challenged by the left and the right. Not many foresaw the sharp turn to the right that followed the 2008 global financial crisis. Orbán, once a dissident who stood for political freedoms during the transition, consolidated authoritarian rule after he returned to power. He systematically dismantled Hungary's democracy.[27]

History in the Marxim Café

Figure 5.9, a takeoff on a classic portrait of Lenin, is from Marxim Café (an ironic portmanteau of Marx and Maxim, as in Gorky) in Budapest, an underground pizza joint frequented largely by students and young people in their twenties, where visitors, seated in booths, peering around red poles and through a haze of cigarette smoke, can view gleefully irreverent posters and artwork knocking once-revered symbols of the past off their pedestal. The menu offers many different pizzas, all identified with jokey names referencing the Soviet past: "The Gulag," "Pre-election Promises," Here, Lenin is pictured in red polka-dot undershorts in a mural that directs guests to

5.9 Vladimir Lenin, Marxim Café, Budapest

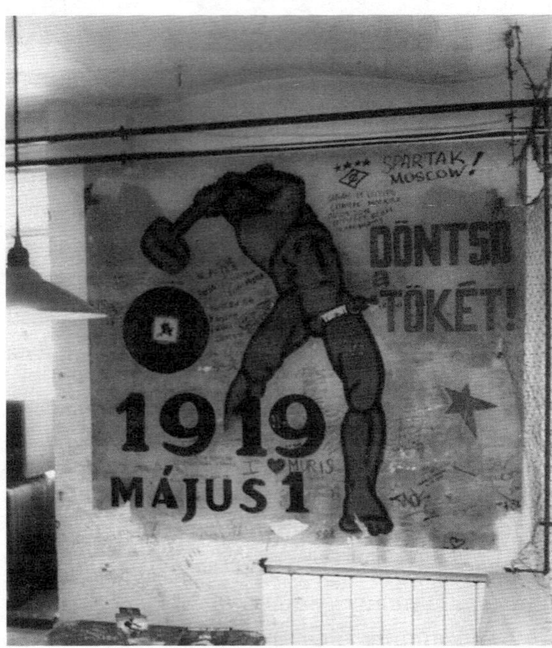

5.10 Poster with graffiti, Marxim Café, Budapest

the toilet. Throughout, graffiti (by customers) adorns both old communist posters and their satirical makeovers, as in figure 5.10's sexualized parody of the heroic socialist male worker.

For all of its irreverence, the ambience of the café, including a ceiling installation that suspends red flags within barbed wire, does not represent a simple, earnest anticommunism. The mood is post-Soviet nostalgia, packaged for young people, tempered by self-aware irony. In 2008, fifteen years after its 1993 opening, it was filled with students and intellectuals. One imagines that the spirit of the place has not strayed far from gatherings of 1980s socialist dissidents and reformers throughout the Eastern bloc, who dreamed of liberation *not* as capitalism but as a politically reformed democratic socialism. The café seems to provide a setting for young people to have intellectual discussions and reflect on the present and future, surrounded by representations of the past. At Café Marxim, you can have your "Pizza à la Kremlin" at a safe distance from authoritarian or dictatorial politics.

Another way of considering the ambivalent playfulness at work in Café Marxim's graffiti and menus or the objects on display and for purchase at cold war theme sites is to consider the cold war fetish object as a transitional object, and to consider these objects on a continuum of unresolved relations. The anthropologist Serguei A. Oushakine has used British psychotherapist Donald Winnicott's elaboration of Anna Freud's work on transitional objects to analyze mourning and loss in post-Soviet Siberia. At particular moments of life, transitional objects provide a critical defense against anxiety, as one sees in the case of a child's security blanket or toy. For Winnicott, it is not the everyday fetishism that is important, but the ability of the transitional object to provide a secure link to the outside, allowing the individual to "map safe trajectories of possible relations beyond the realm of the imaginary. Successful navigation of the ... transition depends on an experience that leads to trust." But in the absence of such confidence, "the transitional object becomes institutionalized as a place of permanent escape." Oushakine's application of psychoanalytic theory to the *politics* of loss is critical here. In the post–cold war context, I would argue that for many, these objects and presentations of the past can enable a coming to terms with sudden rupture, loss, and dislocation.[28] Tangible objects such as keychains of old German Democratic Republic (GDR) traffic light symbols or a Lenin mug can help forge new meanings and new relationships between past, present, and future. We may be drawn to these objects precisely because they unsettle us.

Trabi Safaris and Bond Bars: Spectacle and Rupture in Post-reunification Berlin

If projects of commemoration offer up fetish, kitsch, and nostalgia, much of East German *ostalgie* has been unambivalent in expressing longing for elements of the GDR and a desire to restore East German products that rapidly disappeared after the fall of the Berlin Wall.[29] Perhaps the best-known expression of *ostalgie* is the internationally acclaimed 2003 film *Good Bye, Lenin!* Also the subject of art exhibits and other cultural commentary, *ostalgie* emerged in the difficult times following reunification, and "to many of the former GDR's 17 million citizens, *ostalgie* is more than a fashion trend." It expresses their frustration at the economic uncertainty and patronizing attitude of the West.[30]

Berlin has been an especially fertile site for cultural expressions of *ostalgie*, from the DDR [Deutsche Demokratische Republik] Museum off Alexanderplatz to GDR-themed hotels and restaurants, as well as such consumer experiences as the Trabi Safari, where one can tool around the city behind the wheel of an authentic "little car made out of fiberglass and pressed cotton."[31] (To avoid traffic, I reserved my bright-red Trabi for the earliest available slot on a Sunday morning while most of Berlin slept. Our little caravan had only to contend with temporal nostalgia competition in the form of horse-drawn carriages. I was able to avoid accidents when my vehicle frequently stalled out.) The scholar Daphne Berdahl has argued that attempts to belittle *ostalgie* seem to be aligned with a general disparagement of East German discontent toward the failures of reunification.[32] I will return to this critique, but before turning to expressions of *ostalgie* and the contentious debates about it, it is necessary to recall the history of the changing pre- and postreunification built environments, symbolizing the West's presence in Berlin.

In the era of divided Berlin, before and after the building of the wall, the US and NATO presence structured the landscape in ways that went far beyond Checkpoint Charlie and the presence of troops. From 1959, following the death of US secretary of state John Foster Dulles, a central Berlin road was renamed John-Foster-Dulles-Allee. Roughly parallel to the border with the East, the road traced a promontory overlooking the wall, which was constructed in 1961. The Dulles road, the location of the imposing modernist House of World Culture, loomed over East Berlin as a symbol of the West.

5.11 Trabi Safari

5.12 Trabi Safari

On June 23, 1963, two years after the building of the Berlin Wall, President John F. Kennedy famously declared, "Ich bin ein Berliner" (I am a Berliner).[33] Kennedy's iconic statement of the West's intent to reclaim Berlin was unrivaled until President Ronald Reagan's 1987 exhortation at the site, "Mr. Gorbachev, tear down this wall." In 2006, the John F. Kennedy Museum opened in a space near the east side of the Brandenburg Gate, just across from the US embassy and the DZ Bank building designed by Frank Gehry, all jostling with an array of commanding banking structures reclaiming East Germany for capitalism. Forced by rising rents out of its original location, the John F. Kennedy Museum moved six years later to larger and equally symbolic quarters in a former Jewish girls' school on Auguststraße, in a neighborhood long considered the cultural center of Berlin.

Westalgie

Westalgie kitsch pales in comparison to *ostalgie*'s wistful souvenirs, including mini-Trabant reproductions, brightly colored plastic kitchen tools, and *Ampelmännchen*—little traffic-light men—key chains and T-shirts representing the campaign to save the popular traffic light of the GDR. The Checkpoint Charlie Museum documents attempts to escape East Berlin, from the rare successes to the estimated 245 killed at the wall or by suicide, or found lifeless in the river. Opening in 1962, it came to embrace a human rights ethos, featuring the art of Keith Haring in its permanent collection and placing the struggle against East German repression in a universal continuum of global freedom movements, including the US civil rights movement and the South African antiapartheid struggle. In the image of broader human rights campaigns of the 1970s, the museum aspires to transcend the politics of the cold war's bloc mentality. Its universal humanism hurtles forward, seeing no need to reconcile jarring geopolitical juxtapositions. The museum celebrates Nelson Mandela as well as Reagan, seemingly heedless of the contradiction between its endorsement of the antiapartheid movement and its celebration of Reagan's 1987 "tear down this wall" speech, which was delivered at a moment when Reagan unequivocally supported the apartheid regime in South Africa.

At the old checkpoint, tourists can pass through with reproductions of vintage passports, have them stamped by guards in their respective retro uniforms, and then pause for a photo with the reenactors. Souvenir shops offer toy Trabis and Ushanka military hats with Soviet insignia, and a JFK coffee mug featuring his famous slogan, along with "genuine original"

5.13 Bond Bar and Restaurant, Berlin

5.14 Bond Bar and Restaurant, Berlin

pocket-size chunks of the Berlin Wall. Headlong commercialization has triggered outrage in some visitors at what they view as the trivialization of the danger and suffering of the cold war. Vernon Pike, a former US Army colonel and commander of Checkpoint Charlie, called the site "an unacceptable spectacle."[34] It is not difficult to sympathize with Pike. With the 2010 grand opening of a McDonald's joining an earlier Starbucks decorated with vintage 1970s photos of the checkpoint, the site not only trivializes its history; its ubiquitous tourist stalls and traps (easily the most expensive Starbucks in Berlin) mark the landscape with capitalist triumph.

At times, a defensive *westalgie* appears as a jealous response to the melancholy allure of *ostalgie*. Tourists can drive through West Berlin in Volkswagen Beetles as an alternative to the Trabi drive through East Berlin. Bond Bar and Restaurant opened in 2011, just a block off Kurfürstendamm, West Berlin's upscale shopping street in Charlottenburg. The decor is replete with Bond clichés—the martini (shaken not stirred) and projections of scantily clad, dancing Bond girls in lieu of wall art—and its low-slung lounge seats with pillows evoke the Istanbul of *From Russia with Love* (1962). The owners asserted that unlike East Berlin, their western neighborhood had until recently lacked recognition as a happening place with glamor and fun. The restaurant closed after four years, its hoary high concept failing, perhaps, to make the West as attractive a destination as the free-wheeling East.

In 2014, a twenty-fifth anniversary exhibition, *The Island Looking for the Mainland*, opened in Berlin, a self-described "wistful look back at West Berlin's days as 'the showcase of capitalism.'"[35] In the early 1950s, American officials were preoccupied with West Berlin's survival as an island of capitalist democracy surrounded by communism. Mayor Willy Brandt leveraged US aid to rebuild Berlin in this vision of an "Athens on the Spree, a city state that embodied democracy but was equally admired for its prowess and culture."[36] West Berlin was a unique capitalist haven with no military draft, massive subsidies for excellent free education, and a substantial investment in the arts and culture that attracted bohemians. Although an unabashed celebration of cold war West Berlin, the exhibit pushes back, if inadvertently, against the normalization of Western capitalism in contrast to a backward East. The West's "freedom" is unmasked as ideological, a cold war construct.

The exhibit represents a fascinating response to older institutions such as Berlin's DDR Museum, which focuses on material culture and daily life in the GDR, documenting the Eastern bloc project of creating the good life for the masses—and its competition with the West. Indeed, the ways in which

Western and Eastern utopian dreams of mass society developed together and unraveled together is evident in debates on *ostalgie*. My intention is *not* to intervene in the rich literature and debates among scholars about Germany and the Eastern bloc but rather to examine global fascination with the phenomenon as well as triumphalist Western critiques of *ostalgie*, such as those found in reactions to the film *Good Bye, Lenin!*[37]

The impulse to explore the complexities of daily life in socialist countries animates *Good Bye, Lenin!* Set in 1989, the film tells the story of a young man, Alex, who attempts to re-create an East German social environment to protect his seemingly GDR-loyal mother, who had fallen into a coma before the fall of the wall. Fearing that the shock of political change would kill her, Alex scrambles to rid the apartment of his sister's Western decorations and appliances, and obtain GDR consumer goods and foodstuffs, especially the Spreewald pickles loved by his mother but no longer on the shelves. The film was a smash hit in Germany, winning nine prizes at the 2003 German Film Awards.[38] But *Good Bye, Lenin!* also received sharp criticism for offering, according to some critics, a feel-good nostalgia that minimized the terror and suffering experienced by so many in the former GDR. Such criticism resurfaced with the 2006 release of *The Lives of Others*, a bleak depiction of the East German Stasi intelligence service and the human destruction left in its wake. This is a misplaced debate. A tragicomedy, *Good Bye, Lenin!* has its lighter moments, as it spoofs the GDR while also depicting the pleasures—however limited—of everyday life. The film also offers an important meditation on hegemony and how people come to be invested in an order that they cannot fully believe in. We learn later that it is Alex, not his mother, who has the more limited view, in that Alex's mother, Christiane, is not the devout communist that Alex believes her to be. Alex had grown up believing that his father had left the family for a woman in the West. He learns that his father had fled with a careful plan for Christiane and the children to follow, a plan Christiane was not able carry through, not because of loyalty to the state but because she was terrified of the repercussions should they be caught. She would lose her children. This trauma was the source of her recurrent illnesses that Alex had never understood. Hence, as the philosopher Slavoj Žižek has argued, the state presented in *Good Bye, Lenin!* is hardly benign; it is so powerful and terrifying as to induce madness.[39]

The film's approach to hegemony does not mitigate its insight into the disorienting effect of the sudden collapse of the GDR. The actress Katrin Sass, who plays Christiane in the film, recalled her own experience after the fall of the wall, saying she was "on the edge of the abyss," ending up in an alcoholism treatment program after her career collapsed with reunification.[40] For Sass, the role of a woman awakening from a coma and eventually, knowingly witnessing her son's frantic attempts to re-create the GDR becomes an allegory for the slow adjustment of many Germans to reunification. As director Wolfgang Becker put it, "People lived under this system for 30 or 40 years. They needed time to say goodbye."[41]

Good Bye, Lenin! also explores women's subjectivity, whereas *The Lives of Others* trivializes the main female character as a suffering victim lacking the emotional depth seen in the male characters. The complexity of women's subjectivity is also documented in interviews with East German women. Highly educated women who had previously held positions as university professors and other highly skilled positions fared particularly badly. With their own institutions of employment collapsing and Western institutions refusing to recognize their credentials, many ended up cobbling together new lives with far less pay and prestige in clerical positions as travel agents and similar occupations.[42]

One of the most tangible signs of *ostalgie*'s vigor is the comeback of East German companies and the return of East German consumer products to the shelves to the stores. An emporium located beneath the Berlin-Alexanderplatz railway station in the heart of old East Berlin, 99% *Ostprodukte*, offers East German food and household products along with souvenirs with GDR themes. *Ossie* products are offered through the supermarket chain Netto and through such websites as Mondosarts, named for the type of condom sold in the GDR.[43] Another website, Osthits, marketed canned Trabant exhaust fumes. Thorsten Jahn sold cans of "Trabi Scent" for 3.98 euros in 2005. Detailing the process of holding a piece of cotton against the exhaust pipe of a Trabant, then placing the cloth into cans, Jahn explained, "The smell is something very special and scarce nowadays." Even though the car was notorious for its polluting fumes, Jahn insisted that "it doesn't make people sick," as the cotton filters out toxic particles. Jahn dismissed any suggestion that his Trabi scent was an undignified gimmick for fleecing consumers: "It is political, there are real differences in Germany, and people want to remember the old times."[44]

The commodity kitsch phase of *ostalgie* peaked in the late 2000s, but global patterns of dependence on the tourist economy in deindustrialized areas, along with global fascination with *ostalgie*, promises a continuing market. An ambitious attempt to create a communist-era theme park in Tutow, in the former GDR, acknowledged "a desperate attempt to create jobs and income" in a town blighted by over a decade of unemployment, with over

60 percent of the town's fewer than two thousand residents out of work and young people leaving for the West every day.[45] While the full scope of the project did not come to fruition, the town now has a GDR museum.

A GDR-themed hotel in East Berlin preserves the notion of the austerity and resourcefulness of the former East, cast as a virtue against the gaudy excess and inequality of the West. According to the *Economist*, one thirty-something *Ossie* "can at once speak excitedly about her freedom to travel and rue the passing of East German austerity, in which scarce consumer goods were more valued and less wasted. She points to practices from the GDR now being revived, such as '*Polikliniks*' (one-stop health clinics that share resources), workplace kindergartens and recycling programs modeled on GDR schemes."[46]

For some, these enterprises founded in *ostalgie* offer hope that Germans from the former East and West can meet current economic and societal challenges by drawing on each other's experiences. And if questions of winners and losers in Germany and the rest of Europe remain unresolved, the ardor with which Germans, regardless of ideology, pursued their inquiries into the past has helped make German chancellor Angela Merkel the recognized global leader of liberal democracy.

From History as Inquiry to the Theater of the Absurd

As seen in the acclaim for *Good Bye, Lenin!*, public fascination with *ostalgie* extended globally; the Wende Museum in Los Angeles, opened in 2002, is dedicated to the preservation of East German material culture, and a critically acclaimed exhibition, *Ostalgia*, was held at the New Museum in New York City in 2011.

The cosmopolitan ethos of the Wende Museum can also be seen at the European Solidarity Centre in Gdansk, Poland, a museum, library, and research center that opened in 2014 by the Gdansk shipyards. Built partly with EU funds, it has become a target of Polish nationalists who accuse the museum of inauthenticity. Its expansive, worldly vision—evident in its asymmetrical postmodern architectural design and its exhibits honoring Mandela and probing linkages between Solidarity and other democratic freedom movements—makes it a frequent target of President Andrzej Duda and his Law and Justice Party. A stone's throw away from the European Solidarity Centre, a right-wing nationalist group runs a rival museum, declaring themselves the authentic representatives of the Solidarity movement.[47]

5.15 European Solidarity Centre, Gdansk

5.16 Alternate museum challenging the cosmopolitan orientation of the European Solidarity Centre, Gdansk

Lech Walesa, the world-renowned dissident leader of the Solidarity movement, who, following the defeat of the communist regime, served as Poland's president, has been attacked by the right, accused of collaborating with communists and enabling elites in the postcommunist government to profit handsomely from privatization. As with the internationalist Solidarity Museum, Walesa has been subjected to parochial right-wing slanders equating socialism of any sort with the worst abuses of communist regimes and excoriating the global cosmopolitanism (a term with clear anti-Semitic overtones) of wealthy elites who flourished amid growing economic inequality. Walesa's triumphalist anticommunism may have hurt his own cause. He took to bragging that he backed Mikhail Gorbachev's reforms because he knew all along that the Soviet Union would not survive them. Walesa's self-serving account of how he beat communism played into the hands of the nationalist right. As neoliberalism's reengineering of the global economy left millions unprotected, right-wing politicians' propensity for equating social welfare policies with the purported absolute evil of communism made their religious-based nationalism an attractive political alternative for many in Poland.

Historians and journalists have analyzed Duda's concerted effort to contort public history and memory for nationalist ends that had begun with his election in 2015. He convened a conference of leaders of the nation's museums and cultural institutions in November, putting the force of the state behind his blunt injunction that these institutions galvanize Polish nationalism and discard narratives that shamed Poland. In February 2018, Duda signed into law a bill making it a criminal offense, "punishable for up to three years in prison, for anyone to implicate Poland, or the Polish people in the Crimes of the German Third Reich."[48] Observers have noted that the Polish government is driven by a "feeling of grievance, a sense that the wider world doesn't truly understand the suffering of the Polish people, but also a sense that the Holocaust—in which three million Polish Jews were slaughtered on Polish soil—was giving Poland a bad name."[49] Banning public discussion of the Holocaust, and filling the vacuum of silence with the narrative claiming that Polish people were victims of communism, was a signal expression of this sense of grievance.

Gdansk, where war first broke out in Europe when Germans attacked Poland on September 1, 1939, is also the site of what was intended to be an ambitious World War II museum backed by cutting-edge scholarship and presenting, as one might expect, a continuum of personal, local, and global historical perspectives. "After the Museum of the Second World War was completed—but before it had opened to the public—Law and Justice government officials deemed it too pacifistic and 'not Polish enough,' demanding changes to make it more singularly patriotic." The original director, Pawel Machcewicz, was forced out, and many of the original historians and curators were also fired or left. When the museum opened in March 2017, several exhibits had been modified to reflect official preferences.[50]

Western triumphalism and a chauvinistic anticommunism fueled the rise of the right in other settings. The builders of Nowa Huta, a district in Kraków, built as a shrine to Stalinist central planning, intended its steel mills and Renaissance-style apartments as a model of modernity and the good life. In 2004, the imprint of Western triumphalism was overlaid on an essentially unchanged built environment. Nowa Huta's Central Square was renamed Plac Centralny im. Ronalda Reagana (Ronald Reagan Central Square), an act that sparked significant local protest. To some, the action reaffirmed Poland's geopolitical subservience to the United States. One resident complained, "We always have to kiss Americans' asses."[51] The ceremonial renaming of a former Soviet public space after Reagan was an audacious rewriting of history. Perhaps someone thought that Reagan's unyielding anticommunism made him a fitting choice to exorcise the memory of the Stalinist past. Perhaps they thought the town might benefit from US aid. But the fit was otherwise awkward. Reagan was a union buster, and local residents of a steel town might bristle at seeing his name emblazoned in the town square. Hadn't Polish trade unions played a central, decisive role in bringing down the repressive communist state? As Katherine Lebow has shown, in Kraków as in Gdansk, Stalinism was not simply an ideology, but included practices that could be creatively reinterpreted.[52]

Nowa Huta apartments are gradually turning over from the pensioners who have been longtime residents to younger families who value the affordable space proximate to the city's center. Pensioners frequent the inexpensive communist-era canteens, perhaps out of necessity (prices so low one couldn't cook like this at home), or perhaps defiantly partaking in a communal ritual.

As part of the Crazy Communist tour, I visit Nowa Huta's Restauracja Stylowa. Preserving the elegant if now faded decor of the communist era—red table runners over impeccable white tablecloths and a prominent iron-cast Lenin—may strike a visitor as a benign tourist gimmick, but any symbol of the past in contemporary Poland is fraught. With one of its corner windows drawing customers in with a classic full-body photograph of Lenin, the restaurant was closed by city inspectors on the pretext that it had violated alcohol license rules. It was later allowed to reopen with

5.17 Ronald Reagan Central Square, Nowa Huta, Kraków, Poland

5. 18 Nowa Huta's Restauracja Stylowa, Kraków, Poland

the stipulation that the Lenin poster be reduced in size (showing just his head) in an upper pane of the window. Busts and sculptures of Lenin were once ubiquitous, but with official efforts to diminish his place in history, the head at the top of the window, like many Lenin statues popular in the West, has been decapitated.

In Nowa Huta, just beyond the central square and on a street with a couple of Trabis serving as exhibits on the Crazy Communist tour, one can't miss a billboard advertisement for ArcelorMittal. The world's largest multinational steel manufacturing corporation, with steelmaking operations in nineteen countries and on four continents, took over the plant once known as Vladimir Lenin Steelworks, from its opening in 1954 until 1990. Lebow has unpacked the irony of how, in a Stalin-planned town, workers once took the ideals of workers' collectives and turned them against the repressive communist state, an important precursor to the Solidarity movement.[53] The looming presence of ArcelorMittal marks the perilous journey from the resistance of the workers' collectives, to workers who are nowadays at the mercy of the vicissitudes of the international market. The Kraków steel plant ceased production in November 2019 because of a plunge in global oil prices and weak demand. Plans to reopen in March 2020 were delayed by the COVID-19 pandemic, and the plant was permanently closed in October 2020.

Though the steelworkers of Nowa Huta are examples of the vulnerability of workers to neoliberal economic globalization, they had been privileged compared with most in Poland. In "Poland's right turn" during the early 1990s, Marta Tycner explains, the country's industrial and financial sectors were rapidly privatized, falling into the hands of foreign investors. Workers not on permanent contracts are denied a minimum wage. Nearly half of the workforce have short-term contracts or are self-employed, without pensions, sick leave, maternity leave, or access to unemployment benefits. There is no right to join trade unions, and universal childcare benefits are nonexistent. The state has withdrawn from sectors that it deems unprofitable, such as hospitals and nurseries, railway transportation networks, and post offices, which are vanishing throughout the country.[54]

Tycner notes that the groups most disadvantaged by this situation, those living in the provinces, "and the 20- and 30-somethings who are being offered worse and worse employment conditions," have formed the backbone of Poland's Law and Justice Party.[55]

Yugo-nostalgia

Former Yugoslavs' memories of what they saw as the good life have produced a pronounced Yugo-nostalgia, a term that has come to describe the widespread sense of loss and trauma that accompanied the catastrophic breakup of that nation.[56] Such memories of material stability, national cohesion across ethnic and religious differences, and an embrace of international solidarity as inherent in the Yugoslav presence on the world stage have produced an especially rich field of critical nostalgia.

A 2016 Gallup Poll found that 81 percent of those polled in Serbia and 77 percent of those polled in Bosnia-Herzegovina believed that the breakup of Yugoslavia had harmed their country. Citizens of Montenegro and Macedonia, by majorities of 65 percent and 61 percent, respectively, agreed that the dissolution brought harm. Slovenians were relatively split, with 45 percent believing the breakup had harmed the country and 41 percent believing it had helped. Only citizens of Croatia and Kosovo registered the majority belief that the breakup had helped their country.[57]

Former Yugoslavs in Bosnia fondly recalled consumer goods that had defined the fabric of daily life and leisure: "'Cockta,' the Yugoslav version of Coca-Cola, 'Kiki' candies, or cheap 'Jugoplastika' flip-flops stuffed in a backpack and a ticket for a weekend train to the Adriatic coast." Above all, journalism professor Besim Spahic told Radio Free Europe, Bosnians "miss the stability and harmony of interethnic relations." He continued, "In [Josip Broz] Tito's Yugoslavia, Bosnia was defined as a common state of Serbs, Croats, and Muslims. The focus was on shared values between different ethnic groups. Now the differences are highlighted and blown out of proportion."[58]

The Yugoslavian emphasis on brotherhood and unity not only applied within the country but also resonated with an expansive anti-imperialist internationalism that brought Yugoslavia great prestige as a leader among nonaligned nations and founder of the nonaligned movement at the Belgrade conference in 1961.

In November 2005, the first monument to martial arts expert and film star Bruce Lee was unveiled in Mostar, Bosnia and Herzegovina (a second monument to Lee was dedicated in Hong Kong a day later). Honoring Lee as a symbol of "loyalty, skill, justice, and friendship," the organizers envisioned the life-size bronze statue as a rebuke to the typical use of public monuments to enshrine the country's destructive nationalisms. In a city nearly destroyed by the 1992–93 war that devastated the fifteenth- and sixteenth-century

5.19 Bruce Lee mural in Hong Kong, May 2013. Courtesy of Colleen Woods

Bosniak (Bosnian Muslim) west side of the city, it mattered to the monument's planners that Lee was neither Serb, nor Croatian, nor Muslim, and their design consciously placed Lee's statue facing north, a renunciation of the east-west divide in a city that had been riven by such identities and boundaries. The organizers praised Lee's transnational popularity as an icon of anti-imperialism in the 1970s, embodying underdog characters fighting European and Asian colonizers alike. Lee's influence had truly been universal, reminding them of the hope of their childhood. For young audiences across the globe, from Mostar to Los Angeles, Zagreb, Bombay, and Hong Kong, Lee symbolized a liberated future free from poverty and political repression, and from the armed conflict that raged through the Asian, African, and Central American continents during the cold war.[59]

Staging the Berlin Wall: Affinity, Commerce, and Triumphalism

As suggested by the Mostar monument to Lee, there is nothing inherently problematic about repurposing symbols from one context for use in another. As in Mostar, symbols are creatively employed as part of a cosmopolitan politics of affinity and solidarity. The Berlin Wall, from its tangible fragments to its symbolic appeal, has been displayed and invoked in the service of countless local, national, and even personal political projects.

In *A Wall of Our Own*, Paul Farber—historian and cofounder of the Philadelphia-based public arts and history organization Monument Lab—elegantly explores the ways African American, Japanese American, and Jewish American writers, architects, and photographers have critically engaged the wall. Robert Kennedy declared in Berlin that "we have a wall of our own," referring to US racial segregation as a barrier that undermined national aspirations to freedom. Other Americans, including the photographer Leonard Freed, architect Shinkichi Tajiri, and writers and activists Angela Davis and Audre Lorde, took the Berlin Wall as a point of departure from which to interrogate oppression and to promote ideals of solidarity.[60]

Since its dismantling in 1989, the wall's symbolic power persists, as its remnants, from large panels to small pieces, have been bought and sold, yet another global commodity. As what was left of the wall entered the capitalist marketplace, various chunks became the object of property rights lawsuits from California to Japan, including a dispute in San Bernardino that one of its parties described as a "High-Noon standoff."[61] Wall fragments are displayed at the Reagan Ranch Center. Five slabs relocated to Uijeongbu, South Korea (twenty miles from the border with North Korea), symbolize hopes of reunification. Others display the wall for statements about their own victimization.[62]

Marking Albania's turn to the West after joining NATO and applying for EU membership in 2009, a 2.6-ton graffiti-covered segment of the wall was dedicated in Tirana in March 2013 to commemorate victims of the communist regime. The wall fragment, a gift from the City of Berlin, was displayed alongside a mushroom-shaped bunker and concrete pillars from a notorious labor camp where many lost their lives. The memorial was placed at the entrance of what had formerly been an exclusive neighborhood where the communist elite had lived. With Albania still under scrutiny for compliance with EU regulations, the wall joined the bunker's condemnation of Albania's communist leadership, putting Albania's communist past to rest.[63] None would dispute the crimes of Albania's particularly repressive communist past, but claiming affinity with Europe based on shared victimization is shaky ground on which to build a democracy.

On the twenty-fifth anniversary of the wall's destruction, multiple events and media commentary recontextualized the wall in relation to contemporary social justice projects.[64] But as seen in the fragments of the wall once displayed in the now defunct Newseum at Fifth and Pennsylvania Ave in Washington, DC, the wall has often been presented as a triumphalist trophy.

"Kings of Freedom" and the Freedom to Frack

The 2014 installation of four concrete panels from the Berlin Wall at the University of Virginia in Charlottesville marked a libertarian staging of the wall. With its remnants forming the canvas for the spray-painted graffiti mural *Kings of Freedom* by Berlin artist and DJ Dennis Kaun, a.k.a. KAOS, the diptych painting shows two large portrait heads side by side. On the left, against an orange background, is a wide-eyed male with bright lips, eyebrows, and hair, the hair resembling a punk version of a rooster's comb but evidently representing a crown; on the right is a blindfolded, dull-gray head, wearing more conventional regal headgear, his unhappy expression and drab, statue-like visage accentuated by an explosion of colorful graffiti design. While it is difficult to pinpoint the artist's intention, the text accompanying the installation suggests a stridently libertarian and American exceptionalist reading of the wall. The panels, said to have been painted just days before the wall was dismantled, were purchased by Robert A. Hefner III, founder and owner of the Oklahoma-based oil and gas giant the GHK Companies. Hefner attended the dedication of the installation, situated in a prime location on University of Virginia grounds. The ceremony did double duty, marking the twenty-fifth anniversary of the toppling of the wall and Thomas Jefferson's birthday. Hefner "consider[ed] it a gift to our beloved Mr. Jefferson for his birthday weekend."[65]

At the ceremony, Hefner emphasized "the power of personal freedom," a phrase repeated on the plaque's inscription. For Hefner,

> It's these pieces of the Berlin Wall ... torn down by the free will of the people of Berlin, that serve as full proof that the rights of liberty and freedom that Mr. Jefferson enshrined in the Declaration of Independence are indeed truly unalienable.
>
> Remember, it's the people who tore down the wall—what a great expression of the power of personal freedom and courage. When the Berlin Wall came down, it was an enormous geopolitical earthquake that unleashed waves of events around the world, the aftershocks of which we're still feeling today.[66]

Here, it's worth noting Hefner's geological metaphors as well as his celebrations of Jefferson and the "power of personal freedom" on a site

5.20 Kings of Freedom, Berlin Wall Mural, Berlin artists Dennis Kaun, University of Virginia, Virginia Magazine

built and maintained over much of its early history by enslaved workers. Hefner parlayed his undergraduate degree in geology into his transformation of oil and natural gas exploration and extraction. He was one of the original frackers. His leadership in the energy field earned him a place on the International Council at Harvard's Belfer Center and membership in the Royal Geographical Society of London. The Belfer Center's website notes that during the 1970s, "he was the lone proponent to accurately forecast America's natural gas abundance, and a leader in the efforts to deregulate natural gas prices."[67] By the early 1980s, he was known as an iconoclast who had used the deregulation of the natural gas industry to amass great wealth. As the *New York Times* explained, "Mr. Hefner's success is the direct result of a feature of a 1978 law exempting the sort of deep gas in which he specializes—that found below 15,000 feet—from Federal price controls, while limiting the price of other gas to less than a third of the price he gets. It is not irrelevant that Washington insiders credit Mr. Hefner's lobbying adroitness with winning that provision, or 'loophole' in the phrase of his detractors."[68]

In Hefner's 2009 book, *The Grand Energy Transition,* blurbed by Donald Trump and James R. Schlesinger, economist and former US secretary of energy, former US secretary of defense, and former CIA director, the author continued his advocacy of harvesting natural gas through unconventional extraction—in other words, fracking.

Hefner's acquisition of four massive concrete sections of the Berlin Wall occasioned his view of freedom as a personal accomplishment decontextualized from social and power relations. His ability to purchase and place *Kings of Freedom* on the University of Virginia campus is as much a part of the history of racial capitalism as his beloved Jefferson's Monticello and the university he founded. The self-styled lone wolf had been born into one of the wealthiest and most powerful families in the country. And the source of his family's wealth, the acquisition of indigenous lands for oil extraction, drew directly on the legacy of Thomas Jefferson.

Hefner's grandfather, Robert A. Hefner, was a founder of the Oklahoma oil and gas industry. With a 1902 law degree from the University of Texas, in 1905, he used the 1887 Dawes Act to break up tribal reservations in Indian Territory (later Oklahoma) and acquire an initial thirty-three thousand acres of mineral rights.[69] Theodore Roosevelt, president at that time, drew on the extinctionist/annihilationist legacy of Thomas Jefferson to aggressively enforce the Dawes Act, arguing in 1901 that the reservation system "promotes beggary, perpetuates pauperism, and stifles industry." Reflecting Jefferson's view of productive property, Roosevelt called for efforts "steadily to make the Indian work like any other man on his own ground."[70] His conservationism, preserving public lands as national parks, sites of leisure where white men could reinvigorate themselves by hunting and communing with nature, did not extend to Native peoples, who must be forced to work.

After taking Indian tribal lands to establish oil fields in Carter County, Oklahoma, and incorporating the Hefner Company, Hefner's grandfather became known as "an expert in the legal aspects of the burgeoning industry." As justice of the Supreme Court of Oklahoma from 1926 to 1933, Hefner presided over landmark cases on petroleum law.[71]

His son, Robert A. Hefner II, continued to build the family fortune. He befriended Franklin Roosevelt's son Elliott while honeymooning on Hawaii, and their bond involved work in Washington, DC, and dinners at the White House, where, on one such occasion, Hefner's wife, Louise Good, went into labor. Robert A. Hefner III might have been born there if staff had not cleared snow for a path to the hospital. His success as a lobbyist, facilitated by his access to senior officials in the Reagan White House, seemed destined from birth.

In Hefner's history, "personal power" meant the power to expropriate land and exploit its natural resources and, eventually, the freedom to frack. The month following the dedication on University of Virginia grounds, Hefner published an essay in *Foreign Affairs*, "The United States of Gas: Why the Shale Revolution Could Have Happened Only in America."[72] Hefner attributed the fracking revolution to Yankee ingenuity and America's unique legal system and property laws. Europe, he believed, had been stymied by "misguided energy policy." Even worse, Europe's "hyperactive green movement determined to block the development of shale gas."[73]

Berlin is an afterthought in the text accompanying the mural installation fashioned from panels of the wall. There was evidently just enough room on the plaque for Hefner's libertarian vision of freedom, emphasizing personal achievement. Another plaque would have been needed to recount the circumstances of his family's multigenerational wealth or that Jefferson's privilege and prestige came at the expense of the lives of enslaved peoples and their labor. The inscription enshrines the prescient act of acquisition and the elision of outsize power and privilege through the philanthropic performance: In 1990, Hefner "sent a representative to Berlin to negotiate for a substantial section of the Wall. He believed a portion of the wall would be an icon of the 'power of personal freedom.'" The text offers Hefner's interpretation of Kaun's mural: "Painted on the West German side are two kings: a brightly colored, joyful king, representing freedom, and a largely colorless, blindfolded king, oblivious to the needs and wishes of the people. The East German side remains dull gray cement. Hefner believes these two sides, the colorful, lively West German side and the gray East German side, artistically represent the character of freedom and enslavement."[74]

Presenting a Manichean cold war Germany, Hefner displaces enslavement onto a gray and flat representation of East Germany with an authoritarian king, "oblivious to the needs and wishes of the people." It seems slavery becomes mentionable only when purported to have been enacted by communists, not in any consideration of Jefferson's legacy.

Hefner's libertarian individualism explicitly denies the social, political, and political infrastructure on which privilege is built. The same view is evident at Ramiiisol, Hefner's vineyard outside Charlottesville. A label for the vineyard's 2014 Cabernet Franc bears an image of the Berlin Wall mural art. The vineyard's website boasts of its biodynamic and organic wine production on 140 acres containing the vineyard, organic gardens, and native plants, celebrating Hefner's personal buffer from the environmental damage of fracking, and a harmonious, holistic ecology unavailable to those whose water was poisoned by fracking.[75] The vineyard's website also posts inspirational "sayings" about the power of the individual and the rewards of risk-taking. Inspired in part by Jefferson's failed passion project of making American wines as good as those from Europe, the "sayings" quote notable figures on wine, love, improving the land, and above all, unfettered individualism. Examples include Ayn Rand, "The question isn't who is going to let me; it's who is going to stop me"; and T. S. Eliot, "Only those who will risk going too far can possibly find out how far one can go." A quote attributed to Gandhi is also included: "First they ignore you. Then they ridicule you. Then they fight you. Then you win."[76] By framing Gandhi's story as one of personal persistence rather than collective struggle, like Berlin's Checkpoint Charlie Museum, Ramiiisol transmutes radical visions into a story of the individual rising above society. But this reframing of Gandhi's tribulations along the path to victory echoes Hefner's self-avowed lone-wolf advocacy of natural gas extraction when the industry was focused on oil and coal. As a 1981 *New York Times* story based on an interview with Hefner put it, "geologists scoffed," people said the rocks were not porous enough, that the technology didn't exist. Then Hefner was fought and won through the "loophole" in the 1978 law that brought colossal wealth.[77]

At the University of Virginia, a decade of activism, before and after the 2014 wall installation, has, for many, recontextualized Hefner's Berlin Wall. Attempts by activists to remove Charlottesville's Confederate statues brought hundreds of members of neo-Nazi and white supremacist groups to the city and campus grounds in 2017, resulting in the death of Heather Heyer and injuries permanently disabling several antiracist protesters. Community activists, students, and faculty members documented the university's origins in slavery, demanding that the institution break its official silence on enslavement. They called for the memorialization of the enslaved workers whose labor had built and maintained the institution, even as many were subjected to rape, murder, and other forms of the institution's quotidian violence. A memorial to enslaved laborers now stands on the grounds, equal in size to the circumference of the Rotunda, just a stone's throw away from the wall installation. In July 2020, years of activism and protest by Native American and environmentalist groups in Virginia resulted in the abandonment of the Dominion/Duke Atlantic natural gas pipeline, which would have sliced through Native lands and homes, imperiling fragile ecosystems in the Blue Ridge and Appalachian Mountains of West Virginia, Virginia, and North Carolina. More than simply a symbol of freedom, the sites of the Berlin Wall installation and the commonwealth, sitting atop plundered

Native lands, constitute terrain on which conflicts have been waged over the abiding legacies of racism, slavery, and settler-colonial oppression.

Students surveyed in 2019 about Hefner's wall installation associated it with Trump, the Mexican border wall, and US detention facilities for immigrant and refugee children taken from their families.[78] Others mused about the irony of declarations of freedom on grounds built by enslaved laborers. The Berlin Wall remains an imaginative space for reflection on the past and present. But with the rise of authoritarianism in the United States and eastern and central Europe, and with far right protesters attempting to storm the Reichstag in August 2020 and far right white supremacists storming and occupying the US Capitol in January 2021, driven both by libertarian attacks on the very notion of society—what holds us together as human beings—and by an aggrieved sense of victimization, it is past time to put the stories of triumphalism and victimization to rest.

Patriot Acts

STAGING THE WAR ON TERROR FROM THE SPY MUSEUM TO BISHKEK

Christ, I miss the Cold War.—M (Judi Dench), *Casino Royale* (2007)

In March 2000, the journalist Richard Reeves wrote of a recent taxi ride to Reagan National Airport. It seemed to Reeves that half the drivers in the nation's capital had their radios set to National Public Radio. As Reeves was following Daniel Schorr's in-depth reporting on upcoming elections in Taiwan, the cab driver blurted out, "God, I miss the Cold War." "So do we all," Reeves replied, "right up to the President of the United States." Noting that Bill Clinton at that moment was in South Asia mediating tensions between India and Pakistan over Kashmir, Reeves saw the world as a more dangerous place. The end of the cold war meant the loss of a "certain stagnant security." The Berlin Wall had kept the superpowers apart in Europe, and the US Seventh Fleet prevented Chinese communists "from thinking about invading Taiwan." Soviet backing of India and the United States' and China's support of Pakistan calmed global apprehensions, preventing the contest between India and Pakistan from escalating. Reeves offered a reflective, qualified nostalgia, keenly aware that the cold war was as likely to generate tensions as mediate them. But heading to the airport during the 2000 presidential primary campaigns—when George W. Bush also frequently yearned for the clarity of cold war rivalries—Reeves could identify even with Bush's nod to cold war nostalgia.[1]

The relationship between triumphalist cold war nostalgia and the push for war in the Middle East predated the September 11, 2001, terrorist attacks. Indeed, viewed from the standpoint of the intertwined afterlives of colonialism and the cold war, 9/11 does not constitute the sharp rupture many have suggested.[2] But nostalgia took a fearful turn after nineteen al-Qaeda terrorists hijacked four passenger planes, flying two into the World Trade Center's Twin Towers and one into the Pentagon, with another attempted attack on the Capitol building averted when passengers fought back against the hijackers, saving countless others by forcing the plane to crash in a field near Pittsburgh.[3]

The deadly attacks led to more plaintive longings for the certainties of cold war conflict, and a palpable sense of threat. Reporting from the 2003 Prague NATO Summit, a *Guardian* journalist wrote, "We look back [on] the period of the cold war almost with nostalgia where the mix of deterrence, confidence building and arms control appeared to offer an intellectually coherent approach to a very dangerous strategic situation." For this observer, the destruction of the Twin Towers showed that "previously theoretical risks of non-state actors acquiring nuclear capabilities" had morphed into the alarmingly real prospect of nuclear proliferation.[4]

The sheer volume of post-9/11 references to a supposedly safer cold war global order translated to a new common sense. A 2007 blogger doubled down on nostalgia, reimagining the 1959 Kitchen Debate between Vice President Richard Nixon and Soviet premier Nikita Khrushchev in a whimsical poem that closed with Khrushchev declaring, "You're a lawyer of Capitalism, I'm a lawyer for Communism. Let's Kiss," followed by the obligatory, "God, I miss the cold war." The James Bond film *Casino Royale* reinforced the sentiment upon its release two months later.[5] M (Judi Dench), head of the British intelligence agency MI6, learns that Bond (Daniel Craig) has mistakenly killed a vital asset, exposing the agency to unwelcome public scrutiny. On her way to chastise Bond, she mutters to herself, "Christ, I miss the Cold War." For audiences, M's lament perhaps resonated with post-9/11 news accounts of bureaucratic failures of US intelligence agencies, the quagmire of the occupation of Iraq following the invasion of 2003, and unsettling color-coded terror threat alerts regularly issued by US Homeland Security officials.[6]

Political rhetoric during the so-called war on terror, epitomized by the propagandistic notion itself, indicated a cultural war for the hearts and minds of the American public. Its exponents in and out of the administration deployed political language, even through the medium of popular culture, for political ends. Present and former CIA chiefs and policy makers pursued their mission not only in cabinet meetings or in the White House Situation Room but also in media venues and museums, in attempts to shape public perception through popular cultural channels.

This chapter explores explicit and implicit claims about the history of the cold war invoked during the wars in Afghanistan and Iraq, as well as in defenses of the extension of the surveillance state. First, I explore the synergy between official discourses and cultural institutions on the 9/11 attacks, promoting narratives of US victimization and paranoia in which, as the feminist and literary scholar Anne McClintock has put it, "one finds simultaneously and in condensed form, deliriums of absolute power and forebodings of perpetual threat."[7]

George W. Bush's "axis of evil" rhetoric seeped into popular culture representations of geopolitical conflict. After 9/11, the intelligence community ran with the cultural project of the normalization of the Patriot Act and the creation of the Department of Homeland Security. I discuss the International Spy Museum as a key cultural venture defending the expansion of domestic surveillance under the Patriot Act and promulgating the idea of Islam as a terror threat. This period also witnessed a saturation of mass-mediated cultural productions of geopolitical current affairs. Some noteworthy examples include *Team America*, a live-action feature film with marionettes created by the makers of the animated cable television show *South Park*, and skits from *Saturday Night Live* spoofing North Korean leader Kim Jong Il and other figures. I consider these satirical performances as accompaniments to the official search to name, punish, and humiliate new enemies. While politically ambiguous, these satirical performances recapitulated the bipolar, Manichean framework of the cold war. Taken together, such performances, targeting youth culture, fostered a cultural common sense about the imagined enemy.

After surveying the post-9/11 remapping of a popular geopolitical imaginary in film and popular culture, I turn to sites where the war on terror was actually waged, considering the US presence in the border zones of Afghanistan and Pakistan, as well as in Bishkek, Kyrgyzstan, home of a US military base. Pakistani and Kyrgyz writers have noted that contemporary armed conflict is superimposed on an earlier cold war history and geography. Their local readings of these historically layered spaces, stacking recent military operations and instillations atop a landscape already deeply shaped by past cold war geopolitics, offer accounts of cold war history and memory that belie triumphalist Western assertions about the legacy of the cold war and its relation to the war on terror.

The Patriot Act

The passage of the Patriot Act following the 9/11 attacks, and the establishment of the Homeland Security Administration under the Homeland Security Act on November 25, 2002, enabled the extension and privatization of government security and surveillance on an unprecedented scale.[8] In the wake of 9/11, congressional approval of the Patriot Act in October 2001 rebooted cold war logic in justifying a far-reaching apparatus of internal security and surveillance not seen since the McCarthy era. Some provisions undermined civil liberties, such as indefinite detentions of enemy combatants, summary deportations of immigrants, and government searches of homes and businesses without the consent of the occupant or owner. As historian Mary Dudziak has asserted, the concept of a "war on terror," though unprecedented, also shared critical features of the cold war in that its very definition justified intervention anywhere at home or abroad, anywhere American interests or security were deemed threatened.[9]

A post-9/11 sense of permanent and ubiquitous conflict, argues geographer Derek Gregory, "[has] played a major role in the militarization of the planet."[10] The war on terror acted on an imaginative geography in which, in purportedly wild zones of the global South, wars occur through "greed and sectarian gain, social fabric is destroyed, and developmental gains reversed, non-combatants killed, humanitarian assistance abused, and all civility abandoned." In response to such chaos, "our wars" are conducted by "advanced militaries that are supposed to be surgical, sensitive and scrupulous."[11]

Reliance on private contractors reshaped war-making, from defense contracts to espionage. In his 2000 campaign, Bush insisted that the job of the military was "to fight and win war, not act as nation builders."[12] Privatizing security was Bush's mode of war-making, purportedly without nation-building. In the run-up to the 2003 US invasion of Iraq, Halliburton's CEO, Dick Cheney, helped secure a $7 billion noncompetitive government contract for operations in Iraq before resigning to join the Bush campaign as vice-presidential candidate. The US military disavowed nation-building in Iraq, having outsourced the task to defense contractors and such private security corporations as Blackwater.[13]

The reliance on private military forces, contracted to swiftly enter conflict zones without massive troop deployments and bases, led to the establishment of "lily-pad" bases. Central to the Pentagon's strategy of "fast, flexible, and efficient projection of force," the lily-pad installation replaced the tent cities of the first Afghanistan campaigns. In 2004, Colonel Mike Sumida explained the logic of flexibility at Manas International Airport in Bishkek, Kyrgyzstan, from which the United States had already executed eighteen thousand missions into Afghanistan. "It looks permanent, but it could be unbolted and unwelded if we felt like it."[14]

Like the drone warfare employed by Bush and accelerated during the Obama administration, the lily-pad base promised a new modern warfare with technological precision that would minimize collateral damage and adverse impact on civilian populations. Like secret CIA prisons and hidden black-ops sites, lily-pad bases suggested to the American public that its surgical, measured use of force had a light impact on lands and societies that were, in fact, profoundly transformed through war. While a far cry from massive postwar US installations such as Ramstein in Germany, the lily-pad base shared more with its cold war predecessors than many cared to admit. The Truman Doctrine and National Security Council Paper 68 had emphasized the duty and responsibility of the United States to intervene in all internal and external threats to freedom, even when no direct threat to security was involved. Lily-pad bases served the same objective and were integral to warfare strategies targeting enemies in wars of our own choosing, without boundaries.[15]

From the Patriot Act to the Axis of Evil

Bush's axis of evil speech, given as part of his State of the Union address before a joint session of Congress on January 29, 2002, rebooted cold war metaphors. Sounding echoes of Reagan's "evil empire" rhetoric and the Truman Doctrine, the speech elevated limited and short-term security measures into justifications for permanent and unbounded war. Coined by David Frum, speechwriter and future critic of the Bush administration, the axis of evil formulation rewrote the United States' foreign policy history of the cold war, erasing past alliances with Iran and Iraq, leaving out the US role in the creation of North Korea, and disregarding past US interference with peace and reunification initiatives. Critics charged that the only glue holding together this fabricated axis of nations was that Iraq, Iran, and North Korea were on Uncle Sam's bad side, as states accused of marshaling the threat of weapons of mass destruction. Bush's axis of evil justified the US invasion of Iraq.

Bush opened the speech with claims to triumphalism and vulnerability in the same breath: "Our nation is at war, our economy is in recession and the civilized world faces unprecedented dangers. Yet the state of our union has never been stronger." Bush continued, "The American flag flies again over our embassy in Kabul. Terrorists who once occupied Afghanistan now occupy cells at Guantánamo Bay." But, he continued, "our discoveries in Afghanistan confirmed our worst fears ... our war against terror is only beginning." Vowing to shut down terrorist camps and bring terrorists to justice, Bush pivoted from Afghanistan and, shunning mention of Saudi Arabia (from where most of the perpetrators came), described the need for vigilance against "regimes that sponsor terror from threatening America or our friends and allies with weapons of mass destruction."[16]

Bush's warnings of an axis of evil capitalized on post-9/11 fears to conjure the specter of new security threats. "Some of these regimes have been pretty quiet since September 11," Bush acknowledged, "but we know their true nature." The recent history of Korean reunification talks and the US-Japan-Koreas Agreed Framework was incompatible with Bush's tough talk: "North Korea is a regime arming with missiles and weapons of mass destruction, while starving its citizens." Warning that Iran "aggressively pursues ... weapons and exports terror," Bush declared that "states like these and their terrorist allies, constitute an axis of evil, arming to threaten the peace of the world." Bush's most vivid portrayal of a member of the axis of evil was reserved for Iraq: "Iraq continues to flaunt its hostility toward America and to support terror. The Iraqi regime has plotted to develop anthrax and nerve gas and nuclear weapons for over a decade. This is a regime that has already used poison gas to murder thousands of its own citizens, leaving the bodies of mothers huddled over their dead children.... This is a regime that has something to hide from the civilized world." The only alternative to further "catastrophe," suggested Bush, was mobilization for permanent warfare. The 2002 Axis of Evil address called for further expanding the security state.[17]

As Amy Kaplan has argued, heightened security measures abroad and at the US border entailed new spatial metaphors, with such terms as *ground zero* and *homeland* entering the American lexicon.[18] In the legislation of November 2002 that established the Department of Homeland Security, Bush spelled out the meaning of homeland security in calling for "knowledge gained from bioterrorism research," "stronger police and fire departments," and "stricter border enforcement [to] help combat illegal drugs."[19]

Many Americans found it unusual, if not jarring, to hear the country suddenly referred to as a homeland. Before 9/11, the use of the term was rare in the United States, usually applied to the country of one's parents or ancestors. Rebranding the United States as a "homeland" reproduced the myth of an empty continent, eliding the history of indigenous Americans while simultaneously ignoring the fact that the country was created by waves of forced enslavement and removals as well as voluntary migration and immigration. It further obscured the multinational character of the victims of the 9/11 attacks; the 2,974 victims of the initial attacks (excluding the perpetrators) came from seventy-seven different countries.

The creation of the Department of Homeland Security and the new cabinet position secretary of Homeland Security, critical to enforcing the Patriot Act, constituted the largest government reorganization since 1947, when the Department of Defense was created. Before 9/11, Immigration and Naturalization Services was under the Department of Justice. After 9/11, the US Customs and Border Patrol, US Immigration and Customs Enforcement, and US Citizenship and Immigration Services all came under the umbrella of the Department of Homeland Security.

Moving immigration services from the Department of Justice to the Department of Homeland Security shifted immigration from a matter constitutive of US citizenship to a problem, reframed as an inherent threat to national security. And like the Patriot Act that it enforced, the new Department of Homeland Security blurred the distinction between military and police boundaries.

These new security apparatuses resulted in unpredictable and long-lasting consequences.[20] Scheduled to "sunset" after four years, in 2005 the Patriot Act was reauthorized with changes. In 2011, the Patriot Act Sunset Extension Bill passed; parts expiring in 2015 were restored with the US Freedom Act. In 2016, the Obama administration carried out deportation raids; and in 2019 Immigration and Customs Enforcement announced raids in ten major cities, later holding people in family detention centers in Texas and Pennsylvania and detaining babies and children, separated from their parents.

A more effective response to the 9/11 attacks would have entailed a review of US security and intelligence failures and, above all, an honest assessment of what Chalmers Johnson identified as "blow-back," the disorder unleashed by actions in the cold war and its aftermath.[21] Instead, Bush asked for trust and vigilance in a prolonged mobilization requiring the enlistment of all citizens and allies. Within months of Bush's Axis speech, citizen-warriors

6.1 Luis Jiménez, painting, 2002, International Spy Museum

could immerse themselves in the geopolitical imaginings of a US-led global war on terror by paying a visit to the International Spy Museum on F Street, less than a mile from the Capitol.

The Importance of Being Earnest

Generating support for a sustained war on terror, and the militarization of American society required for a state of perpetual war, entailed a long-term campaign. There is no better entry point for understanding the efforts to secure broad consent for the war on terror than the International Spy Museum in Washington, DC. Combined with myriad projections of cold war nostalgia in popular culture, the museum's glorification of espionage provided cultural validation for the Bush administration's war on terror.

As visitors exit the "Golden Age" of cold war–era espionage exhibit, they confront a startling Luis Jiménez painting (from 2002) of a headless dragon with snakes sprouting out from the torso, slithering in all directions. In the accompanying description, former CIA director James Woolsey describes the image as emblematic of the foreign policy challenges facing the United States in a post-Soviet world: "We've slain a large dragon but we now live in a jungle filled with a bewildering variety of poisonous snakes, and in many ways the dragon was easier to keep track of."

The painting's depiction of serpents suggests that terrorism grew directly from the evils of communism, if not the Soviet Union itself. Another observer could imagine the dragon as a metaphor for the cold war writ large, surmising that current terror threats grew out of certain misbegotten actions of the superpowers in the proxy wars of the later cold war. While the painting is open to multiple interpretations, other features of the museum place it at odds with a serious consideration of cold war history.

Opening in July 2002, just ten months after the 9/11 attacks, the museum was founded by communications tycoon and philanthropist Milton S. Maltz. Maltz, along with George H. W. Bush and Woolsey, sat on the board of directors of the Association of Former Intelligence Officers, a group "dedicated to countering criticism of the U.S. intelligence community coming from the media and congress."[22] In effect, the museum defended an intelligence community under siege for not acting on information that may have prevented the 9/11 attacks. The International Spy Museum's breezy celebration of spying and surveillance lent ideological support to the Patriot Act's vast expansion of the security state.

The International Spy Museum projects the worldview of a unipolar empire with claims to global legitimacy announced in its title. Ostensibly devoted to the craft of espionage, described with a wink as "the world's second-oldest profession," the museum highlights the cold war's "golden age of spying" and asserts a triumphalist continuity between the cold war and the war on terror. Despite its founders' objective of defending the US intelligence community, the museum's website promises an "apolitical presentation of the history of espionage in order to provide visitors with nonbiased, accurate information." The advisory board of directors is "comprised of leading intelligence experts, scholars, and practitioners," who "ensure the authenticity and accuracy of the Museum's depiction of the history and tradecraft of espionage."[23]

Such authenticity is affirmed by the credentials of the board members. Peter Earnest, the ex officio executive director of the International Spy Museum, spent thirty-six years in the CIA, with over twenty years in the agency's Clandestine Service. The next board member featured on the website, David Kahn, boasts a formidable academic background: "The world's leading expert in the history of cryptology, the essential code-making and code-breaking aspect of intelligence gathering. A historian and journalist, he holds a PhD in Modern History from Oxford University, England,

and visiting historian with the National Security Agency. Mr. Kahn taught modern political and military intelligence at Yale and Columbia Universities, and recently retired as an editor for Newsday."[24]

The museum asserts its neutrality (and internationalism) through the involvement of such former KGB spies as Danilovich Kalugin, "a retired Major General in the Soviet KGB," joining fellow board members Dame Stella Rimington, director general of the British Security Service and thus breaker of glass ceilings, as well as codes, as "the first woman to hold the post." Such colorful figures as Antonio Joseph Mendez, the CIA's former chief of disguise, and former CIA specialists in clandestine photography round out the romantic gallery of spies.[25]

Claims to impartiality are bolstered by the authenticity of the lethal gadgets exhibited and accounts of the spies who used them. The museum's "collection of spy-related artifacts, the largest international collection on public display . . . brings to life the stories of the men and women who used these objects."[26] The presentation of the often bizarre artifacts, the stuff of spy novels and films, vouches for their veracity, from the lipstick and umbrella guns said to have felled Soviet agents on the streets of London, to the shoe transmitter, to the 1960s "rectal tool kit" purportedly used by the CIA, which consists of steel blades and files stored in a plastic tube case. Boasting that life imitates art, text accompanying a replica of James Bond's Aston Martin, featured in *Goldfinger*, describes intelligence agencies incorporating Bond-inspired features into their designs.[27]

The realm of fantasy is fertile in its susceptibility to ideology. Along with the museum's waggish trove of cold war artifacts, campy fantasy role-playing games enlist visitors of all ages as active defenders of US national security. Invited to "experience" a spy mission, visitors accepting the mission are assigned a new identity. After a five-minute briefing followed by a sequence of challenges, a blown cover will land the recruit in an interrogation room.

Role-playing scenarios associate spying and surveillance activities with patriotism. Earnest told journalist Stephen Goode that the art of intelligence gathering was indispensable in the nation's founding: "At the museum we show that George Washington, one of our revolutionary leaders and the father of our country, was also the founder of US intelligence gathering. He was a very active intelligence officer, recruited and paid agents, used ciphers and dead drops."[28] For Earnest, espionage is a thoroughly American endeavor. His enlistment of Washington as part of the museum's defense of the Patriot Act indicates that to surveil or to be surveilled is patriotic; surveillance is patriotism.

On the museum's website, schoolteachers can download lesson plans shaped by the patriotic defense of the intelligence community. The seven available in 2019 included "The Enemy Within." In one module, students put themselves "in the shoes" of an FBI case officer during the 1950s Red Scare. Assigned documents from the comic actress Lucille Ball's FBI files, students are tasked with determining whether Ball was a communist. Students read pages of redacted memos and testimony that Ball had attended Communist Party meetings and signed petitions on behalf of the party. The final memo, affirming that Ball has been cooperative and truthful in answering questions from the House Committee on Unamerican Activities, leads to the finding that there is no evidence that Ball was a party member. The lesson: one has nothing to fear from surveillance if one is truthful.[29] Another, fifty-eight-page course module, "9/11: The Intelligence Angle," helps teachers explore "the balance of national security and civil liberties" and how intelligence informs policy decisions and domestic legislation. Released to coincide with the tenth anniversary of the 9/11 attacks, the module ostensibly provided teachers and students the intelligence that national security agencies had at their disposal on 9/11. Students are then asked to role-play their own responses, cultivating an appreciation for the challenges of the art of intelligence.[30]

"Bond in the Classroom; Shaken AND Stirred" moves from an inane unit on the "science of Bond," asking whether a real spy can actually falsify one's fingerprints as Bond did in *Diamonds Are Forever*, to a lesson plan showing teachers how to use Bond movies to help their students understand the general public's fears at the moment a particular film was released. A lesson on the MI6 hacker in the movie *Skyfall* asks students to research a cyber-attack that has occurred in the past three years and to report on how it has affected national security.[31] In these scenarios, threats are real, and complacency is not an option.

The museum's backing of the Bush administration's war on terror draws parallels between the purported new Muslim enemy and anticommunism. As anthropologist John R. Bowen and legal scholar Aziz Rana have argued, post-9/11 bigotry toward Muslims has taken a form distinct from that of bigotry targeting race, ethnicity, and gender. Islamophobia, they argue, resembles anticommunism in that it constructs Muslim identity not as part of an ethnicity or religion but as an ideological choice.[32] To elect an allegiance to Islam—constructed in this view as inherently violent—marks a person as fundamentally other, and anti-American, as the choice sets the person on a treacherous path to hatred and terrorism. Assumptions that Islam is inherently violent and that practicing Muslims have made an ideological choice are augmented by distorted narratives that locate the history of terrorism in the history of Islam.

The museum's assertions of historical veracity assumed a more insidious tone in the speaker series of March 2008, "The Bomber behind the Veil: Muslim Women and Violent Jihad," which featured Farhana Ali, an international policy analyst with the RAND Corporation, the nonprofit think tank. Ali was described as "one of the few researchers focused on these Muslim female fighters." The museum's breathless publicity copy included the warning, "Beware the mujahidaat [Muslim female fighters]." The public was invited to "join Ali, who draws on her background as an accomplished counterterrorism, intelligence, and policy analyst as well as a Muslim woman, for a discussion of the mujahidaat—*their place in Islamic history*, [and] their psychological profile" (my emphasis).[33] With the "truth" of the presentation ensured by Ali's credentials, the museum placed the history of terrorism squarely within "Islamic history," rather than the history of the proxy wars of the later cold war and US officials' support of anti-Soviet mujahideen fighters in Afghanistan.[34] Though the museum invited the public to experience history up close with a bona fide Muslim woman expert, the terms of inquiry rendered a serious engagement with that history unlikely.

Viewing terrorism as rooted in Islam is integral to a popular feature of the International Spy Museum. For fourteen dollars, one can join "Operation Spy," described by the museum as an "immersion interactive experience ... where you are the spy." The mission to "locate a missing nuclear trigger before it ends up in the wrong hands" sends a visitor through a fictionalized world of subterranean passageways, backroom offices, and field outposts.[35]

In three different visits between 2008 and 2010, I signed up for the mission with a team of strangers. We found ourselves in Khandar, a fake central Asian republic, complete with a mock train station lobby with a café menu and scheduled departures for actual cities in central Asia and Europe. Having assumed the role of CIA operatives, we investigated the Zaret terrorist network as a piped-in Hollywood soundtrack played. Our handlers told us that the mission was based on a *real* case. We were working as *real* spies had done. Immediately, we were confronted with a twist in our mission. With multiple potential outcomes depending on how a particular team responds to the theft of nuclear materials, all scenarios involved the questionable allegiances of Nadia Cherat, a Khandar citizen who was recruited as a US agent but whose political judgment is compromised by her loyalty to her family.

As we tracked Nadia, code name Topaz, it became clear that she was withholding information from the US government. Was she a double agent? The mission's outcomes hinged on whether the team believed that Topaz was lying or telling the truth. But in all three scenarios that I experienced, Topaz had not intentionally aided the Zaret terrorist network but had erred in trusting and aiding her cousin, who was revealed to be a member of the network. "Operation Spy" places Topaz in a traditional and backward culture where familial ties are paramount. As we escaped detection accompanied by sound effects of speeding vans and helicopters, we acquired "experiential knowledge" of Topaz's atavistic values, learning that Muslim women are not to be trusted. As a Muslim woman, Topaz had made a set of strategic choices informed by her culture that endangered the free world. Finally, we were hailed as patriots for surveilling and stopping her. Duty required suspicion of Muslim people as the best defense against terrorism.

The premise of "Operation Spy," interrogating whether Topaz can be trusted, enacts what the scholar Moon Charania has identified as a "discursive game" witnessed in Western representations of the loyalty of Benazir Bhutto, twice prime minister of Pakistan and leader of the opposition party when she was assassinated on December 27, 2007. Exploring the West's preoccupation with Bhutto's body and aesthetics, Charania argues that Bhutto was deemed worthy on a democratic neoliberal terrain because, in a conflation of democracy and her self-fashioning, "she is the perfect complement to the 'truth' of modernity and is eminently likeable, hence faithful, to the west."[36]

A 2007 *American Prospect* essay published on the day of Bhutto's death backs up Charania's analysis, describing Bhutto's emergence on the international scene and claiming she was "destined to be an icon," noting that she resembled a "Disney drawing of a beautiful fairytale princess from an animated fable set somewhere in the mysterious orient."[37] Here, Bhutto was figured not as an educated, elite product of a society with a tradition of feminist advocacy for Muslim women's rights but as a democratic martyr arising from the mysterious orient—portrayed as a foil to the similarly stereotyped image of Pakistani women as terrorists or victims of a backward society.[38]

Shopping for Patriotism

After the 9/11 attacks, Bush famously urged Americans not to be cowed by terrorists but to "get down to Disney World in Florida" and go shopping. Visitors exiting the International Spy Museum's exhibits are guided toward a sprawling gift shop. The shop reinforces the museum's grim emphasis on deceit as a tool of the trade, but the world of espionage can also be fun and fit for souvenir consumption. Books about atomic war are displayed alongside how-to spy manuals, such as *I Lie for a Living*, with a foreword by Earnest. Among the espionage tchotchkes and T-shirts sporting the museum's spy motto, "Deny everything," numerous toys and gadgets for aspiring spies, including decoders, traceless breaking-and-entering devices, and lie detectors, entice the consumer.

The entire shop is largely a toy store, with many items marketed to children under twelve, though one imagines that not many parents would give free rein to the surveillance activities promised by the Super Mission 4-in-1 Spy Kit (ages six and up), which includes a "Spy Bug" said to "transmit conversations and noises to your ear bud, through walls." Another popular product, the Tri-Link Alarm System, offers motion detectors to keep people out of your room and protect "your stuff." Along with such popular youth-oriented movie fare as *Alex Rider, Operation Storm Breaker*, and *Spy Kids*, and the museum's own "spies in training" children's programs, including chaperoned sleepover parties, such toys affirm the allure and adventure of espionage, enshrining the spy in the pantheon of American popular culture. Staking out a position above the fray of bygone cold war antagonisms, all the better to cash in on the socialist retro market, the museum sells Che Guevara and Mao Zedong T-shirts. For those willing to imagine themselves as double agents, KGB license plates are available for twelve dollars.

Blurring play and politics, the museum's family experience trades on the nostalgia of baby boomer parents for heroic (and satirical) portrayals of spies and spying in 1960s movies, cartoons, pop songs, and consumer culture. Adult nostalgia for the "coolness" of commodified espionage culture becomes a cultural inheritance to a new generation of American children socialized into the post-9/11 world. On the one hand, the store's wares and their presentation remind us that consumption is ambiguous and complex; we may "buy it" (pun intended), but we are not necessarily completely sold on it, so to speak. At the same time, with such spy products available at many other toy stores, the objects and their consumption send a message about the importance and legitimacy of espionage inside and outside US borders. The cultural romance of espionage, tied to fears of another 9/11-type attack, may well have lent public support to the Bush administration for the US war and subsequent occupation in Iraq, countering charges of shoddy intelligence and, in the end, nonexistent weapons of mass destruction. With documented adventures of spies presented to elicit awe and admiration for their skills and bravery, the fun promised by consumer products normalizes espionage, absolving spies of morally suspect acts of murder or other unsavory doings. As the museum steers visitors away from serious consideration of the political and foreign policy history of the cold war, our participation in the museum's narratives is implicated in the violence disavowed through entertainment, camp, and parody. Though dangerous, spying is also a thrilling spectacle, cool, sexy, perhaps even profitable. But at what cost?

Celebrating the Epistemology of Lying

Spying may be, as the International Spy Museum tells us, integral to the origins of the United States, but the cold war wove new layers of deception deep into the structures of government and society. Andrew Friedman has examined the lived experience of the CIA and the built environment of empire, from the northern suburbs of Virginia to the imperial cities of Tehran and Saigon. In this context, "covert" implies "not merely a secret" but something that is "covered over," intimately related to the "psychological concept of denial and the open secret," which, Friedman argues, is how policy makers experienced and defined life, space, and politics.[39]

The International Spy Museum revels in an epistemology of lying. How do we know the world? By navigating a labyrinth of untruth. From the campy *I Lie for a Living*, written by the museum's director, to the fashion statement, "Deny everything," the cold war security state's "plausible deniability"—melding with a pseudo-Freudian culture in "denial"—amounts to a public crisis of confidence over what is factual. Rather than simply being a result of Donald Trump's authoritarian assault on truth, the present knowledge crisis has more remote origins in the national security state as well as the obfuscations of neoliberal economic policies and practices that obliterated discernible links between expectations (follow rules, buy into best practices) and personal outcomes (lose your job, home, and so on).

History Porn: "Notes from the Real World"

The museum's ultimate tease—promising to immerse you in history only to shut down actual inquiry—defines its James Bond exhibit, "Exquisitely Evil: 50 Years of Bond Villains," which opened in November 2013. The portion marked "Notes from the Real World" features Bond films, each with a panel window the visitor opens to find the "real history" behind the movies.

Behind one window featuring *The Living Daylights* (1987), a photograph depicts Afghani soldiers shouldering Stinger anti-aircraft missiles. The accompanying text explains, "Bond's good relations with Afghan fighters in *The Living Daylights* reflects the reality of the time. CIA, MI6 and several other intelligence agencies supplied arms ... to mujahideen who were fighting to expel the Soviets." Lest the inquiring mind wonder whether those missiles were later turned against the United States, the next installment, from *License to Kill* (1989), dispels concerns. In the film, we are informed, CIA agent Pam Bouvier tries to buy Stinger missiles from the villain Sanchez. "In reality," the text explains, "the CIA ran a multiyear operation to buy back unused stingers from Afghan fighters ... to keep such weapons out of the hands of villains like Sanchez." Giving the villain a Spanish name, the text deflects attention from the history of US funding of anti-American fundamentalists, offering just enough information to make people feel in the know, then shutting down the process of inquiry.

Another feature, "My Bond Moment," measures the exploits of real-world agents against their fictional counterparts. A series of video clips feature former operatives describing their "Bond moment." Robert Baer, author of the 2002 memoir *See No Evil*, the inspiration for Steven Gaghan's 2005 geopolitical thriller *Syriana*, described befriending a group of Russian soldiers during his time in Dushanbe, Tajikistan, not long after the end of US-Soviet hostilities. One night, well into an evening of prodigious vodka consumption, the Russians told Baer they were taking him parachute jumping the next morning. "While I was still completely hung over," Baer explained, "we drove out to an airfield on the Afghan border ... and this Colonel puts a parachute over me." Unsure whether he was making new friends or being singled out for payback against the CIA, "like an idiot," he jumped out of the plane. The parachute opened and Baer somehow landed safely; he recalled his astonishment at bonding with Russians "who had been our enemies just two years before."[40]

Former CIA agent Valerie Plame recorded her "Bond moment" after resigning from the agency in 2003 when she was outed by senior officials in the Bush administration in a high-profile scandal. Plame's husband, US diplomat Joseph Wilson, had been sent to investigate Italian intelligence suggesting that Iraq sought to purchase and import uranium from Niger. Wilson reported to Bush that Iraq did *not* in fact have such a program. When Bush, nonetheless, used the purported sale as evidence of Iraq's possession of weapons of mass destruction, Wilson concluded in a *New York Times* op-ed "that some of the intelligence related to Iraq's nuclear threat was twisted to exaggerate the Iraqi threat."[41] A week later, *Washington Post* columnist Robert Novak cited two senior administration officials who disclosed that Plame was an undercover CIA agent and had suggested sending Wilson to Niger to investigate the Italian report.[42] In 2006, Plame sued Dick Cheney, Karl Rove, and Scooter Libby for ruining her career and denounced Cheney as a traitor for fabricating the case for Iraq's possession of weapons of mass destruction.

In her video clip, Plame explained, "None of my Bond moments ever happened with me wearing a sequined dress or in a casino," but described instead a "brush pass" briefcase exchange with an asset who handed off a briefcase with a floppy disk containing vital intelligence. Bumping into each other as a subterfuge as they rounded a corner on a busy street in an unnamed European city, Plame explained, they completed the transaction in less than four seconds, and no one doing surveillance on the asset "would have been the wiser."[43]

For Earnest, what makes a "Bond moment" is the danger of getting caught. Tasked with planting a wire in the home of a valuable asset, Earnest and his wife attended a formal dinner party at the asset's home. Having instructed his wife to distract the asset while Earnest sneaked to the study, he described slipping under the desk, drilling a hole, and planting the wire. Mission accomplished. The asset never noticed his absence, a receiver car parked outside picked up transmissions revealing the asset as a hostile double agent, and the asset was simply let go without drama. Finally, Earnest explained, he had to think carefully about what he would have done if the asset had walked into the room. But we, instructed by the museum, already know the answer: deny everything.

Disavowal is at the heart of the rebooted James Bond franchise. If *Skyfall* (2012) is up to date in terms of the West's war on terror without boundaries, its plot, down to its visual language, wallows in nostalgia. With Britain under relentless attack from cyber-terrorists with intimate knowledge of British intelligence, Bond responds to the geopolitical crisis outlined by M in her passionate speech defending the relevance of the agency before a skeptical Parliament: "I see a different world than you do, and the truth is that what I see frightens me. I'm frightened because our enemies are no longer known to us. They do not exist on a map, they aren't nations. They are individuals. And look around you—who do you fear? Can you see a face, a uniform, a flag? No, our world is not more transparent now, it's more opaque. The shadows—that's where we must do battle." The world of shadows—the problem of the twenty-first century that M outlines before

Parliament—offers a stark contrast to the cold war, prompting a yearning for the usual suspects and targets of the era's espionage.

At the beginning of the film, which opens in Istanbul, a setting frequently used by the franchise to mark a liminal space between East and West, Bond squares off with mercurial foes as they move through recognizable cold war spaces. *Skyfall*'s main villain, Raoul Silva (Javier Bardem), is headquartered on an island off Macao, a special administrative region, like Hong Kong, of the People's Republic of China. Silva deals in fixed elections, assassinations, and sex trafficking. He gained control of the island by faking an environmental crisis. Managing his empire amid fallen statues sculpted in a monumental social realist style, he forces Bond to fight his henchmen while navigating a massive fallen iconic fist of the revolutionary worker. The shadow places where enemies lurk are littered with shattered, discarded relics of communism.

The film's historical nostalgia becomes self-referential nostalgia for the series itself. Bond even takes the classic Aston Martin DB5, first seen in *Goldfinger* (1964), out of a hidden garage and onto the road. The movie also reactivates the 1960s films' cold war linkage of subversion and evil to deviant sexuality. Silva alternately propositions Bond and strong-arms a woman in a forced sexual embrace. Silva turns out to be ex-agent H, one of M's former top agents, who went rogue. When he became erratic, M turned him over to enemies in China, where he was tortured. Face-to-face with M, he admonishes her for this betrayal in a chilling (if campy) retort: "You have been a bad mommy."

M's warning of invisible, unknowable enemies in her speech to Parliament is belied by her intimate knowledge of this particular enemy, whom she herself trained. Her nostalgic reading of the past amounts to a disingenuous, feigned innocence about an enemy she and fellow officials had a hand in creating, not unlike the US disavowal of the CIA's training of Osama bin Laden. The enemy is mysterious, their world opaque, an assertion that conveniently disregards the fact that they were once allies.

With M marked for revenge by Silva, Bond whisks her away from the compromised parliamentary headquarters and takes her off the grid. When asked where they are going, Bond tells M, "Back to the past, where we still had the advantage." Back to the past means returning to Bond's childhood estate in Scotland. In the final confrontation with Silva, Bond fashions makeshift weapons—explosives made of stainless-steel milk pails filled with rusty nails, crushed light bulbs, and dynamite—to fend off the most technologically advanced Bond villain to date. Stepping away from his guns and myriad gadgets, Bond dispatches his enemy by guile and an old-fashioned hunting knife.

After Silva's demise, Bond returns to MI6 headquarters, staged as a replica of the office from the 1960s films. We learn that the agent with whom Bond has worked most closely throughout the film is named Moneypenny, referencing M's secretary from the earliest installments. The golden age of spying survives.

Performing the Axis of Evil

Beyond the carefully curated International Spy Museum, cultural constructions of the war on terror proliferated, providing numerous occasions for cross-referencing with political rhetoric. Bush's inclusion of North Korea in the axis of evil struck informed observers as bizarre. Under the administrations of Nobel Peace Prize–winning South Korean president Kim Dae-jung (1998–2003) and President Roh Moo-hyun (2003–8), South Korea pursued what is known as the Sunshine policy from 1998 to 2008, with the goal of normalizing political and economic relations and easing military tensions through bilateral and multilateral diplomacy and negotiations.[44]

As part of these efforts, the Truth and Reconciliation Commission of South Korea was created in 2005. Headed by Dong-Choon Kim, a professor of sociology at Sungkonghoe University in Seoul, it was established by the South Korean Assembly as an independent body to investigate human rights violations from 1910 through 1987.[45] Along with emphasizing care for victims, including reparations and medical care, the commission's recommendations focused on memorialization through historical records, monuments, and peace education. In 2005, a Center for Human Rights was established in a former police investigation building in Namyeong-dong, Seoul, where officers tortured hundreds of pro-democracy activists in the 1970s and 1980s in the name of anticommunism. The Center was expanded and reopened in 2019 as a Hall of Human Rights and Democracy.[46] Such acts of remembrance fundamentally challenge continued triumphalist binary framings.

With the momentum toward normalization and reconciliation in Korea, Chung-in Moon, an adviser to both Kim Dae-jung and Roh, blamed US president George W. Bush for abandoning those efforts.[47] And there is a horrible irony in the fact that US actions undermined democracy and reconciliation projects in Korea at the very moment that the United States was expanding its torture and black op sites such as those at Abu Ghraib prison in Iraq and the secret prison at Bagram in Afghanistan.[48]

After Bush's preemptive doctrine toward North Korea unraveled years of diplomacy, the danger of the military tensions between North Korea and South Korea, Japan, and the United States was real. But threats of war, and even nuclear attack, make it all the more imperative to understand the pitfalls of talk of rogue states, and the negative consequences of embargoes and military threats, versus dialogue and diplomatic engagement. As US policy actively undermined Korean projects of reconciliation, US journalistic representations and parodies of Kim Jong Il were not remotely about him or the history of conflict on the Korean peninsula.

The obsessive fixation on Kim reenacted a cold war need for an absolute enemy, with Kim cast as a dangerous and unworthy adversary. Intersecting with news media and political rhetoric, cultural representations and enactments produced popular knowledge about the cold war and historical memory that influenced public opinion and policy.

At the time of the Sunshine policy, media reports that expressed surprise when Kim welcomed South Koreans at the Pyongyang airport in 2000 abounded, delighting in the warmth and "normalcy" of the leader. As reported by the *Independent* of London, "Mr. Kim, it became clear, is not a psychopath or a buffoon, but a humorous, practical, and affable man, who happens to be the leader of the world's last enduring Stalinist dictatorship."[49]

Following Bush's 2002 inclusion of North Korea in the axis of evil, media accounts resuscitated hostile depictions of Kim and North Korea. Despite US–North Korean diplomacy and the Sunshine policy, post–axis of evil depictions of North Korea reanimated derogatory portrayals. Cross-fertilization between conservative press accounts and satirical entertainment performances such as those on *Saturday Night Live* turned public opinion against diplomatic engagement and reconciliation between North and South Korea.

Numerous videos of performances lampooning Kim can be observed through a simple search on YouTube. Parody is always double-edged, sometimes more self-incrimination than a skewering of the object of critique. But context matters. Parodies of Kim trafficked in racist and sexist dehumanization, forms of humiliation akin to the psychological torture and abuse of prisoners at Abu Ghraib in Iraq.[50]

In February 2004 a military report and photographs taken by US military personnel revealed numerous instances of "sadistic, blatant, and wanton criminal abuses" at the US-controlled Abu Ghraib prison between October and December 2003. The acts of torture included "breaking chemical lights and pouring the phosphoric liquid on detainees; pouring cold water on naked detainees; beating detainees with a broom handle and a chair; threatening male detainees with rape ... sodomizing a detainee with a chemical light and perhaps a broom stick, and using military working dogs to frighten and intimidate detainees with threats of attack."[51]

More than sixteen thousand photographs were taken, with fewer than two hundred released to the public. Asking why so many modern states graphically record their atrocities, McClintock has argued that at Abu Ghraib, "US military intelligence, the CIA, the contractors and the interrogators photographed the prisoners as part of a performance of bureaucratic rationalization, to produce the bodies of 'the enemy' and make the prisoners *legible* as enemies, thereby, putatively 'legitimizing' the occupation." Photos were used to terrorize and humiliate, with photographic surveillance itself a form of humiliation and torment.[52]

Parodies similarly engaged in a project of making the enemy legible. In a January 11, 2003, *Saturday Night Live* skit, Kim was played by Horatio Sanz, with Maya Rudolph as the translator's voice. After portraying Kim ranting against "the gun-slinging buccaneer George Bush and his henchmen, Jimmy Carter and Wolf Blitzer," and declaring himself "delusional," the *Saturday Night Live* writers ridicule Kim's interest in American film. Sanz's Kim abruptly interrupts his rant with a film review: "And now, let's take a look at what's new this week on DVD. 'Sweet Home Alabama,' starring Reese Witherspoon. As formulaic romantic comedies go, 'Sweet Home Alabama' is inoffensive, and, I'll say it, charming. Witherspoon finds genuine emotion hidden under a blandly familiar plot, and I'd like to kidnap her and sodomize her. Three-and-a-half stars. And now, back to my angry tirade."[53]

The *Saturday Night Live* skit overlays imagined Korean gibberish with English subtitles. The animated comedy *Team America: World Police* (2004) performs stereotypes of Asian-accented English, portraying Kim as a self-pitying child, desperate for attention. Made by creators of *South Park*, *Team America* centers on a terrorist plot by Kim. Claiming to satirize Hollywood, *Team America* revels in the idea of the United States as police officer of the world.

Those who defend the film's satire insist that it lampoons everyone in a "pox on all of your houses" sendup of global politics. But the film's satire of global affairs fails not simply because it spares George W. Bush but because it endorses Bush's 2002 axis of evil, depicting Kim as "the other" of American democracy and capitalism. The filmmakers claimed that they refrained from "Bush-bashing" because "everyone else was doing that," adding, "We wanted to deal with this emotion of being hated as an American." As Trey

Parker and Matt Stone described the protagonist, an American soldier, "He was a dick. He wasn't an asshole—so too does America have this role in the world as a dick. Cops are dicks, you fucking hate cops, but you need them."[54] In their inimitably puerile fashion, for Parker and Stone, the cartoonish figure of Kim epitomizes threats to global security, allowing US audiences to disregard such destabilizing US foreign policies as the invasion and occupation of Iraq. While the isolation and belligerence of the North Korean regime make it an easy target, the unilateralist policies of Bush are justifiable because another head of state is perceived as more dangerous.

Parodies of Kim took off after the axis of evil speech, continuing after North Korea obtained its first nuclear weapon in 2006.[55] Comedian Danny Cho's 2009 "Kim Jong Il Eharmony" is styled as a commercial for the dating site with Kim as part of a glowing happy couple whose relationship suddenly sours, ending in his girlfriend's assassination when she annoys him.[56] The satiric Onion News Network's "Kim Jong Il Announces Plan to Bring Moon to North Korea" spoofed Kim's aspirations to modernize North Korea, as well as dynastic rule: "From time immemorial man has longed to walk on the moon in North Korea." In a displacement of anxiety about North Korea's nuclear capabilities, the writers mock Kim's technical capacity, showing a chart with five rockets that will be used to move the moon out of its present orbit to North Korea.[57]

What most of these representations have in common is the presentation of Kim as comically and sexually deranged, misogynist yet feminized, a trigger-happy, erratic, and dangerous enemy. As mockery of Kim became a cliché of television entertainment and radio news coverage, sketch comedy sendups and YouTube videos wallowed in stock Asian American stereotypes that far outnumbered dignified media representations by actual actors of Asian descent.

With the aid of mass media stereotyping and compliant corporate news organizations, this Manichean logic calling for the destruction of enemy regimes—while engaging in rituals of demonization and humiliation of "the other"—has become a staple of domestic American politics. First turned against internal enemies—a criminalized and unproductive Black population widely portrayed as noncitizens—the logic of the demonization of political enemies by Republican Party leaders and far right media since the mid-1990s has targeted government, public-sector unions, and the leaders and supporters of the Democratic Party, resulting in virtually unprecedented polarization and dysfunction in US politics. The demonization of political enemies in the pursuit of absolute power resulted in large swaths of the Republican Party leadership and electorate after 2008 refusing to accept or tacitly questioning the legitimacy of Barack Obama's presidency.

Remapping Geopolitics in Post-9/11 Film and Television

These performances shaped the geopolitical imaginations of audiences, along with political and cultural representations in film and television of new military protocols of war. The 2001 film *Black Hawk Down* and the television drama series *24* were released in the immediate wake of 9/11. While their development preceded the terrorist attacks, they offer a critical window into imagined military and official enactments of revenge.

Black Hawk Down, a dramatization of the 1993 debacle of US troop casualties in Mogadishu, was a love letter to the American military. Produced by Jerry Bruckheimer and directed by Ridley Scott, its creators worked closely with the US military. Like the 1999 book it was based on, the film was part of a growing corpus of novels and movies that extolled the basic goodness of the US military against its critics.

Black Hawk Down made uncritical support for the US military a litmus test for patriotism. To one critic, it "seemed to enhance the desire of Americans for a thumping war to avenge 9/11."[58] Finishing first in box-office earnings and holding that status for three consecutive weeks, the film was acclaimed for its unprecedented "realism" in depicting battle.

David Robb, who has studied the official channels of US military–Hollywood collaboration since World War II, argues that *Black Hawk Down* is a case of self-censorship. The filmmakers' requests for cooperation—in the form of borrowed warships, aircraft, location access, and troops—were submitted to the Pentagon with five copies of the film script, to accommodate Department of Defense requests for script modification if needed. In addition, an on-site technical adviser, what Robb calls a "military minder," was part of the collaboration. The Department of Defense loaned the film's producers a platoon of US Army Rangers, flew in military helicopters, and used aircraft from the 160th Special Operations Aviation Regiment with pilots involved in the 1993 operation. In return for the Pentagon's support of the producers of *Black Hawk Down*, Robb says, there was an unstated, mutual understanding: "Let's leave out the whole part about the soldiers being dragged through the streets of Mogadishu. Jerry Bruckheimer knows that if they have that in there, the military's just going to tell them to take it out or they won't help them.... So there's this self-censorship. When you know the government is looking over your shoulder while you're typing, that's a very bad situation."[59]

Bruckheimer sounded like a spokesperson for the US military when he defended the film against charges of racism on *The O'Reilly Factor* on Fox News.[60] Critics objected to the film's depiction of white heroes and the absence of any Somali point of view while depicting a "pornographic" slaughter of Africans in order to portray the film's villain, Somali warlord Mohamed Farrah Aidid, as a Hitler-like figure. Bruckheimer and O'Reilly alike decried Hollywood's "backstabbing" and "political correctness," while critics in the United States and Britain, highlighting historical US support for Somali regimes, charged the filmmakers with rewriting history by turning a debacle into a victory and fueling a growing American appetite for revenge.[61]

As *Black Hawk Down* fueled jingoistic sentiments, the everywhere war moved into Americans' homes and smartphones through video games, television, and films. Through popular culture, the citizen-warrior could immerse themselves in the geopolitical imaginings of a US-led global war on terror in which Americans were at once victors and victims.

Narrated in "real time," the series *24*, premiering on Fox in November 2001 and running for eight seasons, paralleled the structure of the everywhere war. Each episode covered one hour of counterterrorist agent Jack Bauer's life, and each season covered a twenty-four-hour day. Using split screens to represent constant, relentless conflict, the series suggested that the war on terror was being waged everywhere.[62] Critics charged that *24* normalized torture and that it erroneously suggested that so-called enhanced interrogation was effective. Such condemnations, including of the show's negative depiction of Muslims, led producers not to examine the show's assumptions but to seek advice from the military on "ton[ing] down" the torture.[63]

The 2007 movie *Charlie Wilson's War* celebrated rogue characters who go outside the law to achieve their political ends. The film is based on the true story of the eponymous Texas congressman, a rakish backbencher who forges an unlikely partnership during the 1980s with right-wing evangelicals on their anticommunist crusade to get Stinger missiles to militant insurgents in Soviet-occupied Afghanistan. Modeling his identity on a character in a 1969 novel by George MacDonald Fraser, *Flashman*, Wilson fancied himself a reincarnated imperial adventurer who had fought, drank, and womanized his way through nineteenth-century Afghanistan and India.[64] The film contests the fact that US-funded militants became the al-Qaeda and Taliban nemeses of subsequent decades. The film insists that later US conflict with

Afghanistan did *not* arise because the onetime US alliance with anti-American fundamentalists went horribly wrong but rather because the United States departed the country instead of sticking around to build schools and hospitals after the Soviets had been driven out.

Some films were more critical of the US wars in Afghanistan and Iraq and the CIA's use of torture in Guantánamo Bay and its secret prisons. Gaghan's 2005 geopolitical thriller *Syriana*, based on the memoir *See No Evil* by former CIA agent Robert Baer, is deeply skeptical of US policy in the Middle East, challenging American exceptionalism and its assumptions of moral and epistemological superiority. *Syriana* includes a sympathetic Middle Eastern modernizer who lands on the wrong side of the CIA because he stands in the way of its cynical short-term goals. The film also sides with exploited laborers in the transnational workforce building and maintaining US bases.[65]

Against a backdrop of news exposés of the indefinite imprisonment and torture of terror suspects at Guantánamo Bay detention camp, and of CIA black sites—secret locations for the detention and torture of terror suspects—some blockbuster films portrayed US intelligence as using its formidable surveillance capabilities to mete out violence for no higher purpose than to shield top-secret operations from public exposure. The popular Jason Bourne trilogy, based on the novels of Robert Ludlum, was striking in its indictment of the CIA. Bourne (Matt Damon) is a super-agent unwittingly programmed to be a skilled and remorseless killer through a secret CIA collaboration with the global corporation Treadstone, suggesting the privatization of the military and that the US empire now outsources much of its dirty work to shadowy global corporations.

In *The Bourne Identity* (2002), Bourne is sent to assassinate the leader of an African country, but his programmed ruthlessness falters as he recognizes the humanity of the leader, who shields his children from harm's way, leaving himself exposed. The integrity of the leader stands in contrast to the CIA's illegal assault; for some, the fictional assassination plot resonates with a well-documented history of CIA involvement in coups and assassinations that have removed leaders of countries critical of US policies. As Bourne attempts to recover his identity, he retraces his steps as an assassin, finding his victims' families and confronting the pain caused by his actions. Eventually he reaches the person responsible for his brainwashing and learns that his real name is David Webb.

Despite the depiction of endemic corruption in and out of government in *The Bourne Supremacy* (2004) and *The Bourne Ultimatum* (2007), the

CIA—and, by extension, US policy—is absolved in two critical ways. First, Bourne is helped by an insider, Pamela Landy, who, when confronted with his question, "Why did you help me?" responds, "Because I didn't sign up for this. This isn't who we are." Though Bourne had been relentlessly surveilled and hunted by evil high-level officials in the agency, Landy's response tempers the series' portrayal of the agency's sinister actions and values. Second, the possible redemption of the agency ultimately depends on Bourne's prowess as the best agent of all. For all of the repugnant actions and wanton violence it lays at the agency's doorstep, the series has no intention of questioning its legitimacy. Despite everything we might know about CIA assassinations and coups, and more recent evidence of the ineptitude of the agency (as in the failure to connect the dots of warnings before 9/11, or the fabrication of the evidence of weapons of mass destruction), the film lacks the courage of its convictions, stopping short of imagining a more democratic and diplomatic response to matters of war and global security. We still need agents like Bourne, his rehabilitated humanity symbolizing the redemption of the hegemony of US empire. With the public airing of examples of CIA bureaucratic incompetence and human rights violations, cultural production returns to the lone hero reminiscent of the classic Hollywood Westerns, their penchant for violence saving civilization from lawless threats but also marking them as inveterate outsiders. We still need the virtuous vigilante super-agent. US empire may be the problem, but it is also the only solution.

The "Af-Pak" Battle Zone

Super-agents—and, by extension, their high-tech tools—embodied the high-altitude drone strikes of the US wars in Afghanistan, supposedly executed with surgical precision. Our confidence in the super-agent has its corollary in an implicit trust in high-tech wars among the general public as a preferred alternative to the massive deployment of ground troops. Fought in the border zones of Afghanistan and Pakistan—termed "Af-Pak" by the Obama administration—where targeted drone strikes were said to avoid collateral damage and civilian casualties while neutralizing the bad guys, this new mode of warfare flouted international law and relied on a self-serving distortion of cold war history.[66]

The US-led invasion of Afghanistan "combined a long-distance war from the air with a ground war spearheaded by warlords, militias of the Northern Alliance US infantry, and Special Forces."[67] US strikes by drones, or "unmanned aerial vehicles," were carried out by armed MQ-1 Predators and MQ-9 Reapers launched in Afghanistan and Pakistan but remotely controlled by the CIA from the continental United States.[68] US and NATO troops and air missions were launched from the Manas Transit Center, 645 miles from Kabul. According to the historian David Vine, after the start of the war in Afghanistan in 2001, the United States established at least five drone bases in Pakistan.[69]

Bush's 2001 authorization of "kill, capture or detain orders" of terror suspects gave the CIA wide discretion, expanding the scope of the global war's prison-industrial complex involving the seizure, detention, and torture of terror suspects at black sites. A program aimed at targeting "high-value target" individuals carried over into the next administration. With at least forty-six drone strikes in Pakistan by the end of 2008, the program accelerated during the Obama administration, even as extraordinary rendition programs were terminated and black sites closed.[70] By 2010, there had been an additional 180 strikes.[71]

The concept of Af-Pak as a battle zone with precision bombing promotes the illusion that such strikes produce no civilian casualties. But civilian deaths were frequent and often highly visible, as in December 2013, when US military operatives mistook a Yemeni wedding procession for an Al-Qaeda convoy, launching a drone strike with Hellfire missiles that killed at least twelve people in the wedding party.[72] Framings of the United States as both victim and righteous adjudicator in a perpetual global war depended on abstracting the region from its actual history, including the cold war–era US support of Pakistan's military dictatorships, US material backing of a global jihad to combat Soviet communism, and mid-1990s US alliances with the Taliban in pursuit of an oil pipeline. Such amnesia animated an October 2007 *Newsweek* cover story: "The Most Dangerous Nation in the World Isn't Iraq, It's Pakistan," which framed the nation and the region as insular and backward.[73]

Writing after an attempted assassination of Bhutto (and praised as prescient when she was assassinated two months later), foreign correspondent Ron Moreau argued, "Whoever the 'real culprits' of the attack, the truth is that Pakistan's government has only itself to blame. . . . Pakistani leaders created the Islamist monster that now operates with near impunity throughout the country." Noting that "militant Islamist groups that were originally recruited, trained and armed by Pakistan's Inter-Services Intelligence agency (ISI) have since become Islamabad's deadliest enemies," Moreau ignored the inextricable links between ISI and the CIA, instead claiming that "militancy is woven into the fabric of Pakistani society."[74]

Kamila Shamsie's 2009 novel, *Burnt Shadows*, disrupts the myth of a "surgical, sensitive and scrupulous" war on terror conducted by a technologically advanced military by foregrounding the human toll and tragedy wrought by the strategic decisions of policy makers.[75] Situating the region within a longer geopolitical history, the novel's global purview and plot closely track cold war dynamics, from the 1945 bombing of Nagasaki, which inaugurated the nuclear age, to CIA-permeated Karachi, to the late twentieth and early twenty-first-century wars in Afghanistan. The novel opens in the present as a young man in an orange jumpsuit is brought to Guantánamo, notorious for its suspension of basic human rights and constitutional freedoms. The scene shifts to Nagasaki and the doomed, budding romance between nineteen-year-old Hiroko Tanaka and Konrad Weiss, a German who has spent the war years in Japan. Konrad, who had been studying Japanese with Hiroko, is incinerated in the atomic blast. Hiroko survives, with the pattern of the kimono she was wearing at the moment of the blast permanently etched onto her back. Shunned by her society, Hiroko makes her way to Delhi in 1947 in search of Konrad's British half sister, whose husband serves in the British Foreign Service, and Konrad's boyhood friend Sajjad Ashad. As Sajjad tutors Hiroko in Urdu, once again, language study leads to love. Honeymooning in Istanbul to escape the violence of partition, the couple is denied reentry into India when officials claim that Sajjad, as a Muslim, has no right to return.

Exiled from Dilli, Sajjad's home in the Muslim heart of Delhi from the twelfth century, they settle in Karachi. After decades of building a life and raising a son, Raza, their placid existence is disrupted by the threat of nuclear war between India and Pakistan and repression under the US-backed Pakistani military dictatorships, underwritten by the CIA and its alliance with Pakistan's ISI. As the agencies patrol the Pakistan-Afghanistan border, Raza is drawn into the intrigue, deceit, and divided loyalties of private military corporations, where he is framed for a murder he did not commit and sent into the black hole of Guantánamo's state of exception.

Shamsie's narrative stitches together disparate developments that were fatefully shaped by bipolar rivalry. In the spirit of Shamsie's panoramic vision linking the cold war with decolonization and its troubled aftermath, historians would do well to attend to the projects and dreams of those whose lives were uprooted by the period's upheavals and violence.

Hiroko's story is fictional, and the tragedy of lives shattered and rebuilt, surviving the traumas inflicted by bombs and partitions, is seldom recorded in state archives. Yet the quotidian stories of mass displacement are fundamental to the twentieth- and twenty-first-century wars that followed. As Hiroko leaves Japan for India, and then Pakistan, and later for New York after her husband is killed by a trigger-happy CIA driver, we see the brutal afterlife of colonialism perpetuated by cold war geopolitics. With partition a fateful product of colonial policies, military hostilities between India and Pakistan are exacerbated by the US cold war alliance with Pakistan and its hostility toward the nonaligned politics of India. The shattered lives at the center of Shamsie's historical novel compel readers to consider the extent to which the cold war left chaos and human catastrophe in its wake. Hiroko's suffering encapsulates the betrayal of wartime ideals and aspirations of democracy and decolonization by nuclear war, followed by the imposition of US cold war imperatives. If not for US support of Pakistan's military dictatorships, and the CIA's outsize role in the region, Hiroko would not have lost her husband to an assassin. Nor would she have ended up in Karachi, terrified at the prospect of another nuclear explosion. Nor would she face the likelihood of never seeing her beloved son again after losing him to the CIA's secret prison complex.

Shadows of the Cold War in the War on Terror: Notes from Bishkek

Invited by scholars at the American University of Central Asia, I arrived in Bishkek, Kyrgyzstan, on May 5, 2013, Constitution Day. The city's celebration of Victory Day, marking the Soviet defeat of the Nazis and honoring the fallen, was only three days later. Posters and advertisements marking the upcoming national holiday festooned shops, cinemas, and post offices. Schools were closed for the holiday, public parks were mowed, and flowers were planted, their bright colors accenting the monuments that dotted the parks and boulevards. The grand marble public buildings and brutalist cement structures that had apparently seen little upkeep since the collapse of the USSR reinforced the sense that one was in a Soviet city. Still, even as Bishkek's makeover saluted the Red Army's wartime sacrifices, signs of a triumphalist US presence, leaving no doubt of the US cold war "victory," were in abundance.

Far from the coveted Caspian Sea pipeline, Kyrgyzstan never caught the imagination of the West like its larger neighbors, including Afghanistan and China. Yet from the start of US Operation Enduring Freedom against Taliban forces in Afghanistan in 2001 through June 2014, Kyrgyzstan was the site of a key staging ground of the US war in Afghanistan, the Manas

Transit Center, adjacent to the airport near the capital city of Bishkek. With its proximity to Kabul, and less than three hundred miles from Kashgar, China, Kyrgyzstan has been a vital ally in the war in Afghanistan and a key site of US-Russian cooperation—and tensions—in the war on terror. An estimated 5.5 million American and allied troops from twenty-six countries passed through Manas in US- and NATO-led military operations. Manas enabled refueling of fighter jets on a massive scale.[76]

Kyrgyzstan holds the distinction of being the only country to have simultaneously hosted US and Russian military bases. Western press accounts describe the 2003 opening of the Russian Kant airbase, twenty kilometers to the east of Bishkek, as a response to the new American air base. In fact, Russians had reopened the Soviet-era Kant base, built in 1941. Like its neighbor Kazakhstan, known for its cosmonauts and plutonium production centers, Kyrgyzstan was closed to Western visitors during the Soviet period. The Kant base, explained an intellectual who was in his mid-thirties when the Soviet Union collapsed, offered military training to foreigners, including Vietnamese, Cuban, African, and other third-world peoples—"anyone fighting for democracy" and against imperialism.[77]

For over a decade, the Manas Transit Center was the largest US footprint in Kyrgyzstan, but it was not the first American arrival in post-Soviet Bishkek. As an outpost of US triumphalism in the former Soviet sphere, Kyrgyzstan features a palimpsest of US institutions overlaying a decrepit Soviet infrastructure. Hungarian billionaire George Soros and his Open Democracy project partnered with the US government to found the American University of Central Asia (founded as the Kyrgyz-American School) in Bishkek in 1993. The Peace Corps, a slew of Western nongovernmental organizations (NGOs), and scores of investors and mining speculators followed. Direct US aid, supplemented by funds from other US government–financed institutions like the National Endowment for Democracy, was widely considered a major factor in the overthrow of the unpopular president Askar Akayev during the Tulip Revolution of 2005.[78]

In a symbolic gesture rivaling the establishment of the John F. Kennedy Center just east of the Brandenburg Gate in Berlin, the American University of Central Asia moved into the building that formerly housed Kyrgyzstan's Communist Party headquarters in 1993. The building abuts a public plaza and park that also recall the Soviet era. Opposite the school and on the other side of the park sits the rear of the nation's State Historical Museum. The front of the museum faces the picturesque view of snow-capped mountains to the south. For years, a statue of Vladimir Lenin faced the mountains. Yet, controversially, Lenin's statue was replaced under cover of night in 2003 by a monument to Manas, the presumed leader of the ancient Kyrgyz people. Shunted to the rear and now facing the university, Lenin's statue, as locals like to joke, points an accusing finger at the institution. The museum, built in the early 1980s, features panels, photos, and exhibits chronicling the Russian Revolution and its official recognition of central Asian ethno-nations within Soviet modernization. A vast mural on the ceiling depicts scenes from the Bolshevik revolution, the heyday of Kyrgyz Theater in the 1930s, the military victory against global fascism, the heroic space explorations of the cosmonauts, and new threats from the United States in the 1980s, as well as an affirmation of the Soviet commitment to peace. With doves holding peace banners amid a representation of Ronald Reagan as a cowboy riding a nuclear missile, the peoples of the Soviet Union proclaim, "No more Hiroshimas."[79]

Completed a decade before the collapse of the Soviet Union, the mural, a revealing if kitschy document of the Soviet era, is cracking and peeling. More recently, the museum has replaced relics of the Soviet past with Kyrgyz cultural artifacts. Indeed, US projects and institutions inhabit a landscape filled with crumbling roads and bearing visible traces of imperial czarist and Soviet pasts. One readily imagines the certitude of American newcomers deploying ostensibly universal standards of democracy and development, confident that they would sweep aside the past and its crumbling and decrepit infrastructure.

Historians, however, have taught us to see unexpected parallels between East and West that may have a chastening effect on American self-confidence. Kate Brown has illuminated the striking spatial and even historical similarities between US and central Asian landscapes, histories, and development.[80] The flat plains of the central Asian steppes, rising to enormous mountains, and the history of Russian settlement raise comparisons to the American West. Russian settlers moved into the modern-day Kyrgyz Republic in the early 1860s (following the incorporation of Kazakhstan in the 1840s), and the area was annexed by Russia in 1876, roughly during the years that the US Homestead and Morrill Land Grant Acts of 1862 encouraged a rush of white settlers west. With the US settlement came the post–Civil War armies that fought the last wars of Indian conquest and removal. Similarly, Kyrgyz history has seen its share of violent conflict with Russian settlers, including the Kyrgyz uprising that followed the czar's conscription of nomadic peoples into the Russian Army in 1916. However radically divergent the histories of the Kyrgyz Soviet Socialist Republic and the United States appear throughout the twentieth century, their historical similarities of

6.2 Mural, Kyrgyz theater, State Historical Museum, Bishkek, Kyrgyzstan

6.3 "No more Hiroshimas," mural, State Historical Museum, Bishkek, Kyrgyzstan

modernization, settler colonial violence, and multiethnic and multicultural diversity come into focus.

From the perspective of Kyrgyz chroniclers, a shared history and memory is evident. In one mural panel, to the right of a Kyrgyz on horseback with children nestled on both sides, appears a tractor with the label Fordson, a reminder of Henry Ford's dealings with the early Bolshevik state and the seven hundred thousand tractors produced under the Fordson brand before it went out of production in 1928. The Fordson tractor enshrined in the mural is a reminder of a vision and project of modernization harnessing mass production and an equally shared faith that industrial and agricultural development and progress would deliver the good life to the citizens of both societies.[81]

The Manas Transit Center and bases like it were intended to mark a departure from earlier US bases. Meant to efficiently facilitate troop transports and refueling, it was further designed to avoid the adverse impact of US cold war bases whose presence and operation devastated local societies, ecologies, and economies. Accordingly, US officials sought to nurture community relations by sponsoring sports events and scheduling school field trips to visit the base, seeking to project a friendlier image than its cold war–era predecessors.

Yet the Manas air base elicits negative feelings from the Kyrgyz population, with 77 percent citing the United States as the country's biggest problem in a 2012 survey. The base was at the center of several scandals, including the shooting of a local man at the base checkpoint by an American guard, and environmental toxins leaching into the surrounding soil and water.[82] Many take offense at the euphemistic name Manas Transit Center, defiantly calling it the Military Air Base. With the name derived from "The Epic of Manas," a poem chronicling the history of the Kyrgyz people, local people objected to the appropriation of an icon of Kyrgyz cultural identity. As one student queried, "How can an American air base be named after Manas?"[83] Another student's father viewed the name as insulting: "He thought someone was trying to make him the butt of a joke by setting him up as gullible."[84] Like the efforts of the well-intentioned but naïve US Peace Corps volunteer in Robert Rosenberg's novel *This Is Not Civilization*, whose cultural gaffes in Kyrgyzstan escalate to more serious faux pas, the naming backfired.

By 2013, with the base's closure on the horizon and local criticism of the United States mounting, the United States developed plans to expand its embassy, hoping to encourage economic and cultural activities more acceptable to Kyrgyz people than a military base. Facing criticism, and with US companies facing competition from China and Russia over mining rights, some American officials wondered whether they should remain at all. Noting the new construction of several mosques and schools with money primarily from the Turkish government, some wondered whether the country might be conceded to Turkish influence. Rethinking the US presence may be laudable, but the assumptions behind the question are troubling. Viewing Kyrgyzstan as a natural part of a contemporary Turkish world homogenizes the region, erasing both the particularity of the Kyrgyz people and the multiethnic nature of present-day Kyrgyzstan. It also erases the Soviet past.

The pervasive idea that nothing of value or worth remembering happened in the Soviet period is absurd to those who lived through Soviet times. Local artists and intellectuals reflecting on the legacy of the Soviet Union and the country's layered past insist on a recognition of the achievements of the Soviet experiment alongside condemnation of the sordid aspects of the Stalinist past.

Georgy Mamedov, a Bishkek-based writer and curator, outlines a collective project of critical engagement with the legacy of the Soviet Union by central Asian artists in the 2012 exhibition *The Lost Pathos or the Pathos of Loss*. Mamedov writes of Soviet rule, "All its traumatizing and destructive experience on one hand, and inspiring and emancipatory on the other, require comprehensive reflection and understanding which probably can be produced only now, when there is a generation of artists and researchers who can look at the issue of the Soviet, not through the lens of nostalgia and personal traumatic experience of dissolv[ing] of one's identity, but in a way 'objectively,' with sober but engaged eye."[85] Mamedov explains that the curators' interrogations of the past have sparked calls from the current government to close the State Historical Museum. But Mamedov, like others, believes that it should be maintained to critically examine Soviet history.[86]

Mamedov considers the museum an example of Soviet kitsch, appearing, from our present-day perspective, "more racist than intended."[87] Indeed, the State Historical Museum murals tell, in part, a civilizationist story of the development of the Kyrgyz people. But Kyrgyz critics join scholars who insist that this story must be understood in terms of a genuine commitment to decolonization. Unflinching in his depiction of the unsavory aspects of the Russian and Soviet presence in Kyrgyzstan, the historian Benjamin Loring shows that the early Soviet Turkestan Commission established "equal treatment toward the native population in hiring, requisition, taxation, conscription, and other spheres. This policy was neither temporary nor self-serving. It aimed at the permanent disestablishment of colonial privilege in the region." For Loring, "its relatively short lifespan and disappointing outcomes resulted not from a hidden agenda of deception and hypocrisy (as some cold war scholarship has asserted), but rather from weak state capacity and eventually from the exigencies of an 'all-Union' political and economic agenda."[88]

The scholarship on Kyrgyzstan joins recent writing that demonstrates the breadth and depth of the Bolshevik project of cultivating ethno-nations. Historians Ronald Suny and Terry Martin have noted what they call the crowning irony of Soviet history: despite their deep suspicion of nationalism, in the 1920s Lenin and Joseph Stalin adopted wildly ambitious ethno-nationalist projects involving the creation of ethnically specific cultural institutions, from the opera to the press, and the creation of written languages where none had previously existed. The ironic result was that a "radical socialist elite that proclaimed an internationalist agenda that was to transcend the bourgeois nationalist phase of history in fact ended up by institutionalizing nations within its own political body."[89]

A founding member of the collective Former West project, a call to move beyond the bloc mentality, Mamedov argues that "in the post-Soviet period, there has been a tendency to naively homogenize the Soviet Union either as everything was nice, which is dangerous if one is missing Stalin/empire and world power; or everything was bad." But Soviet periods differed greatly, from the revolution to Stalin, Leonid Brezhnev, and perestroika. The Soviet project needs to be analyzed through multiple prisms, including a communist utopian project, an alternative economic project, and "through the unity, equality and social security achieved in the Soviet period." For Mamedov, "perestroika reanimated the true spirit of Leninism." Moving beyond a bloc mentality would require a Western glasnost and perestroika—as well as engagements with critical central Asian perspectives and an assessment of their intertwined histories. According to Mamedov, "The end of the cold war was the end of Europe as well. It was the Soviet political and economic project that created Western European social democracy through reforms."[90]

The transition to a post-Soviet world has been wrenching for Kyrgyzstan in terms of its national identity and material standing. With economic collapse and the mass departure of East German and Russian engineers, people remember living without electricity for three years. In the 1960s, explained one professor, "divided Europe enabled us to conceive of something like a cold war. On this side, there was not a cold war but a wall. For me, it was impossible to go abroad. From this side, it was an Iron Wall, building a wall so that people were not influenced by Western ideas, such as in jamming radio stations. After the Soviet Union, the world became wild. In Soviet times, we produced things, we traveled (within the Soviet Union), we made museums, as if violence didn't exist at all."[91]

Scholars and contemporary observers have commented on Kyrgyzstan's Soviet nostalgia relative to other central Asian countries. One scholar explained that while Soviet "monuments were removed in Turkmenistan and replaced with other statues," "it is different in Kyrgyzstan. Internationalism and multiculturalism [were] a very big part of life. We tried very hard to bring over one hundred different ethnic peoples in Kyrgyzstan together."[92]

Many fondly remember the moral framework of Soviet children's cartoons along with the dependable structure of family holidays and children's camps. "During Soviet times there were Pioneer Camps; now there is nothing for kids to do except to play video games." Lana explained that she felt sorry for Americans. "I thought, poor Americans. They live under capitalism. They don't have the good life. I try to raise my children on Soviet films and cartoons because they are so beautiful. They have good values. . . . I saw an American textbook at a Protestant church that portrayed the Soviet Union as devils and described the Soviet Union as a slave society. The US was invested in brainwashing with different radio stations in different ways. People still don't like capitalism. They don't like having everything determined by money. Young people don't know how much they missed in their parents' lives. It is not just words. Everyday life was more continuous then."[93]

American Studies Kyrgyz–Style

The Soros-funded American University of Central Asia, while sharing the challenges of US and global universities in terms of a lack of funding for the humanities, clearly provides space for creative and critical inquiry on the part of many students and faculty. In 2013, I observed students interviewing a range of family and friends to document the complexity of the Soviet past, as well as considering American studies through the prism of the local presence of US institutions from the military to corporations such as Coca-Cola.

A Kyrgyz American Studies Association conference, held in a former communist summer camp on beautiful mountain Lake Issyk-Kul, mostly draws English-language teachers, but students from the American University of Central Asia offer lively and often brilliant papers examining the impact of US institutions in Kyrgyzstan. Yet with most, if not all, of the participants funded by some form of US or NGO money, a persistent undertone of concern about the sustainability of the projects in the face of growing criticism of NGOs was palatable.

In debates over the presence of NGOs in Kyrgyzstan and the former Soviet sphere more broadly, there has been little assessment of the differences between, on the one hand, the relatively no-strings-attached approach of Soros, which does *not* equate civil society with neoliberalism, and, on the other hand, NGOs that adhere to a neoliberal economic agenda. The conflation of such projects has in part enabled the attacks on Soros by the Viktor Orbán government in Hungary, shutting down Central European University in Budapest.[94] Yet support from NGOs is all too often contingent on a recipient's fealty to a rigid neoliberal agenda, and the actions of numerous NGOs have sparked accusations of political and economic interference.

In past years, Kyrgyz villagers have carried out vigorous protests against foreign mining companies, including South African Talas Gold and the Chinese-owned Asia Gold Enterprises. Protests have also occurred in Bishkek.[95] Contemporary mining overlays a deep history of cold war–era extraction, still visible along a major route between Issyk-Kul, once a Soviet site of torpedo testing, with weapons still produced on the south shore, and Bishkek. The road passes Orlovka village, a strategic place for mining uranium and the wealthiest place in Kyrgyzstan. During the industrial transformation of World War I, rare minerals used in military production kept many people working in factories; decades after its abandonment in Soviet times, the village is very poor. People are trying to develop a nearby ski resort, which is helping the village and offers free skiing to children from the village. In Soviet times, there were several secret cities in the country where weapons scientists worked. After the collapse of the Soviet Union, people didn't know what to do with the weapons scientists. Some were recruited by international organizations such as the International Science and Technology Center.

Given the extensive mining and poor storage of radioactive elements, mountain hazards are a pressing issue in Kyrgyzstan. Many of its one hundred thousand mountain lakes are in danger of lake outbursts from melting glaciers and the spring melting of the mountain snow, outbursts that not only provoke landslides that submerge houses and villages but are highly toxic. Earthquakes are also a major hazard.[96]

Yet ignoring the challenges Kyrgyz people face from legacies of cold war–era extraction and environmental damage, scholars cite a "culture of distrust" and warn of the dangers of "resource nationalism" in a poor country that they claim would benefit from accessing its mineral wealth.[97] Such scholars, along with neoliberal NGOs, draw on what the historian Megan Black has identified as "resource globalism"—the idea that certain materials, in particular oil and materials identified as strategic, are "really the property of all mankind rather than nationalist governments"—and its sister concept, resource primitivism, the idea that multitudes across the globe dangerously misunderstood and undervalued resources. Here, they replicate triumphalist views that deem opposition to capitalism irrational, dismissing Kyrgyz environmental concerns and protesters' questions about who is actually benefiting from the mining.[98]

Promises of investments and support by businesses and NGOs have largely failed to materialize in any way commensurate with the loss of support for infrastructure, education, and public culture that accompanied the collapse of the Soviet state. In 2013, people joked about well-meaning donations of computers to schools without heat or electricity. In the eyes of critics, people are now "free" to choose Western capitalism and corresponding political institutions deemed appropriate by the West. The key for many is that people had no choice; no more choice in Soros's "democracy" and the onslaught of NGOs seeking to regulate and improve Kyrgyz society than they had choice in the dissolution of the Soviet Union, Russian imperialism under the czar, or the Russian Revolution.[99]

NGO Law Monitor considers virtually any attempt to regulate NGOs as "efforts to limit civil society" rather than a rejection of the idea, as the legal scholar Eric Posner has put it, that "the West can impose a political and economic blueprint that will advance the well-being of other countries."[100] In short, "civil society" itself is defined as adherence to neoliberal norms of governance. Human rights monitors were particularly irate at Kyrgyz foreign agent laws, similar to those passed in Russia, "targeting undesirable NGOs."[101]

Disputes about the role of NGOs were central to conflicts in Georgia and Ukraine as well as Kyrgyzstan, where local activists have charged such organizations as Human Rights Watch of having a revolving door with the US government and corporations.[102] The views of these activists align with critiques of human rights projects by such legal scholars as Posner and William Easterly, as well as by the historian Jan Eckel. Eckel has argued that human rights activists, believing in the ethical imperative of intervention, have unwittingly sought "profound changes in the political systems and even social practices of foreign countries."[103]

In a unipolar world, such projects often align with neoliberal agendas. In Bishkek, human rights agendas consistent with neoliberal goals erase histories that challenge Western triumphalism. In contrast, the hands-off approach of Soros-funded human rights and open-society initiatives has enabled searching historical inquiry and mitigated against triumphalist erasure.[104] The cosmopolitanism and intellectual independence fostered by Soros's Open Democracy Foundation is precisely what led to the targeting of the Soros-funded Central Eastern University in Budapest by Orbán's self-proclaimed "illiberal" government.[105]

Whether in geopolitical mappings found in popular culture or in neoliberal scripts on development that condemn local opponents of extractive projects as nationalist fanatics, post-1989 reproductions of Western civilizationist ideas can only be countered by engaging activists, critics, and artists in places where US power has left its mark.

Looking for Lumumba Street

Given my own long-standing interest in transnational solidarity movements, I queried my hosts in Bishkek about their memories of internationalism. I asked about Patrice Lumumba, postindependence prime minister of the short-lived Democratic Republic of the Congo, who was assassinated by Belgian authorities with CIA involvement in 1961, because his death had led to an international outpouring of protests. As documented by the historian Leo Zeilig, after news of Lumumba's death was officially announced on February 13, "as many as 30,000 smashed their way into the Belgian Embassy in Belgrade," with Yugoslav demonstrators shouting, "Lumumba will live forever."[106] In Warsaw, the Belgian ambassador fled for his life. Syrian students and workers took to the streets, and an estimated half a million people demonstrated in Shanghai. Major protest marches also took place in London and Paris.[107] African American protesters at the United Nations in New York held signs declaring, "The murder of Lumumba exposes the nature of colonialism." Ghana's prime minister Kwame Nkrumah observed that Lumumba's murder was "the first time in history that the legal ruler of a country has been done to death with the open connivance of a world organization on whom that ruler put his trust."[108]

Lumumba's assassination reverberated across the globe, altering the cold war landscape as streets were named after him in dozens of cities around the world, including Jakarta, Belgrade, Tehran, and Budapest. Transnational responses rebounded to the Congo when Che Guevara and Cuban troops

6.4 Bishkek, Lumumba Street

clandestinely intervened in Zaire (Congo) on behalf of the beleaguered guerrilla army of Laurent-Désiré Kabila, made up of Lumumba's former supporters.[109]

My questions about Lumumba initially provoked no memories of solidarity with Africans and anti-imperialist wars. Several people responded that the Soviet Union invoked global (as opposed to Soviet) internationalism to deflect criticism at home. I soon discovered that there is a Patrice Lumumba Street in Bishkek. One colleague remembered that her granny had told her that somewhere on her side of town the Soviets had a training camp and school for Africans. On my last day in Bishkek, on the pretext of a tour to see Bishkek away from the center of town, my hosts surprised me by taking me to Lumumba Street. Weaving through streets of factories and car repair shops, we lingered at a residential street, pleasant and nondescript: Lumumba Street. It had not been renamed after 1991, as many in Russia and Eastern Europe had been, nor was it marked as an important site of historical memory.

Driving along Lumumba Street, as we crossed Chuy, a main drag, houses gave way to more factories and auto repair shops. Passing shop after shop, we stumbled onto a vast military training base and the Patrice Lumumba

School; both had trained Africans during the Soviet period. Signs at the base warned,

> Border. Stop. I Will Shoot You.
> No Trespassing. The Forbidden Zone.

Confronting a landscape haunted by the militarism that stood alongside the utopian aspiration for the good life on both sides of the cold war divide, the military base and school on Lumumba Street remind us that the Soviet Union, along with Cuba, provided critical aid to national liberation movements in southern Africa, including those in South Africa, the Republic of the Congo, and Angola.[110] Following the dissolution of the Soviet Union, Cubans training as aircraft mechanics were stranded in Kyrgyzstan, unable to return home. Many married Kyrgyz women, and their presence endures in the Club Havana, an establishment opened in Bishkek next to the Philharmonia Hall.[111]

Like the Kant airbase, the Patrice Lumumba School reveals hidden histories of cold war–era African liberation struggles. One needn't romanticize Soviet internationalism; extensive documentation exists, for example, of racism against African students who studied at Moscow's Patrice Lumumba University and elsewhere in the USSR. But a critical approach must also acknowledge that Soviet training and support were critical to many in the global South fighting anti-imperialist wars. Grappling with that history requires examining the scope of the Soviet experience in and beyond Russia, as well as in the global South—in other words, taking up the challenge of Mamedov to move beyond the bloc mentality.

Spies R Us

PARADOXES OF US-RUSSIAN RELATIONS

It was strange to be in St. Petersburg and Moscow in April 2017. For anyone following the news, it was clear that Vladimir Putin's Russian intelligence service, the GRU, had hacked the US elections, sowing disinformation that contributed to the 2016 election of Donald Trump, and setting in motion Trump's gutting of US government agencies, including the State Department and intelligence communities. Although these developments followed a long-term erosion of US democratic institutions and norms—enabled in part by cold war triumphalism and affinities between Putin-style authoritarianism and Trump's autocratic, white nationalist politics—the results were nevertheless terrifying.

The first time I visited Russia, in May 2008, Putin had tightened his grip over journalists, critics, and the economy, bestowing a bit of trickle-down prosperity by rewarding his circle of loyal oligarchs. The "new cold war" between the United States and Russia was also underway. For the first time since the collapse of the Soviet Union, tanks were paraded on streets to celebrate Victory Day, the defeat of the Nazis. Nostalgia for the military might of empire was palpable.

Despite Putin's consolidation of power and rising tensions with the United States, in 2008 the spirit of glasnost seemed very much alive in some Russian cultural institutions. By 2013, the tide had turned. The Parliament passed legislation criminalizing acts said to offend religious believers after four members of the all-female rock group Pussy Riot were charged in 2012 with hooliganism and inciting hatred against Orthodox Christians. Their transgression had been a punk prayer shouted in the Russian Orthodox Christ Savior Cathedral in Moscow: "Virgin birth-giver of god, please drive away Putin."[1] The new law, in effect by 2014, made it easier to prosecute any who could be accused, credibly or not, of insulting the Russian Orthodox Church.[2] Paralleling these developments, right-wing Russians were forging alliances with the US National Rifle Association and the National Organization for Marriage, whose president, Brian Brown, visited Russia four times in four years and testified in 2013 before the Russian Duma (Parliament) as Russia enacted a series of antigay laws.[3]

Juxtaposing 2008 and 2017 exhibits at the State Museum of Political History of Russia in St. Petersburg reveals a jarring shift from glasnost to Putin-style authoritarianism, and a stark rewriting of history. In 2017, the one hundredth anniversary of the Russian Revolution, Putin's authoritarian government was in no mood for any nostalgia about the promises of education and jobs offered by the Russian Revolution.[4]

The State Museum of Political History of Russia, formerly the Museum of the Revolution, is housed in two Moderne-style mansions. Taken over by the Bolsheviks in 1917, the museum preserves the early Bolshevik headquarters, including Vladimir Lenin's office and the balcony from which he delivered speeches. In 2008, a visitor entered by walking up an oak staircase featuring exquisite stained-glass windows with classic portraits of Lenin in art deco style. Compared with the several museums I visited in the Eastern bloc, the St. Petersburg museum seemed more nuanced in its portrayal of Soviet times, documenting repression as well as the era's scientific, cultural, and material achievements. Past a gift shop full of books, postcards, art, and propaganda posters, the first exhibit contained wrenching letters from political prisoners and guards of the gulags. Other displays replicated the stuff of everyday life, with small, furnished rooms, both rural and urban. Moving chronologically through Soviet history, subsequent exhibits documented artistic, athletic, scientific, and technical achievements, emphasizing the inclusion of women and the greatly admired cosmonauts.

In 2017, a renovation and expansion had changed the entrance. The stained-glass images of Lenin were removed, but I later glimpsed the panels in what

7.1 Vladimir Lenin, State Museum of Political History of Russia, St. Petersburg, Russia, 2008

appeared to be a storage hallway, where they were carelessly draped with a thin cloth. A section of the museum documenting the revolution remained, but the revolution was practically taboo in the featured exhibition, *The Soviet Epoch: Between Utopia and Reality: Section I: 1917–1953*. The exhibition is at least as anti-Soviet as the Museum of Communism in Prague. Even Soviet achievements in literacy and education stemmed from nefarious designs. One panel explained, "Propaganda of Stalin's ideology would have been ineffective in a country where people can't read and write. That's why Bolsheviks primarily considered elimination of illiteracy as the process of influence on people's consciousness and forming a 'new man.'" Ignoring wide documentation of fond memories of children's camps and summer holidays, another panel explains, "A cult of leaders was implanted from childhood through 'Komsomol,' and the Pioneer organization for children."[5]

The anti-Stalinism of the exhibit is to be expected. But the erasure of the revolution is startling. Russia downplayed the one hundredth anniversary

7.2 Shop in vicinity of State Museum of Political History of Russia, St. Petersburg, Russia, 2017

of the Russian Revolution, a stance noted by critics during the centennial year.[6] The civil unrest of early February 1917, noted the writer Ian Frazier, "may not appeal to a leader who faced widespread protests against his own autocratic rule in 2011," as well as in early 2017. Putin emphasized "reconciliation" and "consolidating the social and political unanimity that we have managed to reach today."[7] His claims of unanimity rhetorically airbrushes protests against his policies. And beyond the implicit rebuke of the memory of the revolution, to remind people of the genuine achievements of the Soviet era might occasion a critical nostalgia for education, health care, and jobs—demands on the state that the kleptocratic Putin and his band of oligarchs are unwilling to entertain.

As with the revolution, glasnost, too, had no place in Putin's Russia. Free speech and openness are anathema to Putin, who has dismantled Russia's independent media and infamously claimed that he cannot suppress freedom of speech in Russia because it has never existed. The museum's account of the end of the Soviet era mentions no ambitious political and economic reforms, no calls for openness, not even for a return to the values that had animated the Russian Revolution. Instead, it portrays a vague petering out, with the "USSR gradually falling behind" and "patterns of cultural life unauthorized by the state ... rapidly spreading in society."[8]

Beyond the exhibition on the Soviet era, the museum heaps scorn on reminders of glasnost, disparaging Mikhail Gorbachev and promulgating a narrative of victimization and humiliation through media, especially magazine covers from the international press, including *Newsweek*'s "Crackup" and *Time*'s "A Man without a Country," with a cover photo of Gorbachev. In the museum's handling of the period from 1993 to the present, Boris Yeltsin is denounced as a corrupt and unpopular leader, doing the bidding of the West. The account of Yeltsin's 1996 reelection insinuates US interference: "The first round of the Russian presidential elections. Pre-election spin technologies are applied on a mass-scale. Big-business and oligarchs pay for presidential election campaign.... Boris Yeltsin's rating grows from 5–45%." On Yeltsin's implausible victory, the exhibit features *Time* magazine's July 15, 1996, cover: "Yanks to the Rescue: The Secret Story of How American Advisers Helped Yeltsin Win." Drawing on the memoirs of Yeltsin's opponent, Gennady Zyuganov, whom many believe actually won the election, the museum quotes Zyuganov as recalling, "Few were expecting such total brainwashing from the mass media.... The ruling regime succeeded in implanting a barrier of fear into millions of Russian voters."[9]

Side-by-side videos feature Yeltsin's resignation in a television address to the Russian citizens at twelve o'clock in the morning on December 31, 1999, followed by Acting President Vladimir Putin's Address to the Nation and the 2000 election. The story of Putin rescuing a beleaguered and humbled nation is further highlighted with images from the international press depicting Russian weakness and chaos in the years before Putin came to power.

Traveling with a university-sponsored group in 2017, my approach to US-Russian relations—highlighting comparable histories of settler colonialism, the intersections as well as frictions between different universalizing projects of mass society, and the importance of popular culture as a sphere of conflict and meaning-making—made more sense to our Russian guides than to many of the Americans with whom I traveled. It also opened up many conversations with Russians about our shared plights: their hopes for stability under Putin followed by dismay, turning to fear and outrage with his suppression of the press and embrace of cultural and religious orthodoxy. The state claimed to be "returning" churches to the Russian Orthodox Church when there had never previously existed a separation of church and state under the czarist or communist regimes. For those concerned with preservation of cultural heritage, this was distressing, as tourism had financed the restoration of churches and museums, with fees going to the state-owned buildings. Now in the "private" hands of the Orthodox Church, tourist access was restricted to prioritize religious services, and funds from entrance fees and souvenirs went to the Orthodox Church.

In 2017, in a climate of widespread and sustained mass protests against Putin, ordinary Russians were open in their criticisms. One man in his late sixties said that the best years for the country were during glasnost (notable since younger people tend to conflate the Gorbachev and Yeltsin periods as perestroika shock therapy hell) and that the worst time in the country's history was "now." Indeed, representations of glasnost had been escorted out of museums and cultural institutions.

Changes at the museum in St. Petersburg signaled an abrupt turn to an anticommunist cultural conservatism that had a counterpart on the US right, even sharing direct ties between US and Russian conservatives. These right-wing Christians were but a few of many new actors in US-Russian relations.

New and Old Players in Foreign Policy

The museum's transformation offers a window into a seeming paradox: the increasing ties between the two nations' authoritarian right wings occurring amid a new and pronounced US-Russian cold war. Here, I will not retell the saga of Russian interference in US elections; many accomplished journalists and national security specialists such as Malcolm Nance have told that story. Rather, I argue that narratives about the cold war were critical in refashioning US-Russian relations, and that the heightened anticommunism and antistatism of both former antagonists facilitated the rise of a global, authoritarian right. These processes involved an array of state and nonstate actors, operating at the intersections of politics, culture, and profit-seeking.

In a neoliberal global order defined by weakened state sovereignty, foreign policy-making has defaulted to unconventional actors, whose influence stems from their unaccountability to nation-state governance. Nontraditional foreign policy makers are everywhere and nowhere, a congeries of nongovernmental organizations, popular culture producers, corporations, and social media corporations and their websites—all rivaling the influence of nation-states. First visible in crises involving failed states but echoing throughout the developed world, private actors and nongovernmental organizations (NGOs) increasingly provide relief and social services that governments are no longer able or willing to provide.

But at the same time, as Jan Eckel has argued, what many human rights activists consider an "ethical imperative of intervention" often entails working for "profound changes in the political systems and even social practices of foreign countries."[10]

The neoliberal post-Soviet order has allowed the use of new tools for the intervention of US "soft power," including interventions in elections in the post-Soviet sphere by US politicians, NGOs, and human rights groups.[11] More recently, the United States has become vulnerable to external meddling by foreign intelligence services and internal capture by Trump, who hacked American democracy by manipulating corporate media (cable news) and exploited weaknesses inherent in partisan politics and the political and electoral system. Russian interference in the 2016 presidential campaign, Trump's unwavering praise of (or unwillingness to criticize) Putin, and the Kremlin's hand in Trump's campaign and subsequent actions are but a twist—a ominous twist—in a broader drama involving new techniques of intelligence and information warfare in an era of weakened states, rising economic inequality, and polarized public constituencies.

Yet these striking and even unprecedented dynamics should not obscure deep continuities with cold war and post-1989 US policies. Trump's deception, disinformation, and propagation of "alternate facts" have clear precedents. The assertion of US power abroad has historically always worked through a partnership between corporations and private citizens on the one hand and foreign policy officials and the State Department on the other, with no dearth of examples of direct US interference in the affairs of sovereign nations, whether by covert-action coups or other means. As we have seen, Trump's campaign manager Paul Manafort honed his skills in the sordid world of cold war clientelism, working for Zaire's Mobutu Sese Seko and the National Union for the Total Independence of Angola's Jonas Savimbi, as well as Filipino dictator Ferdinand Marcos.[12]

Long before 2016, a host of actors unsettled the terrain of public discourse and power relations by conjuring a new public constituency, eager for geopolitical intervention based not on facts but on a socially constructed "tabloid geopolitical imaginary."[13] A contempt for diplomacy—the rejection of political resolutions to conflict—was fully evident in the 2008 Republican presidential campaign. That campaign also served as a dress rehearsal for the undermining of truth and facts that may have been decisive in the 2016 election, with catastrophic results throughout the one-term Trump administration. The 2008 John McCain–Sarah Palin ticket anticipated the wild, incendiary rallies of the Trump campaign and administration with the angry populism of Palin's rallies, the Islamophobic smears of Democratic candidate Barack Obama, and the contempt for facts, expertise, and the very idea of the truth among McCain-Palin supporters and surrogates.

Producing Alternate Geopolitical Realities

Cultural production was critical in formulating an alternate geopolitical reality for US publics where political compromise, diplomacy, the rule of law, and conceptions of human rights had no place. Describing the "monster power" of "rootless white males," Steve Bannon, Trump's former senior adviser, intuited that a digital, gaming community of "intense" young men who "disappeared for days and even weeks into alternative realities" could be mined for his far right political purposes.[14] In this case, rather than interventionist instincts directed at Russians, Bannon nurtured progun, antigay, white nationalist alliances with Russians who were eager to cooperate.

Moreover, cultural production was equally critical in the "new cold war" with Russia, from the mid-2000s onward. In the deterioration of US-Russian relations, a host of nonstate actors, from lobbyists to NGOs and popular culture products, reshaped public discourse and power relations. Implicit and explicit claims about the relationship between the cold war and the war on terror are particularly salient in the new geopolitical imaginary. I outline the terrain—the geopolitics of popular culture—before turning to political developments in the new cold war with Russia. Highlighting tensions between diplomats on both sides and the US hawks, I analyze the production of a mode of subjectivity, generated at the intersection of politics (the 2008 US presidential campaign) and the gaming world, in which the possibility of politics and diplomacy is negated.

Investigating the interactions of multiple agents in US-Russian relations, I focus on the imagined political landscape of *Call of Duty* video games as they blend war on terror and cold war scenarios, as well as on constructions of truth and subjectivity in McCain and Palin's campaign. Both were potent and productive sites of meaning-making, effecting a synergy between the corporate narratives purveyed by Activision and its *Call of Duty* cold war gaming scenarios on the one hand and political messaging on the other. I focus on McCain's role in the Georgia crisis, and how his interactions with Georgian politicians exceeded the scope of his office as he challenged President George W. Bush through his aggressive promotion of anti-Russian policies. The 2008 campaign, in its spectacle of vice-presidential nominee

Sarah Palin's populist demagoguery and disregard for facts, expertise, and the very idea of the truth, was a precursor to the Trump campaign.

The troubling conflation between entertainment and politics was evident in Palin's campaign, and in the fierce partisan battles that followed. The former Alaska governor's toxic, influential brand of right-wing populism, stoking hatred of educated elites, the mainstream media, and others deemed "un-American," was a dress rehearsal for the politics of white racial resentment and victimhood that fueled the improbable rise of Trump. Right-wing extremist "woman warrior" politicians such as Palin and Minnesota congresswoman Michele Bachmann traded on their Christian faith and fierce denunciation of purported enemies to woo evangelicals, suburban white women, and gun rights advocates.

Just as different US actors could be found on both sides of the 2014 Ukraine crisis, the abrupt reversal of tensions evident in Trump's pro-Russian policies and gestures might be understood through an anything-goes blurring of gaming and geopolitics in which partisan politics is recast as entertainment.

Gaming the War on Terror through the Cold War

In November 2010, television viewers encountered a one-minute action-packed commercial featuring heavily armed young people and adult civilians (including global NBA superstar Kobe Bryant in Nike sportswear) engaged in fierce urban combat, the rapid fire of automatic weaponry and explosions punctuating the strains of "Gimme Shelter" by the Rolling Stones ("War, children, is just a shot away"), ending with the tagline, "There's a soldier in all of us." Although that sentiment evokes US military recruitment ads, the commercial in fact promoted *Call of Duty: Black Ops*, an installment of the hugely successful Activision video game franchise widely acclaimed as a state-of-the-art first-person shooter game. Upon release, the *Black Ops* edition broke first-day sales records and sold 9.4 million copies in its first week. In its review, the *New York Times* called *Black Ops* "exciting, intense, and engrossing ... the definitive first-person shooter game."[15]

In the commercial's marketing of the allure of fun, fantasy, and empowerment through an equal-opportunity, multicultural orgy of decontextualized warfare, an adorable little plump girl, a hotel concierge, a cab driver, and a short-order cook strike cinematic poses as they do battle alongside Bryant and late-night television host Jimmy Kimmel. Activision, which dominated a multibillion-dollar video game market that has eclipsed Hollywood, beckons to the gaming community and beyond—to the "soldier in all of us." One may wonder how actual combat veterans might react to the ad's avowedly realistic, albeit low-risk, portrayal of military combat heroism as a recreational activity available to ordinary civilians. In any case, the ad's corporate, multicultural, and neoliberal scenario of decontextualized and sanitized war (children, just a shot away) is celebrated as cathartic and patriotic—just a game.

If the ad's scenes of armed civilians waging war against an unspecified enemy seek to enlist a community of gamers, the game itself invites consumers to replay the cold war, stage reenacted victories, and participate in imagined future wars with Russia. Such militaristic Russia-bashing is hardly unique to video games. Vulgar displays and commodifications of what Gorbachev termed America's "winner's complex" proliferated in the post-9/11 years.

I employ the oxymoron "black-ops diplomacy" to designate a popular geopolitical imaginary that views military operations, particularly special-force covert operations, as the default mode of conducting international relations. It is a view of international relations that exudes contempt for diplomacy.

Emphasizing the production of meaning in the intersecting realms of cultural production, media, and politics, I offer a historical interpretation of the relationship between claims about the cold war and the war on terror, along with a methodological discussion of the synergy of meaning-making across and between seemingly unrelated cultural and political spheres, as exemplified by the institutional partnership between the US military and the *Call of Duty* franchise. Outlining the breakdown of US-Russian relations, I read the Activision games against the new cold war with Russia and the 2008 presidential campaign. With attention to the geopolitical context, I note two important but distinct elements of the games themselves: first, the subjectivity encouraged by the first-person shooter mode, zombie modes, and online social sites; and second, a mind-set of people-to-people undiplomacy. Here I discuss the unintended effects of actual foreign policy controversies produced by the games themselves, controversies indicative of the power dynamics of diminished state capacities and new modes of warfare.

The discrediting of diplomacy by foreign policy makers and among the public against a background of escalating US-Russian tensions gained traction through popular culture. Immersive video games and other products were critical for shaping an alternate geopolitical reality dismissive of political compromise, diplomacy, and conceptions of human rights; and these sentiments enabled elites to mobilize consent for an interventionist foreign policy by neoconservative Republicans.

Popular culture was a critical site for the production of narratives about the relationship between the cold war and the war on terror in which Americans were at once victors and victims. The *Call of Duty* franchise mediated between cold war triumphalist claims that "we won" the cold war through military strength on the one hand and fear on the other, emphasizing American innocence and victimhood by conflating Russia and terrorism in a supposed past as well as the future. Over a period that saw the escalation of US-Russian tensions over the expansion of NATO but also spanning years when Russia was an important ally of the United States in the war on terror, the *Call of Duty* franchise released four games between 2007 and 2012 that portrayed Russia as a major US adversary. *Call of Duty 4: Modern Warfare*, released in 2007 and set in 2001, and its sequel, *Call of Duty: Modern Warfare 2*, both depict terrorist attacks on Europe and the United States by an alliance of ultranationalist Russians and separatists in an unnamed but small and oil-rich country in the Middle East. The game's fictitious dictator, Khaled Al-Asad (a crude evocation of Syrian president Bashar al-Assad), suggests an indiscriminate Islamophobia, conflating diverse Islamic cultures and states into a homogenous and violent whole.

Trump, Bannon, and former national security adviser Michael Flynn rekindled the post-9/11 Islamophobia that misrecognizes Muslims as lacking a religious or cultural tradition and as having chosen instead to embrace an ideology of political violence. In February 2016, Flynn tweeted, "Islam is not necessarily a religion but a political system that has a religious doctrine behind it."[16] Resuscitating the cold war logic that labeled the totalitarian Soviet Union a slave society to which its adherents have willingly submitted, Bannon described Islam as submissive, asserting on his Breitbart radio program that it "is not a religion of peace—Islam is a religion of submission."[17]

Enlisting gamers in a figurative war on terror through the activation of cold war tropes that merge fact and fiction, *Call of Duty: Black Ops* (2010) reenacts such past events as US attempts to assassinate Fidel Castro and the US war in Vietnam. The game also features the thwarting of an imagined 1968 toxic chemical weapon attack by the Soviets on the United States. *Modern Warfare 3* (2011) imagines a 2016 surprise Russian invasion of the United

7.3 "World Stands on the Brink." Faux *Time* magazine cover

States (then five years in the near future) in which the player exchanges fire with Russian troops in the streets of Washington, DC, and finds themselves in armed conflict with China in 2025. Like *Metal Gear Solid 2* (2001), which also imagines Russian instigators of terror attacks against the United States, and the 2005 cold war–themed *Metal Gear Solid 3* (set in 1964), all four *Call of Duty* games broke industry sales records.[18]

By 2011, Activision had amassed sufficient clout for *Time* magazine to lend its logo and cover design to advertise the release of *Modern Warfare 3*. The faux magazine cover showed a world "on the brink," with New York City invaded by Russia in 2016.[19] In the context of NATO expansion and repeated warnings about outlaw states, having Russian troops battle in the virtual streets of the nation's capital betrayed a view of the irrelevance of international cooperation. In depicting Russia as a purveyor of military aggression and terrorism, the games effaced Russia's actual support of the US war on terror after 9/11.[20]

A long-developing partnership of the US military and video game industry joined right-wing cable television and talk radio to shape messaging about the war on terror, in what journalist Simon Parkin has aptly termed the military-entertainment complex.[21] The scholar Roger Stahl has documented the extensive use of video game technologies by the armed forces in the training of soldiers.[22] In the 1980s, the US Defense Advanced Research Projects Agency approached video game developers with "the idea of writing video games that could be used to train soldiers."[23] Current and former government and military officials who lent their imprimatur by consulting for the video game industry have included Colonel Oliver North, the unsuccessful US Senate candidate and television commentator known for his role in the Iran-Contra scandal, and members of the Navy SEALs and other special operations units.[24] The US Army has its own consultation bureau to manage solicitations of military expertise by Hollywood filmmakers and the video game industry for project development and production assistance.[25]

The synergy between the *Call of Duty* franchise and the US military included consultation and promotion of *Black Ops 2* by North, who was hired as a consultant, then as a public endorser. In a typical consulting arrangement, Hank Keirsey, a "retired Army lieutenant colonel and decorated combat veteran of the cold war and first Gulf War," had advised initial game development. Overcoming his suspicion of game developers, Keirsey acquired a respect for what he saw as the shared energy and commitment of soldiers and game developers. Impressed by the success of the *Call of Duty* franchise and its implications for envisioning future warfare, the military hired *Call of Duty* writer and producer Dave Anthony. Drawn to Anthony's "out of the box thinking on future threats," military officials had been impressed by his ability to "propose proactive solutions."[26] Reporting on the interface between the military and the Treyarch Group (umbrella owner of Activision) in producing *Black Ops 3*, Keith Stuart noted that the military—through the Defense Advanced Research Projects Agency, the section of the Department of Defense formed in 1958 in response to the 1957 Soviet launching of Sputnik and responsible for emerging military technologies—was interested in "bio-augmentation or human enhancement" involving the use of "various neuro-technologies, including neural implants to improve the performance of the human mind and body." This far-fetched instance of the eternal quest for a strategic advantage for the combat soldier may have originated in *Black Ops 3*, which features augmented special-ops soldiers; players can customize their soldiers with a new cyber system, programmed not only to run faster and jump higher but also to process information faster and more efficiently. Indeed, the collaboration was facilitated by the Obama administration's commissioning of a Brain Research Advancing Innovative Neurotechnologies (BRAIN) initiative, backed by $300 million aimed at developing "reliable neural interface technology."[27]

The New Cold War with Russia and Its Diplomatic Alternatives

As military research and development took inspiration from gaming producers, US-Russian relations deteriorated as the prospects for diplomatic solutions to conflict seemed remote. To be sure, there was no dearth of eloquent advocates for US-Russian cooperation on both sides. Before turning to the role of McCain and the Georgia crisis in the breakdown of US-Russian relations, it is important to recall the aborted vision of diplomacy espoused by Gorbachev and a range of US diplomats.

Gorbachev's critiques of US policy offer vital context for the major flashpoint of conflict over NATO expansion, both internationally and within the United States. Not long after the collapse of the Soviet Union, Gorbachev found himself increasingly at odds with a world overrun with privatization rather than glasnost and perestroika, voicing his objections with a gentle wit and irony. Parlaying his global celebrity to rebrand himself as an avuncular symbol of reform, Gorbachev reveled in the culture of consumption to promote his foundation, a think tank devoted to promoting democracy, humanitarianism, and the crafting of solutions to such global problems as inequality and the climate crisis.

The costs of the triumph of neoliberal privatization are poignantly illustrated in Gorbachev's post-Soviet activities. Critics predictably bemoaned the irony of the former Soviet leader's appearing in advertising campaigns for Pizza Hut and Louis Vuitton. Gorbachev reportedly made $1 million for sitting down with his granddaughter at a Pizza Hut in Moscow in a 1997 advertisement, as customers, seeing him, passionately debate his legacy: he ruined us; no, he brought freedom and hope. In a Capra-esque resolution, the happy diners turn to him, their pizza slices aloft, chanting, "Hail Gorbachev!"[28] In a Louis Vuitton photo advertisement from 2007, Gorbachev sits in a cab beside a half-zipped luxury duffle bag while driving

7.4 Mikhail Gorbachev with granddaughter, Pizza Hut Moscow ad, 1997

7.5 Mikhail Gorbachev, Louis Vuitton ad, 2007

past a remnant of the Berlin Wall. Headline writers could not restrain themselves. Invoking Reagan's 1987 West Berlin sound bite, "Mr. Gorbachev, tear down this wall," a *New York Times* article quipped, "Mr. Gorbachev, show off this bag."[29] For some, the ad conjured a world of espionage and coded messages. Upside down, in Cyrillic, and barely discernible with a magnifying glass, the newspaper poking out from the Louis Vuitton bag read, "The Murder of Litvinenko: They Wanted to Give the Suspect up for $7,000." This referred to the former KGB spy who had died in London the previous November after being poisoned with a radioactive isotope, polonium 210. Before his death, Alexander Litvinenko had accused Putin of ordering his death. The less than subliminal message in the advertisement sparked nervous disclaimers by Vuitton representatives, even as marketing experts opined that the "hidden" message enhanced the "kind of attention and buzz that is regarded as being the measure of success these days."[30] As some pronounced the victory of capitalism or deemed the ad an embarrassing celebrity photo, Gorbachev seemed to have loftier goals than supporting his family and cashing in. He could point to the work of his foundation, dedicated to diplomatic and humanitarian principles. And the indicting text spilling out of the bag echoed Gorbachev's call for a full investigation into Litvinenko's death.[31]

If the ads revealed Gorbachev as a trickster of image-making, his criticism of the inadequate US federal response to Hurricane Katrina's 2005 devastation of New Orleans was scathing. In New Orleans to lend his support to sustainable reconstruction, Gorbachev told local audiences that he would lead a revolution if the US Army Corps of Engineers failed to fix the levees as promised. Praising the rescue and rebuilding efforts of volunteers and businesses in the city's Ninth Ward, Gorbachev charged the US government with negligence: "The . . . state and the federal government should express to the world . . . the intent to rebuild this city." Gorbachev faulted the Bush administration's war in Iraq: "Unfortunately money is easily found for war . . . but not for this kind of trauma, not for this kind of tragedy."[32] Forcefully noting that this was not the first time that money had been squandered on war, Gorbachev acknowledged his own government's self-destructive campaign in Afghanistan as well as previous US global interventions. Where was the victory in capitalism's failure to meet the needs of its people? Gorbachev wondered. He did not hold back on the dire consequences of failed neoliberal policies for New Orleans. Likewise, although rebuffed by the Bush administration, Cuban officials offered to send "some 1,600 medics, field hospitals, and 83 tons of medical supplies to ease the humanitarian disaster" in New Orleans. White House spokesperson Scott McClellan scorned the proposal, saying, "When it comes to Cuba, we have one message for Fidel Castro. He needs to offer the people of Cuba their freedom."[33]

The Katrina tragedy is best understood within a global account of privatization and state disinvestment in public infrastructure and, as Paul Kramer has argued, a US government stretched thin by its war in Iraq.[34] Policies of deregulation, privatization, and the failure of the Clinton administration to address crumbling roads and bridges during the economic boom of the 1990s were symptomatic in the United States of a more serious form of decay, as in the "former East": a fragmentation of sovereignty. Functions of the state were contracted out to the lowest (or best-connected) bidder, disintegrating into a murky array of agencies and administrative zones, with overlapping boundaries and no universal center of competence, engendering a crisis of governability. As historian Clyde Woods has argued, in pre-Katrina Louisiana, the opportunistic unleashing of privatization schemes on an already fractured and inept state of "plantation governance" devastated teachers' unions and public schools, and cleared public housing for private real estate developers.[35] During the Katrina tragedy, lack of coordination by local, state, and federal officials delayed emergency assistance for the victims.

While Gorbachev's aid to New Orleans was part of the ongoing work of his foundation, his calling for a revolution in New Orleans punctuated his displeasure with Bush. By 2005, such scholars as Stephen F. Cohen and Gorbachev himself criticized US triumphalism and squandered opportunities for improved US-Russian relations, warning of a new cold war.[36] In April 2005, Gorbachev was blunt, perhaps also alluding to a signal policy failure of the Reagan era: "Americans have a severe disease—worse than AIDS. It's called the winner's complex." Cohen has asserted that Republicans and Democrats alike conducted two diametrically opposed policies toward Russia during the 1990s, one of which was outwardly decorous, professing to have "replaced America's previous cold war intentions with a relationship of 'strategic partnership and friendship.'" But the real US policy has been characterized by a "winner-take-all exploitation of Russia's weaknesses." Americans' embrace of the triumphalist story included a punishing stance toward Russia. With broken promises, condescending lectures, and demands for unilateral concessions, US policy has arguably been more aggressive and uncompromising than Washington's stance toward the Soviet communist Russia.[37] Equating the expansion of NATO with the expansion of freedom, the US stance seems to have unwittingly fanned the embers of destructive nationalisms.

As tensions mounted, Gorbachev declared in 2008, "We had ten years after the cold war to build a new world order and yet we squandered them.

The United States cannot tolerate anyone acting independently. Every US president has to have a war." Critical turning points for Gorbachev included NATO's promise of eventual membership to Georgia and Ukraine. Gorbachev, like James Baker, secretary of state when George H. W. Bush and Gorbachev declared the end of the cold war in 1989, believed that there had been a clear understanding that NATO, mutually perceived as a cold war creation, would not expand, and certainly not to Russia's borders. Gorbachev recalled, "The Americans promised that they would not expand beyond the boundaries of Germany after the cold war but now, half of eastern and Central Europe are members, so what happened to their promises?" For Gorbachev, promises to Georgia and Ukraine about future NATO membership signaled an attempt to extend the US sphere of influence into Russia's backyard.[38]

Later, as tensions over Ukraine led to the collapse of the Obama administration's 2009 reset with Russia, former US ambassador to the Soviet Union Jack Matlock Jr. argued that the "US and Europe brought on this whole mess in the first place by trying to place military bases outside of Russia." Comparing active American organizing of street protests in Kiev to the prospect of foreigners leading Occupy Wall Street movements, Matlock argued that American policy needlessly provoked Russia by telling Ukrainians and Georgians, "You can join NATO, and that will solve your problems for you."[39] Matlock joined those critics who charged the United States with taking sides in internal disputes and actively fomenting dissent, rather than leaving countries to work out their own paths and choices about political and economic reform.

Dissing Diplomacy in the 2008 McCain Campaign: The Georgia Crisis

A striking instance of NGOs and politicians running their own foreign policy—driven by a poverty of diplomatic imagination—came to light in the "going rogue" persona celebrated by Palin and advanced by McCain during the 2008 presidential campaign. Suggesting a disdain for diplomacy during the campaign, the senator claimed that his rival, Obama, would "condone the positions of our enemies" and "legitimize illegal behavior by sitting down for negotiations without preconditions." The hawkish McCain charged that Obama "thinks that he can negotiate with Iran and get anything he wants."[40] When Palin announced her willingness to attack Russia if she were in the Oval Office, McCain's involvement in the 2008 Georgia crisis prompted questions of propriety from the media, the Obama campaign, and even President Bush.

On August 7, 2008, the Georgian government launched an attack on a rebel group based in the city of Tskhinvali, South Ossetia, a province that had been part of Georgia within the USSR. South Ossetia had declared its independence from the Soviet Union in 1991 as a sovereign state. Georgia's attempt to reestablish control led to the 1991–92 war, which ended with the de facto secession of South Ossetia as well as Abkhazia.

To this day, US press accounts of the 2008 conflict invariably omit the fact that Georgia attacked before Russia, narrating the war as Russian aggression, pure and simple. Many Russians look back on the Georgia crisis as the time their side lost the information war—with international media showing Georgian tanks invading South Ossetia but attributing them to Russia—a lesson that Russian officials would not forget as they vowed to step up their own efforts at information warfare.[41] In fact, in response to the Georgian attack, Russian troops repulsed the Georgian military in Tskhinvali and occupied part of Georgia, including the city of Gori, until August 23. A European Union commission later ruled that Georgia had initiated the conflict by invading South Ossetia in violation of international law. Finding fault with all three parties, the EU report categorically rejected the claim by Georgian president Mikheil Saakashvili that Russia had launched an offensive before the Georgian attack, and also found no evidence of a pending Russian attack. At the same time, the report branded the secession of South Ossetia and Abkhazia from Georgia "illegal and Russian recognition of the two 'states' in violation of international law."[42]

During the 2008 crisis, McCain told Saakashvili, "I know I speak for every American when I say ... today we are all Georgians."[43] McCain's statement prompted widespread skepticism: "Spare me. You couldn't find one American in a thousand who could find Georgia on a map," one journalist opined. McCain assured Saakashvili that "the thoughts and prayers and support of the American people are with that brave little nation as they struggle for their freedom and independence."[44] As he ridiculed Obama's call for a diplomatic solution, McCain emphasized his experience in the region. His presumption of Obama's inexperience and naïveté presaged the senator's role as a relentless critic of President Obama. To his credit, McCain forcefully pushed back against anti-Obama xenophobia on the campaign trail. But further inquiry into McCain's Georgia policy revealed the stakes of his bellicose stance and also exposed sharp tensions within the Republican right over the expansion of NATO.[45]

Randy Scheunemann, McCain's principal foreign policy adviser during his campaign, sat on the board of the neoconservative Project for the New American Century. Headed by William Kristol, the organization had called for a US invasion of Iraq four years before 9/11, with Scheunemann serving as president of its Committee for the Liberation of Iraq. Pat Buchanan, the isolationist purveyor of US culture wars, condemned McCain's involvement in Georgia, as well as NATO expansion. Writing in the *Toronto Star*, Buchanan reported that from January 2007 to May 2008, the McCain campaign paid Scheunemann $70,000—pocket change compared with the $290,000 that Scheunemann's Orion Strategies received in those same fifteen months from the Georgian regime of Saakashvili. Saakashvili's "marching orders to Tbilisi's man in Washington" were to get Georgia a NATO war guarantee. Had he succeeded, Buchanan argued, "US soldiers would be killing Russians in the Caucasus, and dying to protect Scheunemann's client, who launched this idiotic war." For Buchanan, people "like Scheunemann hir[ing] themselves out to put American lives on the line for their clients is a classic corruption of American democracy." Scheunemann's two-man lobbying firm had received $730,000 since 2001 to get Georgia in the NATO alliance, and "he had been paid by Romania and Latvia to do the same." The "lobbying of Scheunemann and friends," Buchanan warned, brought Latvia into NATO, giving "a US war guarantee. If Russia intervenes to halt some nasty ethnic violence in Riga," the United States is committed to come in "and drive the Russians out."[46]

The hostilities between Russia and Georgia were over by August 2008. In September, Vice President Dick Cheney was off to Azerbaijan. There, he met with government officials and oil executives to shore up relations and protect his coveted pipeline.

The World According to McCain and Palin

Facts were a casualty in the 2008 presidential campaign. The experiences of McCain as a prisoner of war in North Vietnam were elevated to unassailable knowledge of war and foreign policy, for which any political or historical criticism was simply irrelevant. During the early 2000s, McCain invoked his authority as a veteran and former prisoner of war who had been tortured to defend his right to use the racist epithet *gook* to refer to his Vietnamese prison guards, and to claim that the American war in Vietnam had been winnable and that the war in Iraq was winnable.[47] Obama "would rather lose a war in order to win a political campaign," McCain snarled, than commit to a US victory in Iraq. Insisting that the United States could win any war if the will to do so existed, McCain asserted that evidence to the contrary was simply an argument for appeasement.[48]

The elevation of McCain's status as prisoner of war as endowing him with absolute authority was symptomatic of the growing hyperpartisanship of American politics. Presidential elections can generate more heat than light, but such claims to knowledge in routine times allow no room for negotiation or political compromise, no consideration of the perspective of one's opponent. In the 2008 election and in the fierce partisan battles that followed, "woman warrior" politicians such as Palin and Bachmann could make reckless, false attacks, such as accusations of Obama "palling around with terrorists" or that Obama was not a US citizen or was a secret Muslim, with no consequences. Little wonder that Trump seized on the "birtherism" conspiracy introduced during the 2008 campaign and cynically fostered by GOP elected officials. Trump weaponized this undebunked lie from 2011 onward.[49]

The 2008 campaign also unveiled the renunciation of political expertise in yet another way. In putting forward an inexperienced, "charismatic" vice-presidential candidate in Palin, the campaign cast knowledge, facts, and logic to the wind as minimal qualifications for a "leader of the free world." In her "authentic" demeanor and word-salad syntax, Palin's evident weaknesses, combined with her evangelical fervor, only enhanced her appeal to many Republicans. To the astonishment of seasoned political observers, her skewed sense of reality resonated with a broad swath of the GOP base.

Following the 2008 campaign, Palin stepped up her role as a climate change denier. Confusing climate with weather, she wrote on Facebook, "Global warming my gluteus maximus," pointing to a picture of her daughter Piper in the snow after her May graduation.[50] As Palin, Bachmann, and Trump severed political speech from the truth, grasping how such claims resonated with large numbers of people required returning to the terrain of popular culture and the blurring of truth within a murky realm of infotainment.

Gaming Neoliberalism: Subjectivity in First-Person-Shooter and Zombie Modes

Like the immersive exhibits at the International Spy Museum in Washington, DC, *Black Ops* and its *Modern Warfare* predecessors are parts of a synergistic field of cultural practices, performances, and enactments that, taken together, reboot binary notions of the cold war, efface its history, and produce a commonsense narrative linking the cold war to the war on terror. Playing through *Black Ops* raised for me the question, What kinds of knowledge, what subjectivities, are created in these enactments? As *Black Ops'* immersive sensory experience undermines historical and political realities, the alternative realities produced by gaming are implicated in the epistemological crisis of helplessness driving polarization and dysfunction in contemporary US politics. One result is a foreign policy imaginary constituting what I call a people-to-people undiplomacy.

Subject position and narrative are interwoven in the *Call of Duty* games. Form and function unite. As seen in the gaming industries' reliance on military consultants, game designers put great stock in authenticity. Some gamers downplay the importance of narrative, noting that after beating the game in the highly scripted first-person-shooter mode, many play in online multiplayer mode. Yet with an eye to manufacturing a realistic experience, game designers strongly emphasize the narrative plot and sweat the details, the visual and aural prompts that move the shooter through the game.

Modern Warfare, the immediate predecessor to *Black Ops*, and *Modern Warfare 2* set sales records and were acclaimed for their story lines and technical advancements. (It bears repeating that both imagine Russian attacks on the US mainland.) In *Modern Warfare*, ultranationalist Russians start a civil war in Russia and plot a coup in the Middle East in order to lure the United States into hostilities. Playing from the perspective of US Marines and NATO allies, the player engages in combat across the Middle East, Azerbaijan, Russia, and Ukraine. Nearly thirty thousand US Marines are killed when Russian terrorists detonate a nuclear device. From there, things get worse. *Modern Warfare 2* jumps to 2016. Ultranationalists have taken over Russia, and the fictional terrorist Vladimir Makarov stages a civilian massacre there, framing a CIA agent and convincing people that the United States is responsible. Russia launches a surprise invasion of the United States, and the player is now fighting Russian troops on the streets of Washington, DC, and on top of the Capitol building. *Black Ops 2*, released in November 2012, revisits the cold war with storylines set in the late 1980s in southern Africa, Afghanistan, and Latin America, then jumping to 2025, when a new cold war with China has ensued after China banned the export of rare minerals, framing the United States for a cyber-attack by an anti-American criminal syndicate.

In first-person-shooter mode, *Black Ops* is tightly scripted, offering the player no moral choices or alternative narratives. Its proximate renditions of history, from its settings to the familiar US foreign policy events and objec-

7.6 Faux Fidel Castro, screen shot, *Call of Duty: Blacks Ops*

tives of the era, reinforces its strong claims to authenticity. Opening with a reenactment of the 1961 US invasion of the Bay of Pigs, the player's missions from 1961 to 1968 include imprisonment and escape from a Soviet gulag, and a journey through Vietnam's Mekong delta. The game boasts its historical veracity with players of *Black Ops* encountering the cold war through meetings with Fidel Castro, John F. Kennedy, and Secretary of Defense Robert S. McNamara. Not unlike George W. Bush going after Saddam Hussein in the second Gulf War, these reenactments promise to undo past policy failures, indulging players in the fantasy of toppling Castro "this time." As the *New York Times* video game reviewer enthused, "I couldn't wait to go back and try to assassinate Castro and kill Russians." Central to the game's alternative reality is a bipolar cold war world in which Asians, Africans, and Latin Americans are peripheral to the "real" fight against the Soviets. Cuba and Vietnam serve as undercard proxies to the main-event fight with the Soviets. The game's celebration of militarism, counterinsurgency, and violence constitutes a fantasy do-over, this time with more firepower.

Significantly, the game replays the cold war through riveting yet maddeningly confusing twists that constantly upend one's sense of reality, experienced through flashbacks tied to key moments in the 1961–68 "cold war." The game takes the form of an espionage mystery that undermines the distinction between hallucination and clarity. As the game opens, the protagonist character Mason (assumed by the player) is under interrogation (with torture) by someone desperate to decode the numbers that are going through my/Mason's brain. The game cuts back and forth between the 1968 interrogation and past incidents, including sit-down meetings with Kennedy and McNamara. With mysterious numbers flashing through my/Mason's head, the interrogators are desperate for him to remember number sequences, forcing us to relive a series of missions. First, I find myself, as Mason, in Cuba at the Bay of Pigs, thinking I have assassinated Castro, later finding out that I killed a double instead. Instead, I/Mason am captured and detained at a gulag in the Soviet Union, where "we" are befriended by Reznev, a Soviet defector. Reznev and I/Mason escape—so I think—with the ultimate goal of capturing a Nazi scientist who is building a chemical weapon for the Soviets. The pursuit takes "us" to Vietnam in 1968. Weirdly, there are no Vietnamese whatsoever. Mason is captured for interrogation. Suddenly "we" flash back to Dallas, seeing ourselves aiming a gun at Kennedy. "Oswald has been compromised." (Yikes! I/Mason killed Kennedy?) I/Mason recover my memory through the interrogators. Or do I? Back at the gulag, I/Mason had initially been brainwashed by General Nikita Dragovitch and programmed to kill Kennedy. They tell Mason that Reznev, who I/Mason thought was working with "us" for the past five years, has been dead the entire time. (With each new revelation, the ground beneath us dissolves, plunging me/Mason deeper into confusion.) Mason looks bewildered. We are at the mercy of the interrogators (and the sadistic game producers). You're on your own, buddy. Now the inquisitors are saying that I/Mason had been rebrainwashed by Reznev to stop Friedrich Steiner, a former Nazi scientist who had defected to the Soviet Union. They ask Mason why he went off mission and killed the Nazi scientist when he was supposed to capture him. Mason is not in good shape. "I was trying to stop them," he stammers—but from what? "The numbers—what do the numbers mean?" The interrogators are still desperate for the numbers.

In all seriousness, the game effects an obscene displacement of the fact that while in 1968 the United States was poisoning Vietnam and its people with Agent Orange chemical weapons, in the game, Mason is the only one able to stop the activation of Soviet sleeper cells in the United States, which are ready to stage a chemical warfare attack in the country. Mason successfully breaks the code and gives the interrogators the location of the Soviet base on a ship, preventing the attack. I/Mason believe we now understand the underlying reality despite the fog of all the brainwashings and flashbacks. But in the final scene, Reznev reappears to undermine any sense of resolution and objective reality.

Filled with double agents, brainwashing, and defectors, the game produces a story and experience evocative of *The Manchurian Candidate* and the novels of John le Carré. Players, as Mason, are not just under interrogation and attack. They've also endured a disintegration of the subject through brainwashing. Blurring illusion and reality, and taking vast liberties with the past under a veneer of historical veracity, the game induces an epistemological uncertainty in its players.[51] Unlike the Jason Bourne character in the Bourne trilogy, who achieves, under extreme duress, a reintegration of the self through sheer strength of will, Mason has a lingering doubt about his own actions and the role of his major Russian nemesis (the very fact of his death is subject to doubt) that suggests the futility of getting at the truth in the cold war. Instead, what's posited as true is that nothing is what it seems. That is the likely takeaway among players for whom the powerful subjective experience offered through the technical brilliance of the game stands in for an engagement with the actual history of the cold war. In the end, the fragmented subjectivity of atomized gameplayers, untethered from historical realities, becomes the sole arbiter of truth.

Neoliberal Zombies

Directed by zombie horror film director George A. Romero, *Black Ops*' zombie mode offers an alternate but reinforcing experience of the fragmented subject navigating a world without stable social or objective moorings. In a campy counter-post-1945 history spanning from World War II to the 1960s, the discovery of Element 115 in a meteorite in Japan has led to the creation of zombies. Romero explained that his idea for the game emerged from research he had done for a World War II movie. He claimed to have found Nazi documents with discussions of Element 115 and outlandish talk of raising the dead.[52]

The alternate reality revolves around four soldiers representing Imperial Japan, Germany, the United States, and the Soviet Union. At one point, zombies breach the Pentagon with Kennedy, McNamara, Richard Nixon, and Castro trapped inside and attempting to fight their way out. At another point, in a self-referential film within the game, soldiers trapped in a room have to rely on four actors who are in a film directed by Romero. But Romero has been infected and is turning into a zombie. A *Black Ops* game extension release included "Call of the Dead," which maps locations from Romero's movies.[53] In hilarious trailers for the map version, Romero tells a zombie,

"Get back to hair and makeup, you don't look dead enough." As the trailer closes, a zombified Romero emerges from the water.

Romero's 1968 *Night of the Living Dead* depicts, as he put it, the "monster within, the zombie being us," taking a stab, as it were, at the dark, racist underside of cold war—and Vietnam War–era America, where the real horror is that Ben, the black hero, survives the zombies only to be perceived as a threat and killed by white law enforcement.[54] Romero's 2011 zombies take on an additional valence. In zombie mode, the experience of relentless assault mirrors assaults on the subject in neoliberal workplaces and institutions. Neoliberalism cannot abide history, effacing human solidarity and the past practices, organic knowledge, and norms of every state or private organization it razes (restructures). Neoliberal practices thus require a malleable subject, commanded to respond to discrete tasks without questioning their logic, purposes, or outcome. While it is cathartic to kill a bunch of zombies, which brings a temporary relief from the onslaught, the exhausted and spent subject learns that the social contract is broken. They are coming to get you, and there is no one out there (no functioning state or civil society) coming to the rescue when your city's water is poisoned, your homes are flooded, or your child is sick and you don't have health care.

Romero has called his zombies "blue-collar monsters."[55] In a totalizing trap, zombies are at once the impersonal force of chaos and the helpless and murderous rage of those infected by its poisons, the working-class teenagers who fought and died in the American war in Vietnam and the economically conscripted soldiers of US campaigns in Iraq, fighting, dying, and returning home to madness and suicide. And as the logic of the zombie is to bring chaos and human apocalypse, at the end of *Black Ops* zombie mode, the earth is destroyed. Destruction is the only solution.

Cruelty and Violence Are the Point

Along with rejecting social and historical reality, the intertwining of desire and violence in the *Call of Duty* franchise resonated with a xenophobic political imaginary in the 2008 and 2016 elections. Undergirding Activision's claims to cold war authenticity, the much-anticipated Berlin Wall installment of *Call of Duty: Black Ops* used actual maps of the city, re-creating landmarks and streets. In a television ad for the game, to the soundtrack of the German band the Scorpions' hit "The Wind of Change," two men—one on each side of the wall—reach out to each other.

Invoking a classic cold war trope where East and West become objects of mystery and longing for each other, guns turn into guitars and a peace dove flies in. But with no foreshadowing and in complete dissonance with the song's lyrics, the ad evolves into an individual expression of violence. The peace dove explodes and the guitars turn back into guns (spewing flames in a simultaneous ejaculation). The climactic resolution of desire in violence is fully borne out by the game.

The history of "The Wind of Change" is drenched in irony. Widely remembered as an anthem celebrating the fall of the wall, the song was inspired by the August 1989 Moscow Music Peace Festival, a two-day hard-rock festival in the one-hundred-thousand-seat Lenin Stadium, where Western heavy metal acts including Ozzy Osbourne, Mötley Crüe, Cinderella, and Skid Row joined local bands like Gorky Park and Brigada-S. The festival inspired Scorpion vocalist Klaus Meine, who had grown up in the shadow of the Iron Curtain, to write the song three months before the wall came down.[56] Expressing hope and peace ("The world is closing in / and did you ever think / that we could be so close / like brothers") after the wall came down, "The Wind of Change" became the soundtrack for the Wayne Isham–directed video featuring the construction and then tearing down of the wall, and indeed, a soundtrack for political and cultural revolution.[57] But the acclaimed advertising video for the Berlin Wall extension of *Call of Duty* not only erases the song's genesis in solidarity with Soviet reform and antinuclear demilitarization, it suggests that history is consonant with libidinal, violent, right-wing populism.

The game's glorified violence coexists with the sociality of online communities forged through multiplayer games and online discussion groups, as well as a vast genre of videos produced by gamers for other gamers that track real-time play-throughs of games accompanied by voice-over commentary, instructions, and advice on how to get through the game. In early 2010, GoldGlove had more than ninety-four thousand hits for a video showing gamers how to play through the Berlin Wall extension.[58] Addressing "my people of the youtubes," GoldGlove exudes the comradery of this genre and its blithe disregard of historical and political reality. Calling for online help in clarifying whether Berlin was divided by North and South or East and West, GoldGlove signals that it matters that this is the Berlin Wall dressed up in historically authentic maps and references—but ultimately it doesn't matter because violence is the main point of the game. Here, it's not simply that viewers lack historical context; the problem is that for the players or enactors, *Black Ops* provides the content as well as the context for knowledge and memory. Here, the phrase "my people of the youtubes" addresses a world in which speech and practice are sundered from the referent of past events.

GoldGlove's genuine solidarity with other gamers and his concern for the PS3 and other gamers who had been denied his Xbox-er's first access to the Berlin Wall game extension—"not fair that you have to wait a month"—accompany his gleeful embrace of violence and reveling in the aesthetic and sensual delights of blood. "Just can't get over that blood sticking snow—when I was playing I didn't really notice but now it is gorgeous—it's just a sexy time."[59] The largely male sociality of the games is also seen in another gamer's commentary on the "There's a Soldier in All of Us" *Black Ops* commercial: "I nearly choked on my beverage when I saw this on the TV the other day. I love the fact that they have basketball star Kobe Bryant and late-night talk-show host Jimmy Kimmel running around with people from all walks of life. Of course, you already know that there are all sorts of people playing with you online, but seeing it represented visually in this way really brings the point home and makes me smile."[60] This online commentator, Les, reads a controversial commercial—deplored by many for its glorification of war—as a warm shout-out to an intimately connected community of gamers. That makes him smile. What happens when friendship is forged and experienced in the context of violence? What happens when violence forges bonds of love and community? And what happens when that dynamic—arguably present in the military and a myriad of institutions—extends its reach into the virtual world? Can diplomacy and politics exist in this community of warmth, solidarity, guns, and dissociation from history?

Meanwhile, in the vacuum created by the decline of diplomacy, warfighting morphs into ever-new forms inspired by the gaming world. As the *Call of Duty* producers' military collaborations envision new neurotechnologies designed to enhance the combat efficiency of the individual soldier, in the gaming world, an atomized, disenfranchised subject plugged into a Borg has ominous potential for fashioning authoritarian subjectivities out of the ruins of states and civil societies weakened and frayed by antidemocratic neoliberal forces, from corporate state capture to the endangered species of print media and investigative local journalism and the spread of disinformation over unaccountable social media companies.

Gaming Interventions

As gaming allowed popular participation in a rebooted, darker cold war, escalating tensions with Russia led to real-world international incidents. Coinciding with an already aggressive Republican foreign policy, the *Call of Duty* franchise had a knack for unintentionally provoking international controversies. The fictionalized Russian enemies created by game designers arguably fueled anxiety among Americans at the prospect of war with Russia over Ukraine in 2014 because they had already been fighting Russians in a campaign across Crimea and Ukraine—and in hand-to-hand combat in the streets of DC and its suburbs—for years in video games.

The lucrative *Call of Duty* franchise touched off several international controversies, resulting in censorship bans by Germany and Cuba of certain games, and Russian allegations of their destabilizing potential for joint counterterrorism efforts and foreign policy. The day after the January 24, 2011, terrorist bombing at the Domodedovo Airport in Moscow, *Russian Times* television reported a troubling similarity between the bombing and the 2009 video game *Modern Warfare 2*'s "No Russian" storyline.[61] It's critical to note that the game, set in 2016, is premised on an imagined US war with Russia. In that scenario, ultranationalists have taken over Russia, and the terrorist Vladimir Makarov bombs a fictitious Moscow airport, inflicting mass casualties on civilians. Makarov and the ultranationalists convince the public that the United States is responsible.

The *Russian Times* coverage, as the *New York Times* reported, disclosed that counterterrorism experts from Russia, Europe, and the United States weighed a causal connection between the fictional gaming scenario and the actual terrorist bombing. In the "No Russian" segment, the gamer plays in character as a CIA agent who infiltrates the ultranationalists for his ultimate mission as a double agent. The character proves his loyalty to the ultranationalist cause by gunning down civilians at the airport. In first-person-shooter mode, the player has no choice but to murder the civilians. *Russian Times* broadcaster Lauren Lister reported that in addition to massive popularity, with sales surpassing $1 billion in its first two months, the "No Russian" segment could be viewed on YouTube without even buying the game. The segment had 870,000 YouTube views by the time of the bombing. While counterterrorism experts cautioned against drawing causal links between the game and the bombing, eerie similarities led them to question whether the perpetrators of the attack "might have trained using the game or others like it." Others worried that "those already radicalized," such as jihadists or al-Qaeda, could be influenced by the game.[62]

The fact that the segment required the gamer in first-person mode to commit an act of terrorism prompted the game's banning in Germany. Fearing for its profits, the franchise rushed out a version that allowed players to opt out of slaughtering innocents. It wasn't just the liberties taken by video games that met with official condemnation. Other offending productions included the 2008 film *Indiana Jones and the Kingdom of the Crystal Skull*. In the film, which is set in 1957, Harrison Ford's archaeologist adventurer matches wits with an evil KGB agent (Cate Blanchett). The stock cold war plot incensed St. Petersburg Communist Party member Victor Perov: "What galls is how together with Americans we defeated Hitler; and how we sympathized when bin Laden hit them. But they go ahead and scare kids with Communists. These people have no shame."[63]

Allowing that responses to video games might be as varied as the people who play them, since the 2007–8 new cold war with Russia, the *Call of Duty* franchise exposed audiences to an open disregard for diplomacy and statecraft. In 2013, an informal Bishkek focus group comprising architects in their early thirties judged the *Black Ops* storyline stupid while admiring its technical brilliance. But rather than seeing it as "just a game," the gamers claimed that *Black Ops* "definitely" represented Americans' perceptions of the cold war. They pointed to the producers' pro-Western portrayal of Cuba, the Soviet Union, and the Vietnam War. The players described the game as poorly translated into Russian. One participant complained that the "characters talk too much and the interrogations take too long and irritate the people who play the game as the 'illogical storyline' unfolds."[64]

With players describing the franchise's World War II predecessors to *Black Ops* as peddling crude versions of Germans and Japanese, and games set in current times positing weak Russians in cahoots with vaguely defined Middle Eastern terrorists, at the very least, the games confirm for these players Americans' general ignorance of Russia and the post-Soviet sphere.

The games' stagings of cultural undiplomacy worked in tandem with the expansion of NATO, and international condemnation of the Ukraine crisis, to promote an anti-American "fever" in Russia that observers contend supersedes that of the Soviet era. Anger toward the United States, reported the *Washington Post* in 2015, is "at its worst since opinion polls began tracking it," with more than 80 percent of Russians holding negative views of the United States.[65] Russian journalists have documented the widespread perception in Russia that after 1989, Russians modeled themselves after the

West but "experienced humiliation and hardship in return." Evgeny Tarlo, a member of Russia's Upper House of Parliament, asserted that after Russia had embraced the West, Russians expected that "they [those in the West] would finally hug and kiss us and we would emerge in ecstasy." Instead, he argued, the West has been trying to destroy Russia.[66]

Spies R Us: *The Americans*

Perhaps Tarlo's sense in 2015 that the West had been trying to destroy Russia had been amplified by viewing the acclaimed FX television series *The Americans*. Premiering in 2013, the series screened popular fantasies of American exceptionalism and triumphalism. With narratives beguiling audiences and critics alike, the dramatic series further illustrated the challenges of maintaining a clear-eyed reckoning on US global relations.

The triumphalism of *The Americans* strangely gained momentum in the aftermath of Trump's election. Set in 1980s Washington, DC, *The Americans* captivated audiences throughout its 2013–18 six-season run. Undercover Russian KGB agents Elizabeth and Philip Jennings have simulated love, marriage, and the storied American nuclear family so convincingly that they have produced real children and live in a typical bourgeois suburban home and neighborhood. Much of the show's frisson derives from interweaving its domestic plot lines with the familiar timeline of the waning cold war. The series was inspired by the widely publicized arrest of a suburban sleeper cell of Russian spies in 2010; a neighbor, shocked by the news, marveled at their former neighbor's perfect hydrangeas. As the first season ended, Ryan C. Fogle, an American diplomat with a poorly fitting blond wig and other disguises, was arrested in Russia in May 2013 while recruiting Russian operatives, inspiring the cheeky *New York Times* headline "From Russia with Wig."

The show rides the whirligig of art imitating life imitating art with meticulous set designs and costumes evocative of 1980s American life. That verisimilitude, combined with real-world acts of espionage, including the much-publicized travails of former NSA contractor and whistleblower Edward Snowden and his attempt to gain asylum in Russia in 2013 after leaking evidence of domestic surveillance programs, lent the series an uncanny relevance for many viewers.

Despite the series' claims of historical authenticity, its fictional portrayals of spies border on the ridiculous. The show centers on the fraught marriage of Elizabeth Jennings (Keri Russell) and her husband, Philip (Matthew Rhys

7.7 Advertisement for *The Americans*

Davies), and their relationship with their children and neighbors. The spies ultimately fail according to the terms set by their Soviet handler—"If you start to think of your marriage as real, you're no use to us."[67] Their covert operation of a marriage muddles through until their ultimate seduction by American culture and the nuclear family ideal, creating a poignant and tragic ending when Philip and Elizabeth are forced to flee to Moscow, abandoning their son, while their college-aged daughter, groomed by Elizabeth in hopes of her joining the family business, refuses to accompany her parents to Moscow.

Elizabeth and Philip give new meaning to the timeworn cold war trope positing communists as sexual deviants, adept at the amoral use of sex to advance their objectives. Ruthless killers, the couple's seduction of unwitting people often ends in murder to head off the risk of exposure. Elizabeth is the more ruthless of the pair, an ideological true believer. Philip is ambivalent, unfulfilled by their sham marriage and seduced, in his own way, by the allure of American culture. Already Americanizing in the first season, he considers defecting. Unhappy, questioning the ideology that binds them, Philip moves out of the house and dabbles in line-dancing and the self-actualization training of EST (Erhard Seminars Training). He warms to the temptation of friendship with next-door neighbor Stan, despite its guarded, instrumental nature—Stan is an FBI agent. But Philip is as capable of murder, mayhem, seduction, and duplicity as Elizabeth, to protect their cover or a mission. By the end of season five, Elizabeth and Philip have each killed sixteen people; Elizabeth has honey-trapped five men in seductions, with Philip seducing only three women, although he had married one of them so he could spy on her FBI bosses and was attempting the seduction of the fifteen-year-old daughter of a senior CIA intelligence operative on the Afghanistan desk.

The KGB executed numerous operations in the United States, but it did not murder anyone in Washington, DC, in the 1980s—or elsewhere in America. The only spy-related fatality was the death of a KGB agent in a Washington hotel in 1941, and that was a probable suicide.[68] *The Americans* obsesses over the purported violence of the Soviet other, in a displacement of the violence endemic to US empire. In 1980s Washington, DC, known as the murder capital of the United States, *The Americans*' dark and often nearly empty streets, where Elizabeth and Philip carry out dead drops and murders, are evocative, a jolting reminder of how empty the streets of DC (and a still gritty New York City) were in the 1980s compared with the 2000s (at least the pre-pandemic 2000s).[69] But the sense of foreboding and danger in the empty 1980s streets of DC—evoked powerfully in the show—was not the result of out-of-control Soviet spies.

The wigs, murder, and mayhem border on camp, but *The Americans* consistently attributes political violence to African Americans, antiapartheid South Africans, and Nicaraguans, all presented as pawns or allies of the Soviet Union. The first pivotal character in this regard is Gregory Thomas, an African American radical and Elizabeth's former lover, whom she fell in love with after recruiting him to the Soviet cause (Philip was husband only in name). Gregory worked in the civil rights movement, and his characterization insinuates that Black militants were directed and controlled by Moscow. While Gregory is portrayed as dedicated to a conflated civil rights and communist cause—explaining why Elizabeth had fallen in love with him—he shares the Soviets' innate ruthlessness, advocating killing the wife of a fallen comrade to get her out of the way, while Philip intervenes to send her to safety in Cuba.

Gregory becomes the mechanism by which Elizabeth and Philip reexamine their relationship. Elizabeth's relationship with Gregory becomes a point of contention between Philip and Elizabeth, prompting Philip to move out of the house. Ultimately, with the mission and Philip's identity at stake, the Soviets frame Gregory for a murder committed by Philip. Gregory has been a loyal comrade and they offer to take him to Moscow, but he refuses, committing suicide by starting a gunfight with a police officer. Following Gregory's death, in season one's finale, after Elizabeth is shot in a setup (by Stan, the next-door neighbor FBI agent, who does not recognize her in disguise), she asks Philip to come home, using their Russian mother tongue. With Gregory out of the way, Philip and Elizabeth realize that they care about each other; both feel newly invested in their relationship and family. *The Americans* kills off the only significant Black character—a poorly realized one at that—as a necessary condition of shoring up the nuclear family. Evoking a very old Jeffersonian idea—that people of African descent have no place in America and must be expelled to achieve American herrenvolk democracy—the show creates the American family at the expense of African Americans.

In season three, Reuben Ncgobo, a member of the African National Congress (ANC) who had studied in Moscow, is recruited by the Soviet Union to thwart a bombing planned by a South African elite intelligence officer at Georgetown University that was intended to frame the antiapartheid movement. In presenting Ncgobo's relationship with the KGB, *The Americans* distorts the ANC, framing it as a KGB subsidiary rather than an independent antiapartheid organization with communists in the fold. Seemingly sympathetic to the antiapartheid cause, the show misrepresents ANC politics and tactics, falsely equating the ANC's armed struggle with the extreme violence of the South African government. When the South African intelligence officer is captured, Ncgobo insists on killing him through "necklacing," a gruesome execution sometimes used in townships against those suspected of police collaboration but roundly condemned by ANC leadership. The misrepresentation of the ANC in service of a plot line animates a racist "both-siderism" that leaves viewers fixated on the violence of the oppressed rather than its most egregious perpetrators.

Nicaraguan Sandinistas are also conflated with the KGB. Appearing in four episodes, the Sandinista character Lucia Chena poses as a political science graduate student from Costa Rica. She befriends Carl, an aide to a member of the House Intelligence Committee overseeing Central America. After getting Carl into drugs by smoking cocaine with him and using him to get Elizabeth into the congressman's office, Lucia follows orders to kill Carl by poisoning heroin he injects himself. Now, communists and Sandinistas are causing Americans' drug problems. Who was actually selling cocaine in the 1980s? Many people, including Reagan administration aide Colonel Oliver North, on behalf of the US government—raising money to aid the anticommunist Contras—*not* the communists and the Sandinistas. And Lucia's demise is witnessed by Elizabeth, who does not intervene as another, more valuable asset strangles her.

Along with vague allusions to Reagan's escalated cold war in Central America and southern Africa, *The Americans* locates audiences in the 1980s through references to the attempted assassination of Reagan, scenes of the Jennings family watching his "Evil Empire" speech on television, and the incorporation of Gorbachev's reforms into the story. Some critics delighted in the show's pronounced late cold war nostalgia, marveling over the forty-plus disguises worn by Elizabeth and Philip and life imitating art. Yet others voiced a critical nostalgia, questioning triumphalism and the risks of American power left unchecked. John DeVore, writing in *Esquire*, took aim at the nostalgia with his own dark dive into the 1980s: "We no longer live in simple times. America is the apex predator of nations, and yet she has no rival that poses an existential threat like the former 'Evil Empire.' Threats abound. . . . The world economy is a cruel pyramid scheme. . . . Even the Earth itself seems to finally be sick of our shit. . . . But in the '80s, it was just Us vs. Them. Is it really better that all the reds are dead?" For DeVore, missing "this bipolar world" is "[our] privilege revealing itself." As "countless lives" were destroyed "over the course of 45 years," most of those casualties were suffered by the "so-called Third World," and "it's not like America wasn't willing to torch a jungle full of people to make a point." For DeVore, the 1980s should have been enough to alert us that we were already living in an "apocalypse." "If you didn't live through the Reagan years, you may not completely grasp how truly insane the decade was. A plague ravaged a vulnerable minority while the powerful laughed. The poor waited with mouths agape for wealth to trickle down, but it never did (and still hasn't). We were going to spend trillions to launch laser guns into orbit to shoot down nukes, for fuck's sake, and name it after a sci-fi film franchise."[70]

Beyond DeVore's rare critical acuity, many critics considered *The Americans'* political topography irrelevant, a mere backdrop to the real psychological drama. The idea that *The Americans* was "existentially truthful" dominated reviews. Todd VanDerWerff wrote on Vox, "It's one of the most deeply emotional shows on television, but it hides those beats within the chilly heart of the spy thriller.... [It] seems to be a series about deeply complicated geopolitical game playing, but is actually a show about the life and death of relationships." This theme was reinforced by the showrunner: "*The Americans* is a very existentially truthful show. It's very truthful not only about spying, but all the metaphors that it gets to through spying—lying and false identity, certainly about the very real challenges of marriage and being a parent. And my suspicion is that for some people, it hits a little too close to home."[71] Critics embraced *The Americans* as a metaphor for marriage and family. As the *New Yorker*'s Emily Nussbaum argued, "'The Americans' is about loss of control. That's what intimacy is: when you're known, you're in danger. To be loved, you have to be known."[72] That many found the show to be an insightful look at the "very real challenges of marriage and being a parent" that hit "too close to home" might suggest that the 1947 creation of the CIA—a secret arm of government—did not simply create the grounds for undermining US democracy, as democracy requires transparency and accountability. Beyond that, perhaps the CIA, in all of its wild ambition for mastering psychology and culture, and its far-reaching literary and cultural ambitions, actually forged a paradigm for a legible form of American intimacy. In a transactional world wrought by cold war capitalism, a world of secrets where families are characterized as in denial and people encouraged to deny everything, and where US cold war violence is continually displaced onto its victims, spies are us.

Private Actors and the Ukrainian Crisis

As fictitious Soviet spies and their third-world counterparts committed murder and mayhem on television, a post-Soviet Russian-US confrontation was developing in Ukraine. While McCain and Palin's foreign policy recklessness and bellicose rhetoric had been held in check by Obama's election (albeit temporarily), it proved only a harbinger of things to come in the involvement of foreign states and social media platforms in purportedly national elections. If McCain had tried to outdo Bush in his aggressive stance toward Russia, the 2009 reset of US-Russian relations announced by Dmitry Medvedev and Obama was undone by a similar cast of characters in the crisis in Ukraine, albeit with a twist.[73] From promoting the failed Orange Revolution of 2004 to the 2014 crisis, US politicians, lobbyists, and NGOs were deeply involved in internal politics in Ukraine. In November 2013, with the United States pushing to bring Ukraine into the EU, the government of Viktor Yanukovych refused to sign on to an EU agreement that would have "driven a deep wedge between Russia and Ukraine." Opposition protests led by Vitali Klitschko drove Yanukovych from power in February 2014. Opposition leader Klitschko's close ties to the State Department and German chancellor Angela Merkel provided the pretext for Russian intervention and the annexation of Crimea in March. Critics saw a nefarious US role in anti-Yanukovych protests through the Belgrade US-financed group, the Centre for Applied Nonviolent Action and Strategies (CANVAS).[74] That group had been funded by the US State Department to stage the revolution that ousted Slobodan Milosevic in then Yugoslavia. Since then, the group had functioned as a "revolution consultancy" for the United States, posing as a Serbian grassroots group backing "democracy." William Engdahl reported for Global Research that Klitschko is "backed by US Assistant Secretary of State Victoria Nuland. Nuland, former US Ambassador to NATO, is a neo-conservative married to leading neo-conservative hawk, Robert Kagan, and was herself a former adviser to Dick Cheney."[75]

Human rights groups, citing abuses by pro-Russian factions, called for intervention on humanitarian grounds. Indeed, the human rights logic of the "imperative to intervene" presents a justification and moral responsibility for intervention as sweeping in scope as the Truman Doctrine and NSC-68. But here, Ukrainians were offered two profoundly antidemocratic choices: Putin-style authoritarianism, on the one hand, and policies protecting global corporate interests, on the other.

Experts on the region such as historian Tarik Cyril Amar pleaded for diplomacy, for the United States "to decode the sabre-rattling of Putin—and help prevent Ukraine from turning into a proxy battlefield." He added, warnings to Putin "without any face-saving offers would be more than useless."[76] The following month McCain sniped, "Russia is a gas station masquerading as a country," undermining diplomatic options and goading Putin.[77]

As tensions between Russia and the United States over Ukraine emboldened hawks in the US government, the 2016 campaign brought another twist with the revelation that Paul Manafort, Trump's first campaign manager, had been working for the pro-Russian Yanukovych for years. A longtime Republican operative and lobbyist since the Reagan administration, Manafort clashed with the State Department in 2006, when "the American ambassador to Ukraine asked Manafort to ask his client to stop bad-mouthing NATO. Manafort flatly refused." According to friends, cash had always been Manafort's prime motivation, but this, to one acquaintance, was "the moment that he crossed over. Where once he could rationalize his work by saying that he was supporting American interests abroad, doing well by doing good, now he seemed suspect."[78]

Manafort's role in the Trump campaign came with the attention and scrutiny he had long avoided. Like other lobbyists and McCain's top adviser, Manafort had operated in the shadows, aggressively promoting the interests of his clients and seeking allies in Congress. The problem was not that Manafort acted as an agent of a foreign government but rather that his client, Yanukovych, was on the wrong side in the eyes of the US foreign policy establishment.

While revelations of Manafort's financial ties to Russia and his pro-Russian, pro-Putin stance led to his resignation as Trump's campaign adviser, by December 2016 he was back advising the president-elect. Two years later he would be tried and convicted for two counts of conspiracy in violation of federal lobbying laws, for money laundering, and for obstruction of justice (in addition to bank and tax fraud convictions).

Hacking Democracy

Fighting back against what many Russians saw as aggressive US attempts to isolate Russia diplomatically and economically, in the 2016 US election, active measures approved by Putin and deployed by Russian intelligence hacked Democratic Party emails, attempted to break into the election websites of at least thirty-nine states, and targeted key segments of the electorate during the campaign with false news stories circulated through phony and legitimate Facebook and Twitter accounts.[79] Rebooting the cold war with a combination of old KGB methods and new internet technologies, Russians showed that they, too, have mastered cyber information warfare and the projection of alternate realities.

As president, Trump consistently refrained from challenging Putin's authoritarian and anti-American policies, with Trump and his major advisers waging open warfare on US intelligence agencies. If a chain reaction of unlikely events and the antimajoritarian character of US political institutions led to Trump's election, the conditions for his autocratic rejection of norms of diplomacy abroad and compromise at home were long in the making and well established. Trump exploited a political system with an electoral college established to entrench the power of slave owners and already riven with partisanship, racial polarization, a contempt for democratic participation, and economic inequality. He asserted limitless executive powers, rejecting any pretense of democratic accountability. His administration laid waste to regulatory agencies and attacked the free press, the independence of the judiciary, and the rule of law. He incited violence by stoking or condoning racial, Islamophobic, and anti-Semitic hatreds, bringing the phrase *stochastic terrorism* into the political lexicon. And if the cold war national security state once offered a carrot-stick social wage, Trump presided over a brave new neoliberal white nationalist order that offers the abandoned white citizen-subject the false promise of protection by an authority figure, reducing governance to the punishment of immigrants and racial and religious minorities, and "deal making" among kleptocrats.

In February 2022, former president Trump praised Putin as Russia invaded the sovereign country of Ukraine, joined by a chorus of right-wing Republicans in the United States and Viktor Orbán in Hungary. The marriage of U.S. and Russian right-wing Christian nationalism has begotten a world where the survival of democracies is far from assured. Russia's brazen attack on Ukraine's democracy, cheered by authoritarians in the United States and abroad, was as shocking as the once unthinkable violent January 6 attempted coup against American multiracial democracy at the Capitol. As Putin and his U.S. and European supporters revel in the use of violence and lies to reshape the global order, thousands of Russian and European protesters in the streets are a somber reminder of past democratic struggles, but also, the mass euphoria and popular aspirations galvanized by the collapse of the Soviet empire. The fate of democracy in the United States and abroad may depend on our ability to remember and revive the democratic and egalitarian visions for political openness articulated by Gorbachev, Václav Havel, and Nelson Mandela, and the millions who welcomed the dawn of a new era with hope.

Epilogue

NOSTALGIA FOR THE FUTURE

In the years surrounding the collapse of the Soviet Union, revolutionaries, dissidents, and reformers called for political openness, a serious reckoning with the cold war past, and far-reaching reforms to address the social, economic, and environmental costs and dislocations of cold war policies. This book has examined the rapid eclipse of those visions, as US policy makers, blinded by triumphalism, refused a critical appraisal of the cold war's complex legacies. Instead, US foreign policy was defined by the projection of unipolar military force and a doubling down on the extractive and ecologically destructive industries (fossil fuels, nuclear weapons, petrochemicals) that had sustained cold war militarism. Adherents of cold war triumphalism celebrated the end of history, assuming a harmonious relationship between capitalism and democracy. For them, the idea that unregulated capitalism was corrosive of democratic institutions was unthinkable.

The deployment of cold war narratives by politicians, policy makers, and pundits continued to shape US foreign policy long after the Soviet collapse, extending the toxic legacies of US empire, domestic racism, and white supremacy at home and abroad. The vacuum left by cold war constructions of the enemy was quickly filled by xenophobic clash-of-civilizations rhetoric, which predated the 9/11 terror attacks, and new, metastasized voicings of racism and white nationalism. The supposed triumph of capitalism and democracy led to the outsized influence of money in politics, with the accumulating ills of vanishing jobs, decaying infrastructure, neoliberal governance, mass incarceration, substance abuse, and deaths of despair. Instead of heeding Mikhail Gorbachev's call for political openness and a redress of environmental damage wrought by cold war policies, many Americans blamed foreigners for their economic woes. Drawn into a vortex of resentment, millions in the United States evince at once a revanchist white nationalism and a waning faith in democratic governance, mirroring what Serguei A. Oushakine has called the patriotism of despair in the post-Soviet context.[1]

Cold war triumphalism fed the hubris of American exceptionalism, free trade, and catastrophic wars in the Middle East. Millions of Americans face an uncertain future. Alarmed by demagogic right-wing media and politicians, they see a nation besieged by external threat. They are not shown the origins of these problems in past projections of hegemonic US power. On the US-Mexico border, refugees from Central America flee violence and poverty in large part attributable to decades of US imperial interventions.

In 2015, far-right politicians in the United States and Europe mobilized against the stream of refugees fleeing armed conflict in Syria, in which the Arab Spring democratic uprising of 2011 against dictatorships throughout the Middle East, some with legacies of cold war-era ties to the United States, met with brutal repression from the regime of Bashar al-Assad. Refugees seeking asylum in Europe, Canada, Australia, and the United States also came from African states, including Libya and Somalia, as well as from ongoing conflicts and instability in Afghanistan and Iraq. Many others fled poverty in Kosovo. Over three thousand migrants died attempting to cross the Mediterranean Sea in crowded and dangerous vessels in 2015. These migrations posed a crisis for EU nations struggling to absorb the flood of migrants. Throughout the union the migration crisis sparked a backlash from far right and nationalist parties.

Less attention was paid to the underlying causes that disrupted the lives of migrants, as they fled upheavals wrought by US and coalition forces in Iraq and Afghanistan, conflicts that destabilized the region. Those conflicts could be traced to their cold war origins. US commentary on the so-called European refugee crisis crested in 2016, during the time of the Republican Party presidential primary. In the end, right-wing politicians from Donald Trump to Viktor Orbán in Hungary rode anti-immigrant xenophobia and racism to power. These nihilistic far-right authoritarians have capitalized on the instability and mass casualties caused by ill-advised imperialist wars of choice. The humanitarian crisis caused by the US debacle in Afghanistan will no doubt further embolden authoritarian governments mobilizing against migrants and refugees.

It is a daunting task, writing this epilogue during a global pandemic and following a white supremacist insurrection at the US Capitol seeking to overturn the results of President Joseph R. Biden's electoral victory. The global assault on liberal democracies and the continuing cataclysms of 2020 have jolted US commentators out of their usual amnesia and complacency. Some have looked to the rise of the New Right, or to the changes unleashed by the 9/11 terror attacks, or the persistence of supremacist ideology, as explanations for the US descent into authoritarianism. I submit that the end of the cold war holds the key to understanding the origin of our current threats to democracy. The brief interregnum that followed of reformist visions of a peace dividend clashed with retooled conceptions of national security, articulated in the search for new enemies, foreign and domestic.

It is clear that people throughout the globe are paying a very high price for cold war triumphalism and the refusal to examine the disastrous effects of the so-called cold war victory for public and planetary health. The pandemic has claimed the lives of nearly six million people. COVID-19 has exposed long-standing racial and social inequalities. If Trump's withdrawal from the international cooperation of the World Health Organization and the Paris Climate Accords appeared to many as extreme acts, as this book has shown, those actions followed decades of Republican Party contempt for the United Nations and for multilateral diplomacy writ large. Trump's rejection of global efforts to address the climate crisis have ample precedent in domestic and foreign policies driven by the interests of the fossil fuel industries.

Varieties of anticommunism, xenophobia, and white supremacy retained as active elements in conservative politics since 1989 have amounted to an attack on the very idea of society—everything, as the late cultural critic Stuart Hall put it, that holds us together as humans.[2] The rejection of society, of a sense of mutual obligation to the collective good, has played out horrifically in the pandemic. In the US response to the pandemic, in addition to the antisocial extremism of Trump and the antimaskers, such pathologies are echoed by the zealous protection of intellectual property rights as corporations producing vaccines have privileged profit over human needs, and as authoritarian, far-right leaders dispute the clear science indicating that rapid global vaccine distribution is imperative for bringing the pandemic under control. As science and public health officials offer clear guidelines to stop the spread of the virus and save lives, Republican politicians have deployed an onslaught of disinformation, racism, and xenophobia, causing millions to deny the seriousness of COVID. Such misguided attempts to encourage vaccine resistance for political gain has proved lethal to untold thousands of Americans and millions across the globe.

Central preoccupations of US cold war triumphalism—rooted in a sense of the righteousness of the US cause and a determined search for new enemies, as suggested by clash-of-civilizations narratives—were on horrifying display in the January 6, 2021 insurrection at the US Capitol as well as the events leading up to it. The insurrection exemplified two manifestations of unequal justice, both shaped by white supremacist ideology. In one, Black Lives Matter protesters and even reporters covering them were criminalized and subjected to unconstitutional police violence and mass arrest. In the other, white criminals and insurrectionists could violently attack police officers and desecrate the Capitol and walk away from the largest crime scene in US history, returning home with a sense of righteous impunity. Their rhetorical justifications for their seditious actions combined clash-of-civilizations rhetoric, anticommunist hysteria, and a false sense of victimization equating the duly elected government with an antidemocratic, authoritarian usurpation. The immediate catalyst was Trump's incessant lie that he had won the election, and that the election was stolen from him. Trump's baseless allegations of election fraud exploited the GOP's racist justifications of the routine suppression of African American voting, using similar unsubstantiated allegations. Incited by Trump's white nationalist rhetoric, which was amplified by conservative media and far right conspiracies, insurrectionists on January 6 stormed the Capitol, some of them intent on violently halting Congress's certification of Biden's victorious Electoral College tally. Carrying a Confederate flag through the Capitol, a building constructed by the labor of enslaved people, rioters surged through the arch of the tunnel bearing signs that said "Stop communism" and "Stop socialism." At a November 14 rally in Washington, DC, which became known as the Million MAGA March, tens of thousands of Trump supporters gathered at Freedom Plaza. Social media celebrity and conspiracy theorist Alex Jones shouted through a bullhorn, "If the globalists think they're gonna keep America under martial law, and they're gonna put that Communist Chinese agent Biden in, they got another thing coming!"[3]

The narrative of Capitol insurrectionists evokes elements of cold war triumphalism, drawing on clash-of-civilizations rhetoric and, in this instance, equating a duly elected government with authoritarian communism. Promulgated by such academics as Samuel Huntington and Bernard Lewis and officially rolled out by the George H. W. Bush administration in its justifications for the first US war in Iraq, clash-of-civilizations rhetoric became a staple of popular culture, a durable if ungainly presence in the dark crevices of the web but also on the *New York Times* best-seller list—in the works of Tom Clancy, with his imagined Asian and Muslim enemies, and the high-profile punditry of policy influencer Robert Kaplan. Stephen Bannon, Trump's former chief strategist and White House senior adviser, has sought to mobilize right-wing Catholics around the "church militant" movement—which places Trump at the forefront of a worldwide clash between Western civilization and Islamic "barbarity." Crusader flags, patches, and other Christian nationalist insignia, along with Trump flags, were commonplace at the Capitol insurrection.

Many insurrectionists, claiming an existential dispossession, exhibited the convoluted logic of cold war triumphalism, which portrays (white) Americans as a morally superior, if not chosen people who have vanquished communism and as potential victims always vulnerable to outside threats. Sedition-minded white supremacist insurrectionists see a coming apocalypse organized by such "globalists" as the Clintons, Bill Gates, and George Soros; their instruments are multinational institutions like the European Union, NATO, and the UN. As noted by Luke Mogelson, "invocations of the new world order often raise the specter of Jewish cabals, and the Stop the Steal movement has been rife with anti-Semitism." At a November 7 rally in Pennsylvania, an elderly woman "gripped a walker with her left hand and a homemade 'Stop the steal' sign with her right. The first letters of 'stop' and 'steal' were stylized to resemble Nazi SS bolts."[4]

Right-wing conspiracists such as Nicholas Fuentes and Alex Jones warned of the "great replacement," contending that Europe and the United States are under siege from nonwhites and non-Christians, and "that these groups are incompatible with Western culture, identity, and prosperity." Emboldened by the Republican Party's acquiescence to their hatred, many white supremacists maintain that the ultimate outcome of the so-called great replacement will be "white genocide." In Charlottesville, neo-Nazis chanted, "Jews will not replace us!" before violent attacks on counterprotesters, killing one of them. The perpetrators of the Christchurch, New Zealand mosque massacre and the El Paso Walmart mass shooting both cited the great replacement in their manifestos. The confinement of the pandemic helped conspiracists promote their theories online. Many COVID-19 skeptics believe that lockdowns, mask mandates, vaccines, and contact tracing are laying the groundwork for the new world order—a genocidal communist dystopia that, Jones says, will look "just like the Hunger Games."[5]

Far-right falsifications of history promote new ideologies conflating local governments with totalitarianism. Unhinged demonstrators who threaten violence against public health and school board officials denounce mask mandates and promotion of inclusive curriculum as "communism." These demonstrators are the thuggish apotheosis of the early 1990s Republican antigovernment rhetoric and privatization policies that have weakened infrastructure, schools, and public health. The war on society, the very idea of the social, had been influentially voiced by Margaret Thatcher and Ronald Reagan. Ironically, in the twisted logic of triumphalism, reckless accusations and charges of communism have persisted despite the assumed victory in the cold war. With no actual communists to be found, the targets of terror became such public servants as school board members, public health officials, and health care workers. Not even the police officers defending the Capitol are exempt from this mass hysteria, a far cry from the post 9/11 tributes to first responders.

Attacking the most elemental functions of government—the promotion of public health, safety, and the common good—ordinary citizens construed such measures as sinister and oppressive. At the Capitol insurrection, one man with a long beard and a Pittsburgh Pirates hat who was facing off against several police officers on the main floor of the Capitol shouted, "I will not let this country be taken over by globalist communist scum!" As reported in the *New Yorker*, the messages of Trump and the conspiracy theorists were "ubiquitous: on signs, clothes, patches, and flags, and in the way that the insurrectionists articulated what they were doing." Rhetoric employed at the Capitol echoed language used in attacks throughout the country. A woman arrested after entering the Michigan capitol building claimed that "extreme government overreach" during the pandemic "had proved that the Democrats aimed, above all, to subjugate citizens." Michelle Gregoire, a twenty-nine-year-old bus driver from Battle Creek, Michigan, told a *New Yorker* reporter, "If the left gets their way, they will silence whoever they want ... and before you know it their guns are confiscated and they're living under communism."[6]

In the wake of Trump's defeat, calls for restoring American leadership in the world remain blind to ways that US cold war policy and its assertion of unipolar power after the collapse of the Soviet Union played a role in worsening the economic immiseration, racial and religious bigotry and xenophobia, and antigovernment hysteria so prevalent today. The triumphalist conflation of democracy and capitalism, exemplified as this book has shown, in the 1992 Republican Platform and the 1994 Contract With America, eroded the social bonds upon which individual and collective survival depends. Renouncing social spending and ceding primacy to market solutions to social problems, such policies have robbed all but the world's most wealthy of a dignified future. The pandemic has underscored that the future of humanity depends on addressing social needs and recognizing our interdependence, amongst ourselves, and with all living species.[7]

As the COVID-19 pandemic rapidly spread to six continents, it was clear that people throughout the globe were imperiled by long-standing contempt by Republican officials for multilateralism. This is compounded by the long record of Republicans of discrediting science, with George W. Bush's withdrawal from the Geneva Climate Accords echoed most recently in Trump's withdrawal of the United States from the Paris Climate Agreement, and then from the World Health Organization at the height of the pandemic. The nation's calamitous response to COVID-19 saw renewed demagogic attacks on science, global cooperation, and the common good, fostering mob anger against public health officials and medical professionals. As for vaccine distribution, the most robust attempts at international cooperation to date remain at the mercy of national priorities and the proprietary rights of corporations. In a global vaccine apartheid, putting profit before technology sharing has endangered the lives of millions worldwide by severely restricting the production and availability of vaccines.

Yet, in the midst of the environmental, economic, and public health wreckage of the US unilateral project, as the last US military and diplomatic personnel left Afghanistan in August of 2021, politicians and pundits focused obsessively on tactics and strategies. Few commentators in the United States bothered to trace the origins of the debacle to cold war interventions that had brought devastation to Afghanistan long before the 9/11 terrorist attacks. Indeed, some continued to invoke cold war triumphalism.

Lamenting the US withdrawal from Afghanistan, Condoleezza Rice, national security adviser in the first George W. Bush administration and later, secretary of state, held out the example of the still unended war in Korea as a *model* of how the US could, indeed should, have remained in Afghanistan.[8] Naturalizing the cold war partition of Korea, Rice characterized the US presence on the peninsula as "reasonable" and achieving a "stable equilibrium." Rice dispensed with cold war dynamics entirely in her assessment of the war in Afghanistan. Summoning what the historian Priya Satia has called time's monster, "a certain kind of historical sensibility [that] allowed and continue[s] to allow many people to avoid perceiving their ethically inconsistent actions—their hypocrisy—in the modern period," Rice assessed the US presence in Afghanistan as a positive force that simply needed more time.[9]

Structuring her commentary around the concept of time, Rice insisted that more time was needed to turn failure into success. "More time for us might have preserved our sophisticated Bagram airbase.... More time would have served our strategic interests." Rice's invocation of "our sophisticated Bagram airbase" willfully erases the torture by US forces and deaths of enemy combatants that occurred at Bagram before the closing of its prison in 2014. She also left out the story of how an airbase built by the Soviets in the 1950s as part of technical aid to Afghans became "ours." For Rice, human rights abuses and the bombing and destabilization of entire countries and regions are mere setbacks within a righteous unfolding of the time of the powerful. Calling for more time to serve US strategic interests, Rice all but admits that attempted US nation-building in Afghanistan served US needs, not the interests of the Afghan people. Her presumption remains that US interests are those of the world, a convergence that will be increasingly evident in the fullness of time.

Lamenting the US withdrawal, Rice argues that "twenty years was not enough to complete a journey from the 7th-century rule of the Taliban and a 30-year civil war to a stable government." Rice takes a page from Bernard Lewis and Robert Kaplan to place a modern political formation born of superpower machinations—the Taliban—in the recesses of an imagined ancient and benighted Islamic dark age. By comparison, the benign US presence had allowed Afghans after 9/11 to "seize the chance to create a modern society where girls could attend school, women could enter professions and human rights would be respected." Rice ignores previous Afghan modernizing projects, in which Afghan women did have constitutional rights and did go to school before cold war interventions destabilized the country. Rice further elides US responsibility in aiding the mujahideen and the role of US and Pakistani funding in supporting the Taliban in the 1990s. For Rice, despite its stumbles, the march of US unipolarity will right the world, if only allowed more time.

But time is up for the vast majority of the world's people. Decades of science denial and unrelenting war driven by continued reliance on fossil fuel and extreme wealth inequality have deprived peoples, regions, and generations of a future. Without a reckoning with the past, there can be no secure and dignified future.

In the copious literature on post–cold war memory, a current trope is that of nostalgia for hope itself: nostalgia for the hope of surmounting the violence of poverty, reductive nationalisms, war, terrorism, and despair. Like the organizers of the Bruce Lee monument in Mostar, Bosnia, for whom the screen icon embodied the hope of their childhood, anthropologist and film-maker Maple Razsa, in his 2010 film *Bastards of Utopia* and his 2015 book of the same name, recalls the sense of empowerment once felt by people in his native Yugoslavia that they could choose a path not dictated by cold war superpowers and make a difference in the world. Exploring the democratic projects of a younger generation, Razsa explains, "I was not specifically nostalgic for the object of Yugoslav socialists' political hopes—the socialist state and economy—but for political hope itself."[10]

Nostalgia for hope itself is intimately bound to nostalgia for the future, and a future can only be reimagined in a symbiotic relationship with the past.[11] Only through an honest reckoning with the past, a clear-eyed account of the causes and origins of current inequities, can we imagine a humane future. Only an honest reckoning with the past will allow repair and reparation. As many throughout Europe and the United States have turned to xenophobic and far-right white nationalism, others have demanded truth and reconciliation about intertwined cold war and imperial atrocities and terror, as a critical path toward antiracist economic and environmental justice.

As historian Kevin K. Gaines has documented, the May 25, 2020, murder of George Floyd in Minneapolis prompted a global outpouring of demands for confronting racist and imperialist legacies, with solidarity protests spreading to fifty countries within two weeks of Floyd's murder.[12] Activists challenged the normalization of police violence and economic inequality, insisting that the continued existence of monuments honoring those colonizers, enslavers, and Confederates responsible for past crimes against humanity helps perpetuate state and vigilante violence against Black, Asian, and Indigenous peoples in the present. Likewise, the most recent wave of hate crimes against Asian-Americans, incited by Trump's frequent references to COVID-19 as "the China virus," has renewed demands for a reckoning with the violent history and legacies of US imperial wars in Asia.

Writing in the *New York Times*, Zachariah Mampilly argues that protests sweeping the globe in 2020 and 2021, including those in India, Yemen, Tunisia, Eswatini, Cuba, Colombia, Brazil, and the United States, are not simply a response to failed government pandemic policies. Like the Occupy Wall Street Movement and the Arab Spring, these protests have denounced governments that refuse accountability and that violate the dignity of their citizens. Protesters, Mampilly argues, have "called for a fundamental re-thinking of the existing post-Cold War social contract between governments and their people," a contract "largely founded upon the notion that market-centric policies would lead to global prosperity and peace."[13]

Protesters challenge not simply the austerity and privatization of neo-liberalism, but its assault on the very notion of human society. Indigenous, antiracist, and environmental activists have rejected neoliberal assertions of an autonomous, inherently self-interested *homo economicus*. Demanding instead a new social contract grounded in the reality of fundamental human connectedness and interdependence, activists call for a politics grounded in care.

Activists see that there is no way forward—no future—without a reckoning with the cold war past and the intricate ways that this history and its aftermath have been bound up with racism, imperialism, and ecological devastation. As the United States maintained, for the most part, a stubborn official silence on its imperial and domestic histories of intertwined racist and anticommunist violence, over twenty countries, including South Africa, Guatemala, and South Korea, and localities in the United States such as Greensboro, North Carolina, and Philadelphia launched truth commissions. Many of these commissions have been criticized for promoting political and legal rights over social and economic rights and justice, arguably legitimizing neoliberal regimes.[14] However constrained by the neoliberal race to the bottom, disempowered citizens, and desiccated democracy, architects of truth and reconciliation projects know that there can be no justice without economic and environmental redress for the profound violence of cold war and imperial histories. The fault lies not in demands for truth, but rather in the terrain of ever-widening inequality on which these projects were enacted. In the hope of reimagining a future, a sustained project of cold war and imperial truth and reconciliation is imperative.

Distortions of truth were built into the foundations of cold war and then intertwined neoliberal and US unipolar projects. The path to security in a possible future will be found not in earlier models of American-style unipolar leadership but in genuine human cooperation and solidarity on global, regional, national, and local scales, focused on meeting basic human needs such as clean water and air through projects of environmental and social justice. Security must be redefined through demilitarization and environmental justice, and a new social contract based on a politics of care. The truth about the past, like the truth of the interdependence of all human and nonhuman life, is not a means to an end. It is the end and the only possible future.

NOTES

Introduction

1 Havel, "Call for Sacrifice," 6–7, republished in Havel, *The Art of the Impossible*, 141.

2 I rely on this literature throughout the book. See, for example, Westad, *Global Cold War*; Bradley, *Imagining Vietnam and America*; Borstelmann, *Cold War*; Vitalis, *America's Kingdom*; Prashad, *Darker Nations*; Joseph and Grandin, *Century of Revolution*; Simpson, *Economists with Guns*; McMahon, *Cold War*; Makdisi and Prashad, *Land of Blue Helmets*; and Chamberlin, *Cold War's Killing Fields*.

3 Engel, *When the World Seemed New*, 484.

4 Conor Cruise O'Brien, "Communist Castaways," *Irish Times*, April 26, 1990.

5 Henry Allen, "Lost in Glasnost: The Cold War May Be History, but the Spoils Are Spoiled," *Washington Post*, March 12, 1990. My approach to the uses and abuses of the past has been shaped by Eric Foner. See Foner, *Who Owns History?*

6 Scribner, *Requiem for Communism*; Sarotte, *1989*. This book is informed by a vast literature on post-1989 former Soviet and Eastern bloc spheres. Kristen Ghodsee's scholarship has been especially important in critiquing US triumphalism and its global impact. See Ghodsee, *Red Hangover*.

7 Buck-Morss, *Dreamworld and Catastrophe*, ix.

8 For exemplary scholarship on shifting constructions of enemies, see Little, *Us versus Them*.

9 Rodgers, *Age of Fracture*.

10 Jodi Kim, *Ends of Empire*; Westad, *Global Cold War*; Singh, *Race and America's Long War*. For exemplary global framings of the intersections of the cold war and

empires, see Lauren Hirshberg, *Suburban Empire*; Monica Kim, *Interrogation Rooms*; and Colleen Woods, *Freedom Incorporated.*

11 I draw on the wealth of new scholarship on the former Eastern bloc that has appeared over the past decade to investigate Western triumphalism and nostalgia in relation to forms of nostalgia in the former Eastern bloc. For some of the important scholarship on these multiple and various forms of nostalgia, see Boym, *Future of Nostalgia*; Scribner, *Requiem for Communism*; Luthar and Pušnik, *Remembering Utopia*; and Todorova, *Remembering Communism.*

12 Important scholarship on US cold war memory includes Wiener, *How We Forgot the Cold War*. Although the different emphases of Wiener's book and my own (forgetting versus nostalgia) may sound opposed, I see the arguments as two sides of the same coin, both concerned with the evasions and distortions of the history of the cold war. See also Schrecker, *Cold War Triumphalism.*

13 Stephen F. Cohen, *Soviet Fates and Lost Alternatives.*

14 Vladimir Radyuhin, "Delhi Declaration Still Relevant, Says Mikhail Gorbachev," *Hindu*, March 1, 2006, updated March 23, 2012, https://www.thehindu.com/todays-paper/tp-international/delhi-declaration-still-relevant-says-mikhail-gorbachev/article3157743.ece. See Sahai, *Delhi Declaration.*

15 "Man of the Year: An Intimate Portrait," *Time*, January 4, 1988.

16 "The Gorbachev Visit; Excerpts from Speech to U.N. on Major Soviet Military Cuts," *New York Times*, December 8, 1988, https://www.nytimes.com/1988/12/08/world/the-gorbachev-visit-excerpts-from-speech-to-un-on-major-soviet-military-cuts.html.

17 Walter Isaacson, "The Gorbachev Challenge," *Time*, December 19, 1988, 16, 17 (from the Vault).

18 Isaacson, "Gorbachev Challenge," 20.

19 *Oxford English Dictionary*, https://www.oxfordreference.com/view/10.1093/oi/authority.20110803095854377.

20 Mark Hosenball, "Centuries of Boredom in World without War; an American Theory," Spectrum, *Times* (London), September 3, 1989.

21 George H. W. Bush, "Address Accepting the Presidential Nomination at the Republican National Convention in New Orleans," American Presidency Project, August 18, 1988, https://www.presidency.ucsb.edu/node/268235.

22 Klein, *Shock Doctrine*. See Slobodian, *Globalists.*

23 Quoted in Stephen Kinzer, "Prenden Journal: For East German Theme Park, the Bad Old Days," *New York Times*, November 9, 1993.

24 Schrecker, *Cold War Triumphalism.*

25 For an important early example, see Hogan, *End of the Cold War.*

26 For models of this approach, see McAlister, *Epic Encounters*; Schwenkel, *American War in Contemporary Vietnam*; and Shibusawa, "Ideology, Culture, and the Cold War." While this book is not framed as a study in memory per se, other important models include Blight, *Race and Reunion.*

27 My debt to scholars in developing intertextual methodological approaches is elaborated in Von Eschen, "Memory." See especially McAlister, *Epic Encounters*; Rosenberg, *Day Which Will Live*; and Friedman, *Covert Capital.*

28 For an excellent analysis of how these tropes operated in 1950s and 1960s American culture, see Jacobson and González, *What Have They Built You to Do?*
29 Warner, *Publics and Counterpublics.*

1. The Ends of History

1 Quoted in Judith Havemann, "Bush Expresses 'Delight,' Issues Invitation to the White House," *Washington Post*, February 12, 1990.
2 Robert Windram, "US Government Considered Nelson Mandela Terrorist until 2008," NBC News, December 7, 2013, http://www.nbcnews.com/news/other/us-government-considered-nelson-mandela-terrorist-until-2008-f2D11708787.
3 For an example of reporting during the 1988 campaign, see Stephen Engelberg with Jeff Gerth, "Bush and Noriega: and Examination of Their Ties," *New York Times*, September 28, 1988, http://www.nytimes.com/1988/09/28/us/bush-and-noriega-examination-of-their-ties.html?pagewanted=all; and Howard Kohn and Vicki Monks, "The Dirty Secrets of George Bush: The Vice President's Illegal Operations," *Rolling Stone*, November 3, 1988, https://www.rollingstone.com/politics/politics-news/the-dirty-secrets-of-george-bush-71927/.
4 Andrew Marshall, "What Happened to the Peace Dividend?," *Independent* (London), January 2, 1993, http://www.independent.co.uk/news/world/what-happened-to-the-peace-dividend-the-end-of-the-cold-war-cost-thousands-of-jobs-andrew-marshall-1476221.html.
5 Denning, *Culture in the Age.*
6 LeoGrande and Kornbluh, *Back Channel to Cuba.*
7 Perry Anderson, *Zone of Engagement*, 281.
8 Harvey, *Brief History of Neoliberalism*; Slobodian, *Globalists.*
9 Schrecker, *Cold War Triumphalism.*
10 Francis Fukuyama, "The End of History?," *National Interest*, Summer 1989, 18.
11 Perry Anderson, "The Ends of History," in *Zone of Engagement*, 279–376. James Atlas, "What Is Fukuyama Saying? And to Whom Is He Saying It?," *New York Times*, October 22, 1989, https://www.nytimes.com/1989/10/22/magazine/what-is-fukuyama-saying-and-to-whom-is-he-saying-it.html.
12 Mark Hosenball, "Centuries of Boredom in World without War; an American Theory," Spectrum, *Times* (London), September 3, 1989.
13 Francis Fukuyama, "The History at the End of History," *Guardian*, April 3, 2007, https://www.theguardian.com/commentisfree/2007/apr/03/thehistoryattheendofhist.
14 Francis Fukuyama, "American Political Decay or Renewal: The Meaning of the 2016 Election," *Foreign Affairs*, July/August 2016.
15 Fukuyama, *End of History*, 44–45.
16 Fukuyama, *End of History*, 352.
17 Patrick E. Tyler, "U.S. Strategy Plans Calls for Insuring No Rivals Develop: A One-Superpower World; Pentagon's Document Outlines Ways to Thwart Challenges to Primacy of America," special to *New York Times*, March 8, 1992.

18 By the time the United States invaded Iraq in 2003, Fukuyama's association with Wolfowitz went back thirty-five years. Both studied with Allan Bloom and lived in Telluride House at Cornell University, first meeting when Fukuyama was an undergraduate and Wolfowitz served on the Board of Telluride. Robert S. Boynton, "Francis Fukuyama: The Neoconservative Who Isn't," *American Prospect*, October 2005, http://www.robertboynton.com/articleDisplay.php?article_id=84.

19 Harvey, *New Imperialism*.

20 Matt Novak, "The White House Screening of *The Hunt for Red October* Had Celebrities, Spies, and (Maybe) a Sex Scandal," Gizmodo, April 26, 2016, http://paleofuture.gizmodo.com/the-white-house-screening-of-the-hunt-for-red-october-h-1772109543.

21 "Tom Clancy by the Numbers," *Time*, October 2, 2013, http://entertainment.time.com/2013/10/02/tom-clancy-by-the-numbers/.

22 Novak, "White House Screening."

23 Vincent Canby, "Connery as Captain of a Renegade Soviet Sub," *New York Times*, March 2, 1990.

24 See Carruthers, *Cold War Captives*.

25 Cahal Milmo, "Ronald Reagan 'Prepared for Historic Cold War Meeting by Reading Tom Clancy Thriller,'" *Independent* (London), December 29, 2015, http://www.independent.co.uk/news/world/americas/ronald-reagan-prepared-for-historic-cold-war-meeting-by-reading-tom-clancy-thriller-a6790036.html#commentsDiv. See also Robert Hutton, "How Reagan Prepped for Gorbachev Summit with Tom Clancy Thriller," Bloomberg, December 29, 2015, http://www.bloomberg.com/news/articles/2015-12-30/how-reagan-prepped-for-gorbachev-summit-with-tom-clancy-thriller.

26 Milmo, "Ronald Reagan."

27 Milmo, "Ronald Reagan."

28 Milmo, "Ronald Reagan."

29 Milmo, "Ronald Reagan."

30 Neil A. Lewis, "Clamor in the East: Gratitude and a Request; in Talk to Congress, Walesa Urges a Marshall Plan to Revive Poland," *New York Times*, November 16, 1989, http://www.nytimes.com/1989/11/16/world/clamor-east-gratitude-request-talk-congress-walesa-urges-marshall-plan-revive.html.

31 Sarotte, *1989*.

32 Quoted in Kris LaGrange, "Ronald Reagan: The Union Buster," UCOMM blog, March 5, 2018, https://ucommblog.com/section/national-politics/ronald-reagan-union-buster. See also Harold Myerson, "How Workers Lost the Power Struggle—and Their Pay Raises," *Washington Post*, October 18, 2014, https://www.washingtonpost.com/opinions/harold-meyerson-workers-lose-the-power-struggle—and-their-pay-raises/2014/10/08/bbe3b0a2-4ee2-11e4-babe-e91da079cb8a_story.html.

33 "George H. W. Bush—Key Events," Miller Center, accessed September 9, 2021, http://millercenter.org/president/bush/key-events; George H. W. Bush, "President Bush's Remarks at the Solidarity Workers Monument," Making the History

of 1989, Roy Rosenzweig Center for History and New Media, accessed September 9, 2021, https://chnm.gmu.edu/1989/items/show/36.

34 David Remnick, "Exit Havel: The King Leaves the Castle," *New Yorker*, https://www.newyorker.com/magazine/2003/02/17/exit-havel.

35 Martin Walker, "Havel's Congress Play a Box Office Hit," *Guardian*, February 22, 1990.

36 Al Kamen, "Havel Asks U.S. to Aid Soviet Democratization; in Hill Speech, Czech Calls for Creating 'Family of Man,'" *Washington Post*, February 22, 1990.

37 Walker, "Havel's Congress."

38 Walker, "Havel's Congress."

39 "Let's Hear It for Hegel!," *Washington Post*, February 23, 1990, https://www.washingtonpost.com/archive/opinions/1990/02/23/lets-hear-it-for-hegel/ed97d6fe-00a0-47f3-90cf-1fd9f940ee24/.

40 Walker, "Havel's Congress."

41 Kamen, "Havel Asks U.S." For Edgar Beigel's reported hearing of "nacho before beans," see Jonah Ben-Joseph, "What Did Congress Hear? About Nacho Chips?," editorial, *Washington Post*, March 3, 1990.

42 Kamen, "Havel Asks U.S."

43 "Upheaval in East: Excerpts from Czech Chief's Address to Congress," *New York Times*, February 22, 1990.

44 "Upheaval in East."

45 Havel, *To the Castle and Back*. See also "Vaclav Havel Obituary," *Guardian*, December 18, 2011, https://www.theguardian.com/world/2011/dec/18/vaclav-havel.

46 George H. W. Bush, "Honoring Nelson Mandela," HuffPost, December 3, 2013, https://www.huffingtonpost.com/george-h-w-bush/honoring-nelson-mandela_1_b_4377877.html.

47 Irwin, *Gordian Knot*.

48 "Hailing South Africa's Communists," editorial, *Washington Post*, February 13, 1990.

49 Joseph Albright and Marcia Kunstel, Cox News Service, "Ex-Official: CIA Helped Jail Mandela," *Chicago Tribune*, June 10, 1990; Frederick Reese, "Looking Back at Mandela's CIA Assisted 1962 Arrest," MPN News, December 6, 2013, http://www.mintpressnews.com/the-cia-helped-apartheid-era-south-africa-arrest-nelson-mandela/167159/.

50 Albright and Kunstel, "Ex-Official."

51 David Lauter, "Query on CIA Tied to Mandela Case Deflected," *Los Angeles Times*, June 13, 1990, http://articles.latimes.com/1990-06-13/news/mn-188_1_mandela-s-arrest; Reese, "Looking Back."

52 "Ex-CIA Spy Admits Tip Led to Nelson Mandela's Long Imprisonment," *Guardian*, May 15, 2016, https://www.theguardian.com/us-news/2016/may/15/cia-operative-nelson-mandela-1962-arrest.

53 Adam Taylor, "The CIA's Mysterious Role in the Arrest of Nelson Mandela," *Washington Post*, May 16, 2016, https://www.washingtonpost.com/news/worldviews/wp/2016/05/16/the-cias-mysterious-role-in-the-arrest-of-nelson-mandela/.

54 Chamberlin, *Global Offensive*, 168. On early US support for the apartheid regime, see Borstelmann, *Apartheid's Reluctant Uncle*.

55 Chamberlin, *Global Offensive*, 182.

56 Sargent, *Superpower Transformed*; Minter, *Apartheid's Contras*.

57 Gleijeses, *Visions of Freedom*, 28–31.

58 Gleijeses, *Visions of Freedom*, 10.

59 Quoted in Gleijeses, *Visions of Freedom*, 513. For an example of Bush and Savimbi's interactions, see White House, memorandum of conversation 8022, Subject: Meeting with Dr. Jonas Savimbi, President of UNITA, October 5, 1989, Oval Office, George H. W. Bush Presidential Library and Museum, https://bush41library.tamu.edu/files/memcons-telcons/1989-10-05--Savimbi.pdf.

60 Jack Kemp, "Should the U.S. Aid Savimbi's Rebels in Angola? He'll Oust Marxists," *New York Times*, December 3, 1985.

61 Gleijeses, *Visions of Freedom*, 10–11.

62 Gleijeses, *Visions of Freedom*, 36.

63 "Excerpts from an Interview with Walter Cronkite of CBS News," American Presidency Project, March 3, 1981, https://www.presidency.ucsb.edu/node/247059.

64 Mamdani, *Good Muslim, Bad Muslim*, 87, 88; Minter, *Apartheid's Contras*.

65 "The Growing Debate over Soviet Ties to Terrorism," *Business Week*, June 1, 1981, 51.

66 Harry Rositzke, "If There Were No K.G.B., Would the Scale and Intensity of Terrorism Be Diminished?," *New York Times*, July 2, 1981.

67 Rositzke, "If There Were No K.G.B."

68 Rositzke, "If There Were No K.G.B."

69 Joseph C. Harsch, "For Once, Kremlin and White House Are in Sync," *Christian Science Monitor*, July 12, 1985.

70 Quoted in "President Assails Terrorist Nations; Unspecified Action Is Threatened," *Washington Post*, July 9, 1985. See also Bernard Weinraub, "President Accuses 5 'Outlaw States' of World Terror," *New York Times*, July 9, 1985, https://www.nytimes.com/1985/07/09/world/president-accuses-5-outlaw-states-of-world-terror.html; Associated Press, "Reagan Sees 5 Nation's as Murder Inc.," *Los Angeles Times*, July 8, 1985, https://www.latimes.com/archives/la-xpm-1985-07-08-mn-9682-story.html; and Reuters, "Reagan Called 'Imbecile,' Libya Accuses U.S. of Backing Terrorism," *Globe and Mail* (Toronto), June 10, 1985. For South Korean commentary, see "A Confederation of Terrorists—a Murder Inc.," editorial, *Hanguk Ibo* (Seoul), July 10, 1985.

71 Jonathan S. Landay, "In Ronald Reagan Era Mandela Was Branded a Terrorist," McClatchy DC Bureau, December 6, 2013, https://www.mcclatchydc.com/news/nation-world/world/article24760045.html.

72 Landay, "In Ronald Reagan Era."

73 Robert Windrem, "US Government Considered Nelson Mandela a Terrorist until 2008," NBC News, December 7, 2013, https://www.nbcnews.com/news/world/us-government-considered-nelson-mandela-terrorist-until-2008-flna2D11708787.

74 Schmitz, *United States and Right-Wing*; Schmitz, *Thank God*.

75 Friedman, *Covert Capital*, 24.

76 White House, memorandum of conversation, Subject: Bilateral Discussion with President Sese Seko Mobutu of the Republic of Zaire, February 24, 1989, Ambassador's Residence, Tokyo, Japan, George H. W. Bush Presidential Library and Museum, https://bush41library.tamu.edu/files/memcons-telcons/1989-02-24--Sese%20Seko.pdf.

77 White House memorandum 5192, Subject: Meeting between the President and Zairian President Mobutu, June 29, 1989, Oval Office, George H. W. Bush Presidential Library and Museum, https://bush41library.tamu.edu/files/memcons-telcons/1989-06-29--Sese%20Seko%20[1].pdf.

78 135 Cong. Rec. H13922 (daily ed. July 29, 1989), secs. 10–12 (Sense of Congress Concerning Angola).

79 Clifford Krauss, "U.S. Cuts Aid to Zaire, Setting Off a Policy Debate," *New York Times*, November 4, 1990, https://www.nytimes.com/1990/11/04/world/us-cuts-aid-to-zaire-setting-off-a-policy-debate.htm.

80 White House memorandum 5192.

81 See Helen C. Epstein's brilliant account in *Another Fine Mess*.

82 Robert Pear, "Mobutu, on Visit, Lauded and Chided," *New York Times*, June 30, 1989. According to the *New York Times*, "The President did not mention Zaire's human rights problems in his public farewell statement to Mr. Mobutu. He praised the African leader for helping to bring about a cease-fire in Angola."

83 Tom McCarthy, "Paul Manafort: How Decades of Serving Dictators Led to Role as Trump's Go-To Guy," *Guardian*, October 30, 2017, https://www.theguardian.com/us-news/2017/oct/30/paul-manafort-profile-donald-trump-dictators.

84 White House memorandum of conversation 1987, Subject: Luncheon Meeting with President Joaquim Chissano of Mozambique, March 13, 1990, Old Family Dining Room, George H. W. Bush Presidential Library and Museum, https://bush41library.tamu.edu/files/memcons-telcons/1990-03-13--Chissano%20[3].pdf.

85 White House memorandum of conversation 5120, Subject: Meeting with President Sam Nujoma of Namibia, June 19, 1990, Oval Office, George H. W. Bush Presidential Library and Museum, https://bush41library.tamu.edu/files/memcons-telcons/1990-06-19--Nujoma.pdf.

86 Gleijeses, *Visions of Freedom*, 89–97, 209–12.

87 On imperial exceptionalism, see the introduction to Woods, *Freedom Incorporated*.

88 Gleijeses, *Visions of Freedom*, 509–11.

89 "Mozambique: Civil War," Mass Atrocity Endings, August 7, 2015, https://sites.tufts.edu/atrocityendings/2015/08/07/mozambique-civil-war/.

90 J. Brooks Spector, "When Mandela First Met America," *Daily Maverick* (South Africa), December 9, 2013.

91 John Kifner, "The Mandela Visit; Mandela Gets an Emotional New York City Welcome," *New York Times*, June 21, 1990, http://www.nytimes.com/1990/06/21/nyregion/the-mandela-visit-mandela-gets-an-emotional-new-york-city-welcome.

92 Spector, "When Mandela First Met America."

93 Spector, "When Mandela First Met America."

94 Kifner, “Mandela Visit.”

95 “Nelson Mandela: First Address to a Joint Session U.S. Congress; Delivered 26 June 1990,” American Rhetoric, September 24, 2021, https://www.americanrhetoric.com/speeches/nelsonmandelauscongress.htm.

96 Maureen Dowd, “The Mandela Visit; Mandela Declines to Rule Out Force,” special to the *New York Times*, June 26, 1990.

97 Landay, “In Ronald Reagan Era.” See also Peter Beinart, “Don’t Sanitize Mandela: He’s Honored Now but Was Hated Then,” ZNet, December 6, 2013, https://zcomm.org/znetarticle/don-t-sanitize-nelson-mandela-he-s-honored-now-but-was-hated-then-by-peter-beinart/.

98 Francis Njubi Nesbitt, “When American Met Mandela,” Foreign Policy in Focus, June 28, 2013, http://fpif.org/when_america_met_mandela/.

99 For a discussion of the role of Arafat and the Palestinian Liberation Organization in the liberation forces of the cold war world, see Chamberlin, *Global Offensive*. On Cuba, see Mahler, *From the Tricontinental*; Gleijeses, *Visions of Freedom*.

100 Landay, “In Ronald Reagan Era.”

101 Memorandum of telephone conversation between George H. W. Bush and Nelson Mandela of South Africa, March 6, 1991, Oval Office, George H. W. Bush Presidential Library and Museum, https://bush41library.tamu.edu/files/memcons-telcons/1991-03-06--Mandela.pdf. On debates at the United Nations over negotiated withdrawal, see Quigley, “United States.”

102 Phillips, *American Dynasty*, 202.

103 “ANC Leader Affirms Control for State Control of Industry,” *Times* (London), January 26, 1990.

104 Mandela quoted in Kifner, “Mandela Visit.”

105 Kifner, “Mandela Visit.”

106 Renwick, *End of Apartheid*.

107 Alan Riding, “European Nations to Lift Sanctions on South Africa,” *New York Times*, April 16, 1991, http://www.nytimes.com/1991/04/16/world/european-nations-to-lift-sanctions-on-south-africa.html.

108 Norman Kempster, “Bush Lifts Economic Sanctions on S. Africa: Apartheid: He Sees ‘Irreversible’ Progress by Pretoria. Opponents in Congress Plan No Effort to Undo the Move,” *Los Angeles Times*, July 11, 1991, http://articles.latimes.com/1991-07-11/news/mn-2867_1_south-africa. See also Andrew Rosenthal, “Bush to Lift South African Sanctions Soon,” *New York Times*, June 20, 1991, http://www.nytimes.com/1991/06/20/world/bush-to-lift-south-africa-sanctions-soon.html.

109 Memorandum of telephone conversation between George H. W. Bush and Nelson Mandela, July 10, 1991, Oval Office, George H. W. Bush Presidential Library and Museum, https://bush41library.tamu.edu/files/memcons-telcons/1991-07-10--Mandela.pdf.

110 Ellis, “Historical Significance,” 261.

111 Ellis, “Historical Significance.”

112 Memorandum of telephone conversation between George H. W. Bush and Nelson Mandela of South Africa, May 3, 1991, Oval Office, George H. W. Bush Presiden-

tial Library and Museum, https://bush41library.tamu.edu/files/memcons-telcons/1991-05-03--Mandela.pdf.

113 National Security Council memorandum of conversation 4461, Subject: Meeting with Gatsha Mangosuthu Buthelezi, Chief Minister of KwaZulu, South Africa, June 20, 1991, Old Family Dining Room, George H. W. Bush Presidential Library and Museum, https://bush41library.tamu.edu/files/memcons-telcons/1991-06-20--Buthelezi.pdf.

114 National Security Council memorandum of conversation 4461.

115 Graham, "Foreign Policy in Transition."

116 John Carlin, "How the Volk Myth Died: It Took Just a Few Minutes to Change the Course of South African History," *Independent* (London), March 13, 1994, https://www.independent.co.uk/news/world/how-the-volk-myth-died-it-took-just-a-few-minutes-to-change-the-course-of-south-african-history-john-1428703.html.

117 Bill Keller, "The South African Vote: The Overview; Bomb Kills 9, Stirring Anxiety," *New York Times*, April 25, 1994, https://www.nytimes.com/1994/04/25/world/south-african-vote-overview-south-africa-bomb-kills-9-stirring-voter-anxiety.html.

118 Mandela, *Conversations with Myself*, 380–81, ellipsis in the original.

119 Andrew Ross Sorkin, "How Mandela Shifted Views on the Freedom of the Market," *New York Times*, December 9, 2013, http://dealbook.nytimes.com/2013/12/09/how-mandela-shifted-views-on-freedom-of-markets/.

120 Bhorat et al., "Economic Policy in South Africa," 21.

121 Hirsh, "Fatal Embrace"; Habib, *South Africa's Suspended Revolution*.

122 Hirsh, "Fatal Embrace."

123 Howard Barrell (2000) quoted in Ferguson, *Global Shadows*, 118; Barrell, "Back to the Future"; Green, *Choice, Not Fate*.

124 Hirsh, "Fatal Embrace."

125 Klein, *Shock Doctrine*.

126 Ferguson, *Global Shadows*, 84.

127 Quoted in Ferguson *Global Shadows*, 117.

128 Ferguson, *Global Shadows*, 84.

129 Bush, "Honoring Nelson Mandela."

2. Out of Order

1 Little, *Us versus Them*, 64–78.

2 George H. W. Bush, "Address before a Joint Session of Congress," Miller Center, September 11, 1990, http://millercenter.org/president/bush/speeches/speech-3425.

3 On US aid to Iraq, see Shane Harris and Matthew M. Aid, "Exclusive: CIA Files Prove America Helped Saddam as He Gassed Iran," *Foreign Policy*, August 26, 2013, https://foreignpolicy.com/2013/08/26/exclusive-cia-files-prove-america-helped-saddam-as-he-gassed-iran/; and Seymour M. Hersh, "U.S. Secretly Gave Aid to Iraq Early in Its War with Iran," *New York Times*, January 26, 1992, https://www.nytimes.com/1992/01/26/world/us-secretly-gave-aid-to-iraq-early-in-its-war-against-iran.html.

4 Lee Lescaze, "Reagan Blames Crime on 'Human Predator,'" *Washington Post*, September 29, 1981, https://www.washingtonpost.com/archive/politics/1981/09/29/reagan-blames-crime-on-human-predator/.

5 Bernard Lewis, "The Roots of Muslim Rage," *Atlantic*, September 1990, https://www.theatlantic.com/magazine/archive/1990/09/the-roots-of-muslim-rage/304643/.

6 Steve Coll, "Days of Rage," *New Yorker*, October 1, 2012.

7 Quoted in Engel, *When the World Seemed New*, 400.

8 Mamdani, *Saviors and Survivors*, 227.

9 Helen C. Epstein, "America's Secret Role in the Rwandan Genocide," *Guardian*, September 12, 2017, https://www.theguardian.com/news/2017/sep/12/americas-secret-role-in-the-rwandan-genocide; Epstein, *Another Fine Mess*.

10 Woodward, *Balkan Tragedy*. Hockenos, *Homeland Calling*, examines the role of émigré and exile communities in fanning the violence.

11 Bowden, *Empire of Civilization*.

12 See Brent Scowcroft, oral history, transcript, November 12–13, 1999, George H. W. Bush Oral History Project, University of Virginia Miller Center. Discussion of Vietnam and bombing is on p. 9.

13 Engel, *When the World Seemed New*, 391.

14 Quoted in Engel, *When the World Seemed New*, 292.

15 Quoted in Engel, *When the World Seemed New*, 480.

16 Engel, *When the World Seemed New*, 412; Untermeyer, *Zenith*, 149.

17 Rabe, *Killing Zone*; Rabe, *Kissinger and Latin America*.

18 Conor Cruise O'Brien, "Communist Castaways," *Irish Times*, April 26, 1990.

19 Amy Goodman, "'How the Iraq War Began in Panama': 1989 Invasion Set the Path for Future Interventions," with Humberto Brown, Greg Grandin, and Lawrence Wilkerson, *Democracy Now*, December 23, 2014, http://www.democracynow.org/2014/12/23/how_the_iraq_war_began_in_Panama; Grandin, *Empire's Workshop*.

20 Howard Kohn and Vicki Monks, "The Dirty Secrets of George Bush: The Vice President's Illegal Operations," *Rolling Stone*, November 3, 1988, https://www.rollingstone.com/politics/politics-news/the-dirty-secrets-of-george-bush-71927/.

21 Kohn and Monks, "Dirty Secrets of George Bush."

22 David Vine, "The U.S. Has an Empire of Bases in the Middle East and It's Not Making Anyone Safer," Foreign Policy in Focus, January 20, 2016, http://fpif.org/u-s-empire-bases-middle-east-not-making-anyone-safer/.

23 Hahn, *Mission Accomplished?*; Von Eschen, *Satchmo Blows Up the World*, 131–33.

24 Sue Chan, "Guess Who Got the Key to Detroit?," CBS News, March 26, 2003, http://www.cbsnews.com/news/guess-who-got-the-key-to-detroit/.

25 Hersh, "U.S. Secretly Gave Aid."

26 Harris and Aid, "Exclusive."

27 Michael Klare, "U.S. Strategy to Defend against 'Rogue' States Needs an Overhaul," *Christian Science Monitor*, April 25, 1995.

28 Vine, *Base Nation*; Vine, "U.S. Has an Empire."

29 *Congressional Record*, vol. 137, pt. 1 (January 12, 1991), S109.

30 On debates at the United Nations over negotiated withdrawal, see Quigley, "United States"; Little, *Us versus Them*, 74–76; Makdisi and Prashad, introduction to *Land of Blue Helmets*, 4; and in the same volume, Chitalkar and Malone, "UN Security Council," 170–76; Hindawi, "Iraq."

31 Klare, "U.S. Strategy to Defend."

32 See John R. MacArthur's important account of this in *Second Front*, 60–70; and Klare, "U.S. Strategy to Defend."

33 Qureshi and Sells, "Introduction," 16.

34 Samuel P. Huntington, "Repent! The End Is Near," *Washington Post*, September 24, 1989.

35 On the administration's views of "a very messy world," see Bush and Scowcroft, *World Transformed*, 355.

36 Peter Beinart, "The New Enemy Within," *Atlantic*, May 2015, https://www.theatlantic.com/magazine/archive/2015/05/the-new-enemy-within/389573/.

37 McAlister, *Epic Encounters*, 219.

38 McAlister, *Epic Encounters*, 219.

39 Khalil, *America's Dream Palace*; Lockman, *Contending Visions*.

40 Lewis, "Roots of Muslim Rage."

41 Qureshi and Sells, "Introduction," 17.

42 See Douglas Little, "Genesis: Containment and the Cold War in the Muslim World," chap. 1 in his *Us versus Them*. For a succinct and excellent discussion of Carter and Reagan's support of Islamist extremist, see Brands, *Making the Unipolar Moment*, 255–60.

43 Melanie Colburn, "America's Devil's Game with Extremist Islam," *Mother Jones*, January/February 2006, https://www.motherjones.com/politics/2006/01/americas-devils-game-extremist-islam/.

44 Wilford, *America's Great Game*; Abdel Bari Atwan, "CIA, George W. Bush, and Many Others, Helped Create ISIS," Salon, October 18, 2015, https://www.salon.com/2015/10/18/america_enabled_radical_islam_how_the_cia_george_w_bush_and_many_others_helped_create_isis/.

45 Atwan, "CIA, George W. Bush."

46 Joe Stephens and David B. Ottaway, "From U.S., the ABC's of Jihad," *Washington Post*, March 23, 2002, https://www.washingtonpost.com/archive/politics/2002/03/23/from-us-the-abcs-of-jihad/d079075a-3ed3-4030-9a96-0d48f6355e54/.

47 Colburn, "America's Devil's Game."

48 See Jeremy Scahill's reflections on his early reporting on Iraq, *Intercept*, December 5, 2018.

49 Barbara Crossette, "Iraq Sanctions Kill Children, U.N. Reports," *New York Times*, December 1, 1995, https://www.nytimes.com/1995/12/01/world/iraq-sanctions-kill-children-un-reports.html.

50 George H. W. Bush, "Address before a Joint Session of the Congress on the State of the Union," American Presidency Project, January 29, 1991, https://www.presidency.ucsb.edu/node/265956.

51 Bush, "Address before a Joint Session," January 29, 1991.

52 Vine, "U.S. Has an Empire."

53 Brands, *Making the Unipolar Moment*, 315.

54 United Nations Development Programme, *Human Development Report 1991*, iii.

55 Andrew Marshall, "What Happened to the Peace Dividend?," *Independent* (London), January 2, 1993, http://www.independent.co.uk/news/world/what-happened-to-the-peace-dividend-the-end-of-the-cold-war-cost-thousands-of-jobs-andrew-marshall-1476221.html.

56 George H. W. Bush, "Address to the Nation on Reducing United States and Soviet Nuclear Weapons," American Presidency Project, September 27, 1991, https://www.presidency.ucsb.edu/node/266636.

57 Marshall, "What Happened?"

58 Jim Mann, "Congress to Probe CIA-Haiti Ties: Intelligence: Members of Both Houses Say They Will Investigate. Reports Say Agency Financed Some Leaders Involved in Coup," *Los Angeles Times*, November 2, 1993, http://articles.latimes.com/1993-11-02/news/mn-52438_1_house-intelligence-committee.

59 On interwar occupation, see Renda, *Taking Haiti*.

60 Tim Weiner, reporting by Stephen Engelberg, Howard W. French, and Tim Weiner, "C.I.A. Formed Haitian Unit Later Tied to the Narcotics Trade," *New York Times*, November 14, 1993, https://www.nytimes.com/1993/11/14/world/cia-formed-haitian-unit-later-tied-to-narcotics-trade.html.

61 Weiner, "C.I.A. Formed Haitian Unit."

62 Bush, "Address before a Joint Session," January 29, 1991.

63 George H. W. Bush, "Address before a Joint Session of Congress on the State of the Union," American Presidency Project, January 28, 1992, https://www.presidency.ucsb.edu/node/266921.

64 Marshall, "What Happened?"

65 Nye, *Soft Power*. I have critiqued this concept in Von Eschen, "Duke Ellington Plays Baghdad."

66 Robin, *Reactionary Mind*, 170–71.

67 Dubois, *Haiti*, 363; Tim Weiner and Howard French, "C.I.A. Formed Haitian Unit Later Tied to Narcotics Trade," *New York Tines*, November 14, 1993, https://www.nytimes.com/1993/11/14/world/cia-formed-haitian-unit-later-tied-to-narcotics-trade.html.

68 National Security Decision Directive 54, September 2, 1982, https://irp.fas.org/offdocs/nsdd/nsdd-54.pdf; National Security Decision Directive 133, March 14, 1984, https://irp.fas.org/offdocs/nsdd/nsdd-133.htm.

69 Walden Bello, "Manufacturing a Food Crisis: How Free Trade Is Destroying Third World Agriculture and Who Is Fighting Back," *Nation*, May 15, 2008, https://www.thenation.com/article/manufacturing-food-crisis/.

70 Bello, "Manufacturing a Food Crisis."

71 Rania Khalek, "Food Emergency: How the World Bank and IMF Have Made African Famine Inevitable," AlterNet, September 8, 2011, http://www.alternet.org/story/152335/food_emergency%3A_how_the_world_bank_and_imf_have_made_african_famine_inevitable; World Bank, *World Development Report 2008*.

72 Bello, "Manufacturing a Food Crisis."

73 Robin, *Reactionary Mind*, 170–71.

74 George H. W. Bush, "Address to the Nation on the Situation in Somalia," American Presidency Project, December 4, 1992, https://www.presidency.ucsb.edu/node/267749.

75 On the period of Soviet support, see Schmidt, *Foreign Intervention in Africa*; and Westad, *Global Cold War*.

76 Charles Mitchell, United Press International, "U.S. Losing Interest in Military Bases in Somalia: Port Airstrip No Longer Are Key Part of Plans for Gulf of Aden Emergency," *Los Angeles Times*, March 17, 1985.

77 Mitchell, "U.S. Losing Interest."

78 Khalek, "Food Emergency."

79 Mark Fineman, "Column One: The Oil Factor in Somalia; Four American Petroleum Giants Had Agreements with the African Nation before Its Civil War Began. They Could Reap Big Rewards If Peace Is Restored," *Los Angeles Times*, January 18, 1993, https://www.latimes.com/archives/la-xpm-1993-01-18-mn-1337-story.html.

80 Fineman, "Oil Factor in Somalia."

81 Fineman, "Oil Factor in Somalia."

82 Khalek, "Food Emergency."

83 Jackson, *Jimmy Carter*.

84 Khalek, "Food Emergency"; Michel Chossudovsky, "Somalia: The Real Causes of Famine," Global Research, February 21, 2013, http://www.globalresearch.ca/somalia-the-real-causes-of-famine/25725.

85 Paul Lewis, "UN Will Increase Troops in Somalia," *New York Times*, March 27, 1993, https://www.nytimes.com/1993/03/27/world/un-will-increase-troops-in-somalia.html.

86 Lewis, "UN Will Increase Troops."

87 Madeleine K. Albright, "Yes, There Is a Reason to Be in Somalia," *New York Times*, August 10, 1993, https://www.nytimes.com/1993/08/10/opinion/yes-there-is-a-reason-to-be-in-somalia.html.

88 Reuters, "The Somalia Mission; Clinton's Words on Somalia: 'The Responsibilities of American Leadership,'" *New York Times*, October 8, 1993, http://www.nytimes.com/1993/10/08/world/somalia-mission-clinton-s-words-somalia-responsibilities-american-leadership.html?pagewanted=all.

89 Havel, "Call for Sacrifice," 6–7.

90 George H. W. Bush, diary entry, July 2, 1991, in *All the Best, George Bush*, 527.

91 Laura Rozen, "Robert Kaplan," Salon, April 17, 2001, https://www.salon.com/2001/04/17/kaplan_3/. See also Richard Cohen, "Bookish on the Balkans," *Washington Post*, May 25, 2000, https://www.washingtonpost.com/archive/opinions/2000/05/25/bookish-on-the-balkans; and Michael T. Kaufman, "The Dangers of Letting a President Read," *New York Times*, May 22, 1999, https://www.nytimes.com/1999/05/22/books/the-dangers-of-letting-a-president-read.

92 Woodward, *Balkan Tragedy*, 198.

93 Woodward, *Balkan Tragedy*, 198.

94 Woodward, *Balkan Tragedy*, 198.

95 Glenny, *Balkans*; Richard Cohen, "Bookish on the Balkans."

96 Woodward, *Balkan Tragedy*, 198.

97 On historical memory, see Ballinger, *History in Exile*, 106–12; and Bergholz, *Violence as a Generative Force*.

98 See Patterson, *Bought and Sold*; and Luthar and Pušnik, *Remembering Utopia*.

99 Michel Chossudovsky, "How the IMF Dismantled Yugoslavia," *Albion Monitor*, April 2, 1999, http://www.albionmonitor.com/9904a/yugodismantle.html.

100 Michel Chossudovsky, "Dismantling Yugoslavia, Colonizing Bosnia," in Jude Wanniski, "The Ignored Dimensions of Balkan Disintegration," Polyconomics, March 31, 1999, http://www.polyconomics.com/memos/mm-990331.htm.

101 See Richard Cohen, "Bookish on the Balkans."

102 Woodward, *Balkan Tragedy*.

103 Memorandum of telephone conversation between George H. W. Bush and President Turgut Ozal of Turkey, December 5, 1992, White House, George H. W. Bush Presidential Library and Museum, https://bush41library.tamu.edu/files/memcons-telcons/1992-12-05--Ozal.pdf.

104 Brands, *Making the Unipolar Moment*, 323.

105 Patrick E. Tyler, "U.S. Strategy Plans Calls for Insuring No Rivals Develop: A One-Superpower World; Pentagon's Document Outlines Ways to Thwart Challenges to Primacy of America," special to *New York Times*, March 8, 1992. For the full document, see Paul Wolfowiz, "Defense Planning Guidance FR 1994–1999," April 16, 1992, https://www.archives.gov/files/declassification/iscap/pdf.

106 Matt Reimann, "Despite Genocide and Rape in Bosnia, U.S. Intervention Was a Tough Sell for the Public," Timeline, April 12, 2017, https://timeline.com/bosnia-genocide-clinton-intervention-eff0412b3b5b.

107 Woodward, *Balkan Tragedy*, 397–98.

108 Reeves, *Running in Place*; Drew, *On the Edge*; Kaufman, "Dangers."

109 See "Bill Clinton's World," *Foreign Policy*, November 30, 2009, https://foreignpolicy.com/2009/11/30/bill-clintons-world/.

110 Robert D. Kaplan, *Balkan Ghosts*, xlix.

111 Robert D. Kaplan, *Balkan Ghosts*, 280. Kaplan's indictment of Papandreou's social democratic politics is echoed in the *Economist*'s June 29, 1996, Papandreou obituary (https://www.economist.com/news/1996/06/29/andreas-papandreou).

112 Robert D. Kaplan, *Balkan Ghosts*, 286–87.

113 Tom Bissell, "Euphorias of Perrier: The Case against Robert D. Kaplan," *VQR*, Summer 2006, https://www.vqronline.org/euphorias-perrier-case-against-robert-d-kaplan.

114 Colum Lynch, "Exclusive: Rwanda Revisited," *Foreign Policy*, April 5, 2015, http://foreignpolicy.com/2015/04/05/rwanda-revisited-genocide-united-states-state-department/; Epstein, "America's Secret Role."

115 Dana Hughes, "Clinton Regrets Rwanda Now (Not So Much in 1994)," ABC News, February 28, 2014, http://abcnews.go.com/blogs/politics/2014/02/bill-clinton-regrets-rwanda-now-not-so-much-in-1994/.

116 Lynch, "Exclusive: Rwanda Revisited."

117 Mamdani, *Saviors and Survivors*, 66.

118 Mamdani, *Saviors and Survivors*, 67.

119 Mamdani, *Saviors and Survivors*, 277.

120 Mamdani, *Saviors and Survivors*, 277. On the political economy of colonial Rwanda and the construction of ethnicity, see Kamola, "Coffee and Genocide."
121 Epstein, *Another Fine Mess*, 26–27.
122 Epstein, *Another Fines Mess*, 28–29; Epstein, "America's Secret Role."
123 Mamdani, *Saviors and Survivors*, 67–68.
124 Epstein, "America's Secret Role."
125 Epstein, *Another Fine Mess*, 29.
126 Mamdani, *Saviors and Survivors*, 67.
127 Epstein, *Another Fine Mess*, 29.
128 Epstein, "America's Secret Role."
129 Epstein, "America's Secret Role."
130 Tim Gallimore, "A Closer Look at Where Rwanda's Lethal Weapons Came From," HuffPost, April 4, 2014, https://www.huffpost.com/entry/a-closer-look-at-where-rw_b_5135559. On the trade and importation of weapons, see Melvern, *Conspiracy to Murder*.
131 Kamola, "Coffee and Genocide."
132 Storey, "Structural Adjustment," 377.
133 Power, *"A Problem from Hell"*.
134 Thabo Mbeki and Mahmood Mamdani, "Courts Can't End Civil Wars," *New York Times*, February 5, 2014, https://www.nytimes.com/2014/02/06/opinion/courts-cant-end-civil-wars.html. See also Eric Posner, "The Case against Human Rights," *Guardian*, December 4, 2014, https://www.theguardian.com/news/2014/dec/04/-sp-case-against-human-rights; Easterly, *White Man's Burden*.
135 Robert Kaplan, "The Coming Anarchy," *Atlantic*, February 1994.
136 Toby Lester, "Beyond 'The Coming Anarchy,'" sidebar, *Atlantic*, August 1996, accessed July 11, 2014, https://www.theatlantic.com/past/docs/issues/96aug/proport/kapsid.htm.
137 Lynch, "Exclusive: Rwanda Revisited."
138 Hughes, "Clinton Regrets Rwanda Now."
139 Johnson, "New World Hawdah," in *Mi Revalueshanary Fren*, 99. The brackets identifying countries are mine. For an extended discussion, see Von Eschen, "Di Eagle and di Bear."
140 Johnson, "New World Hawdah," 99–100.
141 Von Eschen "Di Eagle and di Bear," 204.
142 On US intervention in Somalia, see Michael Wines, "Mission to Somalia: Bush Declares Goal in Somalia 'to Save Thousands,'" *New York Times*, December 5, 1992. The Clinton quote is from Ann Devroy and R. Jeffrey Smith, "Clinton Reexamines a Foreign Policy under Siege," *Washington Post*, October 17, 1993, https://www.washingtonpost.com/archive/politics/1993/10/17/clinton-reexamines-a-foreign-policy-under-siege/794fbbd6-349c-44d4-94b2-65868bd53587/.
143 Devroy and Smith, "Clinton Reexamines a Foreign Policy."
144 The extended version was reported by Charles Krauthammer in "The Greatest Cold War Myth of All," *Time*, November 29, 1993, http://content.time.com/time/magazine/article/0,9171,979706,00.html.
145 Krauthammer, "Greatest Cold War Myth."

3. Losing the Good Life

1 Irving Kristol, "My Cold War," *National Interest*, Spring 1993, 144.
2 Hartman, *War for the Soul*, 276.
3 Kristol, "My Cold War," 144.
4 Peter Pringle, "The Cleaning of America," *Independent* (London), January 15, 1990.
5 Charles Bremner, "America Wakes Up to a New World," *Times* (London), November 4, 1992.
6 Buck-Morss, *Dreamworld and Catastrophe*.
7 Lizabeth Cohen, *Consumer Republic*; Baldwin, *Racial Imaginary*. See Patterson, *Bought and Sold*; and Luthar and Pušnik, *Remembering Utopia*.
8 Nixon, *Slow Violence*, 39–40.
9 "Republican Party Platform of 1992," American Presidency Project, August 17, 1992, https://www.presidency.ucsb.edu/documents/republican-party-platform-1992.
10 Cooper, *Family Values*; Self, *All in the Family*.
11 On the relationship between the growth of the New Right and the need to create new enemies after Soviet communist enemies had become less relevant, see Blee and Creasap, "Conservative and Right-Wing Movements," 274.
12 On the intersections between ideas of free enterprise and the rise of the right, see Maclean, *Democracy in Chains*; Glickman, *Free Enterprise*; and Kurt Anderson, *Evil Geniuses*.
13 Andrew Marshall, "What Happened to the Peace Dividend?," *Independent* (London), January 2, 1993, http://www.independent.co.uk/news/world/what-happened-to-the-peace-dividend-the-end-of-the-cold-war-cost-thousands-of-jobs-andrew-marshall-1476221.html.
14 David Beers, "Brother, Can You Spare $1.5 Trillion: A Lockheed Child's Search for Happiness in a Post-Commie World," *Mother Jones*, July–August 1990, 68.
15 George H. W. Bush, "Address to the Nation on Reducing United States and Soviet Nuclear Weapons," American Presidency Project, September 27, 1991, https://www.presidency.ucsb.edu/node/266636.
16 Sandy Grady, "The Vanishing Peace Dividend," *Daily Press* (Newport News, VA), October 2, 1991, http://articles.dailypress.com/1991-10-02/news/9110010185_1_peace-dividend-missiles-nukes.
17 Grady, "Vanishing Peace Dividend."
18 NATO's plans to cut its 1.2-million-member main army nearly in half alarmed critics, but in the end the plan was scuttled by national opposition and a lack of political will. By 1997, according to Ann Markusen, real-dollar military spending (discounting the private sector) ran at 85 percent of its cold war level. Ann Markusen, "How We Lost the Peace Dividend," *American Prospect*, July–August 1997, 86–95, available at http://prospect.org/article/how-we-lost-peace-dividend.
19 Beers, "Brother, Can You Spare," 68.
20 Cooper, *Family Values*, 315.
21 Graham Peebles, "Worldwide Inequality," openDemocracy, January 29, 2014, https://www.opendemocracy.net/graham-peebles/worldwide-inequality.

Peebles's figures are from the Organization for Economic Cooperation and Development.

22 Chad Stone et al., "A Guide to Statistics on Historical Trends in Income Inequality," Center on Budget and Policy Priorities, last updated January 13, 2020, http://www.cbpp.org/research/poverty-and-inequality/a-guide-to-statistics-on-historical-trends-in-income-inequality.

23 Ryan Vlastelica, "After Ten Fat Years for Stock Investors, a Lean Decade Is Looming," Marketwatch, April 16, 2018, https://www.marketwatch.com/story/the-2010s-were-one-of-the-best-decades-for-stocks-ever-uh-oh-2018-04-11; Jacob M. Schlesinger, "How Alan Greenspan Finally Came to Terms with the Market," *Wall Street Journal*, May 8, 2000, https://www.wsj.com/articles/SB957740787830302I9.

24 Pringle, "Cleaning of America."

25 Pringle, "Cleaning of America."

26 Nathaniel Rich, "Losing Earth: The Decade We Almost Stopped Climate Change," *New York Times*, August 1, 2018, https://www.nytimes.com/interactive/2018/08/01/magazine/climate-change-losing-earth.htm.

27 Rich, "Losing Earth."

28 Cortese, "Regulatory Focus."

29 The quote is from "Editorial: A Chilling Story about Climate Change," *Concord Monitor*, August 26, 2018, https://www.concordmonitor.com/Sununu-and-climate-change-19676534. Rich, "Losing Earth."

30 "Republican Party Platform."

31 See Julie Johnson, "Washington Talk: The Presidency; Tough Words to Translate: 'Kinder and Gentler,'" *New York Times*, January 25, 1989, https://www.nytimes.com/1989/01/25/us/washington-talk-the-presidency-tough-words-to-translate-kinder-and-gentler.html.

32 Steven A. Holmes, "The 1992 Campaign: Republicans; Buchanan's Run Exposes Fissures in the Right," *New York Times*, February 4, 1992, https://www.nytimes.com/1992/02/04/us/the-1992-campaign-republicans-buchanan-s-run-exposes-fissures-in-the-right.html.

33 George F. Kennan, "The GOP Won the Cold War? Ridiculous," *New York Times*, October 28, 1992, http://www.nytimes.com/1992/10/28/opinion/the-gop-won-the-cold-war-ridiculous.html.

34 "Remarks Announcing the Bush-Quayle Candidacies for Reelection," George H. W. Bush Presidential Library and Museum, February 12, 1992, https://bush41library.tamu.edu/archives/public-papers/3935.

35 "Republican Party Platform."

36 Michael Wines, "Bush Links Rivals Plan to Socialism," *New York Times*, February 8, 1991 (ProQuest Historical Newspaper).

37 Douglas Jehl, "Bush Takes Aim at Clinton over Draft, the Economy," *Los Angeles Times*, September 18, 1992 (ProQuest Historical Newspaper).

38 George H. W. Bush, "Remarks at a Bush-Quayle Fundraising Luncheon in Tampa, Florida," George H. W. Bush Presidential Library and Museum, March 4, 1992, https://bush41library.tamu.edu/archives/public-papers/4025.

39 George H. W. Bush, "Remarks to the San Diego Rotary Club in San Diego, California," American Presidency Project, February 7, 1992, https://www.presidency.ucsb.edu/node/266288.

40 George H. W. Bush, "Remarks to the Community in Enid, Oklahoma," American Presidency Project, September 17, 1992, https://www.presidency.ucsb.edu/node/267707.

41 "Republican Party Platform."

42 *Angela Davis Reader*, 66. For the broader history of the culture wars and attacks on the urban poor, see Kelley, *Yo' Mama's Disfunktional*. On the origins of the expansion of the carceral state, see Kohler-Hausmann, *Getting Tough*; and Hinton, *From the War on Poverty*.

43 Dudziak, *Cold War Civil Rights*; Borstelmann, *Cold War*; Biondi, *To Stand and Fight*; Von Eschen, *Satchmo Blows Up the World*; Von Eschen, *Race against Empire*.

44 Omi and Winant, *Racial Formation*, 98–99.

45 "Bush Reaction to Los Angeles Riots," C-SPAN, May 8, 1992, https://www.c-span.org/video/?25979-1/bush-reaction-los-angeles-riots.

46 Omi and Winant, *Racial Formation*, 98–99.

47 Dan Quayle, "Family Values: Address to the Commonwealth Club of California," May 19, 1992, http://www.vicepresidentdanquayle.com/speeches_StandingFirm_CCC_1.html.

48 Douglas Jehl, "Quayle Deplores Eroding Values; Cites TV Show," *Los Angeles Times*, May 20, 1992, http://articles.latimes.com/1992-05-20/news/mn-241_1_dan-quayle. See also Andrew Rosenthal, "Quayle's Moment," *New York Times*, July 5, 1992, https://www.nytimes.com/1992/07/05/magazine/quayle-s-moment.html; Quayle, "Family Values."

49 Rosenthal, "Quayle's Moment."

50 "Republican Party Platform."

51 Conor O'Clery, "Reagan Lifts Party out of Sleaze: Cold War Memorabilia in Nostalgic Sale at a Political Flea Market," *Irish Times*, August 19, 1992.

52 Sharlet, *Family*, 323.

53 Patrick J. Buchanan, "1992 Republican National Convention Speech," Patrick J. Buchanan—Official Website, August 17, 1992, http://buchanan.org/blog/1992-republican-national-convention-speech-148.

54 O'Clery, "Reagan Lifts Party."

55 John F. Harris, "One for the Gipper: Loyalists Toast Reagan amid Nostalgia for '80s," *Washington Post*, August 18, 1992.

56 Harris, "One for the Gipper."

57 O'Clery, "Reagan Lifts Party."

58 Jim Edwards, "'Is Your Washroom Breeding Bolsheviks?': A Look Back at Oddly Charming Cold War Ads, CBS News, November 11, 2009, https://www.cbsnews.com/news/is-your-washroom-breeding-bolsheviks-a-look-back-at-oddly-charming-cold-war-ads/.

59 Jarret B. Wollstein, "Clinton's Health-Care Plan for You: Cradle-to-Grave Slavery, Part 2," Future of Freedom Foundation, February 1, 1994, https://www.fff.org/explore-freedom/article/clintons-healthcare-plan-cradletograve-slavery-part-2/.

60 Skocpol, *Boomerang.* See also Gordon, *Dead on Arrival.*

61 Andrew Rosenthal, "The 1992 Campaign: Issues—Health Care; GOP Tries to Seize a Democratic Issue," *New York Times*, August 5, 1992.

62 William Kristol, "How to Oppose the Health Plan—and Why," Ashbrook Center for Public Affairs at Ashland University, January 1, 1994, https://ashbrook.org/viewpoint/onprin-v2n1-kristol/.

63 The quote is from Limbaugh's December 16, 1993, broadcast, and the charges were followed up on December 27, 1993: "Report: Limbaugh Conservatives Continue 75-Year-Old 'Socialized Medicine' Smear," Media Matters for America, March 5, 2009, https://www.mediamatters.org/rush-limbaugh/report-limbaugh-conservatives-continue-75-year-old-socialized-medicine-smear. For a conservative account of the rise of Limbaugh, see Brian C. Anderson, *South Park Conservatives.*

64 Limbaugh television broadcast, April 4, 1994, in "Report: Limbaugh Conservatives."

65 Quoted in George F. Will, "Inoculated for Exuberance?," *Washington Post*, November 10, 2006.

66 Wollstein, "Clinton's Health-Care Plan."

67 Skocpol, *Boomerang.*

68 The Clinton administration's economic structuring, while greatly reducing the national deficit produced by sky-rocketing military spending under Reagan, reinforced and extended the radical privatization of the Reagan years. The robust market growth for the upper echelons reinforced elite confidence in deregulated market economies.

69 May, *Homeward Bound*; Melani McAlister, "Benevolent Supremacy," in *Epic Encounters.*

70 McAlister, "Benevolent Supremacy."

71 Zaretsky, *No Direction Home.*

72 Christopher Goodwin, "We Have Seen the Face of Evil: It's Still Red," *Australian*, September 9, 1997.

73 Quoted in Richard Corliss, "The Invasion Has Begun: Independence Day Arrives to Lead the Assault of Science Fiction Movies, TV Shows, and Books on the Cultural Mainstream," *Time*, July 8, 1996.

74 On the series, see Mooney, *Opening the X-Files.*

75 Quoted in Mooney, *Opening the X-Files*, 32.

76 Joyce Millman, "'The X-Files' Finds the Truth: Its Time Is Past," *New York Times*, May 19, 2002, https://www.nytimes.com/2002/05/19/arts/television-radio-the-x-files-finds-the-truth-its-time-is-past.html.

77 George W. Bush, Iowa Western Community College, January 21, 2000, "Bushisms," http://home.uchicago.edu/~you/bushisms.html.

78 Millman, "'The X-Files' Finds the Truth."

79 *The X-Files*, season 1, episode 24, "The Erlenmeyer Flask," aired May 13, 1994, on Fox.

80 *The X-Files*, season 3, episode 20, "Jose Chung's from Outer Space," aired April 12, 1996, on Fox.

81 Jonathan Kirby, "Not Just a Fluke: How Darin Morgan Saved the X-Files," PopMatters, October 28, 2007, https://www.popmatters.com/not-just-a-fluke-how-darin-morgan-saved-the-x-files-2496208290.html.

82 Michael Decourcy Hines, "Death in Waco: The Lost Cause; Texas Cult Membership: Many Lives, Shared Fate," *New York Times*, April 20, 1993, https://www.nytimes.com/1993/04/20/us/death-in-waco-the-lost-cause-texas-cult-membership-many-lives-shared-fate.html.

83 For a summation of conspiracy theories, see Jonathan Tilove, "A Quarter Century Later 'Dark Theories Still Hover over Waco," *Austin American Statesman*, April 16, 2018, updated September 25, 2018, https://www.mystatesman.com/news/state--regional-govt--politics/quarter-century-later-dark-theories-still-hover-over-waco-siege/wp35W2dtAWY2tDqVeImvdP/.

84 Tilove, "Quarter Century Later."

85 Adam Lusher, "Waco: How a 51-Day Standoff between a Christian Cult and the FBI Left More Than 80 People Dead and Divided America," *Independent* (London), January 26, 2018, https://www.independent.co.uk/news/world/americas/waco-tv-series-siege-truth-what-really-happened-david-koresh-branch-davidians-cult-fbi-paramount-a8179936.html.

86 Mooney, *Opening the X-Files*, 79–80.

87 Paul Krugman, "Who Broke Politics?," *New York Times*, November 4, 2016, http://www.nytimes.com/2016/11/04/opinion/who-broke-politics.

88 Cooper, *Family Values*, 105, quoting Laura Morgan.

89 Cooper, *Family Values*, 103.

90 Stacey Mickelbart, "Still Nickeled and Dimed a Decade Later," *New Yorker*, August 18, 2011, https://www.newyorker.com/books/page-turner/still-nickel-and-dimed-a-decade-later.

91 Cooper, *Family Values*, 105.

92 Cooper, *Family Values*, 105.

93 Cooper, *Family Values*, 266.

94 "Charitable Choice: The Facts," White House of George W. Bush, accessed September 13, 2021, https://georgewbush-whitehouse.archives.gov/government/fbci/guidance/charitable.html.

95 Cooper, *Family Values*, 271.

96 Osgood and White, *Winning while Losing*.

97 Rosalind S. Helderman and Tom Hamburger, "Guns and Religion: How American Conservatives Grew Closer to Putin's Russia." *Washington Post*, April 30, 2017, https://www.washingtonpost.com/politics/how-the-republican-right-found-allies-in-russia/2017/04/30.

98 See Miller, *Struggle to Save*.

99 Shekhovtsov, *Russia*, xix; Satter, *Darkness at Dawn*, 38; Cheloukhine and Haberfield, *Russian Organized Corruption Networks*, 53.

100 Jeff Sachs, "What I Did in Russia," Jeff Sachs's personal website, March 12, 2012, https://www.jeffsachs.org/newspaper-articles/b4gxflntzkl76ajz2w6yey8ss7sn9m?rq=russia/.

101 Peter Passell, "Dr. Jeffrey Sachs, Shock Therapist," *New York Times*, June 27, 1993.

102 Will Hutton, "Time to Blow Whistle on Karl and Adam," *Guardian*, October 14, 1991.

103 Margaret Shapiro, "'I Can Hardly Believe in Anything': Russian Tumult Stirs Foreboding, Nostalgia," *Washington Post*, July 2, 1992.

104 Shapiro, "'I Can Hardly Believe.'"

105 Shapiro, "'I Can Hardly Believe.'"

106 Shapiro, "'I Can Hardly Believe.'"

107 Oushakine, *Patriotism of Despair*, 220. See also, Alexievich, *Secondhand Time*.

108 Barbara Ehrenreich's *Nickel and Dimed* first appeared in 2001.

109 Daniel Sneider, "Russia's Future Shadowed by Centuries of Conquest," *Christian Science Monitor*, August 10, 1994, https://www.csmonitor.com/1994/0810/10071.html.

110 Ronald Reagan, "Address at Commencement Exercises at the University of Notre Dame," Ronald Reagan Presidential Library and Museum, May 17, 1981, https://www.reaganlibrary.gov/archives/speech/address-commencement-exercises-university-notre-dame.

111 Brown, "Gridded Lives"; Brown, *Plutopia*.

112 Peter Cook, "Can the West Afford to Clean Up the Mess Left by Mr. Marx?," *Globe and Mail* (Toronto), September 18, 1989.

113 Cook, "Can the West Afford?"

114 Rupert Cornwall, "Soviets Learn the Hard Lesson of 'Self-Deceit,'" *Independent* (London), March 8, 1989. The quotes are from "Communism, Exposed," *New York Times*, December 6, 1989. See also Lauren Weiner, "Mexican Schoolbooks Still Glorify Socialism," *Washington Times*, February 7, 1990; and Raymond Whitaker, "The Last Stalinists: Banished to the Four Corners of the Earth," *Independent* (London), September 9, 1991.

115 Andrea Stone, "Coup Sends Chill across the USA," *USA Today*, August 20, 1991.

116 For a range of views, see Charles Bremner, "Warning of Unrest as Hunger Grows in St. Petersburg," *Times* (London), October 4, 1991; and Kitty McKinsey, "Hungarians Yearn for Communist Past," *Ottawa Citizen*, November 3, 1993.

117 Paul Quinn-Judge, "20,000 in Moscow Decry Regime; Protestors Target Yeltsin and Jews," *Boston Globe*, January 13, 1992.

118 Quinn-Judge, "20,000 in Moscow." See also Daniel Sneider, "Soviet Communists Still out in the Cold," *Christian Science Monitor*, March 19, 1992.

119 Jim Hoagland, "Another Breakup in the Old U.S.S.R.," editorial, *Washington Post*, March 3, 1992, https://www.washingtonpost.com/archive/opinions/1992/03/03/another-breakup-in-the-old-ussr/0588d0c9-8bb2-483c-af26-fb5d1a620249/.

120 Paul A. Goble, "For Russia, Another Cruel August?," *Christian Science Monitor*, August 5, 1992.

121 Goble, "Another Cruel August?"

122 Daniel Sneider, "Russia's Future Shadowed by Centuries of Conquest," *Christian Science Monitor*, August 10, 1994.

123 Yurchak, *Everything Was Forever*, 8. See also Scribner, *Requiem for Communism*; Luthar and Pušnik, *Remembering Utopia*; Pence and Betts, *Socialist Modern*; and Todorova, *Remembering Communism*.

124 Jonathan Steele, "The Bitter End of Empire: The Surge of Support for Russia's Right Is a Rebellion against Both Gorbachev and Yeltsin," *Guardian*, December 14, 1993.
125 Faith Brooke, "From the Ashes of the Past, a Cathedral; Stalin Knocked It Down; Now It Is to Be Rebuilt," *Independent* (London), August 24, 1994.
126 This is explored at length in chapters 4 and 7.
127 Grant Stern and Patrick Simpson, "The GOP's Favorite Russian Professor Spent Decades Building Conservative Ties to Moscow," Stern Facts, May 25, 2017, https://thesternfacts.com/how-one-man-influenced-the-republican-partys-transformation-into-the-grand-old-putin-party-141589792320.
128 For a retrospective account, see Mikhail Sokolov and Anastasia Kirilenko, "20 Years Ago, Russia Had Its Biggest Political Crisis since the Bolshevik Revolution," *Atlantic*, October 4, 2013, https://www.theatlantic.com/international/archive/2013/10/20-years-ago-russia-had-its-biggest-political-crisis-since-the-bolshevik-revolution/280237/.
129 Goble, "Another Cruel August?"
130 Steele, "Bitter End of Empire."
131 Steele, "Bitter End of Empire."
132 James Goldgeier, "Promises Made, Promises Broken: What Yeltsin Was Told about NATO in 1993 and Why It Matters," War on the Rocks, July 12, 2016, https://warontherocks.com/2016/07/promises-made-promises-broken-what-yeltsin-was-told-about-nato-in-1993-and-why-it-matters/.
133 Goldgeier, "Promises Made, Promises Broken."
134 Goldgeier, "Promises Made, Promises Broken."
135 Mike Eckel, "'Putin's a Solid Man': Declassified Memos Offer Window into Yeltsin-Clinton Relationship," Radio Free Europe / Radio Liberty, August 30, 2018, https://www.rferl.org/a/putin-s-a-solid-man-declassified-memos-offer-window-into-yeltsin-clinton-relationship/29462317.html.
136 On the origins of resource globalism, see Black, *Global Interior*.

4. "God I Miss the Cold War"

1 Simon Rose, "Clooney's Peace of the Action: The Peacemaker (15,124 mins): Review of the Peacemaker," *Daily Mirror* (London), October 23, 1997.
2 Walter Goodman, "Television Review: Russia's Loose Uranium," *New York Times*, November 19, 1996.
3 Goodman, "Russia's Loose Nukes."
4 DeLillo, *Underworld*, 76.
5 A. M. Rosenthal, "On My Mind: Facing the Risks," *New York Times*, March 16, 1993.
6 "The New Nuclear Clock," editorial, *Christian Science Monitor*, June 1, 1995. See also Jonathan S. Landay, "Tide of Terrorism Spurs Crackdown," *Christian Science Monitor*, April 13, 1995.
7 "Bottling Up Nukes," editorial, *Christian Science Monitor*, February 2, 1995. The editorial called for making permanent the 1970 Nuclear Non-proliferation Treaty, set to expire that year.

8 Matt Bivens and Leonid Bershidsky, "Petersburg Arrests 3 for Trying to Sell Uranium," *Moscow Times*, June 9, 1994.

9 Bivens and Bershidsky, "Petersburg Arrests 3."

10 Rupert Cornwell, "FBI Sets Up Moscow Base to Fight Nuclear Gangsters," *Independent* (London), May 25, 1994. See also Sam Vincent Meddis, "FBI to Open a Moscow Office," *USA Today*, May 26, 1994.

11 "The Nuclear Black Market," *New York Times*, August 22, 1994; Jane Perlez, "Tracing a Nuclear Risk, Stolen Enriched Uranium," *New York Times*, February 15, 1995; Reuters, "A Growth in Smuggling from Ex-Soviet Union," *Philadelphia Inquirer*, February 19, 1995.

12 Brown, *Plutopia*.

13 Masco, *Nuclear Borderlands*, 24–25. On the shared cultures and assumptions of Soviets and Americans, see also Brown, *Plutopia*.

14 Masco, *Nuclear Borderlands*, 24.

15 DeLillo, *Underworld*, 278.

16 DeLillo, *Underworld*, 76.

17 DeLillo, *Underworld*, 77. See Ladino, "'Local Yearnings.'"

18 DeLillo, *Underworld*, 106.

19 DeLillo, *Underworld*, 793.

20 DeLillo, *Underworld*, 121.

21 DeLillo, *Underworld*, 278.

22 Nixon, *Slow Violence*, 2.

23 "Furor on Memo at World Bank," *New York Times*, February 7, 1992, https://www.nytimes.com/1992/02/07/business/furor-on-memo-at-world-bank.html.

24 DeLillo, *Underworld*, 278.

25 Adebajo, *Liberia's Civil War*; Kieh, *First Liberian Civil War*.

26 Nixon, *Slow Violence*, 112.

27 Quoted in Nixon, *Slow Violence*, 110–11.

28 Nixon, *Slow Violence*, 110.

29 Nixon, *Slow Violence*, 113.

30 Klare, *Rogue States and Nuclear Outlaws*.

31 Anthony Lake, "Confronting Backlash States," *Foreign Affairs*, March/April 1994, https://www.foreignaffairs.com/articles/iran/1994-03-01/confronting-backlash-states.

32 "Insecure Nuclear Materials," editorial, *New York Times*, January 7, 1997.

33 Litwak, *Rogue States and Foreign Policy*.

34 Michael T. Klare, "US Strategy to Defend against 'Rogues' Needs an Overhaul," *Christian Science Monitor*, April 25, 1995; Klare, *Rogue States and Nuclear Outlaws*.

35 Klare, "US Strategy to Defend."

36 Richard C. Hottelet, "The Korean Mouse That Roared," *Christian Science Monitor*, April 20, 1995.

37 For an example of nostalgia for the era of containment, see "The Russia-Iran Connection," *Jerusalem Post*, May 21, 1992.

38 Mamdani, *Good Muslim, Bad Muslim*; Coll, *Ghost Wars*.

39 In the years after the 9/11 attacks, US-Chinese cooperation on fighting terrorism and economic interdependence made China a necessary if not entirely worthy capitalist competitor.

40 Quoted in Suettinger, *Beyond Tiananmen*, 95.

41 Suettinger, *Beyond Tiananmen*, 87, 96–99.

42 J. Stapleton Roy and Charles Kraus, "The Communist Domino That Would Not Fall: Chinese Resilience at the Cold War," *Wilson Quarterly*, Fall 2016, http://wilsonquarterly.com/quarterly/the-lasting-legacy-of-the-cold-war/the-communist-domino-that-would-not-fall-chinas-resilience-at-the-end-of-the-cold-war/.

43 Suetttinger, *Beyond Tiananmen*, 87.

44 "Koreans Sign Pact Renouncing Force in a Step to Unity," *New York Times*, December 13, 1991.

45 "Cheney Says North Korean Nuclear Development No. 1 Threat to Asia," *Japan Inc.*, November 30, 1991.

46 Leslie Gelb, "The Next Renegade State," op-ed, *New York Times*, April 10, 1991.

47 Cumings, *North Korea*, 149–50, 151.

48 See Monica Kim, "Empire's Babel"; and Monica Kim, *Interrogation Rooms*.

49 Dong-Choon Kim, *Unending Korean War*; Cumings, *Korean War*; Heonik Kwon, *Other Cold War*; Suzy Kim, *Everyday Life*.

50 Cumings, *Korean War*, 160.

51 David E. Rosenbaum, "U.S. to Pull A-Bombs from South Korea," *New York Times*, October 20, 1991.

52 "Cheney Says."

53 "Kim Il Sung and the Atomic Bomb," *Sydney Morning Herald*, November 3, 1991.

54 "North Korea's Nuclear Ambitions," *Washington Post*, November 25, 1991.

55 R. Jeffrey Smith, "N. Korean Strongman: 'Crazy' or Canny?," *Washington Post*, September 26, 1993.

56 "Pass Notes No 280: Kim Il Sung," *Guardian*, November 9, 1993; "Dear Leader—a Truly Wonderful Human Being," *Irish Times*, July 11, 1994.

57 Smith, "N. Korean Strongman."

58 Heonik Kwon, *Other Cold War*, 2.

59 R. Jeffrey Smith, "N. Korean Strongman."

60 Bill Gertz, "U.S. Diplomacy Not the Answer in North Korea, Two Experts Say; Kim Called 'Evil,' Son Half-Crazy," *Washington Times*, December 10, 1993.

61 Cumings, *Korean War*, 231.

62 Swansbrough, *Test by Fire*, 169. On cold war conceptions of "the Oriental," see Monica Kim, *Interrogation Rooms*; and Jodi Kim, *Ends of Empire*.

63 David E. Sanger, "Carter's Trip to North Korea: Whose Trip Was It Really?," *New York Times*, June 18, 1994, http://www.nytimes.com/1994/06/18/world/carter-visit-to-north-korea-whose-trip-was-it-really.html.

64 "Dictator Makes It Difficult to Predict Korea Moves," *Scotsman*, June 16, 1994.

65 Loretta Tofani, "Kim and Son, Quirky Rulers of N. Korea: The Father Is a Tough Guerrilla Fighter. The Son Is a Playboy," *Philadelphia Inquirer*, June 17, 1994.

66 Tofani, "Kim and Son"; "Dear Leader."

67 Richard Perle, interview, in "Examining the Lessons of the 1994 U.S.-North Korea Deal," *Frontline*, accessed September 14, 2021, http://www.pbs.org/wgbh/pages/frontline/shows/kim/themes/lessons.html.
68 Robert Gallucci, interview, in "Examining the Lessons."
69 William Perry, interview, in "Examining the Lessons."
70 Donald Gregg, interview, in "Examining the Lessons."
71 Bruce Cumings, "This Is What's Really behind North Korea's Nuclear Provocations," *Nation*, March 23, 2017, https://www.thenation.com/article/this-is-whats-really-behind-north-koreas-nuclear-provocations/.
72 Joshua Norman, "The 1993 World Trade Center Bombers: Where Are They Now?," CBS News, February 26, 2013, http://www.cbsnews.com/news/the-1993-world-trade-center-bombers-where-are-they-now/.
73 Robert I. Friedman, "The CIA's Jihad," *New York Magazine*, March 27, 1995, 41.
74 Robert I. Friedman, "CIA's Jihad," 41.
75 Cullather, "Damning Afghanistan."
76 Ben Norton, "We Created Islamic Extremism: Those Blaming Islam for ISIS Would Have Supported Osama bin Laden in the '80s," Salon, November 17, 2015, https://www.salon.com/2015/11/17/we_created_islamic_extremism_those_blaming_islam_for_isis_would_have_supported_osama_bin_laden_in_the_80s/.
77 Melanie Colburn, "America's Devil's Game with Extremist Islam," *Mother Jones*, January–February 2006, https://www.motherjones.com/politics/2006/01/americas-devils-game-extremist-islam/; Dreyfuss, *Devil's Game*.
78 See Westad, *Global Cold War*, 288–330.
79 Jeffrey St. Clair and Alexander Cockburn, "How Jimmy Carter and I Started the Mujahideen," *CounterPunch*, January 15, 1998, http://www.counterpunch.org/1998/01/15/how-jimmy-carter-and-i-started-the-mujahideen/.
80 Norton, "We Created Islamic Extremism."
81 Rashid, *Taliban*, 162, 170–82.
82 "Full Text of Dick Cheney's Speech at the Institute of Petroleum Autumn Lunch, 1999," Resilience, June 8, 2004, https://www.resilience.org/stories/2004-06-08/full-text-dick-cheneys-speech-institute-petroleum-autumn-lunch-1999/.
83 Rashid, *Taliban*, 162–69; George Monbiot, "America's Pipe Dream: A Pro-Western Regime in Kabul Should Give the U.S. an Afghan Route for Caspian Oil," *Guardian*, October 23, 2001.
84 Marjorie Cohn, "Cheney's Black Gold: Oil Interests May Drive U.S. Foreign Policy," *Chicago Tribune*, August 10, 2000, http://articles.chicagotribune.com/2000-08-10/news/0008100507_1_caspian-oil-caspian-sea-gas-journal.
85 "Cheney Pays Visit to Russia's Neighbors: In Azerbaijan, He Says America Has 'Abiding Interest in Region's Stability,'" NBC News, September 3, 2008, https://www.nbcnews.com/id/26522284/ns/world_news-europe/t/cheney-pays-visit-russias-neighbors/#.V4gAUnAfmeA.
86 "Cold War Nostalgia," editorial, *New York Times*, February 3, 1995.
87 See also "Timeline: Nato," BBC, last updated February 21, 2012, http://news.bbc.co.uk/2/hi/europe/country_profiles/1543000.stm.

88 Heather Digby Parton, "Why White House Counsel Don McGahn Has Donald Trump Extremely Worried," Salon, August 20, 2018, https://www.salon.com/2018/08/20/why-white-house-counsel-don-mcgahn-has-donald-trump-extremely-worried/.

89 R. Jeffrey Smith, "The DeLay-Abramoff Money Trail," *Washington Post*, December 31, 2005.

90 R. Jeffrey Smith, "DeLay-Abramoff Money Trail."

91 R. Jeffrey Smith, "DeLay-Abramoff Money Trail."

92 Christopher Buckley, "Megabashing Japan," *New York Times*, October 2, 1994, https://www.nytimes.com/1994/10/02/books/crime-mystery-megabashing-japan.html; review of *Debt of Honor*, by Tom Clancy, *Publishers Weekly*, accessed March 4, 2018, https://www.publishersweekly.com/978-0-399-13954-3.

93 Clancy, *Executive Orders*, dedication page.

94 Oliver Stone, "Who's That in the Oval Office?," *New York Times*, September 22, 1996.

95 Luthar and Pušnik, *Remembering Utopia*.

96 Christopher Goodwin, "We Have Seen the Face of Evil: It's Still Red," *Sunday Times* (UK), September 7, 1997, reprinted in *Australian*, September 9, 1997.

97 Mary Dejevsky, "American Anxiety Takes Wing with Air Force One: The Latest Hollywood Blockbuster Touches a Raw Nerve with Its Portrayal of a Terrorist Assault on the President's Plane," *Independent* (London), July 28, 1997, http://www.independent.co.uk/news/world/american-anxiety-takes-wing-with-air-force-one-1252987.html.

98 Dejevsky, "American Anxiety Takes Wing."

99 Jim Anderson, "U.S. Poll on Russian Elections: Communists First, Yeltsin Nowhere," Deutsche Presse-Agentur, February 21, 1996.

100 Michael Specter, "The Russian Vote: The Overview: Russians Choosing Today: Either Reforms or the Past," *New York Times*, June 16, 1996.

101 Michael R. Gordon, "Russia and I.M.F. Agree on Loan for $10.2 Billion," *New York Times*, February 23, 1996, https://www.nytimes.com/1996/02/23/world/russia-and-imf-agree-on-a-loan-for-10.2-billion.html.

102 Michael Dobbs, "IMF Approves $10.2 Billion Loan for Russia," *Washington Post*, March 27, 1996, https://www.washingtonpost.com/archive/business/1996/03/27/imf-approves-102-billion-loan-for-russia/6820c3ac-496a-482f-a01e-500c2e6a7d40/. See also Richard W. Stevenson, "Did Yeltsin Get a Sweetheart Deal on I.M.F. Loan?," *New York Times*, March 11, 1996, https://www.nytimes.com/1996/03/11/world/did-yeltsin-get-a-sweetheart-deal-on-imf-loans.html.

103 Alessandra Stanley, "The Americans Who Saved Yeltsin (or Did They?)," *New York Times*, July 9, 1996, https://www.nytimes.com/1996/07/09/world/moscow-journal-the-americans-who-saved-yeltsin-or-did-they.html.

104 Simon Shuster, "Rewriting Russian History: Did Boris Yeltsin Steal the 1996 Presidential Election?," *Time*, February 24, 2012.

105 Jason Devaney, "Dick Morris: Bill Clinton Advised Russian President Boris Yeltsin in 1996," Newsmax, September 8, 2016, https://www.newsmax.com/Newsmax-Tv/bill-clinton-advise-boris-yeltsin-dick-morris/2016/09/08/id/747327/; Mike

Eckel, "'Putin's a Solid Man': Declassifies Memos Offer Window into Yeltsin-Clinton Relationship," Radio Free Europe / Radio Liberty, August 30, 2018, https://www.rferl.org/a/putin-s-a-solid-man-declassified-memos-offer-window-into-yeltsin-clinton-relationship/29462317.html.

106 Mark Franchetti, "Soviet Feelgood Films Knock Hollywood off the Screen," *Sunday Times* (UK), July 13, 1997; Shaw and Youngblood, *Cinematic Cold War*.

107 Franchetti, "Soviet Feelgood Films."

108 Quoted in Franchetti, "Soviet Feelgood Films."

109 Franchetti, "Soviet Feelgood Films."

110 Larisa Naumenko, "Keeping Alive Toys of Soviet Youth," *Moscow Times*, March 5, 1997.

111 Franchetti, "Soviet Feelgood Films."

112 Kristen R. Ghodsee, "Why Women Had Better Sex under Socialism," *New York Times*, August 13, 2017.

113 Friend, *The Naughty Nineties*, 443.

114 Hochschild, *Second Shift*.

115 Natasha Fairweather, "Where Has All the Sex Gone?," *Moscow Times*, February 22, 1997.

116 Richard Beeston, "Russians Long for the Good Old, Bad Days," *Australian*, August 3, 1999.

117 Fred Weir, "Russia's Comeback Communists," special to *Christian Science Monitor*, May 25, 1999.

118 "Grim Choices," *Economist*, July 10, 1999.

119 "Text of Remarks Prepared for Delivery by Texas Gov. George W. Bush at Ronald Reagan Presidential Library, Simi Valley, Calif. on November 19, 1999," *Washington Post*, accessed September 14, 2021, https://www.washingtonpost.com/archive/business/technology/1999/11/19/text-of-remarks-prepared-for-delivery-by-texas-gov-george-w-bush-at-ronald-reagan-presidential-library-simi-valley-calif-on-november-19-1999/1e893802-88ce-40de-bcf7-a4e1b6393ad2/.

120 George W. Bush, Iowa Western Community College, January 21, 2000, "Bushisms," http://home.uchicago.edu/~you/bushisms.html.

121 Hirst, *Leo Strauss*, 85–86. For Fukuyama's protest, including the quote, see "Francis Fukuyama: The End of History Man," *Independent* (London), March 25, 2006, http://www.independent.co.uk/news/people/profiles/francis-fukuyama-the-end-of-history-man-6105624.html.

122 See Schrecker, *Cold War Triumphalism*.

123 This included a sustained attack in December 1998 targeting "suspected weapons plants, Iraqi intelligence agencies and fortifications of the military unit known as the Republican Guard." Francis X. Clines and Steven Lee Myers, "Attack on Iraq: The Overview; Impeachment Vote in House Delayed as Clinton Launches Iraq Air Strike, Citing Military Need to Move Swiftly," *New York Times*, December 17, 1998, https://www.nytimes.com/1998/12/17/world/attack-iraq-overview-impeachment-vote-house-delayed-clinton-launches-iraq-air.html.

124 "Text of Remarks."

5. Consuming Nostalgia

1 Jeffrey Fleishman, "It All Started with Communist Condoms," *Gazette Montreal*, November 2, 2002, reprinted from *Los Angeles Times*.

2 Dan Hancox, "Lithuania's Soviet Nostalgia: Back in the USSR," *Guardian*, May 1, 2011, https://www.theguardian.com/travel/2011/may/01/lithuania-soviet-nostalgia-theme-parks; "The Project: 1984 in the Bunker (Back in the USSR)," Vilnius Tourism, December 16, 2007, accessed February 12, 2008, www.vilnius-tourism.it/index.php/ed/55846/.

3 Soviet Café Katvartirka Facebook page, January 22, 2013, https://www.facebook.com/Soviet-cafe-Kvartirka-494905997219878/.

4 See Poiger, *Jazz, Rock, and Rebels*; and Rubin, *Synthetic Socialism*.

5 Jamie Mackay, "European Identity and the Paradox of Anti-communism," openDemocracy, October 3, 2019, https://www.opendemocracy.net/en/can-europe-make-it/european-identity-and-paradox-anti-communism/.

6 Good Orient, accessed August 29, 2007, https://www.goodorient.com. See also "CultRev Retro Chic," *Cogs and Wheels: The Material Culture of Revolutionary China* (blog), March 16, 2007, https://cogsandwheels.wordpress.com/2007/03/16/cultrev-retro-chic/.

7 "CultRev Retro Chic"; Schrift, *Biography*.

8 "FYI: Don't Bring Your Mao Bag to Peru," Shanghaiist, June 23, 2007, https://shanghaiist.com/2007/06/23/fyi_dont_bring/; "Cameron Diaz Apologies to Peru," Just Jared, June 25, 2007, https://www.justjared.com/2007/06/25/cameron-diaz-bag-peru/; Jim Hoft, "Cameron Diaz and Her 'Trendy' Marxist Bag Offend in Peru," Gateway Pundit, June 23, 2007, https://www.thegatewaypundit.com/2007/06/cameron-diaz-her-trendy-marxist-bag-offend-in-peru/.

9 "Actress Cameron Diaz Commits Fashion Crime in Peru," *Pravda*, June 23, 2007; Associated Press, "Diaz's Bag with Maoist Slogan Draws Ire," *USA Today*, June 23, 2007; "The Fashion Pigs," June 28, 2007, monkeysmashesheaven.wordpress.com; Allahpundit, "Celebrity Moron Totes Trendy Maoist Handbag in Peru, Home of the Shining Path," Hot Air, June 22, 2007, https://hotair.com/allahpundit/2007/06/22/celebrity-moron-totes-trendy-maoist-handbag-in-peru-home-of-the-shining-path-n148415.

10 Megs Mahoney Dusil, "Cameron Diaz Style: Huge Fashion Don't in Peru," *Purse Blog*, June 26, 2007, https://www.purseblog.com/celebrities/cameron-diaz-style-huge-fashion-dont-in-peru/.

11 "Actress Cameron Diaz."

12 "Fashion Pigs."

13 "Questions and Answers," Statue Park, official English website, accessed March 2, 2008, http://szoborpark.hu/index.php?Contentld+11&Lang+en; https://www.mementopark.hu/en/home/.

14 *Statue Park: Gigantic Monuments from the Age of Communist Dictatorships* (Budapest: Statue Park Publications, 2007).

15 Visit to Szoborpark, Budapest, February 24, 2008.

16 *Statue Park.*

17 Visit to Szoborpark, Budapest, February 24, 2008.

18 I visited Stalin World in Lithuania in May 2008.

19 *Statue Park.*

20 Kate Connelly, "They Tore Down Lenin's Statue—and Raised One to Frank Zappa," *Guardian*, January 29, 2000, http://www.theguardian.com/travel/2000/jan/29/Lithuania.

21 Adam B. Ellick, "From Zappa to Lenin: Lithuanian Sculptors Chronicle the Times through the Soviet Era to Today," discontinued website, October 26, 2007, accessed November 14, 2009, http://www.balticsww.com/lenin_to_zappa.

22 *Grutas Park Tiesa*, no. 1, April 1, 2002.

23 Visit to Lithuania, May 16–21, 2008. For an excellent critical appraisal of the lack of documentation of the Holocaust at Lithuania's historical sites, see Jonathan Steel, "In the Jerusalem of the North, the Jewish Story Is Forgotten," *Guardian*, June 19, 2008, https://www.theguardian.com/commentisfree/2008/jun/20/secondworldwar.

24 Visit to Grutas Park, Lithuania, May 18, 2008.

25 All quotes were taken from the site during my February 26, 2008, visit; postcards are in my possession.

26 "New Polish Law Equates Communist and Nazi Symbols," RT, November 30, 2009, https://www. rt.com/politics/poland-bans-communist-symbols.

27 See Zack Beauchamp, "The American Right's Favorite Strongman," Vox, August 10, 2020, https://www.vox.com/2020/5/21/21256324/viktor-orban-hungary-american-conservatives; and Rachel Donadio, "How Hungary Ran George Soros out of Town," *Atlantic*, May 15, 2018, https://www.theatlantic.com/international/archive/2018/05/orban-european-union-soros/560480/.

28 Oushakine, *Patriotism of Despair*, 4–5; quotes are from 225–26.

29 The Redstar shop at Szoborpark is linked through the market to the vigorous *ostalgie* of East Germany, where both sell model Trabants made in China.

30 "Ostalgie or Ossification? Nostalgia for the Past May Be More Forward Looking Than It Appears," *Economist*, February 20, 2008, http://www.economist.com/cities/displayObject.cfm?obj_id=2534113&city_id=BER.

31 Berdahl, *Social Life of Postsocialism*, 60. See also Scriber, *Requiem for Communism*.

32 Berdahl, *Social Life of Postsocialism*, 66.

33 Historians seem to have put to rest the footnote that Kennedy actually declared himself a jelly doughnut when saying, "Ich bin ein Berliner."

34 Agence France-Presse, "You Are Now Entering Checkpoint 'McCharlie,'" *Independent* (London), March 14, 2010, https://www.independent.co.uk/incoming/you-are-now-entering-checkpoint-mccharlie-5530596; "McDonald's Arrives at Checkpoint Charlie," *Telegraph*, March 15, 2010, https://www.telegraph.co.uk/news/worldnews/europe/germany/7440503/McDonalds-arrives-at-Checkpoint-Charlie.html.

35 Stadtmuseum Berlin exhibit pamphlet, https://www.en.stadtmuseum.de/exhibitions/westberlin.

36 Krause, *Bringing Cold War Democracy*, 194–95.

37 See Clarke and Wölfel, *Remembering the German Democratic Republic*.

38 Richard Tyler, "A Sensitive Portrayal of East Germany's Collapse," World Socialist Web Site, September 4, 2003, https://www.wsws.org/en/articles/2003/09/good-s04.html.

39 Žižek, *In Defense of Lost Causes.*

40 "Awakening the Inner Socialist," *Age*, January 3, 2004, https://www.theage.com.au/entertainment/movies/awakening-the-inner-socialist-20040103-gdx1bl.html.

41 "Awakening the Inner Socialist."

42 Bruni de la Motte, "East Germans Lost Much in 1989," *Guardian*, November 8, 2009, https://www.theguardian.com/commentisfree/2009/nov/08/1989-berlin-wall; Katrin Bennhold, "20 Years after Fall of Wall, Women of Former East Germany Thrive," *New York Times*, October 5, 2010, https://www.nytimes.com/2010/10/06/world/europe/06iht-letter.html; Trappe and Gornick, "Gender and Work in Germany."

43 "Ostalgie or Ossification?"

44 "Trabant Exhaust Fumes Sold Online," BBC News, July 18, 2005.

45 Tony Paterson, "Border Guards, Kalashnikovs and the Berlin Wall—They're All 'Tourist Attractions' at the Latest German Theme Park," *Telegraph*, June 27, 2004, https://www.telegraph.co.uk/news/worldnews/europe/germany/1465599/Border-guards-Kalashnikovs-and-the-Berlin-Wall-theyre-all-tourist-attractions-at-the-latest-German-theme-park.html.

46 "Ostalgie or Ossification?"

47 Derek Scally, "A Political Battle over History Now Grips Poland's Proudest Memory," *Irish Times*, February 16, 2019, https://www.irishtimes.com/news/world/europe/a-political-battle-over-history-now-grips-poland-s-proudest-memory-1.3795016; Richard Unwin, "Poland's Right-Wing Government Accused of Hijacking Prize-Winning Museum," *Art Newspaper*, March 21, 2019, https://www.theartnewspaper.com/news/poland-s-right-wing-government-accused-of-hijacking-prize-winning-museum.

48 Don Snyder, "Poland Poised to Put 'Bad' Historians in Prison," Forward, September 2, 2016, http://forward.com/news/world/349179/poland-poised-to-put-bad-historians-in-prison/.

49 Rachel Donadio, "The Dark Consequences of Poland's New Holocaust Law," *Atlantic*, February 8, 2018, https://www.theatlantic.com/international/archive/2018/02/poland-holocaust-law/552842/.

50 Cameron Hewitt, "Poland's New World War II Museum: Who Gets to Tell the Story," *Cameron's Travels* (blog), Rick Steves' Europe, November 15, 2018, https://blog.ricksteves.com/cameron/2018/11/poland-world-war-ii-museum/.

51 Quoted in Pozniak, *Nowa Huta*, 82. See Pozniak for an excellent discussion of debates over naming.

52 Lebow, *Unfinished Utopia.*

53 Lebow, *Unfinished Utopia.*

54 Marta Tycner, "Poland's Right Turn: Inexplicable Madness or Rational Response?," openDemocracy, January 7, 2016, https://www.opendemocracy.net/can-europe-make-it/marta-tycner/polands-right-turn-inexplicable-madness-or-rational-response.

55 Tycner, "Poland's Right Turn."

56 Luthar and Pušnik, *Remembering Utopia*. Also see Patterson, *Bought and Sold*; and Stefanovic, *Miss Ex-Yugoslavia*.

57 Gordana Knezevic, "Yugo-nostalgia Prevails in Serbia, Bosnia," Radio Free Europe / Radio Liberty, May 26, 2017, https://www.rferl.org/a/balkans-without-borders-yugo-nostalgia-serbia-bosnia/28511123.html.

58 Knezevic, "Yugo-nostalgia Prevails."

59 Alexander Zaitchik, "Mostar's Little Dragon: How Bruce Lee Became a Symbol of Peace in the Balkans," Reason Online, April 2006, http://www.reason.com/0604/cr.az.mostars.shtml. On the vandalism, see "IMG MGMT: Turbo Sculpture," Art F City, August 24, 2009, http://www.artfagcity.com/2009/08/24/img-mgmt-turbo-sculpture/. On the global importance of Bruce Lee, see Prashad, "Bruce Lee."

60 Farber, *Wall of Our Own*.

61 Andrew Edwards, "Berlin Wall Dispute Arises in San Bernardino," *San Bernardino County Sun*, September 23, 2010; James Keller, "Truro's Dilemma: Whether to Tear Down This Wall: N.S. Town's Officials Consider Moving Berlin Wall Fragments to Diefenbunker," *Montreal Gazette*, November 27, 2006; "Berlin Wall Slabs in Truro Moved to Bible Hill," *Truro Daily*, September 30, 2017.

62 Mark Byrnes, "The Berlin Wall Is Everywhere," Bloomberg, November 7, 2014, https://www.bloomberg.com/news/articles/2014-11-07/the-berlin-wall-is-everywhere.

63 Besar Litmeta, "Berlin Wall Fragment Joins Albanian Memorial," BalkanInsight, March 27, 2013, https://balkaninsight.com/2013/03/27/berlin-wall-fragment-installed-in-albania-memorial/.

64 Farber, "Conclusion, Returns: 1989 and Beyond," *Wall of Our Own*.

65 Robert Hull, "Berlin Wall's 'Kings of Freedom' Art Unveiled on U.Va.'s Grounds as Symbol of Liberty," UVA Today, April 14, 2014, https://news.virginia.edu/content/berlin-wall-s-kings-freedom-art-unveiled-uva-s-grounds-symbol-liberty.

66 Hull, "Berlin Wall's 'Kings of Freedom.'"

67 "Robert A. Hefner, III," Belfer Center for Science and International Affairs, last updated April 1, 2019, https://www.belfercenter.org/person/robert-hefner-iii.

68 Douglas Martin, "The Man Who Digs the Deepest Wells," *New York Times*, November 29, 1981, https://www.nytimes.com/1981/11/29/business/the-man-who-drills-the-deepest-wells.html.

69 "The Hefner Family," Hefner.Energy, accessed May 14, 2019, https://www.hefner.energy/articles/hefner-family-history. On the life of Hefner, see, Trafzer, *The Judge*. On the Dawes Act, see Pevar, *Rights of Indians*.

70 Theodore Roosevelt, "The Struggle for Self-Determination, 1901," available at https://www.digitalhistory.uh.edu/disp_textbook.cfm?smtid=3&psid=720.

71 Douglas Martin, "Man Who Digs"; "Hefner Family History," accessed May 14, 2019, http://www.ghkco.com/history/index.php?page=HEFNER_FAMILY_HISTORY.

72 Robert A. Hefner III, "The United States of Gas: Why the Shale Revolution Could Have Happened Only in America," *Foreign Affairs*, May/June 2014, https://www.foreignaffairs.com/articles/united-states/2014-04-17/united-states-gas.

73 Hefner, "United States of Gas."

74 Text on plaque accompanying installation of *Kings of Freedom* on UVA grounds.
75 Ramiiisol, https://ramiiisolvineyards.com/.
76 "Sayings," Ramiiisol, https://ramiiisolvineyards.com/sayings/.
77 Douglas Martin, "Man Who Digs."
78 I informally surveyed students at the installation in April and May of 2019, as part of a course on Cold War Memory. Aidan Comerford also shared his insights from his own engagement with students at the site. All notes are in my possession.

6. Patriot Acts

1 Richard Reeves, "Old Ideas and Young People Could Mean War," UExpress, March 22, 2000, https://www.uexpress.com/richard-reeves/2000/3/22/old-ideas-and-young-people-could.
2 On this point, see, Jelly-Schapiro, *Security and Terror*, 170.
3 Howard Kurtz, "Keeping Iraq in the Cross Hairs," *Washington Post*, March 18, 2003. On the US wars in Iraq and Afghanistan and the relationships between these wars and previous foreign policy, see Gardner and Young, *Iraq*; Gardner, *Long Road to Baghdad*; and Bailey and Immerman, *Understanding the U.S. Wars*.
4 Timothy Garden, "British and Nato Policy after the Prague Summit," *Guardian*, January 8, 2003, https://www.theguardian.com/news/2003/jan/08/nuclearindustry.uknews.
5 "The Kitchen Debate," *will interpret complx txts 4 food* (blog), August 16, 2007.
6 Gardner, *Long Road to Baghdad*; Weiner, *Legacy of Ashes*; Baer, *See No Evil*; Baer, *Sleeping with the Devil*.
7 McClintock, "Paranoid Empire," *Small Axe*, 51.
8 For differing views of the immediate responses to and concerns about expanded security, see Brad Knickerbocker, "Security Concerns Drive Rise in Secrecy," *Christian Science Monitor*, December 3, 2001; and Gregory F. Treverton, "In Our New World, the Spy Business Must Change," *Christian Science Monitor*, December 3, 2001.
9 Dudziak, *War Time*, chap. 4, "What Is a War on Terror?"
10 Gregory, "Everywhere War," 238.
11 Gregory, "Everywhere War," 239; Gardner, *Killing Machine*.
12 Tom Bissell, "Euphorias of Perrier: The Case against Robert Kaplan," *VQR*, Summer 2006, http://www.vqronline.org/euphorias-perrier-case-against-robert-d-kaplan.
13 On Halliburton contracts, see Anna Fifield, "Contractors Reap $138 Billion from Iraq War," *Financial Times*, March 19, 2003, https://www.ft.com/content/7f435f04-8c05-11e2-b001-00144feabdc0.
14 Anne Scott Tyson, "New U.S. Strategy: 'Lily Pad' Bases," *Christian Science Monitor*, August 14, 2004, https://www.globalpolicy.org/component/content/article/153/26152.html.
15 Gregory, "Everywhere War." On Cold War cartography, see Barney, *Mapping the Cold War*.

16 George W. Bush, "State of the Union Address," George W. Bush White House, January 29, 2002, https://georgewbush-whitehouse.archives.gov/news/releases/2002/01/20020129-11.html.

17 George W. Bush, "State of the Union Address."

18 See Amy Kaplan, "Homeland Insecurities."

19 George W. Bush, "State of the Union Address."

20 See Dudziak, *War Time*.

21 Chalmers Johnson, *Blowback*.

22 Association of Former Intelligence Officers, official website, accessed September 17, 2021, https://www.afio.com/.

23 International Spy Museum official website, https://www.spymuseum.org/.

24 Spy Museum official website.

25 Spy Museum official website.

26 Spy Museum, exhibit placard.

27 Spy Museum, exhibit placard.

28 Stephen Goode, "Earnest Will Open Door to Espionage; E. Peter Earnest Hopes the Soon-to-Be-Open International Spy Museum Will Educate Others about the Importance of Intelligence-Gathering to the Security of the United States," *Insight on the News*, June 24, 2002.

29 "The Enemy Within," Spy Museum official website, accessed December 12, 2021, at https://web.archive.org/web/20160411141651/https://www.spymuseum.org/education-programs/educators/lesson-plans-activities/the-enemy-within/.

30 "9/11: The Intelligence Angle," Spy Museum official website, accessed December 12, 2021, at https://web.archive.org/web/20160411142728/http://www.spymuseum.org/education-programs/educators/lesson-plans-activities/911-the-intelligence-angle/.

31 "Exquisitely Evil: 50 Years of Bond Villains," International Spy Museum, accessed December 12, 2021, at https://web.archive.org/web/20211212162512/http://spy-museum.s3.amazonaws.com/files/Bond_in_the_classroom.pdf.

32 John R. Bowen and Aziz Rana, "Under Western Eyes," in *BR: A Political and Literary Podcast*, December 15, 2016, http://bostonreview.net/war-security-podcast/john-bowen-aziz-rana-under-western-eyes.

33 "Programs: Events Calendar," Spy Museum official website, accessed December 12, 2021, at https://web.archive.org/web/20080305184758/http://www.spymuseum.org/programs/calendar_pages/2008/q1/2008_03_20_prog.php.

34 Mamdani, *Good Muslim, Bad Muslim*.

35 International Spy Museum, accessed October 17, 2010, https://www.spymuseum.org/missions/operation-spy.

36 Charania, *Will the Real?*, 81–84.

37 Quoted in Charania, *Will the Real?*, 75–76.

38 Charania discusses the Western erasure of Muslim women's organizing in her discussions of Malala Yousafzai (67–70).

39 Friedman, *Covert Capital*, 19–20. This dynamic is also captured in Appy, "Eisenhower's Doodle."

40 IntlSpyMuseum, "Robert Baer—My Bond Moment," YouTube video, 1:50, posted December 4, 2012, https://www.youtube.com/watch?v=Kgco4lvorto&list=PL8p1_ubNPTRlyTMfJFOxGTUF4DB28b5pZ&index=5.

41 Joseph C. Wilson, "What I Didn't Find in Africa," *New York Times*, July 6, 2003, http://www.nytimes.com/2003/07/06/opinion/what-i-didn-t-find-in-africa.html.

42 Robert D. Novak, "Mission to Niger," *Washington Post*, July 14, 2003, http://www.washingtonpost.com/wp-dyn/content/article/2005/10/20/AR2005102000874.html.

43 IntlSpyMuseum, "Valerie Plame—My Bond Moment," YouTube video, 1:38, posted December 4, 2012, https://www.youtube.com/watch?v=6X2SmP292wo&index=4&list=PL8p1_ubNPTRlyTMfJFOxGTUF4DB28b5.

44 Moon, *Sunshine Policy*.

45 Dong-Choon Kim, "Korea's Truth and Reconciliation Commission."

46 Visit to Human Rights Center, Seoul, South Korea, July 19, 2012; Kim Jae-heun, "Former Police Torture Facility to Be Turned into Human Rights Memorial Hall," *Korea Times*, December 2018, https://www.koreatimes.co.kr/www/nation/2018/12/119_260988.html.

47 Moon, *Sunshine Policy*.

48 Emma Graham-Harrison, "US Finally Closes Its Detention Facility at Bagram Airbase in Afghanistan," *Guardian*, December 11, 2014, https://www.theguardian.com/world/2014/dec/11/afghanistan-us-bagram-torture-prison.

49 Richard Lloyd Parry, "Profile: Kim Jong Il: The Little God Who Created a Calamity," *Independent* (London), June 18, 2000.

50 See Seymour M. Hersh, "Torture at Abu Ghraib," *New Yorker*, April 30, 2004, https://www.newyorker.com/magazine/2004/05/10/torture-at-abu-ghraib; and McClintock, "Paranoid Empire," *Small Axe*.

51 Hersh, "Torture at Abu Ghraib."

52 McClintock, "Paranoid Empire," *Small Axe*, 59.

53 "A Message from Kim Jong Il," SNL Transcripts, episode aired January 11, 2003, posted October 8, 2018, http://snltranscripts.jt.org/02/02ikim.phtml.

54 Matt Stone, interviewed by Anwar Brett, BBC, accessed September 20, 2021, http://www.bbc.co.uk/films/2005/01/13/matt_stone_team_america_interview.shtml; Heather Havrilesky, "Puppet Masters," *Salon*, October 12, 2004, https://www.salon.com/2004/10/12/parker_stone_2/.

55 See John Feffer, "Infantilzing North Korea: It's Time for Us to Grow Up in Our Assessment of North Korea," Institute for Policy Studies, May 10, 2013, https://ips-dc.org/infantalizing_north_korea/.

56 Arowanafilms, "Kim Jong Il Eharmony," YouTube video, 1:30, posted February 2, 2009, http://www.youtube.com/watch?v=qHkWv1vHtHk.

57 Onion, "Kim Jong Il Announces Plan to Bring Moon to North Korea," YouTube video, 2:16, posted January 26, 2009, http://www.youtube.com/watch?v=bZIgdao1k6o.

58 Evan Thomas, "'Black Hawk Down': Arts and Culture in the Bush Era," *Newsweek*, December 12, 2008.

59 David Robb, "Operation Hollywood: How the U.S. Military Bullies Movie Producers into Showing the U.S. Military in the Best Possible Light," interview by Jeff Fleischer, *Mother Jones*, September 20, 2004, https://www.motherjones.com/politics/2004/09/operation-hollywood/; Robb, *Operation Hollywood*. See also Steve Rose, "The US Military Storm Hollywood," *Guardian*, July 6, 2009, https://www.theguardian.com/film/2009/jul/06/us-military-hollywood.

60 "Defending Black Hawk Down," partial transcript from *The O'Reilly Factor*, January 14, 2002, https://www.foxnews.com/story/defending-black-hawk-down.

61 Mickey Kaus, "What Black Hawk Down Leaves Out," Slate, January 21, 2002, http://www.slate.com/articles/news_and_politics/kausfiles_special/2002/01/what_black_hawk_down_leaves_out.html.

62 On television, media, and the war on terror, see Alsultany, *Arabs and Muslims*.

63 Andrew Buncombe, "US Military Tells Jack Bauer: Cut Out Torture Scenes ... or Else!," *Independent*, February 13, 2007, https://www.independent.co.uk/news/world/americas/us-military-tells-jack-bauer-cut-out-the-torture-scenes-or-else-436143.html.

64 Tom Kenworthy, "Congressman Charlie Wilson Not Holding His Fire," *Washington Post*, August 20, 1990, https://www.washingtonpost.com/archive/lifestyle/1990/08/20/congressman-charlie-wilson-not-holding-his-fire/4597c5fa-1e05-4162-9e4a-e4aefc697f9d/?utm_term=.af9196a8876e.

65 For a superb representation of the excellent scholarship emerging on post-9/11 popular culture, see the introduction and ten essays in Laderman and Gruenewald, *Imperial Benevolence*. See also Shaw, *Cinematic Terror*.

66 Gardner, *Killing Machine*.

67 Gregory, "Everywhere War," 239.

68 Gregory, "Everywhere War," 239.

69 Vine, *Base Nation*, 42.

70 Gregory, "Everywhere War," 239; Gardner, *Killing Machine*.

71 Gregory, "Everywhere War," 241.

72 Mark Mazzetti and Robert F. Worth, "Yemen Deaths Test Claims of New Drone Policy," *New York Times*, December 20, 2013, https://www.nytimes.com/2013/12/21/world/middleeast/yemen-deaths-raise-questions-on-new-drone-policy.html.

73 See Raghavan, *Most Dangerous Place*, 340–68. Raghavan importantly argues that the "trajectory of US foreign policy after 9/11 did not change as sharply from the immediate past as then assumed" (341).

74 Ron Moreau, "Pakistan: The Most Dangerous?," *Newsweek*, October 20, 2007, https://www.newsweek.com/pakistan-most-dangerous-102955.

75 The quote is from Gregory, "Everywhere War," 239. See also Shamsie, *Burnt Shadows*.

76 "Key US Base Supplying Afghanistan Closes," *RT*, June 3, 2014, https://rt.com/usa/163276-us-leave-manas-airbase/. For an earlier report, see Tyson, "New U.S. Strategy."

77 Valeri, interview by author, May 14, 2013.

78 Craig S. Smith, "U.S. Helped to Prepare the Way for Kyrgyzstan's Uprising," *New York Times*, March 30, 2005, https://www.nytimes.com/2005/03/30/world/asia/us-helped-to-prepare-the-way-for-kyrgyzstans-uprising.html.

79 On the cultural projects reflected in the mural, see Igmen, *Speaking Soviet with an Accent*.

80 Kate Brown, "Gridded Lives: Why Kazakhstan and Montana Are Nearly the Same Place," *American Historical Review* 106, no. 1 (2001): 17–48.

81 Buck-Morss, *Dreamworld and Catastrophe*; Westad, *Global Cold War*.

82 "U.S. Vacates Manas Airbase in Kyrgyzstan," *Moscow Times*, March 20, 2014.

83 Interview by author, May 17, 2013.

84 Interview by author, May 17, 2013.

85 Georgy Mamedov, "The Lost Pathos or the Pathos of Loss," Universes in Universe, February 2012, https://universes.art/en/nafas/articles/2012/lost-pathos.

86 Georgy Mamedov, conversation with author, May 14, 2013.

87 Mamedov, conversation with author.

88 Loring, "Building Socialism in Kyrgyzstan," 25; Igmen, *Speaking Soviet with an Accent*.

89 Suny and Martin, introduction to *State of Nations*, 16. See also Martin, *Affirmative Action Empire*.

90 "Georgy Mamedov," Former West, accessed June 30, 2013, https://formerwest.org/Contributors/GeorgyMamedov.

91 Valeri, interview by author, May 14, 2013.

92 Valeri, interview by author.

93 Lana, interview by author, May 15, 2013.

94 See G. M. Tamás's analysis in "The Soros Affair," Lefteast, April 15, 2017, http://www.criticatac.ro/lefteast/the-soros-affair/. For background on the shutdown, see Helene Beinvenu and Balint Bardi, "Hungary Law That Could Close University Faces Uncertainty," *New York Times*, April 12, 2017, https://www.nytimes.com/2017/04/12/world/europe/hungary-central-european-university-soros-orban.html.

95 Kara Downey, "Deep in Kyrgyz Earth," April 10, 2013, accessed June 25, 2016, postsoviet.stanford.edu/discussion/deep-kyrgyz-earth.

96 Tynybekov, Lelevkin, and Kulenbekov, "Environmental Issues."

97 See, for example, Downey, "Deep in Kyrgyz Earth."

98 Black, *Global Interior*. See also "Global Interior: A Conversation with Megan Black about the U.S. Interior Department in the American World Order," Toynbee Prize Foundation, March 16, 2017, https://toynbeeprize.org/posts/megan-black/.

99 Mamedov, conversation with author, May 14, 2013.

100 Eric Posner, "The Case against Human Rights," *Guardian*, December 4, 2014, https://www.theguardian.com/news/2014/dec/04/-sp-case-against-human-rights; Easterly, *White Man's Burden*; "NGO Law Monitor: Kyrgyz Republic," International Center for Not-for-Profit Law, February 17, 2016, accessed June 25, 2016, https://www.icnl.org/research/monitor/kyrgyz; Craig S. Smith, "U.S. Helped to Prepare the Way for Kyrgyzstan's Uprising," *New York Times*, March 30,

2005, https://www.nytimes.com/2005/03/30/world/asia/us-helped-to-prepare-the-way-for-kyrgyzstans-uprising.html.

101 Cholpon Orozobekova, "Will Kyrgyzstan Go Russian on NGOs?," *Diplomat*, October 22, 2015, https://thediplomat.com/2015/10/will-kyrgyzstan-go-russian-on-ngos/. See also Bakybek Beshimov and Ryskeldi Satke, "Kyrgyzstan: The Next Ukraine?," *Diplomat*, March 3, 2014, https://thediplomat.com/2014/03/kyrgyzstan-the-next-ukraine/.

102 "Debate: Is Human Rights Watch Too Close to U.S. Gov't to Criticize Its Foreign Policy?," Amy Goodman with Keane Bhatt and Reed Brody, *Democracy Now*, June 11, 2014, https://www.democracynow.org/2014/6/11/debate_is_human_rights_watch_too.

103 Eckel, "Rebirth of Politics," 257; Posner, "The Case against Human Rights"; Easterly, *White Man's Burden*.

104 Posner, "The Case against Human Rights"; Easterly, *White Man's Burden*.

105 Palko Karasz, "Pressure Grows as Hungary Adopts Law Targeting George Soros's University," *New York Times*, April 11, 2017, https://www.nytimes.com/2017/04/11/world/europe/hungary-george-soros-central-european-university.html?.

106 Zeilig, *Patrice Lumumba*, 131–33.

107 Zeilig, *Patrice Lumumba*, 133.

108 Quoted in Gaines, *American Africans in Ghana*, 122.

109 Guevara, *Congo Diary*.

110 See Jihan El Tahri, dir., *Cuba, an African Odyssey* (Temps Noir, 2007). See also Gleijeses, *Conflicting Missions*; and Gleijeses, *Visions of Freedom*. On early Soviet aid to the African National Congress, see Shubin, *Hot "Cold War."*

111 On the legacies of the Soviet Union in Cuba, see Loss and Prieto, *Caviar with Rum*; and Loss, *Dreaming in Russian*.

7. Spies R Us

1 Jeffrey Tayler, "What Pussy Riot's 'Punk Prayer' Really Said," *Atlantic*, November 8, 2012, https://www.theatlantic.com/international/archive/2012/11/what-pussy-riots-punk-prayer-really-said/264562/.

2 Mark Bennetts, "Putin's Holy War," Politico, February 21, 2017, https://www.politico.eu/article/putins-holy-war/.

3 Rosalind S. Helderman and Tom Hamburger, "Guns and Religion: How American Conservatives Grew Closer to Putin's Russia," *Washington Post*, April 30, 2017, https://www.washingtonpost.com/politics/how-the-republican-right-found-allies-in-russia/2017/04/30/e2d83ff6-29d3-11e7-a616-d7c8a68c1a66_story.html.

4 See Masha Lipman, "Why Putin Won't Be Marking the Hundredth Anniversary of the Russian Revolution," *New Yorker*, November 3, 2017, https://www.newyorker.com/news/news-desk/why-putin-wont-be-marking-the-hundredth-anniversary-of-the-bolshevik-revolution; and Catherine Merridale, "Putin's Russia Can't Celebrate Its Revolutionary Past. It Has to Smother It," *Guardian*, November 3, 2017, https://www.theguardian.com/commentisfree/2017/nov/03/putin-russia-revolution-ignore-centenary.

5 All quotes are from visit to *The Soviet Epoch* exhibit, the State Museum of Political History of Russia, April 7, 2017.

6 See Lipman, "Why Putin Won't Be Marking"; and Merridale, "Putin's Russia Can't Celebrate."

7 Ian Frazier, "What Ever Happened to the Russian Revolution?," *Smithsonian Magazine*, October 2017, https://www.smithsonianmag.com/history/what-ever-happened-to-russian-revolution-180964768/.

8 Photographs and notes from visit to *The Soviet Epoch* exhibit, April 7, 2017, in possession of author.

9 Photographs and notes from visit to the State Museum of Political History of Russia, April 7, 2017, in possession of author.

10 Eckel, "Rebirth of Politics," 257.

11 Shimer, *Rigged*.

12 Tom McCarthy, "Paul Manafort: How Decades of Serving Dictators Led to Role as Trump's Go-To Guy," *Guardian*, October 30, 2017, https://www.theguardian.com/us-news/2017/oct/30/paul-manafort-profile-donald-trump-dictators; Adam Rawnsley, "How Manafort's Work for the 'Torturer's Lobby' Came Back to Haunt Him," *Daily Beast*, February 23, 2019, https://www.thedailybeast.com/how-manaforts-work-for-the-torturers-lobby-came-back-to-haunt-him; Franklin Foer, "Paul Manafort, American Hustler," *Atlantic*, March 2018.

13 Gagnon, "'Invading Your Hearts and Minds.'"

14 Rowan Morrison, "Bannon's 2016: 'Rootless White Males,' 'Pure Evil,' and 'F*cking Hammerhead,'" TPM, July 18, 2017, http://talkingpointsmemo.com/dc/joshua-green-steve-bannon-trump-campaign; Bret Stephens, "How Steve Bannon Rode the Honey Badger into the White House," *New York Times*, July 18, 2017, https://www.nytimes.com/2017/07/18/books/review/devils-bargain-steve-bannon-donald-trump-joshua-green.html.

15 Seth Schiesel, "Suddenly the Cold War Is a Cool Event," *New York Times*, November 12, 2010, http://www.nytimes.com/2010/11/13/arts/television/13duty.html?ref=video-games.

16 Scott Shane, Matthew Rosenberg, and Eric Lipton, "Trump Pushes Dark View of Islam to Center of U.S. Foreign Policy Making," *New York Times*, February 1, 2017.

17 Shane, Rosenberg, and Lipton, "Trump Pushes Dark View."

18 Schiesel, "Suddenly the Cold War."

19 See Gagnon's parallel work on *Call of Duty*: Gagnon, "'Invading Our Hearts and Minds.'"

20 Rashid, *Taliban*; Timothy Mitchell, *Carbon Democracy*; Marjorie Cohn, "Cheney's Black Gold: Oil Interests May Drive U.S. Foreign Policy," *Chicago Tribune*, August 10, 2000, http://articles.chicagotribune.com/2000-08-10/news/0008100507_1_caspian-oil-caspian-sea-gas-journal.

21 Simon Parkin, "*Call of Duty*: Gaming's Role in Military-Entertainment Complex," *Guardian*, October 22, 2014, https://www.theguardian.com/technology/2014/oct/22/call-of-duty-gaming-role-military-entertainment-complex.

22 Stahl, *Militainment, Inc.* See also Dyer-Witheford and Pueter, *Games of Empire*.

23 Parkin, "*Call of Duty*."

24 Dave Thier, "Oliver North Is Selling *Call of Duty Black Ops 2*," *Forbes*, May 2, 2012; Davis Itzkoff, "Oliver North, Now in the Service of TV's KGB," *New York Times*, April 15, 2014, https://www.nytimes.com/2014/04/16/arts/television/oliver-north-now-in-the-service-of-tvs-kgb.html; Stephen Totilo, "*Call of Duty* Creators Say Oliver North Helped Make Their Game More Authentic," Kotaku, May 24, 2012, https://kotaku.com/call-of-duty-creators-say-oliver-north-helped-make-thei-5913092; Robert Burns, "AP Source: Navy SEALs Punished for Secret Breech," *USA Today*, November 9, 2012, https://www.usatoday.com/story/news/nation/2012/11/08/navy-seals-punished/1693453/.

25 See "Telling the Army Story," Army Public Affairs, accessed September 23, 2021, https://www.army.mil/publicAffairs/; and George Washington University Institute for Public Diplomacy and Global Communication, *Take Five Blog*, http://takefiveblog.org/2012/10/09.

26 Parkin, "*Call of Duty*."

27 Keith Stuart, "Does *Call of Duty: Black Ops 3* Predict the Terrifying Future of Warfare?," *Guardian*, May 21, 2015, https://www.theguardian.com/technology/2015/may/21/call-of-duty-black-ops-3-terrifying-future-warfare.

28 Paul McCann, "Gorbachev Is Latest Star in Pizza Hut TV Ad," *Independent* (London), December 4, 1997, http://www.independent.co.uk/news/gorbachev-is-latest-star-in-pizza-hut-ad.1292228.html; Alessandra Stanley, "From Perestroika to Pizza: Gorbachev Stars in TV Ad," *New York Times*, December 3, 1997, http://www.nytimes.com/1997/12/03/world/from-perestroika-to-pizza-gorbachev-stars-in-tv-ad.html.

29 Eric Pfanner, "Mr. Gorbachev, Show Off This Bag," *New York Times*, August 8, 2007, https://www.nytimes.com/2007/08/08/business/media/08adco.html.

30 Dan Levin, "Louis Vuitton Ad Show Gorbachev Accompanied by Subversive Text," *New York Times*, November 5, 2007, http://www.nytimes.com/2007/11/05/business/media/05vuitton.html.

31 Dmitry Sudakov, "Gorbachev's Louis Vuitton Ad Best in a Decade," Pravda, December 30, 2009, http://www.pravdareport.com/society/showbiz/30-12-2009/111507-gorbachev_louis_vuitton-0/.

32 John Pope, "Former Soviet Leader Tours 9th Ward," *Times-Picayune* (New Orleans), October 5, 2007.

33 Mary Murray, "Katrina Aid from Cuba? No Thanks, Says U.S.," NBC News, September 14, 2005, http://www.nbcnews.com/id/9311876/ns/us_news-katrina_the_long_road_back/t/katrina-aid-cuba-no-thanks-says-us/#.VsDMqynfjYc.

34 Paul A. Kramer, "Desert, Storm," *Slate*, September 7, 2016, https://slate.com/news-and-politics/2016/09/how-the-iraq-war-set-the-stage-for-the-hurricane-katrina-disaster.html.

35 Clyde Woods, "Katrina's World."

36 Stephen F. Cohen, "The New American Cold War with Russia," *Nation*, July 10, 2006, republished with a new introduction by the author, June 8, 2007.

37 Stephen F. Cohen, "New American Cold War."

38 Adrian Blomfield and Mike Smith, "Gorbachev: U.S. Could Start a New Cold War," *Telegraph*, May 6, 2008, http://www.telegraph.co.uk/news/worldnews/europe/russia/1933223/Gorbachev-US-could-start-new-Cold-War.html.

39 "Former US Ambassador to Russia: Ukraine Situation Result of US and EEU Aggression toward Russia," Amy Goodman and Juan González with Jack Matlock Jr. (with Joe Biden participating), *Democracy Now*, March 20, 2014; Jack F. Matlock Jr., "Who Is the Bully? The U.S. Has Treated Russia like a Loser since the End of the Cold War," *Washington Post*, March 14, 2014, https://www.washingtonpost.com/opinions/who-is-the-bully-the-united-states-has-treated-russia-like-a-loser-since-the-cold-war/2014/03/14/b0868882-aa06-11e3-8599-ce7295b6851c_story.html; Uwe Klußmann, Matthias Schepp, and Klaus Wiegrefe, "NATO's Eastern Expansion: Did the West Break Its Promise to Moscow?," *Spiegel*, November 26, 2009, http://www.spiegel.de/international/world/nato-s-eastward-expansion-did-the-west-break-its-promise-to-moscow-a-663315.html.

40 "Transcript of First Presidential Debate," CNN, last updated October 14, 2008, http://www.cnn.com/2008/POLITICS/09/26/debate.mississippi.transcript/.

41 On Russian lessons from Georgia, see Evan Osnos and David Remnick, "Trump, Putin, and the New Cold War," *New Yorker*, March 6, 2017, https://www.newyorker.com/magazine/2017/03/06/trump-putin-and-the-new-cold-war.

42 Ian Traynor, "International: Georgia Blamed for Starting Russia War," *Guardian*, October 1, 2009.

43 "McCain: 'We Are All Georgians,'" NBC News, August, 12, 2008, accessed September 12, 2012, http://firstread.nbcnews.com/_news/2008/08/12/4431528-mccain-we-are-all-georgians.

44 "Mccain: 'We Are All Georgians.'"

45 Dan Eggen and Robert Barnes, "McCain's Focus on Georgia Raises Question of Propriety," *Washington Post*, August 15, 2008, http://www.washingtonpost.com/wp-dyn/content/article/2008/08/14/AR2008081403332.html; Rod Dreher, "We Are Not All Georgians Now," RealClearPolitics, August 26, 2008, http://www.realclearpolitics.com/articles/2008/08/we_are_not_all_georgians_now.html.

46 Pat Buchanan, "Georgia's Man in the McCain Camp," *Toronto Star*, September 2, 2008.

47 Bob Collins, "The 'G' Word," NewsCut, July 23, 2008, http://blogs.mprnews.org/newscut/2008/07/the_g_word.

48 Jeffrey Goldberg, "The Wars of John McCain," *Atlantic*, October 2008, http://www.theatlantic.com/magazine/archive/2008/10/the-wars-of-john-mccain/306991/.

49 Chris Megerian, "What Donald Trump Has Said through the Years about Where President Obama Was Born," *Los Angeles Times*, September 16, 2016, https://www.latimes.com/politics/la-na-pol-trump-birther-timeline-20160916-snap-htmlstory.html.

50 Nick Wing, "Sarah Palin: It Snowed in Alaska in May, So There Is No Global Warming," HuffPost, May 20, 2013, http://www.huffingtonpost.com/2013/05/20/sarah-palin-global-warming_n_3306867.html.

51 Another mode of play within *Black Ops*, completely unrelated to the plot but linked in the assault on the subject, is zombie mode.

52 Brian Crecente, "George Romero Explains the Story behind *Call of the Dead* … Then Gets Zombified," Kotaku, May 3, 2011, http://kotaku.com/5798024/george-romero-explains-the-story-behind-call-of-the-dead-then-gets-zombified.

53 moviemaniacsDE, "George Romero's Call of the Dead | Trailer *CoD Black Ops* Escalation Zombie Level (2011) Danny Trejo," YouTube video, 1:53, posted April 27, 2011, https://www.youtube.com/watch?v=fZmoY3JfU1g; Crecente, "George Romero Explains."

54 A. O. Scott and Jason Zinoman, "In George Romero's Zombie Films, the Living Were a Horror Show, Too," *New York Times*, July 17, 2017, https://www.nytimes.com/2017/07/17/movies/in-george-romeros-zombie-films-the-living-were-a-horror-show-too.html.

55 Crecente, "George Romero Explains."

56 Recent claims that the song, atypical for the group, was actually written by the CIA, if true, would simply underscore the fact that the CIA was completely blindsided by the wall coming down as well as the reach of Gorbachev's reforms.

57 Richard Beinstock, "Scorpion's Wind of Change: An Oral History of 1990s Epic Power Ballad," *Rolling Stone*, September 2, 2015, http://www.rollingstone.com/music/features/scorpions-wind-of-change-the-oral-history-of-1990s-epic-power-ballad-20150902.

58 GoldGloveTV, "Berlin Wall—CoD Black Ops First Strike DLC Map Pack," YouTube video, 9:31, posted February 1, 2011, https://www.youtube.com/watch?v=Qm_KhxN6RuA.

59 GoldGloveTV, "Berlin Wall."

60 Les, "*CoD: Black Ops* Commercial 'There's a Soldier in All of Us,'" Stupid Evil Bastard, November 10, 2010, http://stupidevilbastard.com/2010/11/cod-black-ops-commercial-theres-a-soldier-in-all-of-us/.

61 "Russian TV Blames 'Modern Warfare' for Terrorist Attack at Airport," https://mail.google.com/mail/u/0/?pli=1#inbox/QgrcJHsTkLFLLpMkgmlSKdNMxchghkFLNSb?projector=1.

62 "Russian TV Blames 'Modern Warfare.'"

63 Denis Pinchuk, "Indiana Jones Makes Russian Communists See Red," Reuters, May 23, 2008.

64 Author interviews, May 18, 2013.

65 Michael Birnbaum, "Russia's Anti-American Fever Goes beyond the Soviet Era's," *Washington Post*, March 8, 2015.

66 Birnbaum, "Russia's Anti-American Fever."

67 *The Americans*, season 1, episode 8, "Mutually Assured Destruction," aired March 20, 2013, on FX.

68 Aki Peritz, "What *The Americans* Gets Wrong about Russians Spies," *Week*, April 19, 2014, https://theweek.com/articles/447808/what-americans-gets-wrong-about-russian-spies.

69 The population of the DC metro area grew by at least 2,300,000 between 1980, when it hovered at around 3,000,000, to about 5,322,000 in 2020. New York City's population was 8.6 million in 2018, compared with just over 7 million in 1980.

70 John DeVore, "FX Cold War Drama *The Americans* Brings out Some Weird 80's Nostalgia," *Esquire*, April 21, 2016, http://www.esquire.com/entertainment/tv/a44205/the-americans-cold-war-80s-nostalgia/.

71 Todd VanDerWerff, "*The Americans* Is the Best Show on TV: Why Is Nobody Watching It?," Vox, January 18, 2015, http://www.vox.com/2015/1/28/7923027/americans-season-three-premiere.

72 Emily Nussbaum, "'The Americans' Is Too Bleak, and That's Why It's Great," *New Yorker*, March 18, 2015, http://www.newyorker.com/culture/culture-desk/the-americans-is-too-bleak-and-thats-why-its-great.

73 See James L. Goldgeiger, "A Realistic Reset with Russia," Council on Foreign Relations, August/September 2009; and "U.S.-Russia Relations 'Reset' Fact Sheet," Barack Obama White House, June 24, 2010, https://obamawhitehouse.archives.gov/the-press-office/us-russia-relations-reset-fact-sheet.

74 F. William Engdahl, "Ukraine Protests Carefully Orchestrated: The Role of CANVAS, US-Financed 'Color Revolution Training Group,'" GlobalResearch, March 14, 2014, http://www.globalresearch.ca/ukraine-protests-carefully-orchestrated-the-role-of-canvas-us-financed-color-revolution-training-group/5369906.

75 Engdahl, "Ukraine Protests Carefully Orchestrated."

76 Tarik Cyril Amar, "This Is No Second Cold War: Ukraine's Territorial Integrity Must Remain Intact," *Guardian*, February 28, 2014, https://www.theguardian.com/commentisfree/2014/feb/28/ukraine-this-is-no-second-cold-war.

77 "John McCain: Russia 'Is a Gas Station Masquerading as a Country,'" *Week*, March 14, 2014, http://theweek.com/speedreads/456437/john-mccain-russia-gas-station-masquerading-country.

78 Robert Kolker, "Paul Manafort Is Back," Bloomberg, November 28, 2016, https://www.bloomberg.com/news/articles/2016-11-28/paul-manafort-is-back.

79 Snyder, *Road to Unfreedom*, 230.

Epilogue

1 Oushakine, *Patriotism of Despair*.

2 *The Stuart Hall Project*, film premier, Sundance, January 2013; director John Akomfrah; producers Linda Gopaul and David Lawson.

3 Luke Mogelson, "Among the Insurrectionists," *New Yorker*, January 15, 2021, https://www.newyorker.com/magazine/2021/01/25/among-the-insurrectionists.

4 Mogelson, "Among the Insurrectionists."

5 Mogelson, "Among the Insurrectionists."

6 Mogelson, "Among the Insurrectionists."

7 "The New Politics of Care: From Covid 19 to Black Lives Matter." *Boston Review*, April 27, 2020, https://bostonreview.net/politics/gregg-gonsalves-amy-kapczynski-new-politics-care.

8 Condoleezza Rice, Opinion: "The Afghan People didn't choose the Taliban." *Washington Post*, August 17, 2021, https://www.washingtonpost.com/opinions/2021/08/17/condoleezza-rice-afghans-didnt-choose-taliban/.

9 Satia, *Time's Monster*, 6.

10 Razsa, *Bastards of Utopia*, 6.

11 See Charles Piot's *Nostalgia for the Future: West Africa after the Cold War*, which traces the new biopolitics of globalized life in Togo in an eviscerated and privatized state.

12 Gaines, "2020 Global Uprisings."

13 Zachariah Mampilly, "Protests Are Taking Over the World. What's Driving Them?, *New York Times*, October 3, 2021, https://www.nytimes.com/2021/10/03/opinion/covid-protests-world-whats-driving-them.html.

14 Grandin and Klubock, *Truth Commissions*.

WORKS CITED

Adebajo, Adekeye. *Liberia's Civil War: Nigeria, ECOMOG, and Regional Security in West Africa*. Boulder, CO: Lynne Rienner, 2002.

Alexievich, Svetlana. *Secondhand Time: The Last of the Soviets.* Translated by Bela Shayevich. New York: Random House, 2016.

Alsultany, Evelyn. *Arabs and Muslims in the Media: Race and Representation after 9/11.* New York University Press, 2012.

Anderson, Brian C. *South Park Conservatives: The Revolt against Liberal Media Bias.* Washington, DC: Regnery, March 2005.

Anderson, Kurt. *Evil Geniuses: The Unmaking of America: A Recent History.* New York: Random House, 2020.

Anderson, Perry. *A Zone of Engagement.* London: Verso Books, 1992.

Appy, Christian G. "Eisenhower's Guatemalan Doodle, or: How to Draw, Deny and Take Credit for a Third World Coup." In *Cold War Constructions: The Political Culture of United States Imperialism, 1945–1966*, edited by Christian G. Appy, 183–213. Amherst: University of Massachusetts Press, 2000.

Baer, Robert. *See No Evil: The True Story of a Ground Soldier in the CIA's War on Terrorism.* New York: Crown Publishing, 2003.

Baer, Robert. *Sleeping with the Devil: How Washington Sold Our Soul for Saudi Crude.* New York: Three Rivers Press, 2004.

Bailey, Beth, and Immerman, Richard. *Understanding the U.S. Wars in Iraq and Afghanistan.* New York: New York University Press, 2015.

Baldwin, Kate A. *The Racial Imaginary of the Cold War Kitchen: From Sokol'niki Park to Chicago's South Side* Hanover, NH: Dartmouth College Press, 2016.

Ballinger, Pamela. *History in Exile: Memory and Identity at the Borders of the Balkans.* Princeton, NJ: Princeton University Press, 2002.

Barney, Timothy. *Mapping the Cold War: Cartography and the Framing of America's International Power*. Chapel Hill: University of North Carolina Press, 2015.

Barrell, Howard. "Back to the Future: Renaissance and South African Domestic Policy." *African Security Review* 9, no. 2 (2000): 82–91.

Berdahl, Daphne. *On the Social Life of Postsocialism: Memory, Consumption, Germany*. Bloomington: Indiana University Press, 2010.

Bergholz, Max. *Violence as a Generative Force: Identity, Nationalism, and Memory in a Balkan Community*. Ithaca, NY: Cornell University Press, 2016.

Bhorat, Haroon, Alan Hirsch, Ravi Kanbur, and Mthuli Ncube. "Economic Policy in South Africa—Past, Present, and Future." In *The Oxford Companion to the Economics of South Africa*, edited by Haroon Bhorat, Alan Hirsch, Ravi Kanbur, and Mthuli Ncube, 1–25. Oxford: Oxford University Press, 2014.

Biondi, Martha. *To Stand and Fight: The Struggle for Civil Rights in Postwar New York City*. Cambridge, MA: Harvard University Press, 2003.

Black, Megan. *The Global Interior: Mineral Frontiers and American Power*. Cambridge, MA: Harvard University Press, 2018.

Blee, Kathleen M., and Kimberly A. Creasap. "Conservative and Right-Wing Movements." *Annual Review of Sociology* 36 (2010): 269–86.

Blight, David W. *Race and Reunion: The Civil War in American Memory*. Cambridge, MA: Belknap Press of Harvard University Press, 2002.

Borstelmann, Thomas. *Apartheid's Reluctant Uncle: The United States and Africa in the Early Cold War*. Oxford: Oxford University Press, 1993.

Borstelmann, Thomas. *The Cold War and the Color Line: American Race Relations in the Global Arena*. Cambridge, MA: Harvard University Press, 2001.

Bowden, Brett. *Empire of Civilization: The Evolution of an Imperial Idea*. Chicago: University of Chicago Press, 2009.

Boym, Svetlana. *The Future of Nostalgia*. New York: Basic Books, 2002.

Bradley, Mark Philip. *Imagining Vietnam and America: The Making of Postcolonial Vietnam*. Chapel Hill: University of North Carolina Press, 2000.

Brands, Hal. *Making the Unipolar Moment: U.S. Foreign Policy and the Rise of the Post–Cold War Order*. Ithaca, NY: Cornell University Press, 2016.

Brown, Kate. "Gridded Lives: Why Kazakhstan and Montana Are Nearly the Same Place." *American Historical Review* 106, no. 1 (2001): 17–48.

Brown, Kate. *Plutopia: Nuclear Families, Atomic Cities, and the Great Soviet and American Plutonium Disasters*. Oxford: Oxford University Press, 2015.

Buck-Morss, Susan. *Dreamworld and Catastrophe: The Passing of Mass Utopia in East and West*. Cambridge, MA: MIT Press, 2000.

Bush, George H. W. *All the Best, George Bush: My Life in Letters and Other Writings*. New York: Scribner, 2014.

Bush, George H. W., and Brent Scowcroft. *A World Transformed*. New York: Vintage, 1999.

Carruthers, Susan L. *Cold War Captives: Imprisonment, Escape, and Brainwashing*. Berkeley: University of California Press, 2009.

Chamberlin, Paul Thomas. *The Cold War's Killing Fields: Rethinking the Long Peace*. New York: Harper, 2018.

Chamberlin, Paul Thomas. *The Global Offensive: The United States, the Palestine Liberation Organization, and the Making of the Post-Cold War Order.* Oxford: Oxford University Press, 2012.

Charania, Moon. *Will the Real Pakistani Woman Please Stand Up? Empire, Visual Culture and the Brown Female Body.* Jefferson, NC: McFarland, 2015.

Cheloukhine, Serguei, and M. R. Haberfeld. *Russian Organized Corruption Networks and Their International Trajectories.* New York: Springer, 2010.

Chitalkar, Poorvi, and David M. Malone. "The UN Security Council and the Ghosts of Iraq." In *Land of Blue Helmets: The United Nations and the Arab World,* edited by Karim Makdisi and Vijay Prashad, 170–93. Oakland: University of California Press, 2016.

Clancy, Tom. *Executive Orders.* New York: G. P. Putnam's Sons, 1996.

Clarke, David, and Ute Wölfel, eds. *Remembering the German Democratic Republic: Divided Memory in a United Germany.* New York: Palgrave Macmillan, 2011.

Cohen, Lizabeth. *A Consumer's Republic: The Politics of Mass Consumption in Postwar America.* New York: Vintage Books, 2004.

Cohen, Stephen F. *Soviet Fates and Lost Alternatives: From Stalinism to the New Cold War.* New York: Columbia University Press, 2009.

Coll, Steve. *Ghost Wars: The Secret History of the CIA, Afghanistan and Bin Laden, from the Soviet Invasion to September 10, 2001.* New York: Penguin, 2004.

Cooper, Melinda. *Family Values: Between Neoliberalism and the New Social Conservatism.* Near Futures. New York: Zone Books, 2017.

Cortese, Anthony. "Regulatory Focus: *Glasnost, Perestroika,* and the Environment." *Environmental Science and Technology* 23, no. 10 (1989): 1212–13.

Cullather, Nick. "Damning Afghanistan: Modernization in a Buffer State." In "History and Sept. 11," special issue, *Journal of American History* 89, no. 2 (2002): 512–37.

Cumings, Bruce. *The Korean War: A History.* New York: Modern Library, 2011.

Cumings, Bruce. *North Korea: Another Country.* New York: New Press, 2004.

Davis, Angela. *The Angela Y. Davis Reader.* Edited by Joy James. Malden, MA: Blackwell Publishers, 1997.

DeLillo, Don. *Underworld.* New York: Scribner, 1997.

Denning, Michael. *Culture in the Age of Three Worlds.* London: Verso, 2004.

Drew, Elizabeth. *On the Edge: The Clinton Presidency.* New York: Simon and Schuster, 1994.

Dreyfuss, Robert. *Devil's Game: How the United States Helped Unleash Fundamentalist Islam.* New York: Holt, 2005.

Dubois, Laurent. *Haiti: Aftershocks of History.* London: Picador, 2013.

Dudziak, Mary L. *Cold War Civil Rights: Race and the Image of American Democracy.* Princeton, NJ: Princeton University Press, 2001.

Dudziak, Mary L. *War Time: An Idea, Its History, Its Consequences.* New York: Oxford University Press, 2012.

Dyer-Witheford, Nick, and Greig de Peuter. *Games of Empire: Global Capitalism and Video Games.* Minneapolis: University of Minnesota Press, 2009.

Easterly, William. *The White Man's Burden: Why the West's Efforts to Aid the Rest Have Done So Much Ill and So Little Good.* New York: Penguin, 2007.

Eckel, Jan. "The Rebirth of Politics from the Spirit of Morality." In *The Breakthrough: Human Rights in the 1970s*, edited by Jan Eckel and Samuel Moyn, 226–60. Philadelphia: University of Pennsylvania Press, 2014.

Ehrenreich, Barbara. *Nickel and Dimed: On (Not) Getting By in America*. New York: Metropolitan Books, 2001.

Ellis, Stephen. "The Historical Significance of South Africa's Third Force." *Journal of South African Studies* 24, no. 2 (June 1998): 261–99.

Engel, Jeffrey A. *When the World Seemed New: George H. W. Bush and the End of the Cold War*. New York: Houghton Mifflin Harcourt, 2017.

Epstein, Helen C. *Another Fine Mess: America, Uganda, and the War on Terror*. New York: Columbia Global Reports, 2017.

Farber, Paul. *A Wall of Our Own: An American History of the Berlin Wall.* Chapel Hill: University of North Carolina Press, 2020.

Ferguson, James. *Global Shadows: Africa in the Neoliberal World Order.* Durham, NC: Duke University Press, 2006.

Foner, Eric. *Who Owns History? Rethinking the Past in a Changing World*. New York: Hill and Wang, 2003.

Friedman, Andrew. *Covert Capital: Landscapes of Denial and the Making of U.S. Empire in the Suburbs of Northern Virginia*. Berkeley: University of California Press, 2013.

Friend, David. *The Naughty Nineties: The Triumph of the American Libido*. New York: Twelve Books, 2017.

Fukuyama, Francis. *The End of History and the Last Man.* New York: Free Press, 2006.

Gagnon, Frédérick. "'Invading Your Hearts and Minds': *Call of Duty* and the (Re)writing of Militarism in U.S. Digital Games and Popular Culture." *European Journal of American Studies* 5, no. 3 (Summer 2010).

Gaines, Kevin. *American Africans in Ghana: Black Expatriates and the Civil Rights Era*. Chapel Hill: University of North Carolina Press, 2006.

Gaines, Kevin K. "Reflections on Ben Okri, Goenawan Mohamad, and the 2020 Global Uprisings," *The Journal of Transnational American Studies*, 12.1 (2021), 9-44.

Gardner, Lloyd C. *Killing Machine: The American Presidency in the Age of Drone Warfare*. New York: New Press, 2013.

Gardner, Lloyd C. *The Long Road to Baghdad: A History of U.S. Foreign Policy from the 1970s to the Present*. New York: New Press, 2008.

Gardner, Lloyd C., and Marilyn B. Young, eds. *Iraq and the Lessons of Vietnam: Or, How Not to Learn from the Past*. New York: New Press, 2007.

Ghodsee, Kristen. *Red Hangover: Legacies of Twentieth-Century Communism*. Durham, NC: Duke University Press, 2017.

Gleijeses, Piero. *Conflicting Missions: Havana, Washington, and Africa, 1959–1976*. Chapel Hill: University of North Carolina Press, 2003.

Gleijeses, Piero. *Visions of Freedom Havana, Washington, Pretoria, and the Struggle for Southern Africa, 1976–1991*. Chapel Hill: University of North Carolina Press, 2013.

Glenny, Misha. *The Balkans: Nationalism, War, and the Great Powers, 1804–2011*. New York: Penguin Books, 2012.

Glickman, Lawrence B. *Free Enterprise: An American History*. New Haven, CT: Yale University Press, 2019.

Gordon, Colin. *Dead on Arrival: The Politics of Health Care in Twentieth-Century America*. Princeton, NJ: Princeton University Press, 2004.
Graham, Matthew. "Foreign Policy in Transition: The ANC's Search for a Foreign Policy Direction during South Africa's Transition 1990–1994." *Commonwealth Journal of International Affairs* 101, no. 5 (2012): 405–23.
Grandin, Greg. *Empire's Workshop: Latin America, the United States, and the Rise of the New Imperialism*. New York: Holt Paperbacks, 2007.
Grandin, Greg, and Klubock, Thomas Miller, eds. *Truth Commissions: State Terror, History, and Memory*. An Issue of *Radical History Review*. Volume 7, Number 97, 2007.
Green, Pippa. *Choice, Not Fate: Biography of Trevor Manuel*. London: Penguin Global, 2009.
Gregory, Derek. "The Everywhere War." *Geographical Journal* 177, no. 3 (September 2011): 238–50.
Guevara, Ernesto Che. *Congo Diary: The Story of Che Guevara's "Lost Year" in Africa*. New York: Ocean, 2011.
Habib, Adam. *South Africa's Suspended Revolution: Hopes and Prospects*. Athens: Ohio University Press, 2013.
Hahn, Peter L. *Missions Accomplished? The United States and Iraq since World War I*. New York: Oxford University Press, 2011.
Hartman, Andrew. *A War for the Soul of America: A History of the Culture Wars*. Chicago: University of Chicago Press, 2015.
Harvey, David. *A Brief History of Neoliberalism*. Oxford: Oxford University Press, 2005.
Harvey, David. *The New Imperialism*. Oxford: Oxford University Press, 2003.
Havel, Václav. *The Art of the Impossible*. New York: Knopf, 1997.
Havel, Václav. "A Call for Sacrifice: The Co-responsibility of the West." *Foreign Affairs* 73, no. 2 (1994): 2–7.
Havel, Václav. *To the Castle and Back*. New York: Penguin, 2007.
Hindawi, Coralie Pison. "Iraq: Twenty Years in the Shadow of Chapter VII." In *Land of Blue Helmets: The United Nations and the Arab World*, edited by Karim Makdisi and Vijay Prashad, 194–211. Oakland: University of California Press, 2016.
Hinton, Elizabeth. *From the War on Poverty to the War on Crime: The Making of Mass Incarceration in America*. Cambridge, MA: Harvard University Press, 2017.
Hirsh, Alan. "Fatal Embrace: How Relations between Business and Government Help to Explain South Africa's Low-Growth Equilibrium." *South African Journal of International Affairs* 27, no. 4 (2020): 473–92.
Hirshberg, Lauren. *Suburban Empire: Cold War Militarism in the US Pacific*. Berkeley: University of California Press, 2022.
Hirst, Aggie. *Leo Strauss and the Invasion of Iraq: Encountering the Abyss*. New York: Routledge, 2013.
Hochschild, Arlie. *The Second Shift: Working Families and the Revolution at Home*. New York: Avon Books, 1989.
Hockenos, Paul. *Homeland Calling: Exile Patriotism and the Balkan Wars*. Ithaca, NY: Cornell University Press, 2003.
Hogan, Michael J., ed. *The End of the Cold War: Its Meaning and Implications*. Cambridge: Cambridge University Press, 1992.

Igmen, Ali. *Speaking Soviet with an Accent: Culture and Power in Kyrgyzstan*. Pittsburgh: University of Pittsburgh Press, 2012.

Irwin, Ryan. *Gordian Knot: Apartheid and the Unmaking of the Liberal World Order*. Oxford: Oxford University Press, 2012.

Jackson, Donna R. *Jimmy Carter and the Horn of Africa: Cold War Policy in Ethiopia and Somalia*. Jefferson, NC: McFarland, 2007.

Jacobson, Matthew Frye, and Gaspar González. *What Have They Built You to Do? The Manchurian Candidate and Cold War America*. Minneapolis: University of Minnesota Press, 2006.

Jelly-Schapiro, Eli. *Security and Terror: American Culture and the Long History of Colonial Modernity*. Berkeley: University of California Press, 2018.

Johnson, Chalmers. *Blowback: The Costs and Consequences of American Empire*. New York: Holt, 2001.

Johnson, Linton Kwesi. *Mi Revalueshanary Fren*. Port Townsend, WA: Ausable, 2006.

Joseph, Gilbert M., and Greg Grandin, eds. *A Century of Revolution: Insurgent and Counterinsurgent Violence during Latin America's Long Cold War*. Durham, NC: Duke University Press, 2010.

Kaplan, Amy. "Homeland Insecurities: Some Reflections on Language and Space." *Radical History Review* 85 (2003): 82–93.

Kaplan, Robert D. *Balkan Ghosts: A Journey through History*. 1st Picador ed. 1993; New York: Picador, 2005.

Kamola, Isaac A. "Coffee and Genocide." *Transition*, no. 9 (2008): 54–72.

Kelley, Robin D. G. *Yo' Mama's Disfunktional: Fighting the Culture Wars in Urban America*. Boston: Beacon, 1998.

Khalil, Osamah F. *America's Dream Palace: Middle East Expertise and the Rise of the National Security State*. Cambridge, MA: Harvard University Press, 2016.

Kieh, George Klay, Jr. *The First Liberian Civil War: The Crises of Underdevelopment*. New York: Peter Lang, 2007.

Kim, Dong-Choon. "Korea's Truth and Reconciliation Commission: An Overview and Assessment." *Buffalo Human Rights Law Review* 19 (2013): 97–124.

Kim, Dong-Choon. *The Unending Korean War: A Social History*. Translated by Seung-ok Kim. Larkspur, CA: Tamal Vista, 2009.

Kim, Jodi. *Ends of Empire: Asian American Critique and the Cold War*. Minneapolis: University of Minnesota Press, 2010.

Kim, Monica. "Empire's Babel: US Military Interrogation Rooms of the Korean War." *History of the Present* 3, no. 1 (Spring 2013): 1–28.

Kim, Monica. *The Interrogation Rooms of the Korean War: The Untold History*. Princeton, NJ: Princeton University Press, 2020.

Kim, Suzy. *Everyday Life in the North Korean Revolution, 1945–1950*. Ithaca, NY: Cornell University Press, 2013.

Klare, Michael. *Rogue States and Nuclear Outlaws: America's Search for a New Foreign Policy*. New York: Hill and Wang, 1995.

Klein, Naomi. *The Shock Doctrine: The Rise of Disaster Capitalism*. New York: Metropolitan Books, 2007.

Kohler-Hausmann, Julilly. *Getting Tough: Welfare and Imprisonment in 1970s America.* Politics and Society in Modern America. Princeton, NJ: Princeton University Press, 2017.

Krause, Scott H. *Bringing Cold War Democracy to West Berlin: A Shared German-American Project, 1940–1972*. Abingdon, UK: Routledge, 2019.

Kwon, Heonik. *The Other Cold War.* New York: Columbia University Press, 2010.

Laderman, Scott, and Tim Gruenewald, eds. *Imperial Benevolence: U.S. Foreign Policy and American Popular Culture since 9/11.* Berkeley: University of California Press, 2018.

Ladino, Jennifer. "'Local Yearnings': Re-placing Nostalgia in Don DeLillo's *Underworld.*" *Journal of Ecocriticism* 2, no. 1 (January 2010): 1–18.

Lebow, Katherine A. *Unfinished Utopia: Nowa Huta, Stalinism, and Polish Society, 1949–56.* Ithaca, NY: Cornell University Press, 2016.

LeoGrande, William M., and Peter Kornbluh. *Back Channel to Cuba: The Hidden History of Negotiations between Washington and Havana.* Chapel Hill: University of North Carolina Press, 2014.

Little, Douglas. *Us versus Them: The United States, Radical Islam, and the Rise of the Green Threat.* Chapel Hill: University of North Carolina Press, 2016.

Litwak, Robert S. *Rogue States and U.S. Foreign Policy: Containment after the Cold War.* Washington, DC: Woodrow Wilson Center, 2000.

Lockman, Zachary. *Contending Visions of the Middle East: The History and Politics of Orientalism.* Cambridge: Cambridge University Press, 2009.

Loring, Benjamin. "Building Socialism in Kyrgyzstan: Nation-Making, Rural Development, and Social Change, 1921–1932." PhD diss., Brandeis University, 2008.

Loss, Jacqueline. *Dreaming in Russian: The Cuban Soviet Imaginary.* Austin: University of Texas Press, 2013.

Loss, Jacqueline, and José Manuel Prieto, eds. *Caviar with Rum: Cuba-USSR and the Post-Soviet Experience.* New York: Palgrave Macmillan, 2012.

Luthar, Breda, and Maruša Pušnik, eds. *Remembering Utopia: The Culture of Everyday Life in Socialist Yugoslavia.* Washington, DC: New Academia, 2010.

MacArthur, John R. *Second Front: Censorship and Propaganda in the 1991 Gulf War.* Berkeley: University of California Press, 2004.

MacLean, Nancy. *Democracy in Chains: The Deep History of the Radical Right's Stealth Plan for America.* New York: Penguin, 2018.

Mahler, Anne Garland. *From the Tricontinental to the Global South: Race, Radicalism, and Transnational Solidarity.* Durham, NC: Duke University Press, 2018.

Makdisi, Karim, and Vijay Prashad. Introduction to *Land of Blue Helmets: The United Nations and the Arab World*, edited by Karim Makdisi and Vijay Prashad, 1–18. Oakland: University of California Press, 2016.

Makdisi, Karim, and Vijay Prashad, eds. *Land of Blue Helmets: The United Nations and the Arab World.* Oakland: University of California Press, 2016.

Mamdani, Mahmood. *Good Muslim, Bad Muslim: America, the Cold War, and the Roots of Terror.* New York: Pantheon Books, 2004.

Mamdani, Mahmood. *Saviors and Survivors: Darfur, Politics, and the War on Terror.* New York: Pantheon Books, 2009.

Mandela, Nelson. *Conversations with Myself*. New York: Farrar, Straus and Giroux, 2010.
Martin, Terry. *The Affirmative Action Empire: Nations and Nationalism in the Soviet Union, 1923–1939*. Ithaca, NY: Cornell University Press, 2001.
Masco, Joseph. *The Nuclear Borderlands: The Manhattan Project in Post–Cold War New Mexico*. Princeton, NJ: Princeton University Press, 2006.
May, Elaine Tyler. *Homeward Bound: American Families in the Cold War Era*. New York: Basic Books, 1988.
McAlister, Melani. *Epic Encounters: Culture, Media, and U.S. Interests in the Middle East since 1945*. Berkeley: University of California Press, 2001.
McClintock, Anne. "Paranoid Empire: Specters from Guantánamo and Abu Ghraib." *Small Axe* 13, no. 1 (2009): 50–74.
McClintock, Anne. "Paranoid Empire: Specters from Guantánamo and Abu Ghraib." In *States of Emergency: The Object of American Studies*, edited by Russ Castronovo and Susan Gillman, 88–115. Chapel Hill: University of North Carolina Press, 2009.
McMahon, Robert J., ed. *The Cold War in the Third World*. Oxford: Oxford University Press, 2013.
Melvern, Linda. *Conspiracy to Murder: The Rwandan Genocide*. London: Verso, 2004.
Miller, Chris. *The Struggle to Save the Soviet Economy: Mikhail Gorbachev and the Collapse of the USSR*. Chapel Hill: University of North Carolina Press, 2016.
Minter, William. *Apartheid's Contras: An Inquiry into the Roots of War in Angola and Mozambique*. London and Johannesburg: Zed and Witwatersrand University Press, 1994.
Mitchell, Timothy. *Carbon Democracy: Political Power in the Age of Oil*. London: Verso, 2013.
Moon, Chung-in. *The Sunshine Policy: In Defense of Engagement as a Path to Peace in North Korea*. Seoul: Yonsei University Press, 2012.
Mooney, Darren. *Opening the X-Files: A Critical History of the Original Series*. Jefferson, NC: McFarland, 2017.
Nixon, Rob. *Slow Violence and the Environmentalism of the Poor*. Cambridge, MA: Harvard University Press, 2011.
Nye, Joseph S. *Soft Power: The Means to Success in World Politics*. New York: Public Affairs, 2005.
Omi, Michael, and Howard Winant. *Racial Formation*. New York: Routledge, 2014.
Osgood, Kenneth, and Derrick E. White, eds. *Winning while Losing: Civil Rights, the Conservative Movement and the Presidency from Nixon to Obama*. Gainesville: University Press of Florida, 2014.
Oushakine, Serguei A. *The Patriotism of Despair: Nation, War, and Loss in Russia*. Ithaca, NY: Cornell University Press, 2009.
Patterson, Patrick Hyder. *Bought and Sold: Living and Losing the Good Life in Socialist Yugoslavia*. Ithaca, NY: Cornell University Press, 2011.
Pence, Katherine, and Paul Betts, eds. *Socialist Modern: East German Everyday Culture and Politics*. Ann Arbor: University of Michigan Press, 2008.
Pevar, Stephen L. *The Rights of Indians and Tribes*. Oxford: Oxford University Press, 2012.
Phillips, Kevin. *American Dynasty: Aristocracy, Fortune, and the Politics of Deceit in the House of Bush*. New York: Penguin Books, 2004.

Piot, Charles. *Nostalgia for the Future: West Africa after the Cold War*. Chicago: University of Chicago Press, 2010.

Poiger, Uta. *Jazz, Rock, and Rebels: Cold War Politics and American Culture in a Divided Germany*. Chapel Hill: University of North Carolina Press, 2000.

Power, Samantha. *"A Problem from Hell": America and the Age of Genocide*. New York: Basic Books, 2002.

Pozniak, Kinga. *Nowa Huta: Generations of Change in a Model Socialist Town*. Pittsburgh: University of Pittsburgh Press, 2014.

Prashad, Vijay. "Bruce Lee and the Anti-imperialism of Kung Fu." *Positions: East Asia Cultures Critique* 11 (Spring 2002): 51–90.

Prashad, Vijay. *The Darker Nations: A People's History of the Third World*. New York: New Press, 2008.

Quigley, John. "The United States and the United Nations in the Persian Gulf War: New Order or Disorder." *Cornell International Law Journal* 25, no. 1 (1992): 1–49.

Qureshi, Emran, and Michael A. Sells. "Introduction: Constructing the Muslim Enemy." In *The New Crusades: Constructing the Muslim Enemy*, edited by Emran Qureshi and Michael A. Sells, 1–47. New York: Columbia University Press, 2003.

Rabe, Stephen G. *The Killing Zone: The United States Wages Cold War in Latin America*. New York: Oxford University Press, 2012.

Rabe, Stephen G. *Kissinger and Latin America: Intervention, Human Rights, and Diplomacy*. Ithaca, NY: Cornell University Press, 2020.

Raghavan, Srinath. *The Most Dangerous Place: A History of the United States in South Asia*. Haryana, India: Penguin Random House, 2018.

Rashid, Ahmed. *Taliban: Militant Islam, Oil, and Fundamentalism in Central Asia*. New Haven, CT: Yale University Press, 2000.

Razsa, Maple. *Bastards of Utopia: Living Radical Politics after Socialism*. Bloomington: Indiana University Press, 2015.

Reeves, Richard. *Running in Place: How Bill Clinton Disappointed America*. Kansas City, MO: Andrews and McMeel, 1996.

Renda, Mary. *Taking Haiti: Military Occupation and the Culture of U.S. Imperialism*. Chapel Hill: University of North Carolina Press, 2001.

Renwick, Robin. *The End of Apartheid: Diary of a Revolution*. London: Biteback, 2015.

Robb, David L. *Operation Hollywood: How the Pentagon Shapes and Censors the Movies*. New York: Prometheus Books, 2004.

Robin, Corey. *The Reactionary Mind: Conservatism from Edmund Burke to Donald Trump*. New York: Oxford University Press, 2017.

Rodgers, Daniel T. *Age of Fracture*. Cambridge, MA: Belknap Press of Harvard University Press, 2011.

Rosenberg, Emily S. *A Date Which Will Live: Pearl Harbor in American Memory*. Durham, NC: Duke University Press, 2003.

Rubin, Eli. *Synthetic Socialism: Plastics and Dictatorship in the German Democratic Republic* Chapel Hill: University of North Carolina Press, 2008.

Sahai, Shri Nath. *The Delhi Declaration: Cardinal of Indo-Soviet Relations*. New Delhi: Mittal Publications, 1990.

Sargent, Daniel J. *A Superpower Transformed: The Remaking of American Foreign Relations in the 1970s.* Oxford: Oxford University Press, 2015.

Sarotte, Mary Elise. *1989: The Struggle to Create Post–Cold War Europe.* Princeton, NJ: Princeton University Press, 2014.

Satia, Priya. *Time's Monster: How History Makes History.* Cambridge: The Belknap Press of Harvard University Press, 2020.

Satter, David. *Darkness at Dawn: The Rise of the Russian Criminal State.* New Haven, CT: Yale University Press, 2003.

Schmidt, Elizabeth. *Foreign Intervention in Africa: From the Cold War to the War on Terror.* Cambridge: Cambridge University Press, 2013.

Schmitz, David F. *Thank God They're on Our Side: The United States and Right-Wing Dictatorships, 1921–1965.* Chapel Hill: University of North Carolina Press, 1999.

Schmitz, David F. *The United States and Right-Wing Dictatorships, 1965–1989.* Cambridge: Cambridge University Press, 2006.

Schrecker, Ellen, ed. *Cold War Triumphalism: The Misuse of History after the Fall of Communism.* New York: New Press, 2004.

Schrift, Melissa. *Biography of a Chairman Mao Badge: The Creation and Mass Consumption of a Personality Cult.* New Brunswick, NJ: Rutgers University Press, 2001.

Schwenkel, Christina. *The American War in Contemporary Vietnam: Transnational Remembrance and Representation.* Bloomington: Indiana University Press, 2009.

Scribner, Charity. *Requiem for Communism.* Cambridge, MA: MIT Press, 2003.

Self, Robert O. *All in the Family: The Realignment of American Democracy since the 1960s.* New York: Hill and Wang, 2012.

Shamsie, Kamila. *Burnt Shadows.* London: Picador, 2009.

Sharlet, Jeff. *The Family: The Secret Fundamentalism at the Heart of American Power.* New York: HarperCollins, 2008.

Shaw, Tony. *Cinematic Terror: A Global History of Terrorism on Film.* New York: Bloomsbury Academic, 2014.

Shaw, Tony, and Denise J. Youngblood. *Cinematic Cold War: The American and Soviet Struggle for Hearts and Minds.* Lawrence: University of Kansas Press, 2014.

Shekhovtsov, Anton. *Russia and the Western Far Right: Tango Noir.* Abingdon, UK: Routledge, 2018.

Shibusawa, Naoko. "Ideology, Culture, and the Cold War." In *The Oxford Handbook of the Cold War,* edited by Richard H. Immerman and Petra Goedde, 32–49. Oxford: Oxford University Press, 2013.

Shimer, David. *Rigged: America, Russia, and One Hundred Years of Covert Electoral Interference.* New York: Knopf, 2020.

Shubin, Vladimir. *The Hot "Cold War": The USSR in Southern Africa.* London: Pluto, 2008.

Simpson, Bradley R. *Economists with Guns: Authoritarian Development and U.S.-Indonesian Relations, 1960–1968.* Stanford, CA: Stanford University Press, 2008.

Singh, Nikhil Pal. *Race and America's Long War.* Berkeley: University of California Press, 2017.

Skocpol, Theda. *Boomerang: Clinton's Health Security Effort and the Turn against Government in U.S. Politics.* New York: W. W. Norton, 1996.

Slobodian, Quinn. *Globalists: The End of Empire and the Birth of Neoliberalism*. Cambridge, MA: Harvard University Press, 2018.

Snyder, Timothy. *The Road to Unfreedom: Russia, Europe, America*. New York: Penguin, 2018.

Stahl, Roger. *Militainment, Inc.: War, Media, and Popular Culture*. New York: Routledge, 2009.

Stefanovic, Sofija. *Miss Ex-Yugoslavia: A Memoir*. New York: Atria Books, 2018.

Storey, Andy. "Structural Adjustment, State Power and Genocide: The World Bank and Rwanda." *Review of African Political Economy* 28, no. 89 (September 2001): 365–85.

Suettinger, Robert L. *Beyond Tiananmen: The Politics of U.S.-China Relations, 1989–2000*. Washington, DC: Brookings Institution Press, 2003.

Suny, Ronald Grigor, and Terry Martin. Introduction to *A State of Nations: Empire and Nation-Making in the Age of Lenin and Stalin*, edited by Ronald Grigor Suny and Terry Martin, 3–20. Oxford: Oxford University Press, 2001.

Swansbrough, R. *Test by Fire: The War Presidency of George W. Bush*. London: Palgrave, 2008.

Todorova, Maria, ed. *Remembering Communism: Genres of Representation*. New York: Social Science Research Council, 2010.

Trafzer, Clifford E. *The Judge*. Norman: Oklahoma University Press, 1975.

Trappe, Heike, and Janet C. Gornick. "Gender and Work in Germany: Before and after Reunification." *Annual Review of Sociology* 30 (2004): 103–24.

Tynybekov, A. K., V. M. Lelevkin, and J. E. Kulenbekov. "Environmental Issues of the Kyrgyz Republic and Central Asia." In *Environmental Change and Human Security: Recognizing and Acting on Hazard Impacts*, edited by P. H. Liotta, David A. Mouat, William G. Kepner, and Judith M. Lancaster, 407–32. Dordrecht: Springer, 2008.

United Nations Development Programme. *Human Development Report 1991*. New York: Oxford University Press, 1991.

Untermeyer, Chase. *Zenith: In the White House with George H. W. Bush*. College Station: Texas A&M University Press, 2016.

Vine, David. *Base Nation: How U.S. Bases abroad Harm America and the World*. New York: Metropolitan Books, 2015.

Vitalis, Robert. *America's Kingdom: Mythmaking on the Saudi Oil Frontier*. Stanford, CA: Stanford University Press, 2006.

Von Eschen, Penny. "Di Eagle and di Bear: Who Gets to Tell the Story of the Cold War?" In *Audible Empire: Music, Global Politics, Critique*, edited by Ronald Radano and Teju Olaniyan, 189–208. Durham, NC: Duke University Press, 2016.

Von Eschen, Penny. "Duke Ellington Plays Baghdad: Rethinking Hard and Soft Power from the Outside In." In *Contested Democracy: Freedom, Race, and Power in American History*, edited by Manisha Sinha and Penny Von Eschen, 279–300. New York: Columbia University Press, 2007.

Von Eschen, Penny. "Memory and the Study of US Foreign Relations." In *Explaining the History of American Foreign Relations*, edited by Frank Costigliola and Michael Hogan, 304–16. Cambridge: Cambridge University Press, 2016.

Von Eschen, Penny. *Race against Empire: Black Americans and Anticolonialism, 1937–1957*. Ithaca, NY: Cornell University Press, 1997.

Von Eschen, Penny. *Satchmo Blows Up the World: Jazz Ambassadors Play the Cold War.* Cambridge, MA: Harvard University Press, 2004.

Warner, Michael. *Publics and Counterpublics.* Princeton, NJ: Princeton University Press, 2015.

Weiner, Tim. *Legacy of Ashes: The History of the CIA.* New York: Anchor Press, 2008.

Westad, Odd Arne. *The Global Cold War: Third World Interventions and the Making of Our Times.* Cambridge: Cambridge University Press, 2005.

Wilford, Hugh. *America's Great Game: The CIA's Secret Arabists and the Shaping of the Middle East.* New York: Basic Books, 2017.

Wiener, Jon. *How We Forgot the Cold War: A Historical Journey across America.* Berkeley: University of California Press, 2012.

Woods, Colleen. *Freedom Incorporated: Anticommunism and Philippine Independence in the Age of Decolonization.* Ithaca, NY: Cornell University Press, 2020.

Woods, Clyde. "Katrina's World: Blues, Bourbon, and the Return to the Source." *American Quarterly* 6, no. 3 (September 2009): 427–53.

Woodward, Susan L. *Balkan Tragedy: Chaos and Dissolution after the Cold War.* Washington, DC: Brookings Institution, 1995.

World Bank. *World Development Report 2008: Agriculture for Development.* Washington, DC: World Bank, 2007.

Yurchak, Alexei. *Everything Was Forever, Until It Was No More: The Last Soviet Generation.* Princeton, NJ: Princeton University Press, 2005.

Zaretsky, Natasha. *No Direction Home: The American Family and the Fear of National Decline, 1968–1980.* Chapel Hill: University of North Carolina Press, 2007.

Zeilig, Leo. *Patrice Lumumba: Africa's Lost Leader.* London: Haus, 2008.

Žižek, Slavoj. *In Defense of Lost Causes.* London: Verso, 2008.

INDEX

Page numbers in italics refer to figures.